INDIA means BUSINESS

INDIA means
BUSINESS
how the elephant earned
its stripes

Kshama V. Kaushik
Kaushik Dutta

OXFORD
UNIVERSITY PRESS

Oxford University Press is a department of the University of Oxford.
It furthers the University's objective of excellence in research, scholarship,
and education by publishing worldwide. Oxford is a registered trademark of
Oxford University Press in the UK and in certain other countries

Published in India by
Oxford University Press
YMCA Library Building, 1 Jai Singh Road, New Delhi 110001, India

ISBN-13: 978-0-19-807261-4
ISBN-10: 0-19-807261-9

Typeset in Wilke LT Std 9.5/13
by Sai Graphic Design, New Delhi 110 055
Printed in India by Rakmo Press, New Delhi 110 020

Contents

Preface

Once there was an elephant, called India, who was rich, wise, and powerful, and traded with countries in other continents and gave the world many new innovations. Over the centuries, invaders and colonial powers came to plunder and rob it of its wealth, conquer its spirit, and make her a slave to their wishes. The elephant slowly lost her spirit to create new miracles and pioneer ideas and soon became poor and subservient. She then started to withdraw from the world and lived within its own boundaries and slowly started to lose the respect of the modern world.

Meanwhile in East Asia, there were rising tigers called Korea, Japan, Taiwan, Hong Kong, and Singapore who grew and started to move into the markets of the world in the West and, over the decades, became rich, powerful, and relevant. Their people and machines produced great products at cheaper prices and the world began trading with them like never before. India the elephant grew slowly and could not keep pace with the prowling tigers. Then a big change came in the 1990s when the keepers opened up the world to the elephant. The elephant quickly learnt the new ways of the world, became more nimble and powerful, and also relatively richer. She exchanged ideas with the world once again and slowly became a force to be reckoned with. One fine day, the world woke up to see that the elephant was not just large and grey but had developed the tiger's stripes.

This book is about how India the elephant earned her stripes.

The history of the Indian subcontinent begins at least from 600 BC with the Indus Valley Civilization but consolidation of the political landscape was probably the strongest from 300 BC (Mauryan dynasty) onwards. This provided the impetus for a flourishing economy lasting through several centuries, albeit with its share of peaks and troughs. The economy of the subcontinent was one of the largest in the world, at least till the end of the seventeenth and eighteenth centuries, with some estimates placing it at a quarter of the world's output.

A strong economic landscape over many centuries is very closely linked to the social fabric of the entire geographic entity called India— an influence that is felt till today. Economic and social customs were— and still are—closely intertwined and deeply embedded in the warp and weft of community, caste, and occupations, as were influences brought in by invaders and colonizers. There are several unique indigenous business and financial practices that the subcontinent has contributed to global practices, which have withstood the test of time and are used even today.

During the course of research for our previous book, *Corporate Governance: Myth to Reality*, we found very few written sources on the history of Indian businesses, its practices and uniqueness, that spanned from the Indus Valley Civilization through the Mauryan, Mughal, and British period to independent India, and the profound effect it had on the rest of the world. We were inspired to write a book linking Indian business and economic history to modern times and our interpretation on what the future will be, as seen by professionals who have seen Indian businesses closely over the last twenty-five years.

We believe that this book will give a new perspective to anyone having an interest in Indian business history and its transformation into the economic powerhouse that India is today.

Belonging to a generation that has grown up in an age of scarcity, poverty, and despondency, the current times of hope, relative prosperity, and global acceptance makes us appreciate the change in the way the world sees India. This was yet another inspiration to tell the story of India, the ancient civilization and young nation.

This book is made up of many stories told by several people and the list of people we have to thank is very long. Some have been acknowledged in the stories themselves, and some, though by no means all, are Amrit Aggarwal of Spentex Industries for his deep knowledge of *bahi-khata* and other forms of indigenous accounting; Ranjit Roy Chowdhury, former dean, Postgraduate Institute of Medical Education and Research (PGIMER), Chandigarh, and Vasantha Muthuswamy, Indian Council of Medical Research (ICMR), for helping us understand the pharmaceutical sector; Nabanita and S. Radhakrishnan, Defence Research and Development Organisation (DRDO), for their help in understanding defence research and development (R&D); K. Vaidyanath and Nazeeb Arif of ITC; Sandeep Kanwar and Saurav Adhikari of HCL Group; Indrajit Banerjee of Ranbaxy Laboratories; G.N. Gauba of Motherson Sumi; Ashok Banerjee of Indian Institute of Management, Calcutta (IIM-C), for reviewing the manuscript; Gayathri Venkatraman for invaluable document editing support; and last but not least the entire team at Oxford University Press (OUP) for their attention to detail and never-ending patience.

December 2011   KSHAMA V. KAUSHIK
                                                        KAUSHIK DUTTA

Abbreviations

ABLE	Association of Biotechnology Led Enterprises
ACC	Associated Cement Companies Limited
ACMA	Auto Components Manufacturing Association
ACTS	Advanced Computer Training School, CDAC
ADCCB	Amravati District Central Co-Op Bank
AIDS	Acquired Immunodeficiency Syndrome
AIG	America International Group
AIIMS	All India Institute of Medical Sciences
AIIS	All India Institute of Ayurveda
AIR	All India Radio
AMET	Africa, Middle East, and Turkey
AML	Anti-Money-Laundering (Policies)
AMUL	Anand Milk Union Limited
ARV	Antiretroviral (drug)
ASCA	Accumulated Savings and Credit Association
ASSOCHAM	Associated Chambers of Commerce and Industry
AYUSH	Department of Ayurveda, Yoga & Naturopathy, Unani, Siddha, and Homoeopathy
BAT	British American Tobacco
BBC	British Broadcasting Corporation
BCG	Boston Consulting Group
BEL	Bharat Electronics Limited
BIAC	Business and Industry Advisory Committee

BIFR	Board for Industrial and Financial Reconstruction
BIS	Bureau of Indian Standards
BMS	Bombay Milk Scheme
BP	Bharat Petroleum
BPCL	Bharat Petroleum Corporation Limited
BPO	Business Process Outsourcing
BSE	Bombay Stock Exchange
BSNL	Bharat Sanchar Nigam Limited
CAG	Comptroller and Auditor General
CASHE	Credit and Savings for Household Enterprise
CCMB	Centre for Cellular and Molecular Biology
CCRAS	Central Council for Research in Ayurveda and Siddha
C-DAC	Centre for Development of Advanced Computing
CDM	Clean Development Mechanism
CDS	Credit Default Swap
CEO	Chief Executive Officer
CER	Carbon Emission Reduction
CERC	Central Electricity Regulatory Commission
CFTC	Commodity Futures Trading Commission
CFTRI	Central Food Technological Research Institute
CII	Confederation of Indian Industry
CMC	Christian Medical College
CMD	Chairman cum Managing Director
CMM	Compatibility Maturity Model
CMSCPL	Computer Maintenance and Service Company Private Limited
CRISIL	Credit Rating and Information Services of India Limited
CRO	Clinical Research Organizations
CSIR	Council of Scientific and Industrial Research
CSR	Council of Scientific Research
CVIL	Coal Ventures International Limited
DALY	Disability-Adjusted Life Years
DARPA	Defense Advanced Research Projects Agency
DBT	Department of Biotechnology, GoI
DCGI	Drug Controller General of India
DCM	Delhi Cloth Mills
DD	Doordarshan

DFI	Development Financial Institution
DFID	Department for International Development (United Kingdom)
DGCI	Drug Controller General of India
DISMH	Directorate of Indian Systems of Medicine and Homeopathy
DoT	Depart of Telecommunications
DPE	Department of Public Enterprises
DRDO	Defence Research and Development Organisation
DSIR	Department of Industrial and Scientific Research
DST	Department of Science and Technology, GoI
E&Y	Ernst & Young
ECIL	Electronics Corporation of India Limited
EHR	Electronic Health Record(s)
EIC	(British) East India Company
ERDC	Electronics Research and Development Corporation
ERNET	Education and Research Network
ERP	Enterprise Resource Planning
ESG	Environment, Social, and Governance (Standards)
ESOP	Employee Stock Ownership (Share Option) Plan
EU	European Union
FATF	Financial Action Task Force
FDI	Foreign Direct Investment
FIB	Foreign Investment Board
FICCI	Federation of Indian Chambers of Commerce and Industry
FITT	Foundation for Innovation and Technology Transfer (IIT-D)
FIU	Financial Intelligence Unit
FLOSS	Free/Libre and Open-Source Software
FMCG	Fast Moving Consumer Goods
FTSE	Financial Times Stock Exchange
GAAP	Generally Accepted Accounting Principles
GATS	General Agreement on Trade in Services
GCMMF	Gujarat Cooperative Milk Marketing Federation (Limited)
GDP	Gross Domestic Product
GIC	General Insurance Corporation

GM	General Motors
GoI	Government of India
HBS	Harvard Business School
HCL	Hindustan Computers Limited
HGP	Human Genome Project
HIV	Human Immunodeficiency Virus
HLL	Hindustan Lever Limited
HPCL	Hindustan Petroleum Corporation Limited
HR	Human Resource
HRD	Human Resources Development (Ministry)
HUL	Hindustan Unilever Limited
IASB	International Accounting Standards Board
IBA	Indian Banks' Association
IBM	International Business Machines
ICAR	Indian Council of Agricultural Research
IC-FOSS	The International Centre for Free and Open Source Software
ICICI	Industrial Credit and Investment Corporation of India (Bank)
ICL	International Computers Limited
ICMR	Indian Council of Medical Research
ICT	Information and Communication Technology
IDBI	Industrial Development Bank of India
IDC	Indian Software Development Centre
IDFC	Industrial Development Finance Corporation
IFCI	Industrial Finance Corporation of India
IFFCO	Indian Farmers Fertiliser Cooperative Limited
IFRS	International Financial Reporting Standards
IGDMP	Integrated Guided Missile Development Programme
IIIT	Indian Institute of Information Technology
IIM	Indian Institute of Management
IIM-B	Indian Institute of Management, Bangalore
IIM-C	Indian Institute of Management, Calcutta
IISc	Indian Institute of Science
IISCI	Indian Standard Code for Information Interchange
IIT	Indian Institute of Technology
IIT-D	Indian Institute of Technology, Delhi
IL&FS	Infrastructure Leasing & Financial Services Limited

IMDR	Institute of Management Development and Research
IMF	International Monetary Fund
INC	Indian National Congress
IOC	Indian Oil Corporation
IOU	I Owe You
ISFOC	Intelligence-based Script Font Code
IPL	Indian Premier League
IPO	Initial Public Offering
IP	Intellectual Property
IPR	Intellectual Property Rights
ISB	Indian School of Business
ISI	Indian Statistical Institute
ISID	Institute for Studies in Industrial Development
ISRO	Indian Space Research Organisation
ITC	Imperial/Indian Tobacco Company
IT	Information Technology
ITES	Information Technology Enabled Services
ITP	Investment & Technology Promotion (Division), MEA
IVTS	Informal Value Transfer Systems
JUSCO	Jamshedpur Utility and Services Company
KEM	King Edward Memorial (Hospital)
KYC	Know Your Customer
L&T	Larsen & Tubro
LCA	Light Combat Aircraft
LDC	Least Developed Country
LIC	Life Insurance Corporation
LNG	Liquefied Natural Gas
LPG	Liquefied Petroleum Gas
LSSM	Life Sciences and Special Metals, DRDO
LTC	Linux Technology Centre
M&A	Mergers and Acquisitions
MBA	Master of Business Administration
M-CRIL	Micro Credit Ratings International Limited
MCI	Medical Council of India
MDF	Microfinance Development Fund
MDG	Millennium Development Goal
MEA	Ministry of External Affairs
MFI	Microfinance Institutions

MFO	Microfinance organization
MHRD	Ministry of Human Resource Development, GoI
MIT	Massachusetts Institute of Technology
MNC	Multinational Company
MNRE	Ministry of New and Renewable Energy
MoCA	Ministry of Company Affairs
MoEF	Ministry of Environment and Forests
MRTP	Monopololies and Restrictive Trade Practices
MTNL	Mahanagar Telephone Nigam Limited
MUL	Maruti Udyog Limited
NABARD	National Bank for Agriculture and Rural Development
NACUBO	National Association of College and University Business Officers
NASSCOM	The National Association of Software and Services Companies
NBFC	Non-Banking Financial Corporation
NCUI	National Cooperative Union of India
NDTV	New Delhi Television
NGO	Non-governmental Organization
NIF	National Innovation Foundation
NIIPM	National Institute for Intellectual Property Management
NIN	National Institute of Nutrition
NMDC	National Mining Development Corporation
NMTLI	New Millennium Technology Leadership Initiative
NPC	National Planning Committee
NREN	National Research and Education Network
NSC	National Savings Certificate
NSE	National Stock Exchange
NSS	National Savings Scheme
NTPC	National Thermal Power Corporation
OCED	Organisation for Economic Co-operation and Development
OEM	Original Equipment Manufacturers
OFDI	Overseas Foreign Direct Investment
ONGC	Oil and Natural Gas Corporation of India
OSDL	Open Source Development Labs
OSS	Open Source Software
PACS	Primary Agriculture Cooperative Societies

PESB	Public Enterprises Selection Board
PGTI	Professional Golf Tour of India
POSCO	Pohang Iron and Steel Company
PPP	Public–Private Partnership
PRMIA	Professional Risk Managers' International Association
PSU	Public Sector Undertakings
R&T	Research and Technology
RBI	Reserve Bank of India
RIL	Reliance Industries Limited
RINL	Rashtriya Ispat Nigam Limited
RNRL	Reliance Natural Resources Limited
ROSCO	Rotating Savings and Credit Organizations
RPC	Remote Processing Centre
RTI	Right to Information (Act)
S&P	Standard and Poor's
S&T	Science and Technology
SAIL	Steel Authority of India Limited
SBI	State Bank of India
SCSL	Satyam Computer Services Limited
SEBI	Securities and Exchange Board of India
SEC	Securities and Exchange Commission
SERC	Science and Engineering Research Council
SEWA	Self-Employed Women's Association
SEZ	Special Economic Zone
SHG	Self-help group
SIDBI	Small Industries Development Bank of India
SKD	Semi-Knocked-Down (Kits)
SME	Small and Medium Enterprise(s)
SPO	Service Provider's Organization
SRD	Special Drawing Rights
STP	Software Technology Park
STPI	Software Technology Parks of India (GoI)
TBI	Technology Business Incubator
TCS	Tata Consultancy Services
TDS	Tax Deducted at Source (Certificate)
TI	Texas Instruments
TiE	The Indus Entrepreneurs
TIFR	Tata Institute of Fundamental Research

TISCO	Tata Iron and Steel Company
TMC	Toyota Motor Company
TNC	Transnational Corporation
TRAI	Telecom Regulatory Authority of India
TRIPS	Trade-related Aspects of Intellectual Property Rights
UGC	University Grants Commission
UN	United Nations
UNCBD	United Nations Convention on Biological Diversity
UNCTAD	United Nations Conference on Trade and Development
UNICTRAL	United Nations Commission on International Trade Law
USP	Unique Selling Point
UTI	Unit Trust of India
VC	Venture Capitalist
VPN	Virtual Private Network
VSAT	Very Small Aperture Terminal
WEF	World Economic Forum
WHO	World Health Organization
WIPO	World Intellectual Property Organization
WSJ	Wall Street Journal
WTO	World Trade Organization
WWI	World War I
WWII	World War II

1

Indian Business

An Introduction

Modern India is a relatively young country but paradoxically the philosophies, institutions, and business culture are closely linked to the legacies of the past. It is very difficult to arrive at a generalization of the Indian business economy as the roots of business and its culture go back many centuries.

> The economic history of India is not a story with a strong plot which lays bare the mechanism by which a set of progressive, or recessive, circumstances came about. The Indian economy of the 1970s was different to that of the 1860s, but it is hard to say that it had arrived at the end of a journey or had even progressed along a clear path from one point to the other. (Tomlinson 1993: 8)

Around the beginning of the eighteenth century, the landmass comprising the Indian subcontinent was largely an agrarian society with a flourishing overseas trade. There were powerful merchants operating on both the east and west coast, with the bigger ones dealing mostly in commodities like indigo, spices, and textiles, which were in demand with European merchants. They also had a competitive advantage over European traders based on their knowledge of the hinterland and could easily exercise monopoly over certain commodities. These merchants frequently owned large fleets of ships and were rich enough even to finance local rulers in peace and in war; hence the term 'merchant prince' is also used to describe them.

Then there were those traders who operated within a geographical constraint and did not, or could not, expand their network; their operations ranged from local markets and village fairs to supplying the big merchants as they had direct links with the farmers. There were many middlemen involved in the process of making the farmers' produce reach the port cities, operating on a system of brokerage, which later became popular in European countries. Port cities or towns like Surat and Ahmedabad in the west, Patna in the east, and the Coromandel coast were islands of prosperity; their wealth, however, did not trickle down into the vast hinterland.

Most merchants were general merchants dealing in a variety of goods, though some specialized in one or two commodities and became synonymous with that trade. For instance, the Zaveri family of Ahmedabad was—and still is—in the jewellery and precious metals and stones' business, while the Travadis of Surat or Hiranand Sahu of Patna were mainly bankers or *sahukar*s.

Some general merchants were also involved in money-lending, their borrowers ranging from European merchants to kings and rulers. Given the lack of safety in surface transport, merchants devised an ingenious way to remit funds to far-off places. This is the *hundi* system. A hundi is a commercial document like a bill of exchange drawn by a borrower asking the lender to pay a sum of money to the holder or presenter (as the case may be) of the hundi. Soon, the system became so developed that hundis became saleable instruments throughout the country and overseas.

Similarly, non-uniformity of currencies circulating all over the land brought to the fore a set of merchants, usually called *shroff*s or *saraf*s, who specialized in exchanging currencies, creating a virtual currency exchange within India.

The basic character of business at this time was commercial rather than manufacturing. Manufacturing, such as that existed, comprised of artefacts produced by skilled artisans who had limited means and often depended on merchants to finance their operations and buy their produce for onward sale. Since the goods produced by the artisans had a ready demand—some famous products included Dacca muslin, Ahmedabad brocades and jewellery, and cotton textiles from Surat—merchants showed no interest in attempting to transform these ventures into industrial undertakings, even those with substantial means. Ventures requiring low capital and offering low risk dominated the business enterprise of the day and while the merchants became wealthier, the plight of the farm workers or the artisans did not improve dramatically.

Foreign Traders

Despite their superior local knowledge, Indian merchants had serious competition from various foreign merchants operating on Indian coasts for many centuries. The earliest of these were the Arab and Egyptian merchants who were active on the west coast on well-defined sea routes.

By the eighteenth century, the European East India companies, notably the English and Dutch companies and to a limited extent the French companies, gradually took over major trading volumes from India. These companies enjoyed monopoly rights over trade between their respective countries and India by virtue of charters granted to them by their respective governments.

The English operated at Surat, Bombay (now Mumbai), Madras (now Chennai), and Calcutta (now Kolkata); the Dutch at Surat, Cochin (now Kochi), Pulicat, Masulipatnam (now Machilipatnam), and Hoogly; the French at Surat, Pondicherry (now Puducherry), and Hoogly. They also had smaller stations of operations in the interiors.

At that time, demand for Indian goods in Europe was greater than the demand for European goods in India. This led to a problem in payment of goods in India. Since their home governments discouraged export of precious metals or bullion, European traders resorted to a system of comparative advantage. They bought goods in markets that offered a price advantage and sold in markets that had a demand for such goods—all on a huge, international scale.

These are the initial cases of arbitrage trading with India, which till date is the foundation of global trade. Arbitrage represents a differential in production costs, market price, labour, etc., between two markets, and commercial organizations make profits by buying a product or service in cheaper market and selling the same in a second market at higher value. This also made the trading activities of European companies multilateral in character while increasing their geographical reach.

While trade developed into a fairly well-defined activity, politically, the country was far from stable. There was no strong political entity, particularly after the decline of the Mughal Empire, with frequent political fragmentation and alignment. Most of the new states lacked the well-organized treasury and revenue collection system of the Mughals. This made them dependent on the merchant class for money in exchange for the right to collect land revenue from parcels of land. This was equally applicable to European trading companies who were fast acquiring territorial rights. This system was called *potedari*, whereby a ruler would grant a right over land to collect taxes for a sum of money. The Dutch East India Company, meanwhile, had yielded place to the English and French companies.

The British East India Company (EIC) was very influential in the political life of both western and eastern India and with their posturing as honest brokers, stood guarantee for loans by the sahukars and potedars to the local rulers. In the ensuing years of utter confusion and intrigue among rulers, the EIC moved in to dominate local administration, albeit paying token obeisance to the Delhi durbar— still the sovereign on paper. Local traders were active promoters in how things came to this pass; firstly, there was concern for the safety of their merchandise, and, secondly, because they rarely expected protection of any sort from the state and saw their future in working with the foreign powers and hoped they would establish a stable rule.

The role of the house of Jagat Seth, founded by Hiranand Sahu of Patna, is particularly interesting. During the waning influence of Aurangzeb's empire, the house rose to prominence as revenue collectors of the ruling self-styled nawabs of Bengal who were practically independent of the Delhi durbar. Over time (around 1703), Manekchand, one of Hiranand's sons, became the government banker and treasurer and got control of the government mint, including the right to strike coins on behalf of the administration. However, palace intrigues brought distrust between the descendants of Nawab Siraj-ud-daula, and the then head of the house, Jagat Seth. This disturbed the working relationship among the rulers, local traders, and foreign traders that the previous nawabs had carefully nurtured. Playing one against the other, Siraj-ud-daula alienated many elements that kept the balance of his kingdom. Eventually, all the disgruntled elements joined hands to eliminate the common enemy, the ruler of Bengal, Siraj-ud-daula. Robert Clive and W. Watts of the EIC and Jagat Seth were among the main actors. The conspiracy culminated in the Battle of Plassey in 1757 in which Clive, commanding a small force of the EIC, defeated Siraj-ud-daula. Jean Law, head of the French establishment at Kasim Bazar, said: 'They (the Jagat Seths) are, I can confirm, the originators of the revolution: without them the English would never have carried out what they have' (Subramaniam and Ray 2004).

Thus, a mere merchant, notwithstanding the size of his wealth, was responsible for setting in motion a process that would irrevocably change the course of history—of both India and Britain. Similar stories were played out in other parts of the land. Business and politics have for centuries been a heady mix.

THE BRITISH EMPIRE

From then onwards, the rise of the British influence on the Indian landscape was inevitable and inexorable. Their rise coincided with the fall of erstwhile bankers and sahukars of all principalities in the region of Oudh and Bengal. The British hardly needed merchant bankers, being very solvent themselves. The introduction of currency reforms further eliminated the need for traditional banking acumen of the sahukars and shroffs.

The age of merchant princes was certainly over by the time the British assumed firm political power over the subcontinent from the middle of the nineteenth century. They could not anticipate the far-reaching consequences of the changes brought about in a large part by their own actions and worse, neither made any attempts to break new ground in methods of conducting business nor spot new opportunities of profit. However, on a local level, traders and moneylenders still continued with their traditional methods of doing business, largely unconcerned with the changes taking place around them.

Only when the British emerged as the undisputed political power in the land did the business environment stir up, awakened to the possibility of new avenues of profit, owing to improved knowledge of monumental changes taking place in the world over, new directions of opportunity, and its exploitation.

The very reason for colonization of any land is to see how it can serve the interests of the 'home country' and the British were no different. However, the existing infrastructure and administrative machinery were inadequate to serve those needs; in fact, they were unsuitable even to serve the local needs of a land of continental proportions. The new rulers, therefore, lost no time in taking steps to tighten their grip over the entire land and to enhance its capacity to serve British interests. A perhaps unintended by-product was that it provided a business-friendly environment, such as a uniform currency, a systematic banking system, safe modes of transport, and reliable dispute resolution and justice delivery systems.

Setting up of a judicial system was greeted particularly enthusiastically. A body of laws defining the rights and privileges of individuals, rather than traditions and caste-oriented obligations, would guide administration of justice. It was perceived that the new rulers sought to reduce the arbitrariness of the state, a radical departure from the system prevailing so far. For example, the Companies Act of 1850 which, when introduced, was rather toothless but underwent many amendments to make it a workable, effective piece of legislation.

The Indian economy certainly underwent a major structural change over the course of the nineteenth century as it continued to be convulsed by dramatic geopolitical global shifts in technology, market mechanics, or plain old-fashioned politics. Causes and results of the structural change were—and still are—complex, but the Indian colony played a key role in the development of the United Kingdom.

For instance, by the last quarter of the nineteenth century, India was the largest purchaser of British exports, a major employer of British civil servants at high salaries, the provider of half of the Empire's military might—all paid from local revenues—besides being a significant recipient of British capital. About £239–290 million raised in London between 1860 and 1914 was invested in India, more than half of it in the form of government loans. The Indian contribution represented about 20 per cent of all the capital sent to the Empire and about 7 per cent of all the capital exports from Britain (Davis and Huttenback 1986: Table 2.1; qtd in Tomlinson 1993).

REVOLUTION IN THE TEXTILE INDUSTRY

Production of cotton goods marked the beginning of the Industrial Revolution almost everywhere in the world. The industry is dependent on agriculture for the basic raw material and, therefore, the transition from this level to the finished product is a natural progression.

Even at the onset of the eighteenth century, Indian textiles, called 'calicoes', were in great demand in the world for their quality as well as price advantage. However, the use of new machines in Great Britain, running on steam power, produced goods in greater quantity and speed than manual labour—used by Indian artisans—could ever hope to achieve. This, along with tariff protection and subsidy that the British government awarded to its domestic industry, totally reversed the situation. Machine-made British goods, with greater availability and superior quality, severely affected the export of Indian textiles in British and European markets.

Although British 'mill cloth', as it was called, made a few inroads into India's domestic market as well, the bulk of the local population continued to patronize Indian products. D. Gadgil (1954) has argued that it was the development of factory production of textiles in India that gave a real setback to the weavers. Naturally, such factory owners were both Indian and expatriates, and thus, the popular belief that Britain was responsible for impoverishing Indian weavers may not be wholly correct.

The Industrial Revolution in Britain spread to other industries in the country such as iron and steel, and chemicals. Soon, Britain lifted restrictions on export of textile machinery, put in place for protecting the supremacy of the British textile industry. While this completely reversed the balance of trade that existed between India and Britain, it gave a fillip to lucrative trade and paved the way for seeding new ideas for business in India.

This also marked the beginning of the commercialization of Indian agriculture. The Indian farmer no longer cultivated based on local needs; he was conscious of the commercial value of his crop out of his region and even country.

By the 1860s, India had a nascent cotton textile industry. New mills and factories had emerged at regular intervals with numbers rising from ten in 1860 to twenty-eight by 1892 in the city of Bombay alone. Ahmedabad, the other city of textile mills, had eleven mills in 1892, up from only two in 1873. Although the American Civil War brought a period of irrational exuberance in Indian cotton exports—with disastrous consequences for some Indian business houses, the feeling of despondency or erosion of business confidence did not last.

OWNERSHIP OF BUSINESSES

Most of these concerns were joint-stock companies, a concept pioneered by European businesses, and largely under Indian control. Most promoters had a mercantile background that also had trading and banking interests. With their cautious, commercial background, these promoters easily adopted the joint-stock structure of ownership that helped disperse risk more widely than the prevailing sole proprietorship or, in some cases, partnership forms of ownership.

It was the expatriate who popularized the 'agency house' form of organization. An agency house was essentially a partnership firm that acted as a business agent of others from whom it charged a fee for its services. The partners were usually of limited means and the method of financing their operations was akin to the Indian hundi system on an international level. They would accept deposits from EIC employees and, having organic links with some firms back home, arrange for their remittance to specified persons. Over time, such agency houses developed independent lines of business and some also participated directly in overseas trade. Some names like Forbes of Bombay, Parrys of Madras, or Palmers and Andrew Yules of Calcutta made the transition to big business houses.

The concept of an agency house found great acceptance among the newly emerging class of Indian merchants operating on the joint-stock model of ownership. However, in a classic case of wanting to have their cake and eat it too, the promoters seemed unwilling to give up the unbridled control over the enterprise that they were used to in the traditional form of ownership and which was inevitable in the true spirit of a joint-stock company. The managing agency was a neat solution to this problem. The promoter would have a resolution passed at the outset, appointing his family firm as the managing agent almost in perpetuity and with unfettered powers.

Power without accountability—that, for all practical purposes—was the concept of a managing agency. The board of directors had little say in running the company and was largely a rubber stamp or of decorative value.

Thus, the fledgling Indian industry was a continuity of the old trading class which had the necessary resources and business skills with which they ran the family business earlier. The family, in the manner of joint families, would continue to direct the affairs of the company as they did in their family businesses. The adoption of the joint-stock model of ownership was more out of financial conservatism rather than a belief in a pioneering new business concept.

The managing agency system, with all its connotations of a stranglehold on the business, rapidly became firmly entrenched in the business environment of the country, resolutely carrying forward a prevailing social institution.

In expatriate firms, the partnerships controlling the managing agency kept changing as various partners sold out their holdings and moved on. This helped infuse new blood and new ideas, and even fresh funds into the partnership, and helped businesses to thrive. In contrast, the managing agency form perfected by Indian businesses was a family affair. This had inevitable consequences in terms of new ideas or experimentation, which has limited virtue in a joint-family setting. Also, while most expatriate firms did not necessarily hold a controlling interest in the businesses that they managed, which they would do for a fee, Indian managing agencies invariably only ran companies that they controlled. Therefore, they lost out on valuable experience that they might have gained by running someone else's business without risking their own funds.

SPREAD OF INDUSTRY

Most companies started out as textile companies but by the end of the nineteenth century, many businesses had branched out into other machine-based industries, primarily sugar, jute, coal, and even tea and coffee plantations. A pioneer like Jamsetji Nusserwanji Tata also initiated huge projects like steel production, hydroelectricity, and navigation.

Although some sterling companies (companies registered in Britain) engaged in some businesses like tea or jute, the bulk of Indian industry was owned or promoted by Indian businessmen or expatriates.

Figures for this period are revealing; by the end of the nineteenth century, there were as many as 627 manufacturing firms with a total paid-up capital of over Rs 250 million, up from 264 companies with a paid-up capital of less than Rs 110 million only a couple of decades ago. If we include in this category service industries like banking, insurance, navigation, warehousing, etc., the number of companies in the year 1900 was 1,366, with a total paid-up capital of Rs 370 million, up from 505 with a paid-up capital of less than Rs 150 million in the year 1882 (Government of India 1902: 371–2; qtd in Tripathi 2004).

The manufacture of iron products in eighteenth-century India was a well-established trade practised by groups of tribal craftsmen using traditional methods. The methods were simple, using mostly impure iron, and produced most of the requirements of agricultural tools and implements and even weapons. From the late eighteenth century onwards, infusion of European technology such as smelting coal and blast furnaces brought in improvements to local iron-making. The most substantial initial enterprise was at Porto Novo in Madras but it could not sustain commercial viability and had to be shut down in the 1870s. The first modern iron works in India was the Bengal Iron Works Company in 1874 set up by a group of expatriates. In its chequered history, the company changed hands and acquired a new identity but with little change in its fortunes. The most important and successful venture in steelmaking in India arguably is that of the Tatas and is widely acknowledged as a unique example of a large-scale, innovative industrial enterprise that is Indian in all respects.

Although the developn.ent was uneven, with the three Presidency cities of Calcutta, Bombay, and Madras seeing the most amount of investment, the character of Indian business had definitely become industrial. Uneven development is also inevitable in a period of transition. Trading, of course, continued to have a place but mostly as ancillary to manufacturing.

THE INDIAN BUSINESS IDENTITY

Till the end of the nineteenth century, the average Indian businessman was not greatly perturbed by the foreign rulers of the country largely because Indians and Europeans functioned in an interdependent manner—Indians needed British/Indian ships to ply their wares and the foreigners depended on Indian middlemen to navigate their way through the unfamiliar Indian business landscape. There was no real sense of threat, barring occasions of unrest towards Indian textiles in the textile belt of Manchester.

Morris David Morris (1979) puts forth that the payoff structure directed Indian entrepreneurs away from industrial activity and towards the *desh*—the countryside. He argued that indigenous entrepreneurs focused on internal markets and the British focused on the export markets not because of discrimination as has sometimes been asserted but because these two types actually faced idiosyncratic levels of expected profit. The Indians' lack of knowledge of world markets and their knowledge of the interior meant that their realized profit rates were higher there and the exact opposite held for the British in India. By and large, the business community was very supportive of British rule in India because they could see clear benefits of improved infrastructure and administration. Many of them also had close links with the ruling race, as intermediaries or through other close business interactions between Indian and British commercial interests.

But as the industrial base expanded, it brought within its fold many people who had no previous memory of any camaraderie with the ruling race. Also, with time, there developed some degree of indigenous technical expertise, which reduced dependence on European expertise, bringing with it a measure of self-confidence.

Indian industrialists, being supportive of the British rule, expected to be treated fairly and equally as other crown subjects, an expectation which was belied time and again.

For instance, Indians perceived that Manchester exerted an unfair influence and got the government of India to abolish import duties on textiles in 1882. Coupled with the countervailing excise duty imposed on Indian goods in 1894, it was, in the eyes of Indian producers, a blatant attempt to snatch their competitive advantage. They perceived that the Crown was treating different classes of subjects differently and with a racial bias.

Many voices were raised against these measures. The Indian National Congress (INC), founded in 1885, was formed as a sort of organized pressure group to express the views and feelings of pro-nationalists to the government.

Unlike the fledgling 'chambers of commerce', the INC also attracted people from other walks of life. This added impetus to a sense of self-identity, leading to a concept of *swadeshi*—anything indigenous—which rapidly became the vortex for a movement.

Businessmen, whether or not they perceived the full connotation of the movement, were quick to understand its commercial implication. There would be much greater demand for anything they produced. However, textile was the only industry in the country with any degree of maturity to reap the benefits of swadeshi. The movement saw further addition of as many as thity-nine new mills between 1904 and 1910 and the production capacity of many units set up earlier was also expanded.

Bengal witnessed the most strident swadeshi movement—partly because of Lord Curzon's controversial move in 1905 to partition the region into East and West Bengal. People saw in it sinister motives of religion whereby East Bengal would have a majority of Muslims and a minority of Hindus and vice versa in West Bengal.

The movement saw a revival of the Bengali entrepreneurial spirit, which was lying dormant since the 1840s when a series of reverses saw Bengali businessmen bite the dust. Besides the usual cotton mills, there were enterprises using modern scientific knowledge which involved sophisticated modern processes. Some of these were Bengal Chemical & Pharmaceutical Co., which still operates as a company, Calcutta Chemicals, Bengal Lamps, and Calcutta (later Bengal) Pottery Works (Tripathi 2004: 155). There was negligible competition for these industries and therefore demand was sustained easily. The producers actively appealed to the nationalist pride while selling their goods.

Western India, too, had some indigenous industries other than textile such as Alembic Chemical Works in Baroda (now Vadodara) and Kirloskar Brothers in Poona (now Pune).

Perhaps the most famous name in western India—and indeed all over the country later—was that of the Tatas, founded by J.N. Tata.

As was the norm, the house started out with textile mills in 1869 and displayed the founder's legendary originality and perceptiveness in the choice of locations as well as use of technology. Besides, he introduced several labour welfare measures and incentive schemes that were light years ahead of the then prevailing ideas. Jamsetji Tata conceived a steel venture way back in 1882 but had to wait many years for favourable regulatory conditions before he could translate that into action, which came about in 1899. The project was carried through by his son, Dorabji, who, along with associates, identified an area rich in iron ore deposits near Durg in present-day Chhattisgarh. (Although the Tatas did not build a factory there, the government of independent India set up the Bhilai Steel Plant at that place later.) The Tatas finally selected a factory site in Bihar but had no idea how to raise funds for such a huge venture. With a preliminary prospectus, Dorabji approached the London money market. But the British investors were not convinced about investing in such huge investment projects in India and besides, Britain was going through tight money markets. Returning to India in 1907, Dorabji found the swadeshi movement at its height and he therefore appealed to Indians for funds. The response was, to put it mildly, extraordinary. The 'entire capital of £6,30,000 was secured by some 8,000 Indians. And when, later on, an issue of debentures was decided upon to provide working capital, the entire issue, £4,00,000 was subscribed by one Indian Magnate, the Maharaja of Gwalior' (Harris 1958: 190; qtd in Tripathi 2004: 159).˙ Thus, although the steel venture was not conceived in the wake of the swadeshi movement, it was the main plank that helped to set it up.

In the south, the swadeshi movement manifested itself in the establishment of modern banks—Tanjore Permanent Fund (later Bank of Tanjore, 1901), South Indian Bank, Tirunelveli (1903), and the forerunner of Kombakonam, City Union Bank (1904). After the partition of Bengal in 1905, the strident call of swadeshi saw three new banking firms—Canara Banking Corporation of Udipi (later Corporation Bank), Canara Hindu Permanent Fund (later Canara Bank), and Madras Central Cooperative Bank.

Initially, these Indian ventures could not make much headway because the three principal expatriate agency houses in the region— Parry, Binny, and Arbuthnot—had their own banking departments which controlled a major chunk of the banking business. But the house of Arbuthnot fell in 1906 due to a series of badly managed ventures all over the world and the credibility of the other two houses was also badly damaged, as they could not entirely honour their liabilities.

With public trust eroded forever and the groundswell of swadeshi to help, the path was clear for the Indian-controlled banks to prosper. Other than banks, some more business units came into being under the influence of the swadeshi spirit; for example, United India Life Insurance Co., Madras, and Swadeshi Steam Navigation Company, Tuticorin.

Elsewhere in the country, too, swadeshi-inspired banks came into being; the major ones were Bank of India (1907), Punjab & Sind Bank (1908), and Central Bank of India (1911). Bank of Baroda (1908) came about more out of regional chauvinistic pride of the ruler of Baroda than as a response to the swadeshi movement.

Inevitably, only a handful of these banks founded in the heady rush of newfound patriotism were sound institutions, promoted and guided by responsible leadership and managed by competitive staff under good business principles. In the absence of a central regulatory authority, there was cut-throat competition among the mushrooming banking companies, where each house was free to decide their lending and deposit rates or even how much to borrow or lend. In most cases, the paid-up capital was a fraction of the authorized capital and, therefore, such houses were tottering on an extremely thin base. As to the management of banking affairs, with no proven banking model to guide them, most of these banks were little more than glorified sahukars of old. All this was bound to lead to a disastrous end and it did—during a short period of five years from 1913 to 1917, as many as eighty-seven banks with a total paid-up of nearly Rs 20 million failed (Rau 1925: 221–31).

Inquiries instituted into the winding-up revealed that the crisis was due to a combination of factors like lack of prudence while lending, absence of a central bank, weak legislation, and even incompetent auditors. While the industrial sector had gone through refinements in legislation many times, the banking sector operated as an independent sector. In fact, the Company Law of 1913 did not even attempt to define a bank, much less regulate it. It was only in 1936 that a new Company Law, and the formation of a central bank, the Reserve Bank of India (RBI), brought about a degree of order into the financial sector. Till then, the family and other traditional sources continued to be the mainstay of finance for all commercial activities.

WANING SWADESHI MOVEMENT AND WORLD WAR I (1885–1915)

The waning of the swadeshi spirit dampened sales of domestic products. Almost in compensation, business prospects were bolstered by the outbreak of hostilities of World War I (WWI). Imports were disrupted and domestic demand for Indian-made goods went up. However, no new factories were set up because plant and machinery also could not be imported and there was no Indian manufacturer of large plant and machinery. Existing factories worked longer hours and there was an increase in energy requirements.

World War I also put strains on infrastructure like the railway network, which was already severely undercapitalized, leading to delays in shipment, slow trains, and obsolete rolling stock. India also supplied equipment for military campaigns in Palestine and Iraq, and financial stringency and management weakness limited capital investment to solve those problems in the post-war years (Hurd 1983: 740–1). This helped the Tatas to expand their hydroelectric system, a notable exception at a time when no new venture was being promoted. The Tata steel venture, which was till then the target of concerted official hostility and derisive propaganda spread by vested interests of the British steel industry, also supplied most of the government requirements during the war years. At the end of the war, therefore, the Tatas emerged much strengthened and respectable as an industrial house and this helped them add a series of other enterprises. Notable among these were their cement companies, apart from an engineering company, an electro-chemical concern, a construction firm, a sugar company, and a unit to produce soap and allied products.

European-owned companies, mainly in the east, also registered a spurt in growth, with the exception of companies involved in tea plantations since this was mainly an export-oriented business and they had trouble shipping their goods during the war. Jute registered major growth primarily due to military requirements of gunnies, sandbags, corn sacks, and hessians. As a corollary, coal mining also grew to respond to the increased energy demand from the jute industry.

Almost all companies made sizeable wartime profits except those companies that were primarily dependent on the export markets. Few business houses could resist the temptation to float new ventures but unlike the Tatas, not all were equipped to manage these new businesses, called war babies, some far removed from their core competencies. Inevitably, these houses had to resort to rationalization of their businesses.

Indian investments were no longer confined to just cotton and its derivative industries. They expanded to other lines like paper, engineering, shipping, and chemicals. For instance, two prominent Marwari families—G.D. Birla and Sarupchand Hukumchand—opened up jute mills in Calcutta, using wartime profits. This was a clear challenge to the established Scottish monopoly in the trade. The house of Birlas went on to write one of the glorious chapters of Indian businesses over the next century.

The strident and confident mood of the Indian industrialists as a result of gains made during WWI gained further ground in 1915 with the arrival of Mohandas Karamchand Gandhi on the scene. A lawyer by training, Gandhi took up social causes and his doctrine of pacific militancy and saint-like demeanour endeared him to Indian businesses, which, like businesses all over the world, abhorred violence or conflict.

There was increasing involvement between businessmen and politicians, causing further rift between Indian and expatriate business interests. The Indian government, perhaps conscious of the help it got from Indian business during the war years, and in any case not wanting to antagonize them, did not embark on any policies which might have hurt them.

The social composition of business people also underwent a change. People, who were hitherto engaged merely in trade or those who had remained aloof from any business activity—whether in accordance with their respective caste prescription of occupational choices or otherwise—were also drawn into the enterprise class.

At the end of WWI, therefore, industry definitively defined the contours of Indian business, despite its admittedly lop-sided penetration. Invariably, these industries were identified with certain families or groups, mainly due to the system of the managing agency that held sway over the form of ownership—a feature that exists even today.

Native Indian businesses progressively became more conscious of its distinct identity and developed several business associations and chambers of industry and commerce. Formal cartels, informal agency agreements, and political influence were important aspects of business activity in India in the first half of the twentieth century. Relations of industrial houses with the vast and potentially very powerful 'unorganized' business sector was vital to the distribution, sales, and credit systems, especially the up-country merchants, bankers, and credit suppliers who controlled much of the domestic economic activity.

WORLD WAR II AND ITS EFFECT ON INDIAN BUSINESS (1939–45)

The Great Depression of the 1930s that cast its shadow all over the world was not felt very severely in India, maybe because the Indian markets were not well integrated into world markets. But it did dampen business spirits and producers did not have ready answers to problems created by falling or stagnant demand. In the background of insipid business performance, World War II (WWII) was almost a godsend for businesspeople. Imports were once again disrupted and demand for domestic products shot up again. Factories worked overtime to produce up to maximum capacity utilization. Government purchases appeared never-ending, adding to the impetus for production. Most businesses made handsome profits; however, these profits could not be fully utilized for re-investment because the embargo on imports also extended to capital goods in which sector India was far from self-sufficient.

Government purchases also appeared to soak up all available supplies, leading to a widespread shortage of everything, from coal and steel to even foodstuff. In theory, India's share of the cost of war was to be met by taxation in India and reimbursement from Britain but actual government measures to deal with this matter only served to aggravate the situation—it resorted to printing paper money against credit to India's sterling reserves deposited with the Bank of England. This was a perfect recipe for promoting severe inflation, which left fundamental imbalances in many areas that lasted long after the coming of peace.

Nevertheless, businesses enjoyed a period of uninterrupted prosperity for which credit must surly go the proactive measures adopted by the government: strikes and lockouts were banned, several provisions of the Factory Act were relaxed, and steps taken to ensure regular supply of stores and raw materials to manufacturers. To be sure, these measures had many critics but few from the business fraternity.

Inevitably, this period of boom had its underside—plant and machinery, which were in any case old and outdated, faced further wear and tear due to increased work. Upgrading and modernization was difficult—assuming it was on the drawing board of business houses—due to disruptions in imports. At the end of the WWII and through the 1940s, therefore, businesses had to contend with a host of challenges from lack of real-term profits to depreciated plant and machinery, all in the background of increasing political unrest and food famine.

BUSINESS AND POLITICS DURING THE FREEDOM STRUGGLE (1885–1947)

The INC was formed in 1885 more as a pressure group to interact between the ruler and the ruled than as a political entity. Most new and upcoming industrial-businessmen supported INC with funds and/ or participation. While expatriate businessmen remained largely aloof from politics, Indian businessmen increased their engagement with the government, using INC and other budding trade organizations to further the causes of business interests and extract favourable measures such as imposing import duty on Manchester goods or opposing cotton excise duties.

This mutual partnership between business and politics got a further boost with the arrival of M.K. Gandhi (later Mahatma) from South Africa. Gandhi provoked a whole spectrum of attitudes towards him ranging from unwavering loyalty (like G.D. Birla) to active hostility (mainly expatriate businessmen and Indian businessmen who were socially closer to the ruling race).

There were, of course, elements of Gandhi's philosophy that ought to have worried industrialists, such as his dream of a self-sufficient village or his preference of small-scale and cottage industries. But these were not immediately relevant in the larger scheme of things.

At the same time, businessmen did not want to alienate the government of the day and constantly played a balancing act to maintain equidistance between the INC and the rulers. As a slowly unfolding strategy, they wanted to engage sufficiently with the INC to ensure that its thinking on major issues affecting business interests coincided with their own and were prepared to support with funds those programmes that were not confrontational and so long as they could not be accused by the government of encouraging political agitation.

Therefore, Indian businessmen favoured the legislative route to reform despite stiff opposition from Gandhi towards the idea of entry into the Central Legislative Assembly. Within the Assembly, however, the industrialists and nationalist or '*swaraj*-ist' members worked closely together, being bound by community of interests and presented their case as one voice. For instance, in the matter of exchange rate between the rupee and sterling, they took on the government together on the official position which favoured British imports through an adverse rupee–sterling exchange rate and managed to bring about some parity. No other forum could have provided a better opportunity for nationalist business interests and purely political interests to forge a strong and common bond than participation in the Assembly.

In 1935, the British Parliament passed the Government of India Act, creating a federal structure for India and providing a framework for devolution of powers to Indians in governance of the country.

There was a period of relative tranquillity after the formation of Congress ministries in most provinces in 1937. Big businesses, after all, depended on the new government in all provinces for all sorts of concessions; the new government added to a sense of well-being by not adopting a rabid agitational posture or pronounced leftist attitudes.

Just before the adoption of Quit India resolution in 1942, a group of industrialists including stalwarts like G.D. Birla and J.R.D. Tata wrote a memorandum to the viceroy, assuring him of their opposition to open conflict: 'We are businessmen and therefore we need hardly point out that our interest lies in peace, harmony, goodwill and order throughout the country' (Moraes 1967: 213, 219; qtd in Tripathi 2004: 273, fn 9).

As the possibility of transfer of power became more real, the industrialists were more anxious than ever to draw closer to the INC. This went to the extent of their conversion to the concept of a planned economy. The working reports of the National Planning Committee (NPC), constituted by the Congress under the leadership of Jawaharlal Nehru made it clear that planning would be an essential element of economic policy under an indigenous government. And so it came about that in 1944, a group of seven prominent businessmen produced a document called 'the Bombay Plan'. The authors of the document recognized the need for planned development, emphasized state ownership and control of key industries and agreed with the idea of a central directing authority to ensure successful implementation of the economic plans. Private sector, though it will exist, will have to function under tight state direction. The Plan anticipated in several ways the guiding spirit of the First Industrial Policy formed after the transfer of powers as well the Five-Year Plans.

On the question of the Partition of India, most prominent businessmen did not oppose it on commercial grounds. The first Indian businessman to openly support the idea of Pakistan was Ramkrishna Dalmiya: '...to accept Pakistan as being the only solution under the circumstances' (Tripathi 2004: 275). Lala Shri Ram took a clear stand against the idea, in part because he had business interests in the part which might have gone to Pakistan. Ardeshir Dalal, a close associate of the Tatas also pointed out that '[if created] Pakistan will cut itself off from the great economic and industrial future that a self-governing India may look forward to' (Ibid.)

Opposition to the creation of Pakistan was not based on economic benefits that may or may not ensue but rather on an emotional level, including a religious one.

The Indian business class, notwithstanding the strong support or opposition of individual members, had little influence on the developments that determined the political fate of the subcontinent. They were involved only on the periphery of political activities and were engaged in too much of a balancing act to effectively mould events to suit their interests.

INTRINSIC STRENGTH OF INDIAN BUSINESS

By the beginning of the twentieth century, three broadly identifiable business groups had taken shape in the country. One group comprised of indigenous businessmen, mostly families or groups that mainly dealt in traditional or consumer goods such as cotton and derivatives, sugar, cement, etc. The second included the old expatriate firms that rose in strength, coinciding with the consolidation of British political presence. These were involved in pioneering sectors like tea, jute, and coal. The third group represented multinational companies, which, with their global business sense, entered new sectors such as industrial grade chemicals, engineering goods, and even stores.

This is merely a broadly defined structure. There were numerous instances of overlap and inter-linkages with cross-holdings in and by different groups. Then there was the entire network of traders like commission agents, etc., that was interwoven in this fabric.

Towards the end of colonial rule, a merchant was not restricted by law or circumstances to one market or region and could look upon the whole country—or even the whole world—as his canvas. The banking system was more than just rudimentary and, so, business could think of larger investments than what they could raise from their family resources. The joint-stock method of ownership became prevalent although not in its pure form but as an adaptation of the sole-proprietorship or partnership form of absolute control via managing agencies. Legislation and its enforcement were in a mature state, providing much needed security in the growth of business dealings.

In absolute terms, there was a great industrial expansion in India in the early twentieth century. 'By 1939-40, the paid-up capital of joint-stock companies registered in India had increased fourfold from its 1914 level. It increased an additional 50% beyond the 1939-40 level by 1946. The annual rate of increase between 1914 and 1946 was 16.85%' (Ray 1979: 39 [Table 9]). Colonial India was a private enterprise economy in the sense that most decisions about allocation of resources were made by the private sector; the state's annual share of the gross national product averaged less than 10 per cent in every decade from 1872 to 1947 (Tomlinson 1993: 95).

This would lead some to believe that at the end of colonial rule, India had a fairly robust economy, owned by Indians—a truly Indian enterprise class. But scratch the surface and we find that only capital and labour was actually Indian. For other factors of production, notably technology and expertise, the so-called Indian business was dependent mainly on Britain, and later America. In any industry, whether it was textile, sugar, cement, steel, or shipbuilding, there were few instances of indigenous technology being used or any attempts to promote such ventures, for that matter.

Perhaps there was a reason for such reluctance to promote technology. Most promoters of businesses had a trading background, which made them primarily concerned with the financial aspects of a business, unlike the founders of industrial firms in Great Britain and other European countries. The founders in those countries were skilled in their chosen craft—craftsmen, as it were—and therefore more interested in the technical aspect of the business and its innovation.

The house of the Tatas was perhaps the notable exception in attempting research and development in its steel venture for new varieties of steel. This was during WWII and may be because of the exigencies of the war, but some effort was certainly made. The Tatas also actively hired Indian personnel after the mid-1920s and started a vigorous programme of successful training. This gave them substantial savings in labour costs since Indian replacement of foreign technicians were typically paid only two-thirds of the European salaries and more importantly, started a build-up of a base of indigenous expertise.

Tirthankar Roy (2000: 118) argues that India's resource endowments explain both the low investment levels and the resulting lack of productivity growth. The scarcity and the consequent high cost of capital and skilled labour in India meant that India was best suited to be and was a vast world of traditional manufacturing, consisting of tool-based industrial production performed in homes and small offices.

There was little incentive for mills and factory owners to invest their profits into research and development (R&D), especially since importing technology and expertise was so much easier and had very little turnaround time. Besides, there was 'colonial syndrome' wherein Indians perceived anything emerging from the metropolitan country as intrinsically superior. Colonialism had a much deeper impact on the lack of indigenous expertise and technology than people would accept.

While India was the unquestioned world leader in textiles and other handicrafts at the onset of colonial rule, that superiority—India produced nearly a quarter of the world production of manufactured goods in 1750—could not be sustained in the face of the increasing popularity of 'mill cloth' pioneered by Britain. Production techniques used reflected the availability of cheap manual labour and the processes were such as 'could not be used in any country where manual labour possessed value' (Francis Buchanan; qtd in Morris 1983: 559). India had always had weak technological traditions, in part due to a cultural ethos of unquestioning acceptance of an established way of life. This received no fillip during the colonial years either because of lack of official patronage of technical education or because of lack of interest among Indians themselves or both.

This tradition of importing technology continued unabated after India attained independence. India was a country in a hurry and had to catch up with the world in creating an industrial base. As Jawaharlal Nehru said in the 1950s, 'I believe as a practical proposition that it is better to have a second-rate thing made in one's own country than a first-rate thing one has to import' (Miles and Scott: 199). Collaborating with various countries was the obvious choice except that this time India shopped in a wider pool of countries. The erstwhile Soviet Union was a big provider of technology, particularly in steel and armament industries. Automobile industry was another major consumer of imported technology—and one of the slowest to adapt to new innovation. For decades, the country had to put up with Bajaj scooters, Tata trucks, and Ambassador passenger cars, which were at least twenty years behind their economic lifecycles because industrialists felt no imperative to adopt more efficient technology. Globalization in the 1990s and competition from global majors quickly raised the bar and the quality and choice of products improved significantly in a short time.

INDEPENDENCE AND BUSINESS ENTERPRISE

Indian businesses greeted Independence with a mixture of sadness, hope, and trepidation. Apart from the colossal human tragedy due to the horrors of the holocaust following the Partition of India, many businessmen lost sizeable chunks of their business to the newly created states of West and East Pakistan and some were reduced to penury. At the same time, there was no doubt among businessmen that the new dispensation would be more favourable than the colonial regime towards their ambitions and goals. The pronouncements made from time to time by political leaders before independence, however, made it clear to everyone that the state expected to play a far bigger role in business matters. How much and to what degree was still uncertain.

The Congress leadership was still evolving its philosophy with respect to economic thought and had strong proponents of both extreme left and extreme right within its ranks. 'The actual model of development that emerged was a product of a number of compromises among the planners of the day ... Thus, the country started off with a hybrid system of a mixed economy with a strong interventionist state carrying out centralized planning and a small private sector as a mild but important feature' (Kaushik and Dutta 2005a: 159).

The state reserved for itself many sectors and exhorted the public sector 'to reach the commanding heights of the economy'. As independent India's first Prime Minister Jawaharlal Nehru said, '...we are a nation in a hurry ... we are not going to spend the next 50 years arriving slowly' (qtd from memory).

The foundation of heavy industry laid by the public sector was important in giving an industrial base to the country and although one may argue about the efficiency or effectiveness of the public sector, it has nevertheless helped in reducing the steepness of the learning curve of the Indian industry.

Regardless of heavy government presence in most major sectors of the economy that the government had reserved for itself vide a Policy Statement of 1948, the private sector was largely left alone to pursue their existing businesses. Even the much-maligned and much-abused managing agency system, which entrenched family management of public limited companies, did not get the axe decisively and was permitted to continue up to 1960.

It was the post-Nehru regime, led by Indira Gandhi that really constrained and contained the private sector. Understandably, the country could ill afford a purely capitalist economy but the path taken later was not socialist either. Even by the 1950s, the Indian economy was far from any equilibrium and its internal market mechanisms were so damaged because of imbalances left over from 1940s that it was unable to allocate resources effectively. Controls were essential in the short term to shore up this position, and by the time normal conditions were restored the Indian government was committed to centralized planning for political and administrative reasons as well as for economic ones.

Centralized planning was a convenient jargon for government to amass enormous power over the destiny of the private sector. The government took a series of measures, from enactment of restrictive laws like MRTP (Monopoly and Restrictive Trade Practices) Act, nationalization of fourteen major banks, draconian tax rates, and licensing policies that effectively curtailed the vitality of big business. There were years in which tax rates over a certain threshold of income were over 100 per cent which gave no incentive for businesses to expand. The licensing era saw several small and marginal players in almost all industries when the prevailing market mantra was to corner as many licences as one could, never mind if one had no competence in the sector. This led to fragmentation of the market leading to bad economies of scale. Subsequent dismantling of the licence–permit raj has led to the restructuring and consolidation in several sectors, and correcting distortions but in the process much business energy has been lost and a number of businesses, which were successful during the era of protection, quickly died. Newer and focused players entered the field and altered the market dynamics permanently.

INDUSTRIAL AND TECHNOLOGY POLICY FOR TV RECEIVERS

The Department of Electronics and the Electronic Commission acted upon a 'survey' conducted by state owned All India Radio [AIR] in 1970 to estimate the production capacity of TV sets (black & white), which estimated the absorption capacity of the country at 200000 TV sets per year. They therefore recommended an immediate increase in the TV-set production capacity from the existing 40000 sets per year to 200000 sets per year. The Electronics Commission arrived at the following conclusions:

As manufacture of TV sets had already been established on the basis of 'indigenous know-how', no capacity needed to be licensed to large industrial houses or to companies with foreign equity holdings.

The capacity of each of the four out of the five existing large scale private sector manufacturers, except the multinational company Philips, would be doubled.

A capacity of 50000 sets would be reserved for the three public sector companies—ECIL [Electronics Corporation of India Limited], BEL [Bharat Electronics Limited] and HAL [Hindustan Aeronautics Limited]. The Chairman of the Electronics Commission was empowered to settle the exact manner in which this capacity would be divided among the three companies.

A further capacity of 100000 TV sets would be licensed to new applicants in the private sector. Preference would be given to individual scientists, engineers and technicians who had developed competence in the area of TV electronics and to consortia of small scale units.

A wide dispersal of the manufacturing units on a regional basis would be ensured.

This formed the basis of policy guidelines of TV manufacture in 1970 and within which industry had to work. (Parthasarthi 2007: 78–9)

In 2006, the number of TV sets crossed 100 million, a figure even the most ambitious forward-looking public policy guideline could not foresee. This meant that 44 per cent of the population (*National Family Health Survey 2005–6*) had access to TV.

Similar foresight by planners was also seen in the telecom sector. Many planners considered telephone to be a luxury, and investment and expansion of telecommunication was regarded as elitist. Opening the telecom sector to private participation has deepened connectivity— the number of connections were estimated to have increased to 621.28 million at the end of financial year 2009–10 (TRAI 2010). In fact, an entire section of the population has leapfrogged into wireless telephones (584.32 million) with immense boost to business opportunities.

How did independent India acquiesce in such an imperial regime and allow it to thrive is an enduring mystery. Corruption was (and still is) rampant. A centralized planning system gave a lot of business administration power in the hands of the bureaucrats, most of who are from the upper castes. The paradox is that business success is essentially distilled from acquisitiveness, acumen, even greed and sentiments that are traditionally scorned by the literary 'cultured' class comprising the upper castes. (Jawaharlal Nehru once said, '...profit! Oh, how I hate that word' [qtd from memory].) When such people are in charge of shaping the economic destiny of the country, 'their inborn contempt and ignorance of merchants and markets prevent them from both recognizing the failures of the past governmental interventions and promoting the evolution of a market economy in India. Unfortunately, such market evolution is a key factor in determining the future economic prospect of India' (Lal 1999: 41).

Besides a few token noises against the repressive policies, business leaders saw more merit in exploiting the situation to their benefit. There were enough loopholes in the law and enough corrupt government staff for business groups to greatly expand their private enterprises than in the British regime's broad philosophy of laissez faire.

'Bureaucratic controls in India are seen as forming an integral part of a rent-seeking society in which the owners of scarce assets (land, capital) or privileges (such as import licenses) are simply rewarded for this ownership, rather than being forced to earn a return on them by efficient working in an open market' (Krueger 1974).

It is the legacy of this mindset that makes the government of Delhi even in the twenty-first century, armtwist private hospitals and educational institutes to reserve up to 25 per cent of their capacity to free-of-cost serve members of the economically weaker sections of society or try to impose a caste-based reservation policy in employment in the private sector—and in the process opens up new avenues of corruption by government inspectors. Now, if the government were to charge market rates for scarce resources like land or licences, the money can be used to run initiatives of the government in discharge of its obligations to citizens.

Or, if the country had produced sustainable and strong independent institutions, we would look to private and business philanthropy to take forward weaker sections of the society. The economy of newly independent India could not develop without active assistance from the state but the state's ideology, technical competence, and managerial capacity had been found somewhat wanting.

The extent of government intervention in an economy is a dynamic factor, changing with the course of development at different stages. At one extreme is the argument that markets are the best leveller—left to themselves, producers will produce what people want at prices people will pay. At the other end is the ideology that the government should control all aspects of production and distribution. Both these extremes are untenable in the real-world experience of economies. A total laissez-faire approach is as difficult to sustain as total central control. Most economies, therefore, are mixed economies because there are markets and there is government control of varying degrees.

As policymakers in India become less contemptuous and ignorant about trade and commerce, they might begin to substitute *Bania* for 'Brahmin' ideals and might at last begin to dissolve intellectual bulwarks of Indian economic constraints.

LIBERALIZATION AND BEYOND

Although Indian markets were not linked to global markets at the beginning of the 1990s, the Middle East crisis of 1990 had a deep impact on the Indian economy. Firstly, global oil prices rose steeply and oil formed (still does) the largest item on India's import bill; secondly, remittances of foreign exchange by overseas Indian workers was disrupted. This double trouble meant that India's international reserves (excluding gold) fell from 5.23 billion SDRs (Special Drawing Rights) in 1986 to 1.07 billion SDRs in 1990 (Gang and Ansari 1999). India was also facing political instability and all these factors led to downgrading the country's credit rating with the result that India's access to foreign credit was severely curtailed. By 1991, India was very low on foreign exchange and about to default on its international monetary obligations.

The country had to approach international agencies like International Monetary Fund (IMF) and World Bank for a bail out. These agencies set out economic course correction as a condition for lending. Thus India embarked on the long road to liberalization of its economy and markets—not out of any strong political conviction but to implement the mandate of donors. Liberalization, in effect, means a systematic release of market forces from statal, para-statal, and other institutional interferences in the day-to-day working of the economy. The process of freeing up the economy from a socialist mindset has continued through several governments that have assumed power in the last one and a half decades, with minor adjustments to policies based on political convictions of the day. The country substituted the inward-looking trade policy for a more outward looking one, tightly controlled exchange rate with a more market-determined rate and considerably reduced its hostility towards foreign investment.

In the period, 1991–3, most reforms were made in the fiscal area, which was the immediate crisis that needed to be tackled; change was less marked in other areas. Although the atmosphere for control and regulation significantly receded, change was piecemeal and gradual. Some refer to this period of reform as the reform by stealth. 'As of

1990–1, India had not corrected the underlying structural problems of the relationship between the public and private sector and was allocating government resources to activities that in many instances were detrimental to growth' (Krueger and Chinoy 2002: 20). Trade liberalization and gradual opening up of capital account are the pillars of India's economic success following liberalization. The biggest beneficiary, however, has been the services sector which had been poorly regulated rather than the manufacturing sector with access to abundant labour. Services, particularly those in the new economy, never had to face the strict control and archaic laws that older traditional industries had to face, and by the time the government decided to regulate the services, especially software, the economic mood of the country had changed, services had proved their utility to the economy and government policies had become far more business-friendly. Such policies are primarily responsible for boosting India's service export competitiveness, growing at an annual rate of 10 per cent against an average GDP growth of 8 per cent in 2007. An IMF research has found that a healthy and vibrant financial sector is a main pillar of the country's development strategy; the government is deepening India's financial markets further by instituting pension and insurance reforms (Poirson 2007).

However, reforms have been uneven across sectors and regions. There are several infrastructural constraints still plaguing business growth, subsidies in agriculture and fertilizers have not been addressed adequately (a politically volatile issue), administration is not as smooth as a global economy should expect, and labour reforms have yet to be implemented. For all its flaws, the reform process has been successful in several areas—maximum excise duty was reduced from 105 per cent in 1990–1 to 70 per cent in 1994–5, personal income tax rate from 54 per cent to 40 per cent over the same period. Tax reforms have also considerably improved collection—67 per cent reduction in average tariffs during 1988–2001 contributed nearly 90 per cent of the decline in customs' evasion (Mishra, Subramanian, and Topalova 2007). Maximum import duties have come down from 400 per cent in 1990–1 to 65 per cent in 1994–5. In 2009–10, the standard rate of excise duty was 10 per cent while personal income tax was pegged at a maximum of 30 per cent.

One study found a remarkable increase in business investment in India following the market-oriented structural reforms initiated in 1991. Although the study found that a decline in the rate of growth of real public sector investment brought about by reform-related fiscal squeeze, the adverse impact on corporate investment is outweighed by the salutary effects of decline in real rental cost of capital brought about by the reform process and favourable changes in investor perception in the aftermath of reforms (Athukorala and Sen n.d.: 16). Despite numerous studies of the link between trade liberalization and economic growth, research evidence is not conclusive. However, it is fair to say that openness, by leading to lower prices, better information, and newer technologies, has a useful role to play in promoting growth. And this is amply proved by India's experience with the reform process: the total basket of reforms has reduced the government's general deficit from 10 per cent in 2002–3 to 6 per cent of the GDP at the end of March 2007 (5.1 per cent of the GDP in 2009–10) and net FDI has increased from USD 0.1 billion in 1991–2 to USD 5.6 billion in 2005–6 and an estimated USD 11 billion in 2006–7; in 2010–11 equity inflow of FDI was over USD 180 billion. Growth has also reduced poverty rate from 26 per cent in 1999–2000 to less than 22 per cent in 2004–5 (Rodrik and Subramanian 2005). However, according to the Planning Commission, this figure rose to 37 per cent in 2010.

India has experienced a surge in productivity mainly due to an 'attitudinal shift in government' (Rodrik and Subramanian 2005; qtd. in Poirson 2007: 6). Perhaps, the best test of success is the slow and steady upward march of the GDP growth rate from 5.3 per cent in 1994 to 6.8 per cent in 1996–7, to a sustained 8–9 per cent over the past couple of years.

Indian planners have had to suspend their dislike of markets and its auto-correction mode, and have made considerable progress towards reducing the country's business insularity and speeding up integration with world markets.

At the moment India's growth is powered mostly by services and skill-intensive manufacturing activities. 'India needs to broaden its expansion to encompass labour-intensive manufacturing to realize (the) potential (of its demographic dividend)' (qtd in Poirson 2007: 7).

2

Indigenous Business and Financial Practices

The Indian subcontinent had flourishing trade and commerce for several centuries, both maritime and over land, with strong trade links to the Arabian world, central and southeast Asia, as well as European empires. There have been periods of political stability with strong kings whose writ ran over large parts of the land but for the most part in history, Indian trade operated in a politically uncertain, even turbulent environment. This made traders and merchants evolve several techniques and systems of operation that adequately addressed the challenges of those times and constantly adjusted to threats and advantages besides absorbing new knowledge brought about through international trade. For instance, several years before the beginning of rudimentary banking, large temples held part of the wealth of the community in the form of gold and other precious metals and gems. The guarantee of security of such a practice of storing wealth was, quite literally, in the hands of god. The fragility of this security system was quickly exposed when invaders subscribing to different gods, repeatedly looted the community wealth stored in places of worship. Exposure to outside influences and expanding trade and commerce helped to evolve more sophisticated systems of finance and control, some of which are discussed in the following pages.

MERCHANT GUILDS, *SRENIS* OR *NIGAMAS*

One of the earliest known instruments of collective mercantile benefit in India were merchant guilds, formed to protect the interests of traders, artisans, and producers. Guilds were akin to corporate self-governing entities with their own regulations which were duly recognized and even registered by the local authorities.

Guilds or *srenis* or *nigamas* developed in ancient India were a unique social innovation which served a number of useful functions. Thaplyal (2001) discusses the institution of guilds in four time brackets: (i) Vedic period, (ii) Buddhist/Jain period, (iii) Mauryan period, and (iv) Post-Mauryan period. He found that guilds enjoyed considerable autonomy which came, not as a favour from the state, but by their inherent right.

Srenis or nigamas were formed around a trade or a craft and were essentially economic institutions; they could have members across castes and a person could be a member of more than one sreni or nigama. Some srenis and nigamas controlled trade and commerce of various commodities and Kautilya's *Arthashastra* reveals that taxes paid by guilds formed an important source of income to the state.

Thapar says that another early incentive to forming guilds must have been competition; economically it was better to work in a body than to work individually as a corporation would provide added social status and when necessary, assistance could be sought from other members (2000: 73). By gradual stages, guilds developed into the most important industrial bodies in their area.

Over time, srenis were well-regulated and codified entities whose membership sometimes extended over several towns and cities. There were various officers of guilds, who specialized in different works and various guilds, had their law, based on customs and usage regarding matters like organization, production, fixation of prices of commodities, etc. Documentation was considered important and *Arthashastra* mentions a superintendent of accounts who would keep a record of the customs and transactions of the corpus. Most srenis performed the important task of imparting technical education or apprenticeship in the particular trade (but not subjects of religious, philosophical, or higher education, which was the preserve of Brahmins) and routinely carried out administrative, economic, charitable, and banking functions. Some powerful guilds were even known to provide judicial functions in civil cases for their own members.

References to various aspects of formation, operation and duties are found in several ancient texts such as *Arthashastra* (around AD 300), *Yajnavalkyasmriti* (100 BC to AD 300), *Gautama Dharmasutra* (600 BC to 400 BC), *Manusmriti* (300 BC to AD 200), and even the Mahabharata, revealing that srenis formed an important institution of those times (Vyas 1992: 234).

The main purpose of such interest shown by administrators appears to be to establish control over the activities of these corporate organizations and to maintain a check on their earnings and profits. For instance, Kautilya (the original propagator of absolute state control over all affairs of the land) in his *Arthashastra* devised three methods to regulate such corporate organizations, comparable to modern methods: (i) registration of corporations laying down checks and balances on the activities of artisans and craftsmen, (ii) formulation of penal laws to prevent their transgression, and (iii) appointment of special tribunals to administer penal laws relating to artisans and craftsmen.

Further, in order to have effective control over them, guilds were forbidden to transfer their activities from one region to another without notifying the authorities (Jain 1971: 193–6). Thus, business or 'corporate' life in India can be traced back to several centuries and had developed a high level of sophistication of operations. Merchant guilds, probably the earliest democratic institutions of the world, served a very useful role in the regulation of trade and commerce, besides providing socially relevant functions like technical training to youngsters and charity to the poor and needy.

Industry Guilds in Modern Times

The practice of creating trade and industry guilds or associations continues into modern times. In 1830, some traders and craftsmen of Calcutta organized to form the Calcutta Trades Association as a business assembly so as to further common business interests and objectives. In 1834, it became the first in British India to be recognized as a public body with powers to address the government directly and was later called the Calcutta Chamber of Commerce.

By the mid-1830s, all three Presidencies had their chambers of commerce—Calcutta Chamber of Commerce in 1830 (and in 1853, the Bengal Chamber of Commerce), and the Bombay and Madras Chambers by 1836. These chambers were tightly controlled and regulated by Europeans, although some of them did have a few members from Indian business communities. Since European businessmen had a cultural affinity with the rulers, there was a perception (partly real and partly imagined) of more favourable concessions by the government to expatriate business interests through such industry associations.

A growing sense of nationalist sentiment led Indian businessmen to group themselves into industry chambers of their own and probably the first of these was the Native Piece Goods Merchants' Association in Bombay in 1836. Fuelled by a feeling of neglect by the European-dominated large chambers, several other Indian trade associations, such as Bengal National Chamber of Commerce and Bharat Chamber of Commerce, both in Calcutta, and Indian Chamber of Commerce in Cochin, came into being.

However, each of these chambers was still limited in scope and reach (including the expatriate-dominated chambers) and it was only in 1921 that a pressure group consisting of various chambers was formed that claimed to represent the entire Indian business—Associated Chambers of Commerce and Industry or ASSOCHAM. This apex body was again dominated by Europeans who came together to protect their business interests in the country against a growing tide of nationalism.

By this time, the chasm between Indian and European businesses had widened, with both sides petitioning and expecting government policies to favour their own interests. In 1923, when ASSOCHAM opposed the grant of protection to the Indian steel industry, nationalists and industry captains G.D. Birla and Purshottamdas Thakur initiated the process of setting up an apex body of Indian business chambers and in 1927, the Federation of Indian Chambers of Commerce (later 'and Industry' was added) or FICCI was born. The objective of FICCI was to bring merchants from all over India on one platform so as to put forward 'their well-considered and combined views before the government with a force which will carry greater weight than those of the combined European institutions' (Tripathi 2004: 200). The history of FICCI is closely tied to the freedom movement and its policies have been influenced and shaped by nationalists while it has played a major role in helping to evolve the economic policies of the new national government.

Most of the early business associations were formed to protect specific business or sectoral interests. For instance, in 1895, a few Indian engineering firms got together and formed an association called the Engineering and Iron Trade Association to act as a pressure group on the British government to procure orders for iron, steel and engineering goods from firms located in India (the government policy till then was to procure government orders from firms located in the United Kingdom). The association changed its name in 1912 to Indian Engineering Association to exclude traders from its purview and concentrate on manufacturers only since the business interests of the two groups appeared divergent—traders found it more profitable to procure goods from overseas and sell them in the country whereas manufacturers were interested in increasing the local production. A few name changes occurred to reflect the objectives of the association and in 1991, post-liberalization, the association came to be called the Confederation of Indian Industries (CII) to focus on inter-sectoral integration of businesses. Presently, it is a very active not-for-profit business association of India which seeks to create and sustain an environment conducive to the growth of the Indian industry, both within the country and globally.

All the industry associations of India—FICCI, ASSOCHAM, CII, etc.—have undergone restructuring to change the organization in tune with modern times. The membership of the chambers, which had been the exclusive preserve of Indian business groups post independence, has gradually begun to include multinational companies as well. The changing face of the Indian business groups finds expression in the membership and direction of the chambers as well. Just as the second and third generation owners of family business groups have rewritten the way they conduct business, these young leaders have taken over the stewardship of the chambers and associations and are making them more proactive, engaged with all stakeholders, and are now major forums where Indian business interests can find expression.

The common cause of all such associations and chambers is to provide a platform for representing business interests of the members while engaging the government on policy matters such as trade barriers, tax, and other laws. Most of them organize exhibitions, seminars, and trade fairs to promote businesses and deepen engagement levels globally with businesses and industry associations of other countries through collaborations and partnerships. Research, publications, and sponsored studies form an important facet of the associations through which their position and stand on various issues is expressed.

The National Association of Software Service Companies (NASSCOM) is one of the younger associations which was set up in 1988 to deal with the nascent Indian software industry. NASSCOM has been very proactive and a potent force in lobbying for policy-making, including helping in drafting laws and engagement rules for the industry. It has played a major role in creating a brand image for India in the global market for software services by becoming a one-stop platform for all matters relating to the industry in India. It regularly participates in international fairs besides organizing events in India and is a source of good quality data and surveys about the industry. NASSCOM has worked hard in the few years of its existence to create an enabling environment for the Indian software industry to flourish and progress up the value chain in global software services besides acting as a bridge between industry participants and the government.

Indian business houses now also take cross-membership of various industry associations rather than have a single membership with a silo-like attitude. This reduces unnecessary friction and competition among the chambers. Almost all the major chambers now have professional employees as well, apart from the intellectuals working on research.

HUNDIS—INDIGENOUS AND PARA-BANKING

When Europeans arrived in India in the sixteenth century, they found a sophisticated financial market already in place. Indians had developed a system—which they called the *hundi* system—to transmit large sums across the great distances of India and even further.

A hundi is a bill of exchange in a vernacular Indian language, governed by customs and local usage. The word hundi is derived from the Sanskrit root *hund* which means 'to collect'. Hundis have been in use and have evolved over several centuries and were used as remittance instruments to transfer funds from one place to another, as credit instruments to borrow money, like an IOU (I owe you), and for trade transactions.

A hundi is an unconditional order in writing made by a person directing another to pay a certain sum of money to a person named in that order. They were also used as cheques issued by indigenous bankers. There are typically two types of hundis—*Darshini* hundis, from the Hindi word meaning sight and therefore payable on demand, and *Muddati* (or *Miadi* or *Thavani*) hundis from the Urdu word meaning time, implying usance hundis, payable after a stipulated period of time or on a certain date specified in the hundi. Samples of such hundis are still preserved in the Reserve Bank of India (RBI) Monetary Museum.

History of Financial Instruments in India

In ancient India loan deed forms called *rnpatra* or *rnlekhya* were in use. These contained details such as the name of the debtor and creditor, amount of loan, rate of interest, condition and time of repayment, and was witnessed by a person of respectable means.

During the Mauryan period (322–185 BC), an instrument called *adesha* was in use, which was an order on a banker instructing him to pay the money mentioned on the note to a third person—similar to a bill of exchange as we understand it today.

The loan deed used in the Mughal period (from early sixteenth to mid-nineteenth century) was called *dastawez* and was of two types: *dastawez-e-indultabad*, payable on demand, and *dastawez-e-miadi*, payable after a stipulated time.

The most important class of credit instruments that have evolved in India were termed hundis. The origin of hundi is not very clear but it is believed to have been in use for financing long-distance trade in the early medieval period on trading routes such as the Silk Route, the eastern Mediterranean, and the Indian Ocean. Abul Fazl, the great historian, writes in 1596 about the level of sophistication that hundis had achieved by then. Again, Sujan Rai Bhandari, a historian, writes in 1695–6 about the important features of the hundi.

The use of hundis was widespread through several centuries and they are in use even today, though in a morphed form. They are, in reality, the oldest surviving form of credit instruments (Reserve Bank of India 1998).

Origins of Hundis

The hundi network was an institution developed by the trading community for long-distance trade in a landscape that was predominantly insecure and lacked basic infrastructure like roads or effective policing; what little the land could boast in terms of travel routes was frequently overrun by bandits. In such perilous circumstances, it was foolhardy for a businessman to carry cash or other liquid form of wealth to pay for business deals. The hundi network was based on trust and commitment among mercantile families or close-knit communities and groups that were geographically spread out. It is not surprising, therefore, that hundis also had a caste connotation. The position in the *varna* system determined who would pay what rate of interest. For instance, a Brahmin or a *Kshatriya* would pay a lot less than say, a *Shudra*, who was at the bottom of the caste ladder. At the same time, a Brahmin or a Kshatriya was not allowed to engage in money-lending business, which was the preserve of the *Bania* or *Vaishya* (Sharma 2006).

Caste-based or ethnic networks also promoted trust among traders such that hundis were rarely dishonoured despite the huge sums involved in the transactions. Scholars have attributed this in a large measure to a 'community responsibility system'—the whole community of an offending trader was made responsible for his breach of contract, particularly with a member of a different community. Threats of community sanctions and collective punishment made enforcement costs lower (at times awarding a premium for habitual honesty) for long-distance trade partners (Greif 1992).

Firms kept a list of creditable merchants whose notes—*sahjog* hundis—could expect a quick encashment in the bazaar. Such networks or guilds could be found in north and east India in the cities of Calcutta, Allahabad, and Benaras. In south India, the caste-based mercantile organization of the Nattukottai Chettiars in the colonial period had an elaborate system of hundis over long distances (with caste elite firms or *adathis* acting as the clearing houses), collective decisions on standardization of interest rates and caste *panchayats*, with customary sanctions providing the basis of indigenous banking networks spread out in large parts of south India and British south-east Asia (Bardhan 1999). The use of hundis in place of ready money became common in the period of political turmoil in the late seventeenth and early eighteenth century. Hundis helped strengthen ties between distant credit markets.

The hundi was used both as an instrument for remitting funds from one place to another and for raising short-term credit which would be repaid on maturity at another place. The average rate of interest—and discount—on hundis varied from market to market. The difference in interest/discount rates was partly a function of distance, partly of volume of bill traffic between the two cities and partly on the amount of funds available in a given city at a given point of time (Prakash 2006). Another reason for the growth and sophistication of the hundi network perhaps is the growing monetization of land revenue demand in Mughal India. The Mughal Empire had a very efficient system of land revenue collection and enormous sums of money collected as revenue needed to be transferred from the provinces to the capital of the empire at Agra/Delhi and reverse transferred to run provincial administration, trade, consumption, and even to fund military campaigns.

The basic document used by *shroffs* or *sarafs*, as they were variously called (who were real bankers as opposed to *mahajans* who were merely moneylenders), to carry out the large-scale business of remitting funds from one part of the empire to another was the hundi. Sarafs ranged in stature and capacity from small dealers to very large houses with agents or correspondents all over, like the house of Virji Vora of Surat or the house of Jagat Seth of Murshidabad. Often hundis carried seals or stamps of the royal house where it originated, leading to greater confidence in its intrinsic worth. It is reasonable to assume that certain hundis commanded more premium than others, depending on the drawer and drawee. If a hundi was lost, the owner could use the second or third copy (hundis were usually made in copies) and present it for payment. In a sense, hundis worked as alternative, privately issued currency—a reason perhaps why hundis have been banned from official circulation by the government of the day, from the British to the present-day Indian government.

The house of Jagat Seth was reputed to be the greatest banker of the then known world, as attested by several foreign travellers. The Seths had their kuthis (or branches/houses) in all important trade markets all over India and even in the Red Sea and Persian Gulf regions; bills issued by this house were welcome everywhere.

In a raid on Murshidabad by the Maratha army in 1742, a sum of Rs 20 million was looted from the house of Seths. The translator of the Persian chronicle, Seir-ul-Mutaqherin, was struck by the remarkable fact that 'so amazing a loss which would distress any monarch in Europe, affected him so little that he (Jagat Seth) continued to give government bills of exchange at sight of full one crore (10 million) at a time.'

It was this house which sent the Bengal revenues on behalf of the Bengal nawabs to the Mughal emperors from around the early 1730s to early 1740s, amounting to Rs 1.3 million every year by hundis on its kuthis in Delhi/Agra. (Chaudhary 1995: 114–15)

The British East India Company (EIC) was heavily dependent on the advances of Indian bankers for the first five or six decades of its rule (Markovits 2001: 9). Gradually, as the British consolidated its hold over governance in the subcontinent, they established formal banking channels. More importantly, they were less dependent on local money dealers to finance the Raj and district treasury bills had begun to replace the hundi as the basic instrument of official transaction (Bayly 1983: 299). Perhaps, as a further measure of consolidation of British power, in the 1820s and 1830s, it was declared illegal to use hundis. There was no connotation of criminal activity associated with the ban; rather, hundis were considered a challenge to the supremacy of the official banking channels established by the British to ensure successful revenue collection. The hundi was, thus, an integral part of indigenous banking that was used to finance legitimate end uses— including wars that were regularly fought for military/territorial gains by various aspirants of political power.

Hundi and Hawala

Hundi is often erroneously interchanged with the term hawala. The key difference between the two is that in hawala transactions there is virtually no paper trail (except rough noting in an often complex web of transactions). Transactions are carried out by word-of-mouth, involving a great deal of trust and honour amongst the operators. Disputes are settled outside the recognized legal and judicial systems. Settlement of debts can take various forms and not necessarily direct cash transactions. On the other hand, the basis of hundi is a written note, which promises to execute the transaction. Settlement always involves the transfer of money; although a hundi can be endorsed to another person in settlement of mutual debt, the ultimate settlement of a hundi is always in cash.

Informal Funds Transfer Systems in Today's World

This system of funds transfer is still used by many communities, particularly across national borders, at times to avoid bank charges, at others to escape legal scrutiny (for instance, uncomfortable questions about immigration status of sender and receiver), and sometimes to actively engage in illegal transactions like drug dealings, smuggling, or even terrorism. Post 9/11, such informal funds transfer are increasingly within the scrutiny radar of security agencies; however, the anonymity offered by such indigenous systems with little or no paper trail makes it difficult to regulate them, with the result that all informal transfer systems are held to be suspect.

Even today, there is a severe shortage of banking services in rural and semi-rural areas. When people emigrate from their villages to cities or other countries, they frequently need to remit money home. Anyone who has tried to open a bank account knows the difficulty that a migrant will face if s/he tries to use official channels for transmitting funds (with the notable exception of post office [India Post] money orders, which does a wonderful job of outreach to remote areas within India). At the first step, lack of a fixed address or other means of identity will stump their efforts. Such people have little choice but to rely upon informal banking systems.

A study commissioned by the Department for International Development (DFID) estimates the total remittances flowing out of the UK towards developing countries at £1.4 billion and out of this amount, £0.5 billion flowing out through informal mechanisms. The informal value transfer systems (IVTS) in operation include 'what are often known as hundi or interchangeably as hawala systems'. Often funds do not travel physically from one place to another and an accounting system like a chit or other form of confirmation is used. The system requires large pools of cash to be present at both ends for settlement, naturally in different currencies. IVTS offer more attractive rates to people wanting to remit funds across borders than formal operators and mechanisms. They are also more accessible to remitters and recipients with better outreach into smaller towns and villages (Blackwell and Seddon 2004).

Hundi was developed into a full-fledged money market instrument, which was only gradually replaced by the instruments of the formal banking system. Although hundis are not legally recognized in India under the Negotiable Instruments Act 1881, they have been very helpful in the evolution and development of modern instruments like bills of exchange, promissory notes, etc., and exist today in more formal forms. A number of traditional businesses today still transact in hundis despite its lack of legal recognition.

The concept of hundis has now metamorphosed into Bills of Exchange drawn between buyers and sellers which are an integral part of the trade finance and monetary system in modern India.

BAHI-KHATA AND PARTA SYSTEM

Bahi–khata

Bahi-khata is a bookkeeping and accounting system that has been practiced for several centuries; some researchers claim that it predates the thirteenth century descriptive treatise written by Pacioli of Italy. Some others contend that it is an offshoot of Islamic accounting systems brought to India by its Muslim conquerors. Although there is no conclusive agreement on the origins of the bahi-khata, the system has been in use for centuries and has undergone several changes and modifications in response to changing business conditions.

Bahi-khata is a book containing several pages (usually 365, representing the number of days in a year), bound in red cloth, the colour denoting prosperity, with the stitching usually having an artistic pattern, and it is tied up with string.

Most Indian traders followed the cash basis of accounting and this made the *rokad bahi* (cashbook) the most important book of accounts. No alterations were allowed in this khata and in case of error, the *munim* or accountant would have to write the entire cashbook all over again.

Transactions are first entered in the rokad bahi and then posted into the *khata bahi* (ledger). It uses the concept of *naam* (debit) and *jamaa* (credit) for maintaining accounts. This is the reason why bahi-khata is claimed to be a double-entry system of bookkeeping. Latter-day modifications like *nakal bahi* (journal) also record non-cash transactions which allow transactions affecting nominal accounts to be posted into the ledger, which is the forerunner of the modern-day system of accrual basis of accounting.

Indian businessmen hold their business in great reverence and this is reflected in the practice of performing puja (religious ritual) at the beginning of each accounting year, usually Deepavali to Deepavali. The bahi-khata and other account books are decorated with sacred symbols and there is an invocation to god for blessings of prosperity. This practice continues in most business houses of India even today although the context, including the accounting year, has substantially changed. It is not uncommon to find books of account maintained under the modern Western system carrying sacred religious symbols on the first page.

The language used for writing depends on the business; since most of the Indian business was in the hands of Marwaris and Gujaratis in the eighteenth, nineteenth and early twentieth centuries, *mundi* was the language of choice for bookkeeping. The other accounting language was found among Punjabi businessmen which was called *langdi* Hindi. Training in basic accounting methods, business attitudes, and knowledge of the language and script were often received within the munim's family before he was selected for the post. Since the position was one of immense trust, caste affiliations of the person played an important role in selection and were often hereditary. '…the munims are invested with very wide powers. They are not highly paid but their industry, integrity and efficiency are remarkable and proverbial' (Jain 1929: 36). Some commonly used books of accounts are: rokad bahi (cashbook), khata bahi (ledger), nakal bahi (journal), and *satti bahi* (sales/debtors' ledger). The principles of the double-entry system of accounting and the development of accrual basis of accounting integral to the bahi-khata system is now a part of the global accounting language and is practiced all over the world. Though there is a debate on where the accounting language originated, the strength of Indian traditional practices have laid the foundation of strong skills in accounting and financial skills associated with Indians.

The bahi-khata system is still practised in several parts of India, particularly in unincorporated enterprises and even as a parallel system of accounting apart from those mandatory under current laws; these books are also accepted by income tax authorities as proper books of account.

Parta System

The *parta* system of management is a uniquely indigenous management information system that has been developed and used by Indian business houses. Before the terms 'core competency' or 'unrelated businesses' gained currency, Indian business houses would invest in whatever business they thought would be profitable—and which was allowed by the imperial government. This line of reasoning was further buttressed by independent India's licence-raj such that business houses gathered whatever licences the government released—primarily to ensure a presence in those areas of businesses but also to thwart competition. The result was that most business houses had large, multi-unit, multi-product establishments with cross-holdings, which made the task of control very important.

The parta system was developed to keep track of the return on investment in a particular project and is widely credited to the legendary G.D. Birla but which other business houses adopted as well. 'Parta' is an abbreviation of the question in Hindi: *'Kya* cost *parta hai?'*, meaning 'What is the cost?', which is a key question of an investor trying to ascertain the profitability of a venture. The basic rationale of a parta system is embedded in the principles of costing, including marginal costing where the focus is on total and incremental cost of production. As resources were scarce, Indian businesses always focused on keeping costs low and monitoring costs to derive profits.

Parta is a system of accountability where the manager of each division or unit has to draw up a series of estimates for any investment, new or old, and serves as a constant tracking system. A master parta plan is prepared, which contains information like:

$$\text{Parta} = \text{Selling Cost} - (\text{Manufacturing Cost} + \text{Administrative Cost including Finance Cost}) = \text{Net Profit}$$

The master parta plan may run into several pages, depending on the nature and size/value of the project. This is then broken down into monthly partas, containing targets, which are adopted in consultation with the chief executive officer (CEO). This, in turn, is broken down into daily reports for micro-management.

The daily reports, including any difference between targets versus actual, are sent up the line to the top management, depending on the extent of involvement of senior management in the project. If results are consistently short of targets by designated dates, a review meeting of the senior-most people is held and suitable corrective action is decided (Taparia 2005). The parta management system is designed for a production-oriented business where daily output targets can be fixed and measured. There is also the underlying assumption that 'whatever is produced will be sold'.

The parta system is useful as an information system in a multi-unit group for control and monitoring, particularly where new projects are being implemented. It aims to keep a strict vigil on project costs to prevent or at least reduce cost overruns.

However, it is a largely top-down control mechanism with the result that managers (read non-family) do not have a sense of ownership with the process. Their role is limited to supplying numbers on a daily/ monthly or periodic basis rather than participate in fixing norms or other aspects of the process.

With the increasing use of digital information technology, the parta system has morphed into principles of marginal or differential costing, where the focus is now on determining and monitoring incremental costs and companies who deal with a large number of manufacturing parts like in an automobile or consumer electronics, where such principles are critical to the success of the business. Modern day Enterprise Resource Planning (ERP) and other large Information Technology (IT) systems have inbuilt capability to track such costs and also deliver daily cash, inventory reports, which is the basic foundation of the parta system, to manage businesses.

Principles drawn from the parta system in the modern form are used by successful businesses in India and outside to understand, monitor and control costs, and improve oversight of critical business functions of cash, and inventory movements.

CHIT FUNDS AND *NIDHI* FUNDS

Chit Funds

A 'chit' is an old indigenous financial instrument that combines savings and borrowings among a small group of persons called the members of the chit. It is in the nature of Rotating Savings and Credit Organizations (ROSCO) that have existed all over the world, especially among poor rural communities. In India, it originated in the villages of Tamil Nadu and Kerala about a century ago and has since reached such levels of sophistication that chit funds are regulated by a special law called the Chit Funds Act, 1982. Chit funds started as a grain pool when farmers would contribute a specific amount of grain from their produce, usually every six months to coincide with the cropping season. These amounts would be written on pieces or 'chits' of paper. A farmer who had a bad crop could dip into this common pool, which would again be noted on his chit. Gradually, chits began to be used for money procured from selling that produce and the periodicity was also adjusted; consequently, this system of pooling and lending came to be called 'chit funds'.

It is a financial mechanism that gathers small, scattered savings, and converts it into a usable pool of capital for the collective benefit of subscribers. It involves regular periodic subscriptions, called prize money, made over to a foreman who is a person or company that manages the chit, cash, costs, and assets for a definite period. Each subscriber or member is entitled to the prize money, determined by draw of lots or bidding auction or any other agreed method. There will be as many periodical instalments as there are members, which mean that even when a subscriber 'wins' the prize money, he is bound to pay the rest of the periodic instalments.

Chit funds, like most ROSCOs, are perhaps the most efficient form of financial intermediation as they instantaneously convert small savings into loans without any paperwork or storage costs. The rate of interest earned by members, whether in savings mode or in borrowing mode, is the result of market forces of demand and supply among the members.

As an example, let us say ten members get together and pool Rs 1,000 a month each. That makes the kitty or prize money Rs 10,000 a month and the whole fund is Rs 1,00,000 in ten months. Two or more members may have an immediate need for money. They 'bid' for the prize money of Rs 10,000 of that month. The bidding is in reverse—the lowest bidder wins the prize money. If the lowest bid of a member is Rs 6,000, it means he is willing to forego Rs 4,000. This sum that he loses, called the discount, is set apart to meet the expenses of running the chit or for distribution among the members or both. The winner, also called prized subscriber, will still have to pay his share of Rs 1,000 a month for the remaining term of the chit.

It is easy for a chit fund to turn into a debt trap for desperately poor people who join chit funds that also have relatively well-off people. The better-off ones who do not immediately need money are the ones who really benefit from such a scheme; if they keep up with the instalment payments, they get back their full money when the chit is closed, besides the amount of money forfeited by bidders during the tenure of the chit fund. Chit funds can also slide dangerously into gambling with disastrous consequences—depending on the level of desperation, a bidder can make ridiculously low bids, as much as 40 per cent of the chit amount, whereby he has straightaway lost on the full deal. This situation can get worse with mala fide intentions of some members who may enforce lower bids by making false bids so that the desperate member makes a still lower bid. Trouble also strikes when one or more subscribers disappear after collecting the prize money, leaving the chit fund with a big financial loss to recover from.

The auction or bidding process is central to running a chit fund and the success depends on the 'spread' between the prize money and discount, and, of course, on completion of the term of the chit. Barring unscrupulous operators muddying the waters, chit funds are a wonderfully simple and effective financial instrument for delivering credit, particularly where formal banking systems do not reach. Despite central legislation imposing strict conditions on its running, chit funds remain an unorganized business. An Ernst & Young (E&Y) study of 2004 puts the size of chit fund business at over Rs 20 billion.

Chit fund businesses have a higher history of failure than other similar types of businesses and the government has stepped in with some tough legal provisions.

Some of the provisions are considered unduly restrictive and enacted as a response to particular failures. For instance, the provision of disallowing any other business to be carried out by a chit fund may be a response to funds that collapsed because its foremen diverted chit fund monies to other uses (Sudarshan Chit Fund in 1976 went bust because the foreman had siphoned off the funds to finance the allied business interests of the chit fund company like shipping, hotel and transport businesses). But to put a blanket ban on all funds and deny them an avenue to bolster their funds' position seems rather unfair. Another provision is the security deposit to be lodged with the registrar as a precondition to grant of permission to start the fund—this provision goes against the basic principle of chit funds which is to provide immediate funds without too much paperwork as bringing in a government official into the process will almost certainly erase that advantage.

Studies have shown that small and marginal businesses, besides poor people seeking loans for other reasons, often rely on informal sources of money more than the formal financial sector. A roadside vendor looks for a source where he can borrow money in the morning to buy raw materials, etc., and return it in the evening with the stipulated interest. As long as he makes a certain sum of money that is more than what he has to repay, he is willing to pay the obviously high rates of interest that the moneylender charges. Ease of access is a huge factor and the lower transaction cost compensates him adequately for the high, even extortionate interest rates.

Laws must be alive to ground realities—despite a reputation of being 'cheat funds', to put a name to the disillusionment of members of failed funds, chit funds fulfil a very vital need in society, particularly considering the dismal record of formal banking channels in reaching out to the marginal sections of society. Well-meaning laws that are tough to observe in practice will only make such businesses go underground, leaving its members even more vulnerable to mismanagement.

Nidhi Funds

There is no official definition of the word '*nidhi*', which in Sanskrit means, 'treasure'. Nidhi is a name given to businesses that are formed with the objective of cultivating the habit of thrift and savings amongst its members. Such companies function for the mutual benefit of members by receiving deposits only from individuals enrolled as members and lend only to individuals also enrolled as members.

Nidhi companies are recognized as Non-Banking Financial Companies (NBFCs) and are governed by the regulations of the Reserve Bank of India (RBI) and the Ministry of Company Affairs (MCA). Nidhi companies are very popular in south India and have been around for over a century, operating under different names such as nidhi fund, permanent fund, benefit funds, or mutual benefit funds. At a time when banks on a national level commanding investor or depositor confidence were rare, nidhi funds served communities well by providing many financial services that we now take for granted. Moreover, nidhis also provided a much-needed escape from the clutches of the unscrupulous moneylenders.

Nidhi funds are in a category called ASCAs (Accumulated Savings and Credit Associations) where funds are built up from members' contributions but these are not rotated among members immediately (as in chit funds) and only upon need-based requests of the members.

Nidhi companies operate under the fundamental principle of mutual benefit where a corpus is built up out of contributions or savings of members and such monies are then lent out to members against the security of jewels or property and sometimes certificates like National Savings Certificate (NSC), National Savings Scheme (NSS), fixed deposits, etc. A unique feature of nidhi companies is that one has to be a member in order to be a borrower. For that reason, they usually operate on a limited geographical scale.

There are several nidhi companies that have withstood the test of time—Chennai Sri Ekambareshwar Saswatha Nidhi Ltd tops the chart at 133 years, followed by The Egmore Benefit Society (130 years), The Mylapore Hindu Permanent Fund Ltd (128 years), and The Sriman Madhwa Siddhanta Onnahini Permanent Nidhi (120 years) (Ramesh 2007). But there have been several instances of nidhis collapsing and leaving behind a trail of destruction with inevitable regulatory mechanisms setting in. Besides, failure in the NBFC sector per se has also extended to nidhi companies. As a start, any company wanting to carry on the business of nidhi should have the word 'nidhi' as part of its name and, conversely, the word 'nidhi' will not form part of the name of any company, firm, or individual engaged in borrowing and lending money without incorporating the laws governing nidhi funds. Further, nidhis are not expected to engage in the business of chit fund, hire purchase, insurance, or any other business including investment in share and debentures. Nidhi companies are not allowed to advertise for mobilizing resources or pay brokerage or incentives for mobilizing funds. They are expected to circulate privately among members their loan and deposit schemes.

The government set up in the year 2000 the first committee chaired by P. Sabanayagam to exclusively look into the functions of nidhis and make recommendations for regulating performance. Some of the major recommendations are:

- Ratio of net-owned funds to deposits must be 1:20;
- Parking of funds in deposits in nationalized banks—not less than 10 per cent of deposits received by a nidhi must be placed in an unencumbered deposit in a nationalized bank;
- Sanction of loan against specified security and as a percentage of the value of a property offered as security;
- Fixing ceiling limits on interest paid by nidhi companies on its deposits;
- Restriction on opening of branches;
- Applicability of prudential norms for income recognition and classification of assets in nidhi companies.

Predictably, these recommendations were met with protests from the Chamber of Nidhis and an expert group was set up to look into such grievances. Another committee, the A.R. Rao Committee, gave its recommendations after addressing all grievances in 2005. The recommendations remain substantially unchanged and gives a time-table to nidhis for compliance. The nidhi business has for a long time filled in the gaps left by formal banking channels towards the needs of the middle and lower classes; there is certainly a case for regulating, supervising, and exercising control over its fiscal discipline but without stifling its vibrancy. Both nidhis and chit funds are governed by the RBI as NBFCs to bring about accountability and assurance.

Both chit funds and nidhi funds are a prototype of microfinance that has been popularly used in India and Bangladesh since the 1990s. Microfinance or microcredit is the extension of small loans to people who are below the bar of acceptability as borrowers of mainstream banking because of reasons ranging from being landless or with no assets to offer as collateral or having uncertain revenue streams such as hawkers, casual labourers, etc. A self-help group, the basic unit under a microfinance system, often evolves out of existing chit funds and nidhi funds and scales up operations so that it becomes a part of the structured microfinance mechanism. Microfinance is really an extension of nidhi funds except that the amount of funds involved is often very small or micro as compared to nidhi funds. All such schemes fill in the large gaps left by formal banking channels to serve the financial needs of the people.

India has a long history of migration and invasion and has absorbed diverse ideas while adapting them to suit the local environment; all the while maintaining a core strength that keeps its people grounded while carrying out their duties or occupations.

Modern technology, communication facilities, and new financial instruments have made global trade and commerce possible on a larger scale than ever before in history. However, it has also brought with it large-scale business frauds like Enron, WorldCom, etc., and caused massive losses to millions, which in turn have created an almost continuous cycle of regulation. The decline in the quality of financial reporting is directly related to the internal control culture and environment within an organization.

Control and discipline have always been central to running a successful finance function, whether in the age of handwritten cloth-bound ledgers or sophisticated paperless transactions of the digital age. The best ethics and values come not from impersonal rules and regulations but are distilled from the collective ideals of individuals and communities.

With the onset of modern finance and accounting systems, business managers still struggle to meet the competing demands of a range of stakeholders. Paradoxically, technology often makes simple tasks more fraught with risk.

Temples used to be the nerve centre of villages in ancient and medieval India, where social, economic, and educational activities were held in addition to devotional and spiritual programmes. The influence of religion is still strong in India and the spiritual climate is such that a person sees oneself as a part of a larger system and not as an independent individual. Deeply embedded in the Indian psyche is the concept of *dharma*; dharma is an ancient Sanskrit word that can be broadly translated as a prescribed duty for particular occupations and castes. In the business context, dharma means ethics and values, a concept endorsed more recently by Mahatma Gandhi who articulated the seven sins to avoid and the sin that relates to the business world is 'business without ethics' (or, commerce without morality). The connection between business and spirituality is particularly enhanced in the prosperous business community of Jains whose business practices are deeply anchored in their religious beliefs. Concepts that are increasingly fashionable in business schools and with regulators, such as environment sustainability, ethical investing, business social responsibility, nurturing human capital, etc., have been part of Jain culture for centuries and keep them centred as they seek business fortunes all over the world (Shah 2007). Therefore, rather than dismissing ancient practices as outmoded, Indian businesses may profit from delving into the past as an anchorage to modern commerce.

3

Role of Family Business in Indian Economy

The operating structure of Indian business, before the onset of modern business entities, was almost exclusively that of a family enterprise. Since a joint family system was the pivot of the Indian social structure, the cultural and familial dimension spilled over into the business domain as well. Traditionally, caste played a significant role in determining which families or communities would be exclusively in trade or business and even defined the kind of business they would be involved in. This carried on for generations. Most businesses started out as trading operations and were run by a single family or a partnership of two or more families. Businesses operated within the confines of resources that could be mobilized by the families; the structure of these businesses in later years under the British rule moved to a managing agency system or as a limited liability corporation.

The history of many older business families is closely linked to the nationalist or independence movement or as a reaction to British economic policies. The Birla group's jute business started as a rebellion against the closed club of British cartels in jute, just as Walchand Hirachand's foray into shipping was out of nationalist sentiments. Likewise, Jamshetji Tata built the iconic Taj Mahal hotel partly to avenge his indignation at being refused admission to a British establishment.

G.M. Rao, founder and chairman of GMR Group, in an interview said that, 'Today 65% of the top companies on the National Stock Exchange (of India) are family-owned businesses. We need to think about their governance. These companies are becoming so big that if the family gets estranged, it could impact the national business environment' (Kumra 2007: 63). Prophetic words indeed!

In 2009, Ambani Brothers' Reliance Industries Limited (RIL) and Reliance Natural Resources Limited (RNRL) were engaged in a battle over the pricing of gas, a scarce national resource. The disagreement pulled several agencies into its ambit—public sector companies, government, and even the Supreme Court, besides sparking off a national debate on the definition of national assets and whether private players can be allowed the power to impact the lives of all citizens in a country.

In January 2009, Ramalinga Raju, founder of Satyam Computer Services Limited (SCSL), a new-age blue-chip company, sent shock waves throughout the country with his astounding confession that the company's profits were inflated over the past several years and cash as reflected in the books was 'non-existent'. It caused mayhem in the stock markets, already reeling from a slowdown of 2008, impacted the very image of corporate India by raising doubts about the quality of corporate governance, besides sparking a nationwide debate on the role of various regulatory agencies responsible for corporate oversight. This also prompted an unprecedented government intervention, taking over the management and the board of the scandal-ridden company, and later selling it to the Mahindra Group in an auction. This attempt to restore confidence in Indian business and the regulatory system has been the first of its kind and reflects the magnitude a failed business has on one of the fastest growing economies.

The proportion of family enterprises to widely held companies is said to be around 64 per cent in the US, 75 per cent in the UK, and more than 90 per cent in India, Latin America, Far- and Middle East.

A Moody's–ICRA survey in 2007 revealed that seventeen of the thirty Sensex (Bombay Stock Exchange [BSE]) companies are family-controlled; the remaining thirteen companies include government-owned banks and state-owned enterprises.

R.K. Hazari, a noted historian, has estimated that most of the prominent industrial firms on the contours of Indian business during the 1950s were in the hands of just eighteen Indian families and two

British houses. Since then, those businesses have undergone several separations/mutations, changes, and some of them have even gone into oblivion.

Amongst the top ten groups in terms of assets in 1969 were the Tatas, the Birlas, Martin Burn, Bangur, Thapar, Modi, Mafatlal, and the ACC. In 1999, the only groups to be amongst the top twenty-five in India were the Tatas, the Birlas, and the Thapars (Pande et al. 2010). Except for the Tatas and the Birlas, the remaining eight did not feature in the top twenty-five in 2009.

The landscape of Indian businesses has seen significant changes over the last decades and businesses that were not sustainable or could not adapt rapidly to the changes in the environment ceded their pole positions to newer groups. Groups like Mafatlal, DCM-Shriram, Walchand, and Sarabhai have faded away from their former glory and new family groups like Sunil Mittal's Bharti Group, K.P. Singh's DLF Ltd, Om Prakash Jindal, Adani, Jaiprakash, and Mahindra rule the business landscape, along with stalwarts from the past such as the Tatas, the Birlas, and the Ambanis, who sustained their businesses through many changing faces of the business environment. The state of play and the pecking order changes every decade and makes Indian family businesses very vibrant to change where status quo is not an option for these business houses.

EVOLUTION OF BUSINESS CONGLOMERATES IN INDIA

A conglomeration of entities has been characteristic of the Indian business landscape since the nineteenth century, initially brought in by the British-era managing agencies and later replicated by Indian family business groups and public sector or government companies. Family businesses quickly took to the Western concept of a limited liability, introduced in the nineteenth century, and adapted to that business style accordingly—the concept of limited liability for the shareholders allowed families to raise much more resources than their own contribution and at the same time retain a tight control over the business through a managing agency. This adaptability has continued into modern times as well. 'The shareholding pattern was designed in a way that business owners usually controlled a company even with very small holdings due to the support extended by financial institutions. These managements faced a severe threat of losing control, especially to foreign companies, following liberalisation of the economy. Promoters, therefore, started increasing their stakes almost immediately after liberalization' (Rao and Guha 2006: 11).

One of the key characteristics of a corporate entity is the separation of ownership and management. However, Indian promoter-run companies or family firms do not completely fit Western economic theories that view firms as independent, isolated, and autonomous actors in an open and free market. Control over a company may be exercised through funds and investment companies that the promoter family manages and so, in the Indian context, 'promoter holdings' may be less meaningful than 'holdings of the controlling group'. Most large Indian companies are an amalgam of family-owned and public companies.

> Although the Ambani family controlled over 45% of the shares in Reliance Industries, the individual family members held minimal holdings. In reality, approximately 34% of RIL shares were not technically promoter family holdings but the stake maintained through a complex web of around 400 investment companies that were characterized officially as 'persons acting in concert'—a strange brew unique to India. (Singh and Goodrich 2006)

After India's independence in 1947, growth of family business groups was seen in government policy circles as synonymous with concentration of wealth, making them prime candidates for regulation. For four decades from 1950, the growth of business groups was regulated by a few principal legislative instruments which were restrictive in nature. Some of these acts, which are withdrawn or superseded today but were the tools of control for the government, include the Industrial Development and Regulation Act, 1951 (the primary law on licensing which restricted the number of manufacturers for a specific product), Monopolies and Restrictive Trade Practices Act (MRTP), 1969 (laws restricting growth and market size share), and Capital Issues (Control) Act, 1947 (laws on how an equity should be priced based on net assets or past profits as against market-driven valuation on future prospects). There were sections of the Companies Act, the laws which govern the rules of corporate India, which contained restrictions on growth by limiting inter-corporate deposits, inter-company investments, directorships, etc. These pieces of draconian legislations in effect created what is known as the 'licence-permit raj', allowing near-absolute government control over private enterprise activity in the country.

The law called Foreign Exchange Regulation Act (FERA) of 1974 made it mandatory for foreign companies with a stake over a threshold to seek government permission or sell the excess shareholding through a public listing. In the absence of current account convertibility, every small foreign exchange transaction needed the approval of the Reserve Bank of India (RBI). Due to changes in these laws in 1977, about sixty companies including Coke and IBM, left India rather than share their proprietary technology with others (India was IBM's largest business in Asia in 1976.)

In 1970, the marginal rate of income tax in India, including surcharge, was a whopping 93.5 per cent and additionally there was a tax of 8 per cent on one's wealth. Income tax rates came down to 66 per cent in 1976 and have since lowered to about 35 per cent in 2010. These high tax rates till the reforms in the 1990s gave very little incentive for businesses to expand and create wealth. Corruption and evasion of taxes was rampant and the 'black money', money on which tax was evaded, was nearly as big as the real economy. Therefore, a conglomerate or group structure of family business (the only credible private structure) developed partly as a protective response to such restrictive government policies, where a separate entity was created for each licence.

Till the 1990s, raising finances to run large businesses was a key challenge for the private sector, particularly since nationalization of banks in the 1970s had ensured that business houses did not have an internal bank to fund group activities. Additionally, Indian promoters in this era preferred using public money either from government-owned banks or financial institutions such as IFCI (Industrial Finance Corporation of India), IDBI (Industrial Development Bank of India), LIC (Life Insurance Corporation), and ICICI (Industrial Credit and Investment Corporation of India Bank), several state financial institutions, besides UTI (Unit Trust of India), or less frequently from the public, to run the enterprises they controlled. These institutions were the providers of long-term credit in exchange for seats on boards of borrowing companies, in effect investing taxpayer money into the private sector with apparent government oversight. Access to such resources depended largely on the perceived commercial activities of the promoter group and since multiple entities could raise separate debt from these institutions and government banks and then list in a stock exchange, promoters created a number of entities with separate businesses but under one common control. This helped the group leverage assets and capital better than putting all businesses in one entity.

There is no single or common reason for the prevalence of groups or conglomerates in India. Business literature has a theory that business groups are responses to institutional voids in an economy (Foss, Lando, and Thomsen 2000; Archibald 1987; Leibenstein 1968). In a developing country like India, there are significant gaps in knowledge of information, risk, labour, capital, and market intelligence. Market imperfections lend a competitive edge to business groups who can tap into indefinable networks, in-house talent, and incremental privileged knowledge. Reasons could range from a need for maximum control of resources through minimum capital commitment or as a de-risking strategy, to fill an institutional gap or to harness latent talent available within the group.

Gautam Thapar, the third-generation promoter of the Thapar Group and founder of the breakaway Avanta Group, in an interview while replying to a question from Wharton Business School as to why ownership in family businesses in India is not normally divorced from management by the third or fourth generation, unlike in Western economies, said:

I think we need to make a distinction between public ownership in a family business through a stock market listing, and family ownership of business in general. In the first case, a large part of the reason this divorce doesn't happen in India is the nature of our capital markets, the size of the economy and the nature of the institutional investors in our markets. Despite our vibrant equity markets, we have no debt capital markets to speak of. The size of individual market sectors in the Indian economy is small, and it is only now beginning to get to a scale and size that makes large investments possible. For years, the only institutional investor was the government of India. Given a choice 35 to 40 years ago, many family-owned businesses would not have opted for raising equity in capital markets, but were forced to do so due to tax and non-availability of capital. (Indian Knowledge@Wharton 2009)

Khanna and Palepu (2000: 887) of Harvard Business School (HBS) found that diversified business groups added value in which affiliated firms enjoyed substantial autonomy in gaining superior access to critical resources such as foreign capital and technology, including access to international capital markets. This was possible due to a group's organizational arrangements which were assumed to replicate the functions of institutions that are missing in emerging markets. Ashok Banerji, a senior professor of finance and control in the Indian Institute of Management Calcutta (IIM-C) has said that another reason for corporates in India to have a conglomeration is due to the lower reliability of the value chain in a production process. As the reliability of suppliers in key product intermediates and ancillaries is fairly low, all large manufacturers have gone in for integrating in unrelated areas of the product chain, which is not the most efficient business model as these feeder units are mainly captive and lack focus than if they were self-sustaining units. He cites the example of ITC, which for its cigarette manufacturing had to acquire printing and packaging companies, like Triveni Tissues, which are unrelated to the main product but are key inputs to the process, as the quality of printing and packaging was inconsistent and imports were expensive (Interview with the authors).

Another study conducted by Ghemawat and Khanna (1998) noted two general rationales for diversification: concerned information impactedness and entrepreneurial scarcity, both pointing to a business group's internal mechanism for allocation of resources such as capital, information, and entrepreneurship. The other came from specific policies, such as taxation, that distorted the market processes and forced firms to increase diversification by taking advantages of economies of scope. The two sampled organizations reduced their diversification as policy distortions were wholly or partially removed and market mechanisms were introduced.

R.K. Hazari (1967) argued that a business group could be represented by a series of concentric circles and so allocated group companies between inner and outer circles. Units assigned to the inner circle had decision-making powers and those in the outer circle were companies where the group had 50:50 or minority equity participation. He identified twenty business groups which he referred to as 'complexes' but did not classify any group as large. A commonly held view of groups is to regard them as pyramids. A corporate pyramid works something like this: a business family holds a controlling stake, say 51 per cent, in a company at the top of the pyramid, which may or may not be publicly listed. This company in turn holds a stake in a second tier of companies which or each of which hold(s) a stake in a third tier. In this way, the family controls the entire pyramid from top to bottom or the interlocking grid of companies even though its financial stake is diminishing in companies further away from the core holding company, say 26 per cent (51 per cent of 51 per cent) in the second tier or ring, 13 per cent (51 per cent of 26 per cent) in the third tier/ring, and so on. Thus business groups can raise money from outsiders without ceding control, which is a mix of diffused ownership and entrenched management.

The Securities and Exchange Board of India (SEBI) requires listed companies to provide consolidated group accounts but this does not lead to consolidation of all entities that are controlled by a group. Very often, the holding companies through which families exercise control are not listed, making it difficult to obtain complete information from public sources about the total group.

Connections between and among individual companies may be formal—as in shared management and personnel, or through inter-corporate deposits—or informal, through the guiding hand of a central controlling authority of the group.

A survey had found that many Indian family-controlled groups have complex corporate structures. Furthermore, it is common to see inter-group cross-holdings of shares (Moody's–ICRA 2007: 2). In such cases and despite regulatory requirements to disclose promoter share-holding, it can be difficult to assess ownership and control—which potentially impact(s) credit quality—on the basis of public information (Ibid.: 4). Many families in India exert control with less than 50 per cent shareholding. The study notes that promoter shareholdings range between 26 and 90 per cent, with a median of 50 per cent (Ibid.). The study covered thirty-two Indian companies across sixteen prominent family groups, covering a broad cross-section of Indian industry and accounting for 40 per cent of the total Sensex market capitalization.

Khanna and Palepu (2000) also found that group dynamics can increase the long-term prospects of the affiliate and invoke trust among the investors; contrarily a failed business has a cost that reaches beyond the affected business into the whole group. This actually works as an added comfort to lenders and investors.

In March 2007, a decade and a half after the licence–permit raj was dismantled, the aggregate share of promoter holdings in the listed sector stood at over 60 per cent (CMIE [Centre for Monitoring Indian Economy] Prowess data), indicating the high confidence in promoter-led companies.

Since liberalization, many groups have divested unrelated businesses and concentrated on core competencies. Yet the trend to invest in several different industries still remains strong among Indian family businesses but increasingly for business reasons. From the traditional groups like the Birlas and the Tatas to Reliance, Bharti Group (Bharti Airtel), Mahindra, etc., a number of businesses are unrelated but are managed through common ownership and supervision.

Growth of large business groups in the 1990s and beyond is in part due to the easing of controls over sector-related policies, a more benign tax and duty regime, and de-reservation of sectors to permit private sector participation (such as in petroleum refining or oil exploration, telecommunication, and defence).

Ram Kumar Kakani (2001) says that there is a link between financial performance and corporate characteristics (including product diversity) of the 240 large Indian corporates studied over a span of twelve years. He argues that like in the developed world, most conglomerates are value destroyers in the developing world too; due to the presence of a number of product portfolios with poor market power, the conglomerates have destroyed more shareholder value than their focused counterparts. One of the examples in the study, which was released in 2001, is the comparison drawn between the BPL Nambiar Group and the Videocon Group. The BPL Nambiar Group was regarded as a success story as it was focused on the electronics sector, while Videocon had ventured into unrelated sectors apart from electronics, like pharmaceuticals, power, etc., had destroyed shareholder value and had a low profitability. This was the case in 2001, but in 2010, the BPL Nambiar Group is a marginal player in the electronics space and is not even a shadow of its glorious days. Meanwhile, Videocon Group, the conglomerate, has sustained value and the flagship company, Videocon Industries Limited, a group company, is among the top 100—the most valuable private sector company according to the *Business Today* rankings. Presently, the group is over USD 4 billion in sales and is rated by the Boston Consulting Group (BCG), the global consulting organization, as among the top 100 Global Emerging Giants.

> The combined assets of Mukesh Ambani Group in 2009 stood at Rs 20,04,690 million and those of his brother, Anil Ambani at Rs 14,13,040 million, compared to the unified Reliance Group founded by their father, Dhirubai Ambani in 1997 at Rs 1,93,450 million. The brothers in their respective empires have more diversified businesses: from oil, industrial infrastructure, retail, sports, etc., for Mukesh, to telecommunication, finance, media, power, etc., for Anil Ambani than earlier Reliance Group. More value has been created by diversity of businesses by this group than many others who were focused on a few core industries.

There are a number of studies that debate whether a focused business creates more value than a conglomerate in India but there are too many exceptions to the hypothesis to make any conclusion either way.

The changing business environment of liberalized India has brought forward several new and first-generation businessmen but a number of old business families have also largely kept pace with new opportunities. Several old groups have entered new economy business and offered robust competition, besides creating shareholder wealth.

Ownership concentration has always been very high in India, but the relationship between a high level of promoter ownership and a firm's performance has been a matter of debate.

Indian corporate laws are closely modelled on the Anglo-Saxon model which recommends dispersed shareholding as one of the important considerations for good corporate governance. But in India the holding pattern of promoters really does not indicate the presence or absence of good governance practices. As Satyam Computer's promoter holding fell from over 25 per cent in 2001 to less than 5 per cent in 2008, the ownership evidently became widespread, conforming to the recommended norms, which subsequent events exposed as hollow.

Tata Consultancy Services Limited (TCS), a company with majority ownership by the Tata Group, is the largest Indian software company. Tata Sons, the holding entity, usually has a very small ownership in the companies within the group, to which TCS is an exception. This is a true reflection of the inherent entrepreneurial spirit of traditional Indian family conglomerates to be able to survive and succeed in a restrictive, liberal, or competitive environment.

Berle and Means (1932) suggested that there exists an inverse correlation between diffused ownership and firm performance; in other words, professional managers acting on behalf of a scattered ownership do not act in the best interests of the shareholders by optimally utilizing corporate resources to enhance profit and therefore shareholder wealth. When companies are listed, the issue of promoter holdings becomes one of corporate governance and potentially creates a conflict between two categories of shareholders—promoter shareholders and non-promoter shareholders; however, in India, a high promoter holding has not been a barrier to adding shareholder value. In fact, promoters who have achieved critical parameters in terms of size or other key milestones tend to increase promoter holdings to combat takeover threat and yet manage to deliver good returns to minority shareholders. Analysing cross-sectional data from the mid-1990s, Jayati Sarkar and Subrata Sarkar (2000) find that company value actually declines with a rise ranging from 0–25 per cent in the holding of mutual funds and insurance companies after which there is no clear effect. On the other hand, for development financial institutions' (DFI) holdings, there is no clear effect on valuation below 25 per cent, but a significant positive effect above 25 per cent suggesting better monitoring when stakes are higher.

Despite the government policy of actively managing the macro- and microeconomic growth of large business houses, the Tata and the Birla groups have maintained the top two positions all through the period of regulatory intervention. The J.K. Singhania, Thapar, and Mafatlal groups also retained their positions in the top ten businesses for eighteen years from 1972–90 (Rajakumar and Henley 2007). However, a number of the groups, which were at the top of the list of distinguished corporates in the 1990s like the Singhanias, the Mafatlals, and the Modi Group, have moved to significantly lesser prominence in the 2000s and other groups which innovated and changed gears with the markets emerged at the top of the rungs. These groups include Essar, DLF, Bharti Airtel, GMR, Fortis, Adani, and Sterlite, which featured in the Forbes list of the top twenty-five richest Indians in 2010.

INDIAN FAMILY BUSINESSES AND POLITICS

The biggest advantage that Indian family businesses have is their ability to adjust to the prevalent political dispensation and its impact on the business environment. Some may argue that it is the Indian businessman's flexibility that led to the destabilization of the existing ruling order in the 1800s; others will counter that such businessmen were only trying to maximize their returns—in other words, following their prescribed dharma or path of enlightenment.

Businessmen everywhere prefer political stability and support the structure that is most conducive for a stable environment. Therefore, the business class by and large supported the British Raj. Indian nationalism even up to the end of World War I (WWI) was limited to trader-industrialists pressing for economic concessions or at least similar terms of business in line with other crown subjects. The early stages of the Indian National Congress (INC) constituted nothing more than a platform or pressure group to deliver the views of the Indian public to the ruling elite and since businessmen did not see any threat to the prevailing order, the upcoming industrial class largely supported the Congress with funds and participation. When Gandhi returned to India, there was growing stridency, even militancy, in the nationalist movement and soon, the business establishment was sharply polarized into 'for' and 'against' camps. The Ahmedabad mill owners, belonging to the same caste as Gandhi, were the first ones to come under his influence, followed by businessmen with a traditional outlook such as Kasturbhai Lalbhai, G.D. Birla, and Jamnalal Bajaj. But even they did not want to alienate the government and likewise the British government looked to merchant-industrialists to counter the growing threat of nationalism.

After the end of the non-cooperation movement of 1921, industrialists across the spectrum preferred the legislative route to reform even though Mahatma Gandhi was opposed entry into the assembly.

Indian businessmen had

> a four-pronged strategy: i) keep aloof from the confrontational-agitational aspects of the freedom struggle, ii) support with funds such constructive programmes that were indirectly linked with the Congress organization but did not come under its direct purview, iii) influence policy formulation by the Congress to ensure that its thinking on major issues affecting business interests remained in tune with their own, iv) act in unison with the nationalist-minded elements in the legislatures to garner support for the demands of Indian industry. (Tripathi 2004: 261)

As the prospect of full independence became clearer, industrialists became anxious to influence the economic policy of the Congress and in 1944 seven prominent businessmen (Purshottamdas Thakurdas, J.R.D. Tata, G.D. Birla, Lala Shri Ram, Ardeshir Dalal, A.D. Shroff, and Kasturbhai Lalbhai) representing all sections of the Indian business interests along with economist John Matthai prepared a document known as the 'Bombay Plan'. The authors recognized the all-pervasive role of the government in all aspects of economic activities and the First Five-Year Plan (1951–56) of independent India that was drawn up was quite close to the Bombay Plan.

However, the policy that the new Indian government followed was a socialist one and in policy, at least, the official position was generally antagonistic to business groups. Still, even in the heyday of the so-called licence–permit raj, most business groups prospered, partly due to a vast protected market and partly due to their ability to work the system to their best possible advantage. Some business groups were able to receive favourable treatment during the licence–permit raj while there is evidence of the so-called Bombay Club lobbying for restricted entry of multinational companies. The relation between business groups and the state is very complex and conventional populist wisdom of mutual rent-seeking is a rather narrow view.

It is a worldwide phenomenon that there are close links between a policy-making state and business houses or business interests either through powerful industry organizations or directly as elected members to the legislatures. The dual role of businessmen as politicians is a relatively new concept in India and goes against the age-old established varna or caste system that advocates one vocation at a time. An entrepreneur's political participation behaviour is a complex matrix of factors such as his age, the size and maturity of his business, and how effectively he can delegate business duties, extent of government control over his industry, etc. 'An entrepreneur's motivation to participate in politics is shaped by the institutional environment in which they operate' (Bartels and Brady 2003).

In mature democracies, businessmen influence public policy by lobbying for elected officials and providing campaign finance to professional politicians. In immature democracies, businessmen often employ an alternate strategy—running for public office themselves in order to further their business interests despite high opportunity costs of doing so (Gehlbach, Sonin, and Zhuravskaya 2006).

In the Indian context, as long as the sanctity of property rights and access to resources vests in politicians or political parties rather than in standalone institutions, we can expect a close interaction between businessmen and politicians, particularly if businessmen have to ensure sustainability of investments beyond the time horizon of a particular political dispensation. Engaging politicians of all ideologies in today's era of coalition politics is a business reality in India whether through political donations, direct entry into state legislatures and Parliament or otherwise. Indian family businesses can mitigate the high opportunity cost of fulltime participation in politics, based on traditional close-knit families where one or more family members can be spared to join politics while the business matters may be handled by other members.

In 1960, companies were allowed under Section 293(A) of the Companies Act to donate to political parties if its Memorandum permitted such contribution, later subject to a ceiling of Rs 25,000 or 5 per cent of the average net profits of the past three years. In 1969, the Indira Gandhi government banned company donations to political parties ostensibly to stem corruption but even so, funds were raised by placing advertisements in souvenirs of political parties. This was of course only the visible component of political donations; the bulk of donations were hidden from public view. In 1984, the Rajiv Gandhi government lifted the total ban on company donations although there was a somewhat improbable ceiling imposed. A subsection 4 to Section 293(A) of the Companies Act was inserted in 1985 which explained the objective as 'permitting the corporate sector to play a legitimate role within the defined norms in the functioning of our democracy.

The Tata Group and the A.V. Birla Group, two of the country's largest and most respected business houses, have separately set up electoral trust funds to make political donations. The Electoral Trust was set up before elections in 1999 with the objective of making political contributions more transparent, non-discriminatory, and non-discretionary and is open to contributions from both Tata and non-Tata companies. Distribution is in two phases; in the first phase to parties (not individuals) who hold more than 5 per cent seats at the start of elections in proportion to the number of seats and in the second phase to parties who secure more than 5 per cent seats in the election, again in proportion to the seats won.

Grasim Industries, the flagship of A.V. Birla Group, set up General Electoral Trust which receives contributions only from the A.V. Birla Group. The trust considers the overall business interests of the contributing companies in each state while disbursing funds.

Several companies make direct donations to political parties through cheques. Bharti Airtel Group also has a separate trust called Bharti Electoral Trust through which it makes donations.

These are examples of how companies are trying to engage with politics in a transparent manner while protecting their legitimate interests and also to make a crucial distinction between funding politics—which is in everyone's interests—and funding politicians, which may expose the company to accusations of bribery or buying favours, which is also an accepted behaviour for businesses in an Indian society.

Business necessarily has to work closely with the government everywhere to find a mutually symbiotic balance. Britain—which has shaped several of India's institutions—always had a system where business worked with government alliance, where Crown-chartered corporations were the great money-makers that expanded the British raj over most of the world. It is all too common in India to view politics and politicians with cynicism and weariness but for businessmen who actively participate in politics, it can be the purest form of corporate social responsibility. Prime Minister Manmohan Singh, addressing the CII's annual general meeting in 2007, prescribed the remedy to the dichotomy of business and politics when he said, 'Businessmen who enter politics must erect a Chinese wall between their political activities and their businesses' (Singh 2007).

THE NEXT GENERATION OF INDIAN FAMILY BUSINESSES

The new generation of businesses of old families has been working hard to bring in a more transparent image to traditional businesses. Capital markets, no matter how imperfect they may be, have been setting a higher premium to businesses that have a transparent operation and a clean image. This has brought about a change in the corporate behaviour of old businesses. Higher levels of education of the descendants of the founders help them visualize that a globalized economy creates a worldwide market and they need to play by modern rules for expansion beyond their immediate boundaries. The other major reason to bring in greater transparency and reduce transaction costs is due to the use of information technology by the government of India and the state governments in ensuring greater compliance, especially of taxation laws.

The trend today is for scions to get good education, often a management degree from a foreign school. This helps to expand the worldview of the successor, appreciate better the dynamics of business, and also inculcate a sense of respect for educated professional staff

In 1980, Bajaj Auto was the leader in the scooter segment, having successfully learnt to survive in the licence–permit raj of the day. Even in the initial years of liberalization, Bajaj Auto retained its pole position in the scooter segment, although it lost the lead in motorcycles. Further liberalization brought in the threat of cheaper imports and greater FDI into rival companies like Hero Honda. Rahul Bajaj, at the helm of affairs of the group, used his position as the head of the so-called Bombay Club to try and insulate his business from further erosion.

His eldest son, Rajiv Bajaj, came back to the country in the early 1990s, fresh from education in a US business school. He concluded that the existing factories—of which his father was very proud— were too entrenched in old ways to attempt reform and so set up a greenfield factory to experiment with ideas of modern management. One of these was a radically different mix of workforce—80 per cent diploma engineers and 20 per cent skilled workers, as against 80 per cent skilled workers, 20 per cent daily wagers, and no engineers at all in the company's existing factories. The engineers helped to produce newer designs at one-third the price of what would have to be paid to foreign designers and enabled the company to compete with market dominant Hero Honda. Success in the new factory led to duplication in other factories of the company through VRS (voluntary retirement scheme) and other schemes (Swaminathan 2005).

According to the Management Disclosure and Analysis report, 2006–7 of the company, the total manpower productivity of the group was dramatically raised:

Year	Vehicles Produced/Person/Year
1998	73
2000	83
2005	166
2007	266

Rajiv Bajaj, in 2009, also brought about another major change due to shifting consumer preferences. Bajaj Auto, in 2009, discontinued the manufacture of scooters, which was its traditional mainstay, and moved on to manufacturing only motorcycles and commercial vehicles. This is a gigantic move as the term 'Hamara Bajaj' meaning our Bajaj, the famous ad line of Bajaj Scooters is etched into the psyche of most Indians and it is a tectonic decision to discontinue this product line due to falling demand.

working in the business. Adopting modern methods of management and being open to newer ideas directly impacts the economic growth.

Growing urbanization, exposure to Western culture, and a modern education system has shaken the bedrock of the joint family social system in India. Its effects—some good, some not so good—are also felt as a corollary in the way Indian family businesses are now run. There is a lot more modernity, openness to outside influences, and willingness to experiment with newer methods of management, including financial management which may also lead to dilution of control. Before independence, there were several instances of different business families coming together to jointly control one or more companies or groups as a response to challenge the entrenched European dominance of business enterprise.

> In 1936, in an effort to fight competition from European companies, ten cement companies belonging to four prominent business families, the Tatas, Khatans, Killick Nixon, and F.E. Dinshaw groups were merged to form the Associated Cement Companies Limited (ACC). This merger happened before the term 'mergers and acquisitions' (M&A) was even properly coined. The stock traders in Mumbai for many years referred to ACC as the 'Merger'. ACC's website states that the merger was a result of the efforts of these groups 'to face competition for survival in a small but aggressive market mingled with the country's nationalist pride ...'

This cohesion came apart after independence when the common perceived threat diminished. Cohesion diminished not only between families but also within individual families such that practically there is no large family group in the second generation and beyond that has not seen some kind of division. The Dalmias were perhaps the first prominent business house to break up after independence and since then most business houses—Birlas, Modis, Sarabhais, Bangurs, Singhanias, Thapars, Goenkas, etc.—have split up or reorganized themselves. A family business is not always run solely for the financial bottom-line. Many families look to their businesses for emotional sustenance as well, whether because they have nurtured it or because they have inherited it. Often, it gives the owners a sense of purpose or even a continuance of family values. This is usually a positive thing but can often leave owners with a fuzzy line of where family boundaries end and business domain begins. This type of attachment to the business can act as 'psychological handcuffs' which can prove detrimental to the business (Wasserman 2006).

For a business to flourish, it must accommodate the interests of all stakeholders—employees, customers, government, society at large, etc.—rather than the narrow confines of majority and minority shareholders. Besides, what is good for one may not necessarily be good for the other. For example, refusal to infuse outside funds into the business may be good to prevent dilution of family holdings but the company will suffer from lack of growth due to constraints of funds.

Rahul Bajaj, the head of India's leading family business Bajaj Group, sums up the angst of family businesses having incompetent family members: 'It is easy to get rid of an outside manager, but how do you get rid of a family member? You must either do what is right for the business or the family. Either way you will end up with an unhappy family or a weak company' (Das 1999).

Succession typically involves two or more people whose time horizons and outlooks on life are very different. With a parent and a child typically in their sixties and forties respectively, generational gap can all too often turn into cultural warfare.

In India, the cultural context of succession often overshadows the individual wishes of the owner, as in the case of the Birla family.

The vast Birla family has, over the generations, faithfully followed traditions while creating and bequeathing wealth. The third generation also saw a fairly amicable (though not without its controversies) partition of family properties among the claimants. However, things changed dramatically when Priyamvada Birla, childless widow of M.P. Birla, who controlled the estimated Rs 50 billion group assets died in July 2004, leaving all her assets to her chartered accountant and financial advisor—and an outsider—R.S. Lodha. Apart from commercial ventures, M.P. Birla had built several charitable trusts and institutions which formed part of the estate. The family expected to either inherit or take control of this branch of property and was shocked at this instance of 'unfamily'-like behaviour.

The turn of events may yet have been accepted by the family members but for a 25 per cent holding in Pilani Investments, the holding company that holds shares in practically all other M.P. Birla companies (a complex structure perhaps created as a tax-handling mechanism) which led R.S. Lodha to say to the shareholders of Birla Corporation he is in full authority. It is the intrusion of an outsider into an exclusive family domain that caused maximum angst among family members. This will has brought together members of the diverse Birla family who are fighting a court battle against an outsider's claim to the property that they see as rightfully belonging to them.

John L. Ward, clinical professor of family businesses in Kellogg School of Management and one of the leading experts in the world on family businesses, posits that 'Succession planning is important but less problematic in India. The greater question is continuity planning' (Madhavan 2010). Continuity planning is investing in the culture and governance of the business for the long-term future. He also finds that in general, transfer of leadership from '…the senior generation to the next generation works a lot better in India. But the number one challenge in India is rivalry and conflict between siblings (Ibid.).

Some owners prefer to let the subject of succession evolve; they give plenty of room to discuss issues among competent sons, daughters, nephews, and nieces so that consensus can be reached while the present owner is still in the saddle. This pragmatic approach ensures that the business faces few cataclysmic changes at the time of change of guard. The hardest transition for a family-oriented business is moving from a parent–child to a peer relationship. This is a key dynamic in a family relationship and is in many ways the unique selling point (USP) of the business, a key competitive advantage, as it were, in privately held or family-controlled companies that enhances business performance. The inter-personal relationship of people who comprise the distinctive work unit of a family business is also often the most neglected and least protected. Modern managerial education is geared to teaching managers to look at problems and solutions in a rather linear manner, the focus being on rational decision-making. Relationship dynamics and human risk profile issues are considered 'soft issues' and are rarely reflected in a person's educational or training background. However, these issues assume increasing importance in proportion to the size of the business and the number of non-family people that are within the sphere of influence of the family business because these are issues that can affect the very survival of the business and with it the fortunes of many more people than the immediate family.

In the absence of a clear-headed and deliberate process of succession, the question may be precipitated by a crisis, in which event it is likely that a 'fix-it' solution is adopted which need not be the 'best-fit'. Rahul Bajaj, head of the Bajaj group of companies, says: 'If you can separate the two key issues—ownership, which comes with voting rights, and management of the company—from each other in your lifetime, then there is no problem' (*Business Today* 2005).

G.M. Rao, founder and chairman of the global infrastructure business GMR Group, realized that if family members start fighting they are no longer focused on the business and called a family meeting to address this issue:

> In the end we agreed to a family constitution model that outlines succession, conflict resolution, our values, and our mission. It says what qualifications are needed to enter the business, as well as our media and political policy. It even talks about what happens in case of a divorce. All these things are needed to be addressed in detail to protect and delink the business from the family. (Kumra 2007: 63)

Even so, the next generation's success in running or sustaining the business momentum is dependent on a complex matrix of factors like changing business environment, financial matters, regulatory issues, interpersonal equations within the business, etc. However, one of the most difficult issues for the Indian families is, when does the founding generation let go of the control in favour of the next generation?

Spentex Industries is presently looked after by the third generation, running a business enterprise of textiles with a presence in five countries and a turnover of about Rs 13.5 billion. It was founded in the mid-twentieth century by Chiranjilal Choudhary who built the business from modest beginnings. True to Hindu traditions which prescribe duties for various stages of life, Chiranjilal Choudhary handed over the baton of the business to his son and grandsons more than twelve years ago and devoted his life to meditation. In the true spirit of *'vanaprastha'* (literally meaning 'going to the forest'), Chiranjilal Choudhary physically left the family business and with his wife proceeded along the path of meditation and discovery of the inner self. In this land fabled for saints, it is still very unusual to find a successful businessman who voluntarily hands over succession to the younger generation although he is still hale and hearty and capable of running the business for several years more.

With the energy that the present-day young owners bring, Spentex Industries today is one of India's largest cotton yarn spinning companies, proving that succession at the right moment can transform the outlook and prospects of a family business.

Gurcharan Das, a noted businessman and author, in his essay 'Indian Business Families' (2002) says,

Splits occur when the third generation grows up. The head of the family then needs all the skills of a diplomat. 'Govern a family as you would cook a small fish, very gently,' says a famous Chinese proverb. 'When things begin to go sour, the family is the place where the most ridiculous and least respectable things in the world happen. People begin to take hints that were not intended and miss the hints that were intended. Family life is no longer an adventure, but an anxious discipline in which everybody is constantly graded for performance. Brothers deal with brothers with a smile, but they make sure they bring a witness,' says a member of a prominent business family which has recently split and who prefers to remain nameless. We have seen this spectacle repeatedly in the past ten years among the Modis, the Walchands, the Raunaq Singhs, the Bhai Mohan Singhs and a dozen other joint family firms who have separated.

The split in the Shriram Group (DCM) has left their companies in a financial mess. Vivek Bharat Ram, co-promoter of DCM Daewoo, did not have the cash to subscribe to the expansion of the car company's capital; as a result, his family's share in the company has declined from 34 per cent to 10 per cent. Arun Bharat Ram defaulted in paying Rs 700 million, the final instalment for taking over Ceat's nylon cord division. Vinay Bharat Ram defaulted in 1996 in repayment of inter-corporate deposits. Siddharth Shriram's Siel troubles are partially forcing him to divest unprofitable businesses. Siel Ltd is leaving fertilizer distribution and divesting equity in compressors and in India Hard Metals. 'After the split the companies suddenly realised that they were unable to negotiate attractive terms from banks and financial institutions as they used to as one family' (Gupta, Gollakota, and Srinivasan 2007: 243).

However, split has not always proved to be a bad thing in Indian business families—often it has led to release of energy in a positive manner; although there could be a period of instability and flux during the process of change of guard. Smaller and leaner businesses can grow at a different pace with better focus of attention by the owner and a single power centre; the Ambani brothers are classic examples of this theory.

The original business mutates into newer entities but retains the family name and the goodwill of the family brand helps all new

After the death of Dhirubhai Ambani, the largest Indian private sector business, the Reliance group of companies split into two groups headed by the two heirs, Mukesh and Anil Ambani, in a deal crafted by their mother under advice of a family mentor. The over three million investors seemed to agree that smaller companies are easier and more profitable to run—at the time of demerger, the market value of the undivided group was around Rs 1,000 billion. One year later, in May 2006, the Mukesh Ambani-led group had crossed a market capitalization of Rs 2,000 billion, while the Anil Ambani-led group had a market cap of Rs 1,000 billion. At the beginning of the last quarter of 2007 Mukesh Ambani group's market cap had crossed Rs 5,000 billion and Anil Ambani's group had crossed Rs 1,750 billion. Both groups have moved beyond their original businesses into new and exciting ventures, which promise great revenues. Mukesh Ambani has committed resources to India's burgeoning retail sector and real estate development, besides concentrating on its core oil and gas exploration, crude refining and petrochemicals. Anil Ambani has catapulted his inherited businesses to India's top telecom status and the largest private sector mutual fund. He is further expanding the energy business and is integrating the telecom business with entertainment, a sector poised to grow at 18 per cent CAGR (compounded annual growth rate) over the next few years.

Both the companies have entered into different verticals after the demerger, which has enhanced the valuation of the group. In 2010, Mukesh Ambani featured as the fourth richest person in the world, according to the Forbes list. Anil Ambani was placed 36th in the same list.

owners to carry on its legacy, along with the privilege of access to the indefinable network among the business community distilled over the years.

In fact, the very concept of an Indian business is changing. One definition is that if majority shareholding is in 'Indian' hands, it is an Indian company. The reason why most Indians are proud of L.N. Mittal's achievements is that although his investments are spread all over the world and very little in India, he holds an Indian passport. Or consider GE or IBM, the US-based businesses which have invested vastly in India, developed local vendors, hired Indian staff, paid Indian taxes—in other words, do everything that a home-grown Indian company will do for local value addition. Or consider Infosys, a true-blue Indian company by most accounts, which earns nearly all of its revenues by selling solutions to overseas customers.

On the flip side, will Jaguar or Land Rover be considered Indian brands because the Tatas currently own them?

R&D and Technology in Family Businesses in India

Investment in innovation is a key determinant to economic growth. When entrepreneurs devise innovations, it raises the productivity of the business and in consequence, the economy. It is also true that innovation is a positive sum game, that is, innovation can be reapplied over and over again to other areas. However, the downside is that such innovations may lay waste or make obsolete certain existing investments.

Schumpeter (1912) calls this destruction of value of some businesses caused by creativity in others as 'creative destruction'. While the overall positive outcome of innovation may be true for the economy as a whole, individual businesses tend to resist the force potential of creative destruction because most of its wealth is tied up in existing stock. The businessman then ends up seeing the creative destruction as 'creative self-destruction' and is induced to 'manage' innovation cautiously (Randall and Yeung 2003). But this attempt will not stop independent firms from innovating and upsetting the applecart, provided they have access to funds to invest in R&D.

This theory was well played out in the Indian economy before liberalization when firms—public or private—kept using technology for which they had paid and for which their manufacturing processes were aligned, even if it was obsolete in the rest of the world. The protected Indian business in the automobile market ensured that new technology did not come into India. Local firms had little need to invest in innovation in an assured market. This protectionism may have helped large businesses but it has had the effect of keeping the Indian economy behind the time horizon of global businesses like the Ambassador cars modelled after Morris Oxford of 1948 which ruled the Indian roads for decades. Since the 1980s, once the Suzuki Motors' joint venture with the Indian government called Maruti Udyog Limited

(MUL) launched their ever popular 800 series, Ambassador cars were no match for the technology, look, feel, or driving pleasure that this new 'little wonder' brought to the Indian consumer. Ambassador got pushed out of the market in a few years and today has more nostalgic value than being serious competition.

Technology continues to be disruptive and no single company has control over the total breadth of technology required to carry out their own business. This leads to collaboration for survival and taking this to the next level is collaborative innovation, where companies, individuals, research organizations, etc., outside of a sponsoring company, come together to solve complex problems or provide new insights or share research results to create a competitive advantage for the sponsoring company. The boundaries of an organization get extended to create intellectual bases outside of the organization.

An added dimension is that most Indian businesses have risen from the trader class of yore and as and when opportunity presented itself, some have evolved into industrialists, that is, owners of industrial enterprises. This does not by and large change the driving force of Indian businessmen—which is, returns on investment. Therefore, the route to obtaining technology has usually been to enter into joint ventures with foreign firms that possess the required technology.

Joint ventures offer, in principle at least, an opportunity for each partner to benefit significantly from the comparative advantages of the other. In India, often having the right contacts, being in the right networks, and knowing the rules of the game is crucial to business success. The diversity in customs, religion, and preferences make India a complex place to serve and these factors are expected to be handled best by local partners while foreign partners can offer advanced process and product technology, management knowhow, and access to foreign markets.

Joint ventures in India have had a chequered history with some successes and some failures. Success of a joint venture essentially depends on how porous is the barrier between the local firm and foreign partner—for the local firm, the extent of absorbing technology, systems, and processes and for the foreign partner, the real benefit on the ground of access to the local partner's knowledge of markets, networks, or contacts.

Another dimension to the success of a joint venture is how well both partners have thought through the contract terms and whether they have factored in real-time growth because growth is the greatest dynamic which may alter the relationship balance between the two parties. Joint venture relationships are often fragile and difficult to negotiate and, once negotiated, to hold together. Yet many do succeed and, indeed, thrive.

The Samvardhana Motherson Group has over fifty joint ventures and their joint venture with Sumitomo Corporation is over twenty-seven years old. Vivek Chaand Sehgal, the founder of the group along with his mother, Snehalata Sehgal (hence the name of the group), says that their strategy is to grow through joint ventures with companies having cutting edge technology or acquiring companies with such advantages. The group has very few failed joint ventures as both parties strive to create value and wealth for each other and the basic platform is based on trust and respect. Chaand also sits on the management board of Sumitomo Corporation, which is a reflection of the value and respect one of the largest Japanese companies has for this Indian group.

While joint ventures were the preferred mode of technology transfer in the years following liberalization, the past couple of years have seen several overseas acquisitions by Indians firms. Tata Steel's USD 13.6 billion acquisition of Corus and Hindalco's USD 6 million acquisition of Novelis have brought Indian M&A (mergers and acquisations) deals to the global forefront and along the way have broken the myth that Indian overseas business is only about IT and outsourcing.

RISE OF THE NEW-AGE OWNER-DRIVEN BUSINESSES

In the last decade, the evolution of family businesses in India into giant global corporations and hence their influence over the economic well-being of the nation is a matter of pride and concern. Hence, any uncertainties or risks whether relating to acquisitions by these companies like in the case of Tatas' of Corus Steel, UK, or Birlas' of Novelis, USA, or succession issues in Reliance, or corporate failures like Satyam, not only rock the economy but also bring in government machinery with utmost speed to mediate and work towards a solution to the crisis.

This recent influence over the Indian economy has been triggered by a new breed of entrepreneurs, especially in information technology and other new economy enterprises, who are well educated and have global exposure and perspective.

Globalization and entrepreneurship are related. Foreign-born entrepreneurs are being agents of globalization by investing in their native countries, and their growing mobility is in turn fuelling the emergence of entrepreneurial networks in distant locations. Indian-Americans have the highest median income of any national-origin group in the US, and almost 40 per cent of Indians have masters, doctorates, or other professional degrees, five times the US national average. Added to this, Indian entrepreneurs, who comprised 8 per cent of software entrepreneurs in Silicon Valley, California, quickly adopted the business patterns of their American surroundings, but still keep a wide range of professional ties with their home country, which often results in starting their own business in India, taking advantage of access to cheap labour (Nafziger and Ojede 2007). Tarun Khanna, a professor in HBS, opines that India and China have through modern times been somewhat asleep but both societies 'have woken up' and the results could reshape business, politics, and society worldwide. He says:

> In some sense people in these societies are running faster than their rules and laws can keep up. So they are creating the rules as they go along. And entrepreneurship is, after all, doing things in new ways, ahead of social norms and customs, and establishing the rules and laws. In both countries, these processes are unfolding not just in the mainstream business sector but in society at large and even in politics and civil society. (Lagace 2008, n. pag.)

The post-liberalization software boom in 1991 was brought about by policy changes, inflows of capital into India, and also depreciation of the rupee in that period which helped fuel growth. The other major governmental intervention came through the software technology park (STP) scheme which was designed to overcome the challenges an Indian software exporter faced due to poor infrastructure, especially in the area of telecommunications access.

These establishments, which were based on the cost efficiency models through infrastructure sharing, sharing of satellite links and other access modes, reduced cost and cycle time of delivery of services, and enhanced the quality and dependability of the infrastructure. This played a significant role in drawing smaller firms into delivery of IT services. Indian firms, due to improving infrastructure, took advantage of the cost arbitrage between India and the Western countries. The Indian Software Development Centre (IDC) was used as the pivot to develop or maintain software and the smaller 'onsite' presence at the client's premises in the US or Europe helped keep the costs down. This era saw the emergence of highly profitable IT companies having significantly higher margins compared to both their global peers or Indian companies in manufacturing businesses. This in turn led a number of educated Indian software and other professionals to leave their jobs whether in India or overseas to start their own ventures.

The National Association of Software Services Companies (NASSCOM), the premier association of software companies in India, whose membership base constitutes over 95 per cent of the Indian IT industry's revenues, and which employs over 2.24 million professionals, played an integral part in the emergence of India as an IT powerhouse. In 2009, 75 per cent of the NASSCOM's members belonged to small (STPI) companies having a turnover of less than USD 10 million, showing the emergence of a number of new economy entrepreneurs on the Indian business landscape.

In a television interview in February 2010, Narayana Murthy, Infosys' chief mentor, said that two of the biggest game changers in recent times for Indian businesses have been—allowing up to 100 per cent foreign direct investment (FDI) in high-technology sectors and current account convertibility. These policy changes along with other liberalization initiatives gave a kick start to the Indian economy since the 1990s.

Entrepreneurship in this age rarely happens in a closed environment and is often a result of a network of relationships both social and business, information advantage, and mobility of resources and capital. In India, the organizations that foster and incubate new businesses or ideas have been traditionally weak or nonexistent. This led to entrepreneurs relying on and building informal networks to foster new ideas and innovation.

One set of informal networks that has received particular attention in recent years is diaspora, or cross-border networks, constituted by ties between expatriates from developing countries who are based abroad and entrepreneurs who live at 'home'. These studies have argued that expatriate networks seem to be vital in overcoming information barriers in cross-border business (Gould 1994; Rouch 2001; Rouch and Trinidade 2002) and are also an important channel for driving knowledge transfer across countries (Saxenian 2002, 2006; Kerr 2008; Nanda and Khanna 2010). The informal networks or the diaspora of Indians, especially those in the Silicon Valley, played a great role in the quantum leap in entrepreneurship amongst young Indians that one has seen in the past two decades.

A study by William R. Kerr (2009) explores, among other things, the ethnic composition of US innovation and the study states that 99 per cent of the US innovations can be attributed to nine distinct ethnicities—Anglo-Saxon, Chinese, European, Hispanic, Indian, Japanese, Korean, Russian, and Vietnamese. While the share of the Anglo-Saxon and European ethnicities declined from over 90 per cent of the US domestic patents in 1975 to 76 per cent in 2004, the share of Chinese and Indian ethnicities increased in these thirty years from 2 per cent to 9 and 6 per cent, respectively. The immigrant inventors, like the Indian and the Chinese, are more concentrated in high-technology industries such as information technology and pharmaceuticals.

The increase in the level of patents of the Indian diaspora over the last thirty years has created a new concentration of knowledge and technical know-how. Over a period, the diaspora exploited this knowledge base by linking with the Indian mainland for development, research and detailed engineering or codification of intellectual property. The social networks played a major role in the transition and created a number of entrepreneurs both in India and the US to feed into the boom.

The new-age Indian entrepreneur has had to deal with a number of variables in his business which was global in nature but the output had to be generated locally in India to keep the advantage of costs. The customers were usually global, the technology was cutting edge or processes were built under high levels of sophistication (like CMM [Capability Maturity Model] Level V) and most of these enterprises were funded at an early stage by a venture capital fund, which brought in sophistication in management systems besides bringing in a culture of corporate governance and sharing critical information outside the band of 'founders'. Founders were more amenable to setting aside a part of the company for employees in the form of Employee Stock Option Schemes (ESOP) to share in the growth and vision of the owners.

A study by Ashish Arora and Suma Athreye found that,

> The adoption of ESOPs and the charting of career paths in management for technically qualified professionals by leading software firms have also had at least one unintended outcome. Technically qualified persons now view entrepreneurship itself quite differently. It is a logical extension of the managerial tasks that they would in any case hope to do with the growth in their careers, with an added element of risk that nevertheless promises large rewards. This partly explains why the ex-employees of HCL and Wipro have been active entrepreneurs; TechSpan, NIIT, Pertech Computers, Global Infotech, InfoTech Enterprises, STG and Infogain were all set up by ex-HCL employees, [as were] product-based ventures such as Jamcracker, Microland, e4e ventures, Tarang software, iLantus, Jumpstart, Qsupport and Mindtree consulting have been set up by ex-Wipro employees. Other leading software firms are alive to these concerns. Recent plans announced by TCS indicate that they too will start a venture capital fund to encourage start-ups by employees with innovative ideas. (Arora and Athreye 2001)

The effect has been cascading—as the erstwhile employees turned into entrepreneurs and then venture capitalists, funding and mentoring of start-up businesses became a normal phenomenon, which in a traditional business model only happened for the family members. Larger companies like the HCL Group to smaller Internet–based job search companies like Info Edge (Naukri.com) have been investing in and incubating new companies involved in innovative technology or ideas. There are others like Saurabh Srivastava and Mohit Goyal, ex-promoters of IIS Infotech, which was sold to Xansa Plc., who started the Indian Angels Network and The Indus Entrepreneurs (TiE), which created the bridge between the entrepreneurs of Indian origin in the US and those living in India for sharing and collaborating on business and technology.

New-age owners have completely altered the business landscape of India in a short span of time and have helped raise the general standard of conduct of traditional businesses as well.

INDIAN FAMILY BUSINESSES IN THE GLOBAL ECONOMY

A survey of family-controlled companies in India shows that the surveyed groups have shown good recent financial performances, with mean compound revenue growth of 28 per cent from 2001–2 through 2006–7 and mean compound post-tax profit growth of 47 per cent (Moody's–ICRA 2007: 7). A critical factor in grooming Indian businesses to compete globally is the maturity of the stock markets. Today, it is far more beneficial for owners to focus on increasing the sustainable value of their firm than to strip the company of its assets for personal use. Maximizing shareholder wealth and, consequently, declaring handsome dividends for all shareholders is a more attractive option in modern times. In one of our conversations with Mukesh Ambani, owner of India's largest private entity, he said that a business multiplies wealth many times over than cash in the hands of the owner. It makes business sense to stay invested in the business.

Family companies in India are generally susceptible to excessive indebtedness, as they seek to expand without diluting ownership or control. The Moody's–ICRA studied companies, however, have shown conservativeness; with average debt–equity at 0.5x since 2001. Many Indian companies have issued foreign currency convertible bonds, with the assumption that these will be converted into equity though the report says that it remains to be seen whether the family-owned companies will resort to more debt funding to prevent dilution (Ibid.). It also helps that laws are more realistic now than they were a couple of decades ago. With almost punitive rates of taxes, most owners paid themselves a pittance and let the company absorb expenses including living expenses of owners like electricity, personal staff, fuel costs, food, etc., through euphemistically named 'staff houses'. Foreign exchange laws were draconian, offering little opportunity to travel overseas to explore development initiatives, in fact almost actively pushing out entrepreneurship from the country.

Today, more enlightened companies pay their owner CEOs a salary that is comparable in Indian markets for such talent, if at all available, but is still much lower than US or Europe and promoters are less likely but not immune to charge their companies with their personal and household expenses.

The Forbes 2008 list of richest people around the globe included four Indians in the top ten. All of them control their own businesses. In the survey, India is also said to have the largest number of billionaires in Asia with a combined wealth of USD 340 billion. They too control their business empires. In 2010, India still has 52 billionaires in USD terms despite global slowdown and its effect on the stock indices.

Family-owned businesses, particularly those who have resolved their power centres within the family, are far more nimble, with faster response time to take advantage of the fast-paced and volatile global environment, and are more likely to stay afloat and succeed.

Opening up the economy has ushered in an explosion of entre-preneurship activity and there are as many new garage start-ups as big, registered companies. While the new start-up may be by first-generation owners, very soon in its lifecycle such businesses will be confronted with all the challenges of established family businesses outlined in the above sections.

Most research on family businesses is based on Western societies; there is very little research done in the Indian context except anecdotal evidence. For instance, the rate of survival for family businesses is usually considered to fall by one-third with every succeeding generation. However, CII pegs the rate for India as 13 per cent for businesses to survive into the third generation, while a slimmer 4 per cent move into the fourth generation. Families that survive across three or more generations often have institutionalized systems and processes of governance in place, making them stronger to combat the forces that challenge their continuity.

What is often overlooked is that while family businesses spilt up very often as they grow, it is not indicative of success or lack of it in any of the subgroups. Joint families require a huge effort to continue after a generation or two in modern times, even in the non-business domain. Expanding families bring several more divergent views to the table and jostling of such divergent views contributes to the wear and tear of the family fabric.

The rising Indian economy has given a shot of confidence to all businesses; it has also helped shake up several moribund PSUs and family business houses into gearing up to modern methods. The resilience that Indian businesses have shown in the turbulent busi-ness environment after independence—socialism, licence–permit raj, liberalization, and lack of protection—indicates that Indian business in whatever form is capable and willing to deal with the global economy on very equal terms.

The social background of owners of family business is now very varied; the strict compartmentalization engendered by India's caste system is not very relevant anymore. Chasing material wealth through business is no longer considered beneath dignity and this shift has brought in newer entrants into business with newer ideas of management, enterprise and finance.

Keeping in mind Indian traditions distilled over hundreds of years, one can safely say that while there may be splits and demergers in family businesses, each breakaway segment has an equal chance of success as the original. In traditional management theory, this is the notion of past dependence: where you can go next depends on where you have gone in the past. Indian IT and other companies have changed that notion forever.

4

State-owned Enterprises or Public Sector Undertakings

State-owned enterprises or public sector undertakings (PSUs) are government-controlled companies, statutory corporations set up by an Act of Parliament, or departmental enterprises of the government (like in the defence sector, railways, or department of telecommunications). In India such enterprises constitute an important segment of the economy. Starting from independence in 1947 when they were charged with the responsibility of 'reaching the commanding heights of the economy', today they account for more than 50 per cent of the gross domestic capital formation. There are nearly 240 central PSUs and probably a few thousand at the state level. Even though the country has made rapid progress towards a market economy in the last one and a half decades, some of the most important spheres of the economy are dominated by the public sector—approximately 56 per cent of the finance including banking and insurance, 85 per cent of crude oil production, 75 per cent of refining, 79–100 per cent in various segments of electricity, and a monopoly in defence production, space, and atomic energy.* 'By the late 1970s, it is estimated that 62.1% of the total "productive capacity" was in state-owned enterprises as was

---

* *Sources*: http://indiabudget.nic.in, www.india-seminar.com, and various news reports.

26.7% of employment. By contrast, industrial value added originating in public sector enterprises was only 29.5% of the total' (Bardhan 1984: 102).

The PSUs show tremendous variations in terms of purpose, managerial attitudes, embedded skills and knowledge, size, and mix of activities. This makes recommendations or even analysis across PSUs very difficult and most reform activities have focused on individual sectors. Perhaps the biggest contribution of PSUs lies in creating a diversified industrial base and also creating capacity in several core areas. However, this is largely a mixed bag.

> ...the strategy virtually ignored consideration of scale economies, vastly restricted domestic and import competition, constrained technological upgrading through licensing and purchase of foreign technologies. (It further) encouraged capital-intensive production and discouraged employment generation that was further constrained by the high costs of hiring and firing imposed by our restrictive labour laws. The consequence was a high cost and globally uncompetitive industrial sector which was also out of tune with India's capital scarcity and labour abundance. (Srinivasan 2000: 6)

Like in any other form of company, in PSUs there is an overlap in the role of ownership and management. Diffuse ownership leads to poor monitoring by non-dominant owners, a feature common to both private and public companies. The crucial difference between the two sectors is the quality of oversight of the dominant owner. A large investor, who is protected by the government using taxpayers' money, as most PSUs are, tends to have a higher degree of moral hazard than privately owned large investors (Kaushik and Dutta 2005a: 178–9).

> [This is the] flip side of the agency theory, which is the gap between owners and managers ... [where] the owner is the government, generally faceless and too diverse to take decisions for the sustained benefit of the company. The managers are government employees[usually operating under assured employment and thus without fear of losing their jobs for delivering poor results]. This is a case of disconnect of accountability on the part of both the owner and the manager, causing severe moral hazard. Accountability that is diffuse is actually non-existent. (Kaushik and Dutta 2005b)

In India, PSUs are rarely accountable to shareholders—which is mostly the government; further, ownership is sometimes assumed by certain elected representatives of the people, the politicians and through them the civil bureaucracy. Thus, many PSUs have civil servants at the board level. However, civil servants are trained and skilled for administering the governmental functions; running commercial enterprises requires altogether different skill sets.

Most governance tenets are aimed at private sector entities, recognizing them as powerful engines of growth; the Organisation for Economic Co-operation and Development (OECD) principles also primarily focus on publicly traded companies and on developing vibrant and efficient capital markets. Funds generated by PSUs are further invested in other PSUs, government securities, and other government initiatives, all falling within the realm of 'public money'. The concept of public money can also be extended to borrowings from public sector banks by private or public entities. The principles of governance borrowed from developed countries exclude this large band of users of public money from complying with corporate governance practices as they are not listed entities (Kaushik and Dutta 2005b).

A company needs to constantly watch for trends, technology changes, skill depletion and upgrade, customer preferences, etc., to be relevant in the market. This is possible only if there is a person or a group which is strongly committed or incentivized to track these changes and take quick corrective action—and whose continued relevance or survival in the organization is linked to how successfully these tasks are performed. The organizational nature of an average PSU leaves little scope for this kind of quick manoeuvre or response to market situations. Economic change over the past one and a half decades is, however, forcing PSUs to shape up and reform in order to be in the reckoning. The reform of the public sector has largely taken the route of disinvestment or listing in stock exchanges in India or overseas for a significant minority stake. Disinvestment, privatization, or deregulation of PSUs is a public policy process whereby a government reduces its role as an owner and manager of business enterprises in the interest of other economic players such as the domestic and foreign investors. In fact, India has followed a sequenced deregulation pattern since the mid-1970s when the government reduced the number of sectors reserved exclusively for the public sector which enjoyed a monopoly till then.

The government-shareholder is using disinvestment as a route to (i) mobilize non-inflationary resources for national governance, and (ii) to create greater commercial orientation in the management of PSUs.

According to the OECD *Economic Survey of India 2007*, public sector ownership in industry is still extensive in India. In the so-called organized sector of the economy, state-owned enterprises produce 38 per cent of business-sector value addition. There is a large number of loss-making public enterprises, particularly at the state level and, on average, the productivity and profitability of publicly-owned firms have been lower than in the private sector. Privatization would thus appear to offer considerable possibilities for improving productivity. Public companies should be controlled by a government investment agency, rather than by a sponsoring ministry, so as to separate the ownership and policy-making functions.

Disinvestment of the public sector should logically follow the same rationale propounded for privately-held companies—dispersed shareholding avoids concentration of economic power and promotes better oversight and monitoring. However, disinvestment is an emotionally volatile and political subject, and arguments abound over whether to disinvest at all, by how much, in what kind of companies or sectors, etc. The reforms process in India is usually noisy, messy, confusing, and sometimes ridden with corruption; the process sometimes works brilliantly (like in the telecom sector), while at other times, it fails. Sometimes when privatization is not feasible or politically achievable, some governments seek to improve the performance of state enterprises by negotiating a performance contract with the managers. A World Bank study finds that this strategy rarely works (Shirley 1998). This is because a well-designed and enforced performance contract is as politically costly as a well-designed privatization one and if there is no political will to do the latter, the former is not likely to succeed because it is perceived as a soft alternative to privatization. This study was conducted over twelve state-owned enterprises in six countries (including India's NTPC [National Thermal Power Corporation]) and extensively in China. India has had varying degrees of success with privatization of PSU entities.

The public sector reform agenda in India is premised on:

- Increased efficiency: Improving the input–output ratio within the public sector;
- Decentralization: Creating more flexible and responsive decision-making bodies;

- Increased accountability: Increasing pressure on staff to perform well, reduce inefficient or corrupt practices, and be more responsive to recipient groups;
- Improved resource management: Increasing effectiveness of human, financial, and other resources;
- Marketization: Using market forces to cover relationships within the public sector, between citizens (consumers) and the PSU, and between the public and private sector. The rationale is that market relations will drive down costs and increase efficiency and/or effectiveness of service delivery.

The presumption and prevailing wisdom demanding privatization of PSUs is that the private sector is more efficient and will deliver better results and the problems of the public sector will be eliminated by competitive market forces. The premise of benefits of disinvestment are yet to be fully ascertained; a sizeable enough body of empirical evidence on which hypotheses about the impact of privatization can be tested is only available several years after the process is rolled out.

An IIM study of 2003 compared the performance of state-owned enterprises with that of private sector firms in respect of technical efficiency in eight different sectors over the period 1991–2 to 1998–9. Judging by the average levels of technical efficiency, no conclusive evidence of superior performance on the part of the private sector was found (Mohan and Ray 2003). The study adjusted companies for scale and still found no significant advantages of size in performance efficiency.

In the coming years, there may be very few 100 per cent government-owned firms with the government encouraging even the less promising PSUs to list at least partially on the bourses. The rate of return on capital employed is increasingly becoming an important factor in PSU management and budgetary support in the form of non-plan loans to loss-making units is being phased out. The PSUs are now also under the purview of the Board for Industrial and Financial Reconstruction (BIFR) which can recommend restructuring or closing down of non-performing units.

However, the reform process must be fully completed in a sector before its benefits can be felt. For instance, partial privatization in the power sector—only in distribution and not generation and transmission—has not really helped the sector achieve the complete benefits of privatization.

GOING GLOBAL

Pressure to stay relevant, not to mention competitive, is forcing several large PSUs to shake up their style of management and emulate the dynamics of the private sector. The government acknowledges problems endemic to running the public sector and has embarked on a programme of privatization. Privatization tackles three major problems of PSUs—(i) incentives (to succeed), (ii) priorities (of economic success), and (iii) access (to investment money). India already has a fairly robust stock market and an independent and reasonably assertive stock market regulator, conditions necessary for listed companies to develop, implement, and maintain better corporate governance norms. Even partial listing on the bourses is likely to extend the benefit of moving into a corporate mindset for a PSU, although for lasting benefit, the essence of privatization is transfer of management and control from government into independent hands.

As a first step, 'enterprization' (a term used by Joel Ruet in the context of reform of the power sector, in particular state electricity boards), that is, turning public bodies from de facto administrations into full-fledged commercial enterprises, subject to the checks and balances, has helped in efficiency improvement. Enterprization, as distinct from corporatization, is essentially the bringing in of a management culture or the way a profitable corporate entity is run. Central to adopting a management culture is the sense of ownership that key employees have with the organization and the extent of real authority and accountability. It follows then that a large degree of autonomy is necessary for enterprization to take root in PSUs.

The reasons for increased commercial focus are varied, ranging from securing supply lines, finding new markets, building alliances, etc.—equally applicable to the private and public sector; it is best captured in the address of the President to the joint session of Parliament in February 2001, 'The public sector has played a vital role in the development of our economy. However, the nature of this role cannot remain frozen to what was conceived 50 years ago—a time when the technical landscape and the national and international economic environment were so very different' (qtd in Ministry of Finance 2003).

In recent months and years, some PSUs have proved that key constraints often cited as affecting performance such as operational autonomy or political interference need not always hold back from delivering great performances. The global 500 list of the biggest companies of 2007 includes five Indian oil companies, four of which are in the public sector—ONGC (Oil and Natural Gas Corporation), Indian Oil, BPCL (Bharat Petroleum Corporation Limited), and HPCL (Hindustan Petroleum Corporation Limited). The process of strengthening PSUs was a conscious policy decision when the government identified nine PSUs that had the potential to emerge as global giants and named them *navratnas* or nine jewels. That list has since been expanded to more than nine, besides several 'mini navratnas'. The purpose behind such identification was to give them greater autonomy and delegation of powers to incur capital expenditure, enter technology joint ventures or strategic alliances, restructure their organizations, raise capital from domestic and international market, in short to give them power and authority to compete on commercial lines.

Going global needs very different levels of skills and mindsets, not to mention very large war chests. The PSUs sometimes form a loose or formal consortium to get the benefit of collective bargaining, as some steel and coal companies have done; SAIL (Steel Authority of India Limited), NTPC (National Thermal Power Corporation), Coal India, RINL (Rashtriya Ispat Nigam Limited), and NMDC (National Mineral Development Corporation) have come together to form a special purpose vehicle called Coal Ventures International Limited (CVIL), which has an equity capital of Rs 35 billion, going up to Rs 100 billion, as war chest to try and acquire some international facilities to secure supplies of coking coal for the steel and power sectors. The seriousness of intent can be gauged by the fact that this company has the mandate to clear proposals up to Rs 15 billion at the board level itself—all PSUs, including navratnas have to get Cabinet approval for investments above Rs 10 billion (Sasi 2008).

STAFF ATTRITION

One of the biggest challenges facing PSUs is to retain staff, particularly at senior levels. Technical expertise in PSUs is often of a more superior quality although considerations like efficient utilization of resources, avoiding overruns of time and cost, and working within a tight delivery schedule are not very well developed.

Paradoxically, while technical efficiency and capital flows are not a constraint, it is often the human resource element that holds back the public sector. Indeed, in India, PSUs are often used to implement public policy initiatives and social objectives of the government. '(While) PSUs can align their objectives with those of public policy, (they) cannot be held responsible for achieving them in entirety or for eternity. That would violate the very reason for being a company' (Kaushik and Dutta 2005a: 178).

> The Hindustan Fertilizer Factory was set up in West Bengal in 1986 at a cost of $1.2 billion and had employed 1,550 workers by 1994. It had all the accoutrements to be found in a modern industrial enterprise such as a canteen, a personnel department, engineers, electricians, plumbers and painters to maintain the equipment. The only thing missing was fertilizers: the factory had produced none since its establishment. (Balasubramanyan 2001: 10)
>
> The Talcher unit of Fertilizer Corporation of India, the state-owned fertilizer factory, (has) celebrated its silver jubilee but has yet to produce its first kilogram of fertilizer. A few years ago, its workers went on strike, demanding higher wages ... the government gave into their demand. (Forbes 2002: 131)

PSU employees are not incentivized to deliver differential performance in a large part because there is no additional reward for superior work and no punishment for underperformance either. India also has some of the most rigid labour laws which is actually a product of political thinking over the years that assumes 'poor' labour to be always right and 'rich and cruel' employers to be always wrong. Once hired, the staff is often a fixed 'asset' with no question of flexibility for the employer to align HR requirements to business fluctuations or fire employees for underperforming.

Compounding this problem is the looming skill shortage in the entire Indian economy. It is now accepted that the Indian education system has failed to keep pace with the growth in the economy. Before the process of liberalization made the expansion of MNCs and privately owned companies possible, the public sector was the first employer of choice for a large number of Indian middle class professionals. The booming economy and rapid expansion of the private sector in hitherto reserved sectors have created a major problem of employee attrition in PSUs. Only in the last decades have Indian private sector companies invested in large projects. The talent pool available to handle large projects was always limited in the private sector, whereas public sector managers always had experience and solid grounding in handling mega projects. The telecommunication industry witnessed growth following the entry of private players led by engineers and managers from the Department of Telecommunications (DoT), who left the government to join more lucrative and challenging roles in the private sector. A similar situation was also in the insurance sector where there was no significant skill in the Indian private sector as insurance till 1999 was completely government-owned.

The recruitment style of the PSUs is often self-perpetuating and self-defeating; they rarely pay market rates for quality people and are often forced to accommodate political mandates in recruitment policies. There has been a steady process of downsizing and stalled recruitment in PSUs which is likely to compound the problem. The average age in the public sector is 47–8 years and this is quite likely to create a crisis in a decade when people of experience retire (Bhagat 2006); also, the general trend is that when a senior employee joins another company, the whole team follows soon and this leaves a vacuum that is very hard to fill.

An ASSOCHAM study in 2007 had estimated that the domestic petroleum and power sector would grapple with a maximum attrition rate of a whopping 35 per cent in 2008. India's energy sector is slated to witness major expansion activities and calls for fresh requirement of a professional and skilled workforce of over 25 to 35 thousand. PSUs like ONGC, IOC (Indian Oil Company), Oil India, BP (Bharat Petroleum), NTPC, Power Trading Corporation, and Power Grid Corporation are some companies identified where executives and below-executive cadre will in all likelihood jump ship to better paying opportunities offered by the new private sector entrants. The public sector itself is undertaking major expansion programmes and will need not only a fresh infusion of talent but also the ability to retain existing employees (ASSOCHAM 2007). Attrition hits PSUs especially hard because it is more difficult for them to compete in the talent market given the fixed and low levels of pay (in some cases only half of what the private sector offers). The ONGC, for instance, lost about fifty employees a year till 2004. The figure went up 600 per cent to 300 in 2006 (of which around 225 were engineers with technical skills). The NTPC loses 100 engineers to private sector firms and expects the figure to double to 200 a year by 2012 when private power projects become fully operational. According to A.K. Khandelwal, chairman and MD, Bank of Baroda, the banking sector is not spared either and public sector banks lose around 1,000 employees every year (*Financial Express* 2007). The 239 central PSUs employed a total of 1.649 million people at the end of 2006; the comparable figures for the previous four years were: 1.992 million, 1.866 million, 1.762 million, and 1.7 million (Government of India 2006).

PSUs are lobbying with the union government to ask the pay commission—perhaps for the first time—for a differential pay structure favouring employees with technical experience so as to retain them. While there may be no significant advantage of technical performance of the private sector over the public sector, economic efficiency is another matter altogether, helped in no small measure by better performing employees getting paid better money for working as hard. The rate of growth of the private sector is very fast and it seems a good fit between the underpaid public sector staff—particularly senior staff—and the talent vacuum in the private sector. In a slightly different context but relevant to staffing, a former deputy chairman of the planning commission noted that '(instead of occupying the commanding heights of the economy), by and large the state-owned sector had become an appendix to the private sector, meant to ensure its smooth running by providing the needed infrastructure and the basic production facilities. As a result, instead of striking a path of its own, the state-owned sector has to subordinate itself to the logic and requirements of the private sector' (Bala 2006: 15).

TELECOM

The telecom sector is one of the fastest growing and most exciting sectors of the Indian economy. It sees keen participation and competition from public, private and foreign companies. Looking back a decade and a half, telecommunications was a part of the services rendered not even as a utility or by a government-owned agency but as a full-fledged government department. Tariffs were set on non-commercial lines under the assumption of universal service obligation which heavily subsidized general users. Long-distance national and international calls were priced at exorbitant rates to subsidize local calls and rural users. Even so, teledensity in March 1990 was only about 0.46 per 100 persons against the then prevailing world average of eight per 100 persons.

Since easing of regulatory constraints through the 1990s and beyond, the country's telecom network has become the third largest in the world (OECD 2007). Teledensity stood at 621.28 million users at the end of financial year 2009–10, with mobile phones having a larger share than fixed landlines (Radhakrishnan, Prahlada, and Kumar n.d.). The trigger for such dramatic transformation was opening the sector to private investment and simultaneously remodelling government-owned telecom services. Up until 2000, the government carried out all telecom-related services through DoT, including policy-making, licensing, and service provision. These functions were separated and the business of providing telecom services was transferred to a newly-created corporate entity called Bharat Sanchar Nigam Limited (BSNL). Mahanagar Telephone Nigam Limited (MTNL), the other government-owned company formed in the early 1980s, provides telecommunication services in Delhi and Mumbai.

Since its inception in 2000, BSNL has brought about phenomenal transformation in India's telecom sector from manually operated technology to a completely chip-based digital high-speed era. Today, BSNL is India's largest telecom company. With its formidable network coverage of the entire country, BSNL, commanded 24 per cent of the mobile market share as of 31 March 2008 even without serving two of the highest cell-phone density metros of Mumbai and NCR region; its share of fixed line phones is higher at over 85 per cent and provides the complete range of telecom services. It is the pioneer in rural telephony, working on 80 per cent of the Rs 25 billion (USD 0.58 billion) market, under the Rural Telephony Project of the Government of India. While being spun off from a government department to a corporate entity, BSNL took on a massive workforce of over 3,00,000 employees, the highest ratio of employees to phone connections in India—a large portion of whom were not geared to a service-oriented industry that telecom has become. Moreover, BSNL runs several training institutes all over the country which provide both induction and in-service training to enhance skills, improve customer orientation, and deepen the skill base available in the telecom sector in the country. Government agencies and PSUs traditionally have strong technical skills and this plays a major role in BSNL's ability to maintain a nationwide network of the entire range of telecom services using the latest technology. The vastness of network ensures that its engineers and technicians have experience in working in challenging circumstances in all kinds of terrains.

Despite being a legacy operator with an inherited government work culture, BSNL has rewritten the rules for the entire telecom industry in the country providing quality services at low tariffs. This provides stiff competition to other private operators to continually innovate, thus sparking greater efficiency and raising the bar of performance. This synergy also helps BSNL to continually improve its work culture, particularly its customer interface that will help retain or bring back customers into its network.

Being a 100 per cent government-owned PSU, BSNL has to follow government-mandated guidelines on most operational matters and this makes the company response to changing market conditions slow and cumbersome, often losing crucial market share in the process. At present, BSNL enjoys a mini navratna status and is working hard to be crowned a navratna which will give the PSU greater autonomy in decision-making on technical, functional, and financial matters.

Both MTNL and BSNL have been primarily responsible for bringing down telephone tariffs, especially for mobile phones in India. In early-2000, BSNL's launch of services was at a much lower tariff than the private operators, who had to bring down their tariffs. In Delhi and Mumbai, MTNL played a similar role as BSNL to bring down tariffs for the common man.

SPACE

India's 'space programme' has always been closely guarded and firmly under government wraps. This bastion is also slowly opening up to the private enterprise; in 2007, the Indian Space Research Organisation (ISRO) began outsourcing some non-critical components to the private sector. This is expected to free scientists' minds from routine work so that they can concentrate on research and development. Today, ISRO is also trying to tap the global satellite launch market (Paris-based market research firm Euroconsult estimates the launch market to grow to USD 145 billion over the next 10 years). Launch vehicles account for roughly two-third of the cost of a space mission and this is the segment where ISRO reckons it can beat global competition on cost alone by 25–35 per cent.

Through increasing sourcing from industry, ISRO not only expects to build technical and technological capability in the country in building more critical sub-components, systems, and modules but also to bring down costs further through increased competition.

ISRO has already launched satellites for Germany, Belgium, Italy, South Korea, Malaysia, Israel, Russia, and Singapore and has proved India's capability and reliability in this sensitive and high-value market. India has quietly and consistently built up its space programme since 1963 with increasing indigenization at all stages—at first to reduce dependability on foreign space agencies and now to be globally cost-competitive enough to target 5–10 per cent of the satellite launch market and even component-building market. When costs come down, satellites can benefit larger numbers of humanity by making telecommunications more affordable, reducing digital divides, enabling a level playing field in education, delivering satellite-linked quality healthcare services, etc.

DEFENCE

Yet another closed department of the government, which is facing winds of change, is the defence sector. Speaking at a FICCI seminar in 2006, Pranab Mukherjee (the then defence minister) had said that India is the largest importer of defence systems in the world with the average capital defence acquisition in the past three years amounting to Rs 450 billion/year (≈ USD 10.5 bn) and is likely to go up to a whopping figure of Rs 1250 billion/year (≈ USD 30 bn) by 2010 (Mukherjee 2006). Domestic production has been minimal and till recently only ordnance depots and some PSUs were involved in weapons system development. The Indian industry has participated in defence production on the sidelines since the 1970s and increasingly through DRDO (Defence Research and Development Organisation)-initiated programmes, Integrated Guided Missile Development programme (IGDMP) in the 1980s and the Light Combat Aircraft (LCA) programme in the 1990s, which has greatly increased industry capability to produce world-class goods. Some private companies like L&T, Tata Power, and even IT giant Wipro have started work for producing military equipment. However, it is still not enough to enable Indian defence production to be independent or at least not totally dependent on foreign suppliers. Another limiting factor is the huge investment required to enter defence production and with no reasonable guarantee of purchase by the only buyer, the defence establishment.

This is where an offset clause in defence purchase agreements helps the local economy. 'Offset' is a term commonly used to refer to consideration required to be created by the seller through industrial participation of the buying country. That is, foreign agencies getting orders, usually above a certain size, have to spend a part of the order value by procuring products and services from companies in the buying country or otherwise investing in them.

Presently, government policy requires that all defence contracts above Rs 3 billion must have a minimum offset value of 30 per cent and must be discharged in India concurrently, and this limit may also be raised in cases of very large orders.

Israel is an example of a country which has used a strong offset policy to become a major arms exporter from a virtual non-entity a few years ago. With defence imports targeted to reach Rs 125 billion over the next few years, the size of the local defence industry will also sharply rise. The then defence minister estimated that USD 10 billion would flow back into the country during the Eleventh Plan Period through offsets in defence deals (*Businessworld* 2007). While most defence analysts cautiously agree that the Indian private industry can absorb the offset orders—some of them have a separate defence vertical—it could also spur the sluggish defence ordnance factories and other public sector companies to raise the bar of performance to stay relevant. Defence production of any credible value requires large investments, which the public sector has at its command; private industries offer the benefit of being dynamic and more conscious of time and cost overruns and more likely to adopt modern manufacturing methods and tools. The logical way forward is public–private partnership (PPP)—DRDO (along with its allied defence research agencies) has already entered partnerships with Indian industries which encompass thirty ordnance factories, forty PSUs, thirty major private industries, and over 800 small and medium-scale industries.

POWER

One of the most important infrastructure elements of the country is the power sector. Over fifty years of monopoly, rent-seeking, and even corruption have rendered power one of the most vulnerable infrastructure constraints of the country. Indian citizens are used to treating water and electricity as free resources; electricity has particularly become a political commodity and tariffs are set by the government with little relevance to cost of production or market fluctuations.

The share of different types of power generation in India is: thermal-based (64.6 per cent), hydropower (24.7 per cent), nuclear power (2.9 per cent), and renewables (7.7 per cent). Power is a concurrent subject in India; states have a greater share of generation and transmission assets and almost the entire distribution network is under their control. Most states have unbundled the state electricity boards and separated the generation, transmission, and distribution functions—some states have privatized the distribution function. Private participation is allowed in generation, transmission, and distribution. According to Ministry of Power data, transmission and distribution losses including unbilled, unpaid, or incorrectly billed amounts are approximately—33 per cent of the total availability (the global average is around 7–8 per cent). It is this segment that is most in need of reforms and states have had different degrees of success.

Till March 2011, the government was still the dominant player in the power sector (Ministry of Power n.d.):

- State Sector: 82,452.58 MW (47.49 per cent);

- Central Sector: 54,412.63 MW (31.34 per cent);
- Private Sector: 36,761.19 MW (21.17 per cent).

Reform of the power sector is still an ongoing process and various initiatives are being tried out at all segments of the supply chain; the premise is that competition from more players will bring efficiency to the market and provide incentives for cost reduction. Issues such as free electricity to the agriculture sector, charging market rates to the domestic sector, and meeting demands of the industrial sector through the grid rather than expecting industry to generate it require strong coordination of political and economic vision. Without resolving the backlog of contentious issues and providing reasonable conditions for earning profits, this sector cannot attract private investment at a level required to derive benefits of competition. As of now, the government and public sector remain the dominant players in the power sector.

FINANCIAL SECTOR

The Indian financial sector has two broad categories: (i) an organized sector, and (ii) a traditional sector known as informal credit market. The organized financial sector has one of the highest shares of public ownership in India, and it thus also enjoys a commanding share in all sectors of the economy. The credit–deposit ratio (which is a good proxy for credit–GDP ratio in India) is around 70 per cent (Thorat 2010). This is through three main segments of the financial system: (i) commercial banks, (ii) term-lending institutions, and (iii) non-banking financial companies (NBFCs), working under the Reserve Bank of India (RBI) which is the apex institution in the financial system. State-owned banks often serve as a channel for the proliferation of the soft-budget constraints of other firms and perhaps unwittingly foster the fiscal mismanagement of loss-making PSUs.

As the economy grows in size and complexity, the financial sector will have to provide the means for providing momentum of funds flow. The efficiency with which such funds are collected and transmitted depends on the width, depth, and diversity of the financial system; the fundamental strength of the financial sector will be particularly tested in converting non-productive savings (in the form of gold, etc.) into productive assets flowing into the economy.

The broad category of institutional shareholding amounts to close to one-fourth of the total market capital. This, however, is not a homogeneous group and within it are included foreign institutional investors, banks, financial institutions, and mutual funds, making it highly unlikely that they will act in a coordinated manner. Of these institutions, mutual funds often represent corporate investments rather than individual investors, several being promoted by India's business houses. Therefore, it calls into question the conventional governance remedy of institutions playing a monitoring role.

The financial sector is a sector which has seen real reforms in the past one and a half decades, much more than most other sectors. Some factors that have adversely affected the viability and profitability of banks and financial institutions prior to 1991 were: interest rates on government securities were artificially pegged at low levels and were unrelated to market conditions; subsidies or concessional availability of bank credit was limited to certain sectors; interest rates were administered; a captive market existed for government securities; and excessive reliance on central bank financing. Moreover, transactions among the government, RBI, and commercial banks were governed by fiscal priorities (read political) rather than sound principles of financial management or commercial viability.

> Bank supervision and accounting rules were lax—for example, income was booked on the accrual principle but was matched by huge receivables, so it was difficult to ascertain the real state of assets and liabilities. 'The real rate of return to the banks on their assets in the latter half of the 1980s was estimated to be about 0.15 per cent ... reflecting the poor quality of their loan portfolio. (Krueger and Chinoy 2002: 24)

Reforms introduced from the 1990s saw a phased implementation of international best practices, greater operational autonomy, interest rate deregulation, gradual reduction of RBI's dual role of owner and monitor, use of information technology to upgrade recovery, restructuring, and service, aimed at restoring vitality in the banking system.

As part of financial restructuring, banks were recapitalized by the government to meet prudential norms; the exercise is estimated to have cost nearly 1 per cent of the GDP (Gross Domestic Product) and in March 2006, the capital adequacy ratio stood at 12.4 per cent, which is as good as the global standard (the US has 13 per cent). Some part of the equity has been divested to private shareholders and banks listed on the stock exchanges are subject to disclosure and market discipline standards as other listed entities.

Commercial banks' net profits were 0.9 per cent of the total assets in 2005–6; the ratio of non-performing loans to total loans, which was 15.7 per cent as of March 1997, declined to 3.3 per cent by March 2006, and non-performing assets declined to 1.2 per cent of net advances during 2005–6 (Reddy 2007: 8). Moreover, LIC and GIC (General Insurance Corporation), the insurance behemoths, have also got greater operational freedom and permission to appoint fund managers in India and abroad and to invest up to 60 per cent of their funds in approved market investments rather than only government securities.

Permitting foreign and private banks to operate in India has helped raise competition and brought about efficiency. Liberalization has enabled the emergence of financial conglomerates, integrating banking, insurance and other businesses to achieve synergy and efficiency. Post-reforms, the Indian financial sector has transited to a regime of market-determined interest rates, some degree of free exchange rate, partial capital and current account convertibility, and an auction-based system in government securities market. Although these measures have helped to integrate Indian financial markets into global markets, it is a long way from becoming a global player as some other sectors have already done. Global pressures bring about efficiency like little else and efficiency of the financial sector directly raises the efficiency of capital, that is, the entire economy.

McKinsey & Co., with support from the Indian Banks Association (Indian Banks' Association), tracked 14 leading Indian banks and their customers in five surveys and found that Indian banks achieved the highest pre-tax returns on investment across Asia at 17.9 per cent in 2006, compared to those in Malaysia (16.3 per cent), China (15.1 per cent), and Thailand (9.1 per cent). This performance helped Indian banks post the highest returns to shareholders as measured by stock market banking indices. Between January 2000 and October 2007, Indian banks delivered returns to shareholders of 36.76 per cent (compounded annual growth rate), compared to 24.03 per cent for the entire Indian stock market (McKinsey & Co. 2007). In the same period, Chinese banks achieved returns to shareholders of 17.57 per cent, while British banks managed only 9.34 per cent. All those ranked better than 7.16 per cent by all shares on the FTSE (Financial Times Stock Exchange) index and 4.54 per cent on the Dow Jones index, as tracked by the same report.

While a booming economy has helped Indian banks achieve these figures, it is also the result of better lending choices. For decades, public sector banks were required to lend to the 'priority sector' where returns are few and chances of bad debts high; more operational freedom has made banks assess their customers wisely and profitably.

The robustness of financial sector reforms will, however, be tested while financing the infrastructure sector. The unique features of infrastructure projects—long gestation periods, assets that are not easily transferable, vulnerability to regulatory and political changes, and, in general, a higher risk profile—make its financing different from other sectors. Financing of infrastructure projects is largely cash-flow-based and not asset-based and this requires strong due diligence for risk analysis and risk-mitigating mechanisms. Financing infrastructure growth to keep pace with GDP growth of over 8 per cent per annum will form a major chunk of lending for banks and financial institutions requiring long-term commitment of both equity and long-term debt; specialized PSU lending agencies like IL&FS (Infrastructure Leasing & Financial Services Limited), IDFC (Industrial Development Finance Company), ICICI, and IDBI are emerging in the forefront of such lending in India.

The future of banking will be dominated by technology-based banking, IT, and electronic fund transfer systems. Products offered by banks have moved beyond conventional banking to provide 24-hour banking and more value-added services. This change is led mostly by private and foreign banks and PSU banks lose on customer base due to slower response time and constraints imposed by the regulator. These changes are also challenging for the monitoring and regulatory mechanism to enable proper growth of the sector.

CONCLUSION

The strength of the public sector is in the magnitude, infrastructure, resources as well as sectoral penetration it has achieved. From the brief snapshots above, it appears that public sector enterprises are also uniformly grappling with similar problems as the private sector. It is clear that government as the owner and often the regulator is aware of the shortcomings and trying to draft policies and take other proactive measures to improve efficiency and capital utilization. Collaboration among PSUs and between the public and private sector is on the rise and the country has come a long way from the era when business was regarded with suspicion. The public sector faces challenges that are vastly different from the private sector concerns; for instance, it is subject to a lot more scrutiny and not always of the helpful kind. The PSUs are vulnerable to competitors who may try to obtain sensitive and classified business information by asking politically-motivated questions or queries under the Right to Information (RTI) Act.

One and a half decades of reforms have greatly improved the performance of the public sector but this is an ongoing exercise. In areas like power and other infrastructure like roads and railways, reforms have only made a modest beginning in removing systemic constraints.

This is evident from the analysis of the Comptroller and Auditor General of India (CAG). As on 31 March 2006, 116 central government companies and corporations had accumulated losses of Rs 841.55 billion. Out of these, equity capital of eighty-two companies had been completely eroded and the combined share of losses of these companies was Rs 816.17 billion. Forty-six of the eighty-two companies were referred to the BIFR (Board for Industrial & Financial Reconstruction) and eighteen companies have been approved for closure, winding up, or sale, while a revival package has been approved for twelve companies. (CAG 2007)

According to the *Public Enterprises Survey 2009–10*, conducted by the Department of Public Enterprises (DPE), profitability of 217 central PSUs reveal the following facts:

Table 4.1 Financial Ratio of Central Public Sector Enterprises

Particulars	2007–08	2008–09	2009–10
Net Profit to Turnover	7.41	6.59	7.50
Net Profit to Capital Employed	11.21	10.57	10.17
Net Profit to Net-worth	15.60	14.28	14.02

Source: Department of Public Enterprises, *Public Enterprises Survey 2009–10*, Vol. 1, Box 3 Financial Ratio.

The public sector will continue to play a major role in the economy although the private sector will also increase its presence. The traditional strength of PSUs, that is, monopoly, is practically nonexistent in a post-WTO (World Trade Organization) world and blurring national boundaries have increased both opportunities and competition for all businesses. The PSUs have been instrumental in creating basic economic infrastructure in the country and developing a deep bank of technical skills; clearly, though, it can better deliver value only by sharpening its commercial orientation. Moreover, PSUs are increasingly adopting stock market-mandated corporate governance norms either voluntarily or as part of the listing agreement.

There are winds of change that are flowing through the public sector as the belief is getting stronger that the country may not be willing to subsidise loss-making ventures or guarantee jobs of people achieving lower than the acceptable benchmark of productivity. Airports, ports, roads, power, and even defence production have been privatized, which were earlier treated as unquestionable holy cows. Some banks like the Canara Bank have gone through extensive change and makeover to be customer-focused. Air India and Indian Airlines have been merged to create synergies and stem any losses or inefficiencies. As we get more integrated with the global economy, the concept of government business running inefficiently or in losses for perpetuity will disappear. Many PSUs are turning themselves around and embracing the change.

Despite all adversity, the faith of people in the public sector is undiminished. The quality of products and services of a PSU is taken at face value and usually not questioned. This is a quantum leap of faith in India, where people are used to double guessing the product, service, bill, or contract of private players. This is truly the value of the public sector in Indian lives.

5

Influence of Global Business on India

The Indian subcontinent has been a part of the global trade network throughout recorded history. Coastal India, in particular, has witnessed robust commerce and true integration of influences wrought by international trade along established sea routes. Trade along land routes has shaped the socioeconomic environment in the northwest regions.

The Dutch East India Company was established in 1602 when the Estates-General of the Netherlands granted it a twenty-one-year monopoly to carry out colonial activities in Asia. It is widely recognized as the first multinational corporation (MNC) in the world and the first company to issue stock. It remained an important trading concern for almost two centuries, paying an almost 18 per cent annual dividend for almost 200 years, until it became bankrupt and was finally dissolved in 1800, its possessions and debt being taken over by the Government of the Batavian Republic.

FOREIGN NATIONAL COMPANIES IN BRITISH INDIA

By the onset of eighteenth century when Britain had established political supremacy over the Indian subcontinent, Indian commerce consisted of handloom textiles, considered among the most superior in the world then, and other handicrafts or farm products. Fresh business ideas from Europe gradually broadened Indian businesses into new areas like jute, coal, and tea and coffee plantations, besides introducing revolutionary technology in the established sector of textiles. Multinational companies and their subsidiaries played a pioneering role in introducing and developing those industries for which Indian houses did not show much enthusiasm or even lacked the technical and managerial expertise to venture into. The United Kingdom dominated the foreign trade and investment in India; a study shows that as much as 14 per cent of all British investments were made in India and other Asian countries during 1865–1914 (Bagchi 1972). They also introduced modern technologies capable of large-scale production in their businesses creating significant economies of scale and introduced several managerial and marketing practices that were used in their home countries but not in India. Imperial Tobacco gave away free samples of cigarettes to promote its use, advertised their wares through decorative visual displays in village markets, and held various events to publicize their products (Basu 1988: 12–22). Tea companies invited common people to free tea tasting events especially in eastern India in an effort to open up a virgin market by changing the habits of an entire country.

Unlike most Indian firms that were strictly controlled by the promoter, a managing director (MD) of such multinational companies reported to the board, and had significant autonomy and independence over its operations and decision-making. This phenomenon of close control and intense management by Indian promoters still continue in a fair degree but there is a noticeable change towards more inclusive decision making, which in today's context is brought about by globalized nature of Indian businesses and the challenges they present. The multinational subsidiaries influenced changing ways of doing business among Indian businesses. Joint-stock form of ownership found instant acceptance among Indian merchants because it helped disperse risk more widely than the prevailing form of ownership, which was mostly proprietary, and risks were concentrated in the hands of the family.

By the end of World War I (WWI) in 1918, United Kingdom looked rather weak as a power and United States and Japan had become stronger political and economic entities. This also impacted foreign direct investment (FDI) and more US companies started operating in India like General Motors in 1928, Ford Motors in 1930, and Colgate Palmolive in 1938. Japan also rose as a significant trading partner, particularly in cotton.

Nonetheless, British business interests remained as strong as ever. India was still a hot spot for investments by British companies during this period. Between 1930 and 1945, as many as 28 new manufacturing British subsidiaries started their operations in India. With the continued interest of British investments and the additional interest of American, Japanese and other European countries, the total inward stock of foreign direct investment was about $1.0 billion by 1929. India ranked third among the favourable hosts to foreign direct investments in 1929. (Nayak 2006: 13)

Following the partition of Bengal, from 1905–08, a new movement of self-reliance blew across called the swadeshi movement, whose basic principle was to create jobs for millions of Indians, whose livelihood were lost as a consequence of cheap imports into India following the Industrial Revolution in the UK. The strategy was to boycott British made goods and work towards revival of the domestic industry and indigenous production techniques. The concept of substituting machine by labour is embedded in the everlasting image of Mahatma Gandhi and his spinning-wheel. Though the movement took epic emotional and political proportions leading to repealing of the order of the participation of Bengal in 1908, there is no conclusive evidence of the degree of economic success of the movement so far it relates to British businesses.

The rise of the swadeshi movement did not significantly reduce the prominence of the global businesses in India, although there was a marked increase in the number of Indian businesses. The defining ones were Bengal Chemicals by Prafulla Chandra Roy in Calcutta, which still operates and is a leader in cleaning fluids and naphthalene products. The other one is Tata Steel, founded by Jamshetji Tata in Bihar, which is one of the largest steel manufacturers in the world today.

Most expatriate business houses did not factor in the looming threat of Indian independence in their investment decisions in India and got along with their business in the hope of a long inning. There were exceptions of course, notably Sir Victor Sassoon, head of E.D. Sassoon & Company, who shifted his headquarters from Bombay to

Shanghai in as early as 1931. In his words, 'there will be less scope in India for a foreigner in future because of cut-throat competition with Indian firms, which have less overhead charges and because of the anti-foreign prejudice. It looks as if India under swaraj will have a great deal of internal trouble' (Tripathi 2004: 223). However, Sir Victor soon came to rue his judgement when China under Communist takeover forced him out of the country while his Indian operations continued to flourish for more than a decade after shifting base to China. Independent India, in its restrictive phase of the late-1960s and 1970s, did live up to Sir Victor's fears but in the 1930s, that fear among multinationals and expatriate houses was not a popular sentiment. Bird & Heilgers, one of the most prominent export houses based in Calcutta, had a different take on the rising tide of nationalism. Edward (Tom) Benthall, perhaps the most dominant figure in the Birds' management, in his conversation with Gandhi during the latter's England visit for the Round Table Conference in 1931, refers to the 'suffering of the European business community' in the last ten years and says that the government officers were 'anxious not to be accused of favouring Europeans' and 'giving concessions to Indians where in equity Europeans had a prior claim'. And Europeans, who had received many concessional advantages in the past because of their access to the government, 'must in future expect that to be reversed' but expected that 'we were not deliberately discriminated against' (Ibid.: 209). The Parrys, operating mostly in south India, now owned by the Murugappa Group of Chennai, also did not let the looming Indian independence affect its business operations. In fact, they reacted by making suitable changes to their structure and personnel, more Indianization of the workforce and for good measure, shifted their seat of management and control from London to Madras (Chennai) within a year of independence and registered the company under the Indian law.

At the time of independence, the old foreign firms, which were mainly British, were holding on to their interests without losing hope in the business climate of the newly independent India. Figures indicate that expatriate firms grew at a slower pace than Indian firms but scholars attribute this to a number of reasons. One, of course, was the buoyancy and confidence that Indian businesses were experiencing with favourable conditions and few restrictions vis-à-vis foreign firms.

The Chelmsford–Montague Declaration of 1917 that promised a greater role for Indians in the governance of their country came as a wake-up call for the business community. With rising nationalism, the entry barriers in new industries were more or less the same for all prospective businessmen, Indian or European.

Another factor is that most industries in which foreign firms had interests had reached certain maturity and the initial aggressive entrepreneurship, which caused the expansion, gave way to settled management. Indians, with their community linkages to raise finances and with greater understanding of market realities, were not content acting as agents or sub-agents of British companies alone but wanted to be business owners themselves. These factors perhaps explain why Indian interests were gaining in strength and British interests were stagnating or declining.

INDEPENDENCE AND FOREIGN COMPANIES

When Indian independence became a reality, most of these foreign firms changed their approach to their business interests in India. Several such firms gradually withdrew from the country by either selling out to Indian businessmen or by the government taking over such businesses that had become bankrupt, sick, or faced labour trouble. Rising labour militancy in Bengal, where most of these business houses were located, saw several businesses affected—although Indian firms were equally impacted.

Indian businesses houses, taking advantage of the support and encouragement that the national government provided, including restrictive entry rights through grant of licences, asserted its influence and dominance in the Indian business landscape.

Prominent agency houses like Parry's and Binny, both from Madras, had already started the process of Indianization before independence and gradually even came under the control of Indian institutions. Similar in vintage to Parry's, Binny was formed in 1812 by John Binny and was a pioneering textile company in India. Binny still operates as a public listed company under Indian ownership having gone through processes of mergers and re-organizations.

Meanwhile, the wholly owned subsidiary of 100 per cent British American Tobacco, Imperial Tobacco Company, continued operations as though India were still an outpost of the British Raj—the senior managers were mostly expatriates working in junior grades at the head office and practiced a centralized, top-down tone of management. Imperial Tobacco was in a monopoly business and those leading the company continued in the early days of independence as though 'newly independent India would collapse and request to be governed again, as part of the white man's burden' (Haksar 1993: 9). The company also seemed to believe that without revenue from the imperial government, the government of independent India would be hard pressed to administer the affairs of the country. In fact, there was great indignation over changes that took place in the cigarette and tobacco excise duties and over restrictions on the import of tobacco leaf, following the foreign investment policy put forth in 1949. Real change in the functioning of the company or in understanding its responsibilities and obligations as a corporate guest to its host country was slow in coming but over the years, the Indian management turned the company whose main revenues came from tobacco into a 'rainbow identity' of diverse products and service offerings and for years, the company has been a pillar of the Indian stock market indices.

Most other expatriate businesses, in the initial years of independence, were tightly controlled by their parent companies till the enactment of FERA (Foreign Exchange Regulation Act) in 1973, which forced them to dilute their holdings to 40 per cent. Several subsidiaries adapted to the new realities by changing their names such as Unilever calling itself Hindustan Lever Limited (HLL) or Imperial Tobacco Company (ITC) changing the 'Imperial' to 'Indian' or just to ITC.

THE RECEPTIVE PHASE OF FOREIGN INVESTMENT, 1948–67

Following independence in 1947, the government made huge investments in state-owned enterprises following its decision to follow the path of 'mixed economy', which is the reflection of the desire of independent India best described by Jawaharlal Nehru speaking at the opening session of the 1956 Economic Commission for Asia and the Far East, '...we are not going to spend the next 100 years arriving gradually, step-by-step, to the stage of development which the developed countries have reached today. Our pace and tempo has to be faster' (qtd in Misra 1978: 162).

The bulk of new investments of independent India were in infrastructure industries, something that British India had neglected, with the possible exception of a rail network, which was formed in 1853 and is now one of the largest networks in the world.

However, in this phase, foreign investment was considered essential for supplementing domestic capital and more importantly as a means of securing technical, scientific, and industrial knowledge—areas in which indigenous efforts have been traditionally negligible, if not nonexistent. The framework of industrial policies of this era, needed foreign capital to supplement domestic savings and be used for higher investments.

The Industrial Policy Resolution of 1948 (IPR 48) welcomed the inflow of foreign capital but visualized a law to ensure that majority ownership and effective control remained in Indian hands, perhaps because of insecurity caused by the long shadow cast by turn of events during the dominance of Dutch, French, and English East India Companies in colonized India. It stated that all individual cases of majority foreign participation in Indian companies will be under the scrutiny and approval of the government and even had clauses that Indian personnel should be sufficiently trained so that they could replace the expatriate managers within a time frame. This caused a sense of fear and discomfort amongst foreign businesses in India about the future and they started looking for assurances from the government.

On 6 April 1949, Prime Minister J.L. Nehru made a statement to the Indian Parliament in relation to IPR 48, which till date remains the most comprehensive document on the role of foreign capital in India in that period. He said foreign private capital was also important because 'in many cases, scientific, technical and industrial knowledge and capital equipment can best be secured with foreign capital' (Dhar 1988:5). The prime minister, in order to deal with the growing uncertainties amongst British businesses, said in the same statement:

> I should like to add a few words about British interests in India which naturally form the largest part of foreign investments in India. Although it is the policy of the Government of India to encourage the growth of Indian

industry and commerce (including such services like banking, shipping and insurance) to the best of their ability, there is and will still be considerable scope for the investment of British capital in India. These considerations will apply equally to other existing non-Indian interests. The Government of India has no desire to injure in any way British or other non-Indian interests in India and would gladly welcome their contribution in a constructive and cooperative role in the development of India's economy. (Ibid.: 6)

Nevertheless, under IPR 48, foreign investors had reasonable assurance of unrestricted remittances of profits and dividends, non-discriminatory treatment, and fair compensation in the event of acquisition of their business. However, as the years went by, the Indian government grew more assertive—and more restrictive—in terms of the number of industries where foreign capital was permitted.

The foreign exchange crisis of 1957–8, arising out of fiscal imbalance caused by taking large unserviceable foreign debts for funding industrial and infrastructure activities resulted in relaxation of restrictions and forming policies to encourage foreign investment by offering incentives and concessions; several double taxation avoidance treaties were signed during this period, and corporate and personal taxes as well as royalties were rationalized. These concessions did not come voluntarily but were guided by the World Bank and similar institutions, which were lending and working on the bailout. The World Bank's view on the role of foreign capital was evident in its 'Report of the Banker's Mission to India and Pakistan' in 1960. The report observed that borrowing governments, in order to qualify for all the potential sources of aid to the full, would have to create conditions which would attract foreign private capital. Below are two views:

> The form in which the World Bank wanted foreign capital to participate in the Indian economy was, however, made abundantly clear much earlier when the Government had sought the Bank's assistance for financing the Rourkela Steel Plant in 1956. The Bank insisted that the German collaborators who were supplying technology should have more leverage than had been offered to them in the proposed project which was to be in the public sector. (Dhar 1988: 10)

> It is generally believed that the government's policies to nationalize companies in certain industries and its informal pressures on foreign companies to increase local equity participation in India reduced the flow of FDI (foreign direct investment) into India during this period. Contrary

to this popular perception, this study finds that FDI to India during this period actually rose and reached its peak in 1961. From 1948 to 1961, the amount of FDI stock grew from 2558 million INR [Indian Rupee] to 5285 million INR, an increase of nearly 143 %. Similarly, the number of foreign collaborations with Indian companies grew significantly. The number of joint ventures increased from 34 in 1951 to 464 in 1961, an increase of nearly 14 times in a period of 11 years. (Nayak 2006: 13)

According to the Department of Industrial Policy & Promotion, between 1991 and March 2011, India received USD 146 billion as FDI of private equity capital. The fundamental change in this period from the earlier periods is in the underlying industrial sectors that attracted these investments, reflecting a structural shift in the balance of India's economic power compared to what the founding fathers had envisaged, which was primarily based on manufacturing and capital goods industries.

THE RESTRICTIVE PHASE, 1968–79

In the early- to mid-1960s, as a result of the Government of India's invitation to foreign investors with an attractive tax regime and liberal incentives on free remittances of profits saw a net outflow of foreign exchange leading to another foreign exchange crisis.

This time, the government set up a Foreign Investment Board (FIB) in 1968 to approve foreign investment and set strict norms of equity partnership between foreign and Indian investors. There were several layers of authority through which an application had to pass, including in some cases the Parliament, before foreign investment could be allowed.

The government decided that the link between foreign equity investment and securing access to foreign technology was not very strong. As examples to bolster the argument, the government pointed to several public sector companies, in which foreign equity was a rare exception, which had been able to secure whatever technology they needed in any industry ranging from drugs, to engineering, electronics to petrochemicals.

The enactment of FERA in 1973 further tightened restrictions on operation of foreign companies. Foreign companies (except some in the tea industry) had to dilute their holdings to 40 per cent or below and then they were free to expand their operations like any other Indian company. Besides, the government took a dim view on the fairness of foreign technology agreements and under FERA 1973, included several clauses designed to address such 'anomalies':

- Where the government or a public financial institution possess equity holdings in a company with less than 50 per cent aggregate non-resident holding, the government would retain the right of transfer to any R&D or design engineering consultancy organization, wholly owned by the government, any documentation or techno-logically relevant information acquired through technology import agreement;
- The government would have the right to direct the foreign company to license the imported technology to other parties after the expiry of the agreement (with suitable compensation);
- The collaborator under agreements involving royalty payments would be obliged to pass on, during the duration of the technology transfer agreement, all improvements to technology made by it;
- A foreign company with less than 50 per cent aggregate non-resident holding should use a specified indigenous brand name on the products which it manufactures for the domestic market, using technology covered by the agreement.

In an attempt to force foreign companies to share technology, in 1976, a committee was formed which decided that all foreign companies had to hire Indian consultants; even where foreign consultants were clearly needed, Indian consultants had to be appointed as prime consultants. Sumit K. Majumdar argues that

> The decline in the role of foreign firms in India was further exacerbated by the introduction of the FERA in 1973. While it promulgated after the hike in oil prices, to save foreign exchange which was needed to pay for critical imports such as food and petroleum, at the same time the maximum shareholding that foreign firms could have in Indian companies was limited to 40 per cent. This was so that outflows repatriated to foreign owners could be minimized. Nevertheless, the consequences were dysfunctional. (Majumdar 2005: 4)

He refers to an anecdote of an American businessman's remark, at a meeting with the then Indian Prime Minister Indira Gandhi, 'My issue, Madam Prime Minister, is with the government's insistence on limiting foreign ownership in companies to 40 per cent. Consequently, multinational companies have lost interest in India. And your country is neither getting investment nor technology' (qtd in Majumdar 2005: 4).

The above observation sums up the state of play in India at that time. It took many decades before India could free herself from the clutches of fiscal policies that were inward looking and geared to give greater powers of scrutiny to the government and an industrial policy that was tilted in favour of a select few with licences.

However, there was some silver lining to the dark clouds of misdirected economic policies in early 1970s, the Electronics Committee, a precursor to the Electronics Commision and Department of Electronics, headed by Vikram Sarabhai (one of the brightest scientists India has ever seen and father of Indian Space programme) was asked to review the dominance and effect of IBM (International Business Machines) and its subsidiary ICL (International Computers Limited) on the Indian computer industry. The panel found that a bulk of IBM's revenue came from renting out computers rather than manufacturing new machines. The little manufacturing that was done was largely import of 'as is' machines, that is, second-hand machines imported from IBM subsidiaries in other countries which had almost exhausted their effective lives, stripped down and worn out parts replaced, given a new number, and sold or rented to Indian customers. The other manufacturing activity consisted of assembling 'key punches', a kind of glorified calculating machine, which would soon be obsolete because personal computers would soon replace it (Parthasarathi 2005: 81–2).

IBM withdrew from India in 1978 as they were not willing to dilute their shareholding or make necessary investments for manufacturing. IBM re-entered India later and is today a US business employing over 90,000 people in India (2010 figures), making it one of the largest software companies operating in India.

Following the Electronic Committee's report, Government of India in 1975 created its own company called Computer Maintenance and Service Company Private Limited (CMSCPL) to maintain and service mainframe computers imported into India and reduce IBM's stranglehold on the industry. In 1978, following IBM's exit, the company took over 800 installations of IBM, including some of the employees. It then started servicing computers manufactured by other companies. Later, the company was called CMC Limited and is currently owned by the Tata Group who bought the company in 1990s during the privatization process. In 2011 fiscal, CMC Limited has clocked a turnover of nearly Rs 80 billion, a fairly long journey from a humble beginning.

This was the first wave of large-scale Indianization of foreign or multinational companies. Foreign companies also had to be registered under the Indian Companies Act to carry out significant operations in India. Sales or branch offices of foreign companies had to virtually close down, as the registration process with the government was very onerous.

Prior to 1991, the government exercised a high degree of control over industrial activity by regulating and promoting much of the economic activity. The development strategy discouraged inputs from abroad in the form of investment or imports, while the limited domestic resources were spread out by licensing of manufacturing activity. The result was a domestic industry that was highly protected—from abroad due to import controls and high duties, and from domestic competition due to licensing and reservations. Industrial policy was dominated by licensing constraints by virtue of which strict entry barriers were maintained ... This and other policies led to a very high degree of bureaucratization of the economy. Also, many sectors, like textiles, were reserved for the small scale sector, thereby making it difficult for domestic firms belonging to these sectors to enjoy economies of scale, and making these sectors unattractive to MNCs. (Beena et al. 2004: 127)

This protective umbrella allowed Indian companies to grow, manufacture and sell whatever they produced, usually on their own terms. Therefore, Indian companies found little incentive to innovate or bring in new products and ideas as the industrial policies ensured that they had virtually no competition. There was little necessity for Indian products to benchmark themselves against international excellence. Import controls and high protective import duties made Indian companies uncompetitive in the global markets, this coupled with a protected domestic market made Indian businesses risk averse and complacent. The Indian manufacturers and markets were rapidly losing its global relevance.

This restrictive phase had the effect of isolating the country from global markets and as a consequence, it led to breeding inefficiency, complacency, slow growth, and even obsolescence in technology among Indian businesses.

THE LIBERALIZATION PHASE—1990S ONWARDS

The beginning of the 1990s saw yet another foreign exchange crisis brought about largely due to the closed economic policy of the government. By January 1991 the current account deficit was running at an annual rate of about USD 10 billion and inflation had reached 13 per cent. PSUs were incurring huge losses, corruption was rampant owing to the deeply entrenched licence–permit raj where even junior bureaucrats could decide the economic future of the country. There were shortages in just about every product or service created by artificially restricting production through a licensing process. This ranged from telephones, sugar, and cement, to petroleum products and of course foreign exchange. The Monopolies and Restrictive Trade Practice Act (MRTP) restricted investment and dominant market shares in many key industries. The threshold of domination was very low stemming from the past history of foreign companies in India that did not help producers achieve economies of scale but at the same time, created synthetic shortages. Only companies with licences thrived and the rest of the population paid the price.

During this period, there was flight of NRI (non-resident Indians) deposits of about USD 1 billion, looming external debt and the country faced a political and emotional embarrassment of mortgaging the nation's gold reserves with the Bank of England for loans besides seeking an emergency grant from International Monetary Fund (IMF).

As in the 1960s, it was the foreign exchange crisis that forced the government, albeit at the behest of donor agencies, to change the economic policy that eventually opened up the economy. However, during this period, the government decided to allow market forces to guide the economy rather than follow another restrictive phase.

The new industrial policy took an about turn in 1991 and reserved only eighteen sectors that were closed to foreign companies. That list has since been pruned; the policy on FDI is reviewed on a continuous basis and several measures have been taken. (As of April 2011, only nine sectors like multi-brand retail, agriculture, real estate and housing, legal services, lottery, gambling and betting, and railways are closed to foreign investment.) Foreign equity participation up to 51 per cent was approved automatically where equity inflow was sufficient to meet the costs of imported capital goods whereas 100 per cent equity participation was permitted in the power sector. No permission was required to hire foreign consultants and the requirement of hiring Indian consultants was also scrapped. Multinational companies were allowed to explore and develop gas fields and set up petro-gas projects. Indian companies were allowed to use foreign names for products made locally, paving the way for a common global brand value for companies.

The years 1992–3 also saw partial convertibility of the Indian rupee on trade account, setting the stage for Indian companies to set shop overseas. Telecom, roads, and partly insurance was also opened up, import licensing requirements for most imports were removed, and several export restrictions were either removed or relaxed.

The process of the integration of Indian markets into global systems was firmly underway.

FOREIGN COMPANIES IN 2000 AND BEYOND

The process of liberalization has been continuing for over fifteen years and several strictures that were earlier considered 'holy cow' are now either nonexistent or scarcely recognizable. However, not all foreign or multinational companies fared well after liberalization. Hindustan Unilever Limited (HUL) is a shining example of a company seizing opportunities to expand and grow. Then there are companies like ICI, Siemens, and Philips who have operated in India for over fifty years but are now struggling to keep up the momentum against an onslaught of Asian, US, European, and even Indian companies fiercely competing in the Indian marketplace. The very contour of the term 'foreign' or 'multinational company' has undergone a change. Today, the term makes a reader pause and think where the company is coming from. It could well be an Indian company that has acquired operations overseas like Airtel-Bharti's acquisition of Zain Telecommunications, Tata's acquisition of Tetley or Jaguar Land Rover, or Aditya Birla taking control of Novelis in the US, etc. Indian businesses are on a global shopping spree, and some Indian companies are becoming recognizable in countries like Ireland, UK, USA, continental Europe, and also in the southeast Asian countries. However, in today's wired and connected world, it is difficult to precisely define a multinational company by the virtue of its origin—businesses are so highly interlinked that very few companies can truly claim a particular nationality. Companies may also find that businesses in countries other than the headquarters contribute more to the bottom line than the 'domestic' business.

Local conditions can also affect the global operations of a business and also determine the strategy of companies re-entering India. When Coca-Cola left India in the restrictive phase of the 1970s, local manufacturers of the cola beverage like the Thums Up brand filled the vacuum. When Coca-Cola re-entered the Indian market in 1993, it came back to a totally different market. Apart from domestic, indigenous competitors, it had to deal with Pepsi, which had already entered the Indian market and was aggressively increasing its market share. Domestic competition came from leading domestic brands called Thums Up, a cola drink, Limca, a lemon drink, and Gold Spot, an orange one, etc., owned by the Parle Group, who controlled about 60 per cent of the Indian market at that time. Coca-Cola bought these brands from Parle in the 1990s to create a two-way battle with Pepsi for the cola market in India. The reported acquisition price of USD 60 million was quite large at that time but may appear small in today's context of mega deals. Parle continued its business of bottled drinking water, where it is a leader in India, while Coca-Cola achieved limited success in that segment. Thus, for Coca-Cola, business in India had come a full circle—from being a monopoly to facing intense challenges from product competitors as well as civil society groups over allegations of the high level pesticide content in its beverages prompting the company to improve its Indian and global safety standards. These were eventful changes that helped both the company and the country. Between 1993 and 2011, Coca-Cola has invested over USD 1 billion into India and continues to promote education, water conversation projects, etc. as a part of its corporate social responsibility.

RUNNING OF FOREIGN OR MULTINATIONAL COMPANIES

Despite the restriction of holding not more than 40 per cent stake, MNCs managed to run their Indian operations through their parent companies. The popular mode of dilution of equity to stay within prescribed limits was to issue fresh shares and ensure that subscribers were widely dispersed with little threat of takeovers.

The Imperial Tobacco Company started to broaden its shareholding base only in 1954 and that too with only 6 per cent of the shares being sold to the public; the level of foreign shareholding remained at 94 per cent for several years until 1970.

The MNCs usually have deep pockets, due to which they can operate and hire the best talent in the country at more attractive pay than most Indian companies, transport technology across countries, advertise with big budgets, and have the ability to absorb losses for long periods, which helps them stay the course, particularly in industries with long gestation periods.

The MNCs operating and competing in the Indian market have had a positive impact on the performance of Indian companies as well. The MNCs combine deep pockets with streamlined operations, a strict control on costs and deliver products of proven quality, often competitively priced, particularly if they wish to buy its market share. With this basic formula, MNCs invigorated Indian companies that during the licence and permit era up to the early 1990s had lost the inclination to compete for the buyer's attention because they were used to operating in an economy where demand was always greater than supply.

In the initial years of the spread of the MNCs, the underlying assumption was that management practices and processes are uniformly effective across countries and as countries evolve and develop, they will emulate the values and cultures prevalent in the home countries of the MNCs—that is, largely Western culture. The predominant view was of a unipolar, monolithic economic culture, expounded by carriers of the MNC home nationalities. And there is reason enough for such a view. In 1959, only six of the fifty largest international corporations were non-American and the world saw no reason why such progression would not continue. However, Japanese ascendancy put this train of thought into a spin. The Japanese work culture, with strict top-down approach, attention to detail, and collectivist social and cultural habits had a huge impact on the way organizations were run. By 1993, 60 per cent of the largest corporations were other than American, representing fifteen countries. In 2010, only six of the largest twenty global companies were US companies while China has three companies in the Fortune 20 list of the largest global companies, signalling a gradual shift in the global economic equations.

There is a greater interplay of cultures and attitudes that shape an MNC's outlook today than twenty-five years ago. It is also a moot point whether a company can be identified with a particular nationality anymore. The largest corporation in the world today, measured by sales, is Wal-Mart, a retail behemoth. Till 2002, only 16.3 per cent of its revenue was international, and most of this was from the North American region. Today the company operates in fifteen countries and its global opeartions contribute 27.4 per cent of its sales, a significant change in the mix since 2002. Despite its steady global expansion, Wal-Mart was regarded as a regional multinational entity, not a global one. In 2006, Wal-Mart, in order to seek newer markets, entered into a joint venture with Bharti Enterprises, the Indian telecommunications giant to enter the retail market following the heels of its very successful foray in China.

The largest companies in the world are redefining their strategies and businesses outside their home base that is critical to sustained success creating newer markets and buffering risks. Ranbaxy Laboratories Limited was an Indian pharmaceutical company, where the controlling stake of the Indian promoter, the Singh family was sold to Daiichi Sankyo of Japan for a whopping USD 4.6 billion in 2008. Ranbaxy defined itself as an international company with a large Indian business. The dynamics of global businesses is evolving and businesses around the world are seeking newer markets, newer products, and newer safety mechanisms against business risks in a bid to globalize.

'Globalization' of a multinational entity depends on the business it is in, that is whether they pursue a global strategy or a market or country-specific strategy depends on its core business. For instance, stringent local and regional regulations may prevent pharmaceutical or defence companies from adopting a global strategy.

A common thread among multinational companies, however, is their uniform and underlying philosophy: producing products of the highest quality at the lowest possible costs for the maximum satisfaction of customers. The twin concerns of adhering to parent company ethos and norms while keeping in tune with local labour, regulations, market and infrastructure conditions requires a sophisticated degree of coordination and skilful handling of various interfaces. The name often used to describe this phenomenon is 'glocal', a combination of global and local. A glocal orientation gives an MNC the necessary distance perspective so that it can focus on business issues instead of getting bogged down by local issues and disputes.

Multinational companies with large businesses in several countries tend to become trans-national organizations, that is, organizations to which national boundaries cease to matter (Ohmae 1990; Bartlett and Ghosal 2002 [1989]). Such trans-national companies build competitive advantage through knowledge transfer across borders as well as production centres in host-country subsidiaries.

Rugman (2005) argues that in order to evolve towards the transnational solution, managers should pursue an incremental, path-dependent trajectory of change. The selectivity required to manage the transformation towards a transnational company has three facets. First, respect for the firm's specific administrative heritage, (where) the MNC should build upon its existing strengths responsible for initial stages of international success. Second, extensive socialization, meaning substantial attention is devoted to the physiology and psychology of the organization, rather than merely to sweeping changes in anatomy or organizational structure. Third, selectivity in terms of the roles assigned to national subsidiaries, given the strategic nature of their location and their contribution to new, non location-bound knowledge development.

However, these are guided by purely commercial considerations in the pursuit of delivering maximum value at the most competitive price while managing its affairs with a global mindset.

The ground level experience, however, is not always smooth. Most MNCs tend to bear the imprint of the culture of the country of origin and aligning home and foreign cultures both in real time and at ground level is always a challenge that different companies try in different ways. For instance, Ford Motor Company is run along cherished American principles, prominent among which is individualism. Bellah et al. (1995) argue that individualism is at the core of American culture; it believes in individual advancement independent of community, family or social status, and values success as the real goal of human endeavour. It also believes that people are naturally inclined towards maximizing self-interest. This philosophy underpins its culture in all its businesses across the world.

On the other hand, Japanese culture puts a greater value in community and hierarchical relationships, that is, it is more of a collectivist culture. It highly values the concept of *Kaizen*, a continuously improving process, which means continuous improvement is a way of life and no stage is good enough to stop trying to improve further. This translates into thoroughness in the whole process of production from planning to finish. Good Japanese factories can often trace their product faults back to the design phase and maintain very small rework area. The Japanese priority most often is process orientation (Chen 1995: 225).

This philosophy is the guiding force behind the hugely successful joint venture Maruti Suzuki India Limited (formerly, MUL) in India, which even twenty-six years after bringing in its first car, is by far the largest and the most profitable car maker in India and its most significant subsidiary.

It is very important for the success of an MNC or a trans-national company that managers must recognize that some parts of the firm (particularly the downstream end) may operate regionally, whereas some other parts (particularly the upstream part) may function globally.

Indian work culture is more aligned towards the Japanese and other Asian cultures rather than the US or Anglo-Saxon ones. Indians believe in collectivism, have a strong sense of hierarchy, and look upon the workplace as an entity from which a person draws economic and emotional sustenance. They also tend to form strong friendships within the organization that spill over into their personal lives as well. While this is good in many ways, it can also affect a dispassionate and arms-length appraisal of performance, which is crucial to maintain competitiveness. Where Indian work culture differs significantly from Japanese or Korean cultures is in the obsession with process. Indians tend to rely a lot on the instinct and 'feel' of a matter rather than codifying the steps involved in the process, which often leads to inconsistency in the quality of end products. Indians also have a tendency to drift with events rather than try and get on top of the situation, giving an impression of an overriding belief in fatality; the much-talked about Indian 'otherworldliness' helps in putting work in its proper perspective but also prevents a total focus on the end product (Sinha 2004).

Indians, however, are known to be both collectivists and individualists. In matters of personal advancement and betterment, they display a high degree of individualism, perhaps because of deeply engrained religious values that proclaim that god will judge each person based on his *karma* on earth. But in community or familial situations, they display a strong degree of collectivism. This identity with a community or a group determines his behaviour towards those 'within' and 'without' the group. This tendency makes Indians form cliques that are often so strong as to impair professionalism at work.

A striking feature of most MNCs is the low number of expatriates that the Indian unit employs. Most employees are Indians but often achieve far greater efficiency than in a typical Indian business. This speaks volumes about traditional, indigenous managerial styles as compared to the influences that overseas companies bring.

Organizations that extend boundaries to include employees' families are desired and respected in India. For instance, units of the Steel Authority of India (SAIL), like the Bhilai Steel Plant, have built self-containing townships for their employees which include quality schools, excellent healthcare facilities, and markets. In short, the employer assumed all the responsibilities that a head of a family is traditionally expected to shoulder, including giving priority or preference to the employees' children while recruiting additional workforce.

This ethos is replicated not only in several public sector enterprises but also in private family groups like the Tatas, Birlas, Thapars, etc. Though in a number of such factories, which are located in undeveloped parts of the country mainly for tax exemptions, without such facilities it would be virtually impossible to have a quality workforce, especially managerial staff.

That such values are not consistent with efficiency and performance-oriented, profit-focused companies is amply demonstrated by the strategy of Tata Steel when it decided to embark on an extensive modernization programme in 2000 to prepare itself to become a world-class company. Along with identifying and eliminating inefficient and uncompetitive plants and shop floor processes, the company examined each managerial and shop floor job as well to assess its potential to add to the value chain. Those that did not measure up were let go. The policy of providing employment to one dependant of every employee who had put in twenty years or more of service was dispensed with and this brought down the employee strength from 78,000 in 1974 to 43,000 in 2004. The company had almost become entwined in managing ancillary activities like highly subsidized health facilities, canteen food and other township amenities so that its corporate advertisement by-line was almost disquieting— 'We also make steel'. These activities were either curtailed or handed over to private operators like JUSCO (Jamshedpur Utility and Services Company), a 100 per cent subsidiary of TISCO (Tata Iron and Steel Company) with an agenda to transform itself from being a cost centre of the steel company into a profit centre in its own right by offering its services to others as well. The dividends of these measures have amply paid off with Tata Steel emerging as a streamlined fighting ship, successfully taking over the European giant Corus Steel to become one of the five largest world players in steel.

RESEARCH AND DEVELOPMENT (R&D) IN MNCs AND JOINT VENTURES

Indian businessmen have traditionally shown little interest in upgrading or evolving new technology. Most promoters of companies at the time of the British raj had a trading background which made them primarily concerned with the financial aspects of the business, unlike founders of industrial firms in Great Britain and other European countries who were often skilled in a chosen craft and therefore more interested in the technical aspects of the business. It was easier for Indian businessmen to buy or contract out the research and development (R&D) than to invest in the long, often frustrating, process of developing own technology. Even the government policies tacitly supported the easy path of transfer of technology from global partners to Indian companies rather than encouraging these companies to create their own technological excellence.

This trend still persists among businessmen, whether in an Indian business or in a joint venture and traditionally the outlay for R&D amongst Indian companies and the Indian government is abysmally small.

In the manufacturing sector, MNCs usually do not reveal or transfer the core technology so as to maintain parent company superiority;

besides, the Indian company is usually contractually bound not to conduct R&D in certain core areas and must 'confine itself to either components testing or making cosmetic improvements or submitting suggestions to the head office for further processing' (Sinha 2004: 225). This is a major reason why foreign arms manufacturers are resisting the government of India's offset policy particulars of 30 per cent in any defence purchase deal.

However, the striking reality is that apart from government investments in laboratories and universities, most research in India is carried out by multinational companies. R&D is a cost-intensive, often frustrating, investment which requires deep pockets and staying power. Synergies and networking with other teams working on similar projects immensely helps achieve results and this is where MNCs score over individual researchers. Internationalization of R&D is a combination of pull and push factors (UNCTAD 2005). The critical factors to offshore R&D in India range from growing competition, rising costs of R&D in developed countries, and scarcity of engineering, to scientific manpower and with increasing complexity of R&D. The compelling reasons that countries like India present as a destination for R&D include the growing availability of science and engineering skills and manpower at competitive costs, globalization of manufacturing processes, and substantial and fast-growing markets in some developing countries that increase their attractiveness as locations for R&D.

Improvement in information technology further facilitates greater fragmentation in R&D, allowing 'teams' to work globally on a project to improve efficiency. Foreign companies or MNCs investing in R&D in India have been instrumental in revitalizing this area. In R&D, personnel costs are the highest and MNCs are better able to win the global war for talent since they generally pay better salaries, are able to provide global mobility and provide better technical exposure to research personnel. Competing Indian firms thus have to match the MNC offer closely or risk losing out on top talent and this raises the bar in the whole economy.

Several MNCs have opened design and R&D centres in India in the past decade; in particular the software industry R&D in India is an embedded part of the global R&D chain with important bits of work being done here. The process of contracting R&D work to India may have started with the notion of cost savings—Indian scientists cost substantially less than their Western-educated counterparts—but gradually, global R&D is attracted to India for other factors as well. Much more study and research is needed to find out the reasons for this but we put forward the hypothesis that it has its genesis in the Indian 'virtues' of frugality. Years of impoverishment and the necessity for austerity have taught Indians how to squeeze maximum value out of anything. Making something last a long time, recycling and reusing are so much a part of the Indian psyche that it has spilled over into the working styles as well. This hypothesis has been somewhat vindicated by the introduction of Nano, the world's cheapest car from Tata Motors.

The sectors that have seen maximum FDI in R&D are IT–ITES (information technology and information technology enabled services), pharmaceuticals, and some engineering sectors despite the perception of weak IP (Intellectual Property) protection laws in India. This is because R&D projects are covered by the Contract Act (governing relationships between parties), IT Act, rigorous pre-contract due diligence, and documented compliance with international standards (including security management systems)—all areas with proven strength. These statutes and provisions have been actively used to defend and protect sensitive information shared in the course of BPO (business process outsourcing) projects, thus raising the credibility of Indian operations (Boston Consulting Group 2006). Submitting data of trials to authorities to get approvals for commercial exploitation of R&D, however, is a different matter. This is dealt with differently by different firms including the option of submitting such data in other, more regulated markets like the US and European Union (EU), which have better data protection laws. Therefore, the adequacy or otherwise of India's IP protection laws really does not impact R&D projects.

POSITION OF INDIAN ENTITIES OF MNCS IN THE GLOBAL WORLD

The scribe asked, 'what is in a name?' but companies spend serious money on branding to fit in with its current corporate philosophy. In a reverse sweep of sorts, multinational companies which changed their names to fit in with the nationalist flavour prevailing in the 1960–70s are increasingly reverting to a common corporate name that can be recognized globally. For instance, after fifty-one years of existence as Unilever's subsidiary in India, Hindustan Lever Limited (HLL) changed its name to Hindustan Unilever Limited (HUL) in 2007. This was still not completely in keeping with its global rule of naming its subsidiaries in various countries—Unilever Nepal in Nepal, Unilever Japan in Japan—where Unilever comes first and then the country name in an effort to create a uniform corporate brand across the world of 'One Unilever'. In India, however, the country name comes before Unilever, reflecting 'the company's commitment towards its local roots while leveraging the global scale and reputation of Unilever with its consumers and stakeholders in India', as the company's chairman Harish Manwani puts it (*Times of India* 2007c). Perhaps it also has to do with the fact that the Indian entity is the single largest operating company in the Unilever world in revenues and also contributes significantly to the Asia–AMET (Africa, Middle East, and Turkey) region's growth of Rs 177 billion in revenues for the year 2010.

The really big players in the 'poster boy' of Indian economy, the IT–ITES and pharmaceutical sectors, are not just publicly traded Indian companies but also Indian subsidiaries of multinational companies. On the flip side, Indian companies that have gone multinational also try to distil a global identity through names; most companies use terms like 'UK Development Centre' or 'India Development Centre' to identify more closely with the local business environment.

INDIAN COMPANIES BECOMING MULTINATIONAL BUSINESSES

Since the late 1990s and early 2000s, the trend has been for Indian companies to acquire foreign companies rather than merely entering into a technical collaboration. Increased overseas acquisitions can be considered a response mechanism of Indian firms to forces unleashed by liberalization and lifting of most restrictions in the Indian economy. Indian companies suddenly found themselves exposed to global competition and quickly realized the inadequacy of their technical and other capabilities. They had to immediately ramp up their competitive strength and 'Indian companies realized that adopting a long-term competencies-building strategy with larger investment in R&D,

advertising, etc., is relatively riskier and costlier than pursuing the route of overseas acquisitions.' An October 2007 study found that for the past one and a half decades, Indian multinationals began to aggressively use overseas acquisition as a preferred expansion strategy into the world market. The progression of Indian multinationals from adoption of greenfield overseas foreign direct investment (OFDI) to brownfield OFDI testifies to the fact that their internationalization strategies have become more sophisticated and complex over time (Pradhan 2007).

Overseas acquisitions by Indian firms are a result of several factors—higher economic growth, rising foreign exchange reserves, continuing liberalization of FDI regime, increasing bilateral trade and investment treaties with foreign countries, etc.

Unlike most international M&A (mergers and acquisitions) transactions that typically feature stock swaps in the financing arithmetic, Indian acquirers have for the most part paid in cash for their targets, helped by a war chest of internal resources and borrowings. Share swaps have not yet emerged as a favoured payment option generally. One of the reasons could be that several Indian companies are owned or controlled directly by the promoter shareholders who also constitute management. The promoter on his part would not like to dilute his holdings and therefore control over the operations, while the seller may have doubts about the 'professionalism' of management in case of a share swap deal. Where the foreign sellers are private equity funds, settling accounts through the equity route in Indian companies would amount to foreign direct investment, which is subject to a host of regulatory issues.

Settling in cash at today's interest rates also makes financial sense—the cost of equity is presently higher than that of debt, so paying in cash brings down the cost of acquisition (India Knowledge@Wharton 2006).

The software industry is a good test study of how the low-cost advantage that India has is not sustainable over a medium term. It then becomes imperative for Indian software firms to look for other means to be distinctive and focus on value to the customer. Competing on the basis of cost arbitrage is a losing battle and other factors like exchange rates can also play havoc with margins. Unless companies move up the value chain and move to providing solutions rather than providing manpower, the comparison with Indian global companies will be disadvantageous. Many IT companies are investing in and launching products and solution sets, so that their relationship with the customer is that of a sustainable partnership.

Likewise, HCL Technologies Limited created HCL BPO to offer a credible and sustaining BPO service. HCL believes that a combination of offshore, near shore and onshore facilities is essential because a variety of regulatory or business factors makes it impossible to sustain a 100 per cent offshore facility alone. A cost-saving factor by itself gets quickly levelled out and does not allow the business to expand beyond a point. In order to penetrate the UK market, HCL wanted to associate with a blue-chip British iconic brand and HCL BPO, located at Belfast, Northern Ireland, was born as a 90:10 joint venture with the British Telecom. Most global or Fortune 500 companies have a significant presence in the European market. From India, the company's language capability is limited to English; from its Belfast subsidiary employing people who speak several European languages like French, German, Italian, Spanish, Portuguese, and Dutch, the company is able to deliver in several European languages and consolidate its business proposition. HCL is among the top six employers in the private sector in Northern Ireland. Similarly, HCL BPO has a centre in Malaysia which also operated a dedicated product support helpdesk for an important client in Malaysia; the facility has since expanded to provide multi-Asian language support, besides doubling up as a disaster recovery site. The company is now located in thirty-one countries around the world.

Bharat Forge was a small company in the 1990s with a workforce scarcely distinguishable from farm labour when it decided to upgrade its operations to expand to global strength. By 2007, it had become one of the world's largest automotive components' manufacturers, holding nearly 45 per cent market share in India, with a largely 'white-collar' workforce. The company acquired businesses worldwide and entered into joint ventures in countries like China (whose market is nearly four times bigger than India's) in line with a 'dual-shore' supply model. This means it can supply all components to a client from two plants—one in India and one closer to the client. The plants in the US and Europe reduce supply chain risks while the flagship plant in India, with economies of scale and relatively low-skilled workers, help keep the costs down.

Indian collaboration with overseas companies has an interesting pattern to it. Barring high-profile acquisitions like Tata's Corus Steel and ArcelorMittal (if it can be called Indian), most acquisitions are of a relatively smaller value. Reasons for acquisitions are primarily to complement skills that India does not possess, to ensure supply lines of raw materials like ONGC Videsh acquiring stakes in gas/oil blocks around the world. The result is a smart leverage of an existing low-cost production base and moving more processes of acquired companies to such a low-cost production base while combining it with access to new markets and R&D efforts.

While it is early yet, overseas Indian acquisitions have been largely successful. According to Gene Donally (2008), of Pricewaterhouse-Coopers, an Indian company acquiring an overseas business uses the intuition of Indian culture (of tolerance and assimilation) and does not attempt complete change as demonstrated by Tata Tea's acquisition of UK's Tetley Tea; they left the management in place, including cultures and mores. Tatas have not fundamentally altered the operation of Tetley Tea except to align it to the business and corporate values of the house of Tatas. Dealing with people when you cross borders requires a different touch and feel embedded in mutual appreciation and respect. Tata Group may have been able to imbibe and assimilate these factors in its corporate fabric as it was reflected in May 2011, when its UK company Jaguar Land Rover, for the first time in its over sixty years, declared a profit after tax of over £1 billion.

The Imperial Tobacco Company to ITC Limited

The story of change from a narrow-focused, insular, non-priority, and single-product foreign company of the 1940s to the respected multi-product Indian company of today.

The Imperial Tobacco Company was in a monopoly position at the dawn of Independence and was backed by the mammoth BAT (British American Tobacco) Industries. The management saw no reason to change its ways to adjust to the changing realities, the philosophy being: the customer does not know what he wants, we know what is best for the customer. It was also a highly centralized company and the main job of depots or regional office managers (most of whom were expatriates) was to write reports and letters to the head office with little decision-making or initiative displayed or even allowed in the job.

Changes in Business Environment From 1948 to 1951, the business environment changed rapidly, with rising costs, increase in cigarette excise duties, levying of a tobacco excise, customs duties, and restrictions on import of tobacco leaf and then a total ban on manufactured cigarette imports. This had a major effect on the company's tobacco operations.

It was also an era of centralized planning, a time when even petty government officials could decide what and how much a company, particularly a foreign company, could produce, what businesses it could diversify in and how much expansion could be permitted.

The Company Response The company responded by initiating a policy of Indianization and upgrade of its workforce. The management undertook a comprehensive inventory of the work practices that threw up several areas that required to be tightened to develop a competitively superior management that would provide growth opportunity to all capable people. As much as a third of the workforce consisted of unionized staff and this section was gradually moved up from the shop floor and supervisory positions.

Indianization of the workforce was undertaken as a gradual process with more and more Indians occupying senior managerial positions including, for the first time in 1969, an Indian Chairman of the Board.

The company was forced to radically change the cigarette blend with reduced imported content throughout its product portfolio, although more as a response to events rather than a measured strategy by reading trends and forecasting future events. The result was that the company finally had an Indian product for the Indian market, shaped by the specific Indian environment.

Since the 1950s, and up to the enactment of FERA in 1973, BAT had given up only 6 per cent of its shares and there was virtually no trading in that 6 per cent. With FERA, BAT decided to take a trans-national rather than a traditional multinational outlook and recognized the realities of independent India's economic ambitions. British American Tobacco's 94 per cent was reduced in stages to below

40 per cent, first with disinvestments and then with dilution. This later went to below 34 per cent when equity increases were offered to the Indian public, directly and through public institutional investors; BAT also did not take up a subsequent convertible debenture rights issue when these were offered to the public, resulting in a proportionate reduction in the overseas shareholding with an increase in equity on conversion.

The company that emerged from the macro-level of re-organization was ITC Limited, an essentially Indian company, with Indian leadership and management, its earnings deployed within the country rather than repatriated overseas, with a corporate style relevant for India and engaging in several social, economic, and commercial obligations necessary for a responsible corporate citizen.

From a Tobacco Company to a Rainbow Identity   What really propelled the company to its present position of eminence was its ability to recognize the limitations of the tobacco industry and proactively embark on a diversification drive that ensured leadership not only in the tobacco business but also as a front runner in several other ventures.

There was further change of management that saw the company transform itself once again from the Indian Tobacco Company to ITC limited. The company anticipated that smoking and health were likely to become major health concerns following Western trends, and notwithstanding significant contributions to indirect taxation revenue, the company expected the tobacco and cigarette industry to have a growth of only forty more years.

Besides, in the 1970s, the company was under sustained attack by a competitor who tried to paint the company as being 'foreign' and 'anti-national', which created ripples not only in the press but also affected public—and therefore government—perception. It was, therefore, necessary for the company to be seen as moving in tandem with national priorities.

Two major strategies followed were:

(i) One was to enter an industry that earned foreign exchange for the country. This led to major investments in the hotel and tourism industry, a division that has proven to be immensely successful;

(ii) The second was to enter a core sector industry where the government found it difficult to attract private investments. Accordingly,
the company invested Rs 440 million in 1975 in setting up a
paper industry.

The ITC Group's high command, that is the board of directors,
oversees the business of the company, followed by the corporate
management committee which acts like a venture capitalist for the new
or existing businesses, and to which the divisional or business heads
are answerable for return on investment. Each business line is run
like an autonomous division, operating independently, formulating
their operating policies, and doing their own planning and reviews of
performance, within the framework of group guidelines.

The ITC Group functions as 'the banker of first resort' with interest-
bearing investible surpluses of the business pooled, either for central,
new investment decisions or for new investments by individual
businesses.

A cornerstone of the ITC Group is to know the business inside-out
in any venture it enters—and as a corollary, to aim to be the market
leader in that segment. The group works on the principle that the
annual rate of growth in gross/net turnover and volume share must
be higher than that of the industry within a predetermined gestation
period. Thereafter, growth should not be lower than that of the industry
in order to maintain the market share.

The focus of the managerial setup is on decentralization, with
businesses operating independently and managers given a great degree
of operational freedom to function as 'proneurial managers', that is,
professional entrepreneurs. This policy of creating several top teams
has gone a long way in developing a bank of general managerial talent
in the country to deal with complex business issues that are universal
across businesses.

The upside of ITC's approach to management is that it has built a
sustainable model of interdependent disparities or inter-linkages. By
creating interdivisional synergies, the group has been able to harness
latent energy and talent from within and deploy it with tremendous
success across seemingly unrelated business. For instance:

• The lifestyle business which deals with the fickle world of fashion used engineers from the tobacco business to set up 'just-in-time' production techniques;

- Chefs from the hotel and hospitality business contribute to developing product formulations in the food and ready-to-eat business;
- Historically, Imperial has had one of the best distribution systems in the country. This is tapped to provide channel synergy for other businesses;
- Cross-linkages help to insulate against gestation costs, which in India, are anyway longer than in several other countries.

The risk appetite of the company has increased from the mid-1990s and has seen the company enter several seemingly unrelated businesses that are as diverse as fashion garments, golf courses, ready-to-eat snacks, and now agriculture retail. The company always had a close relationship with farmers for its tobacco business.

It is increasingly engaging the rural community in other crops as well. The company believes in helping rural communities to build capability rather than provide charity, which end up weakening the receiver. To this end, the company has successful models like e-*chaupal* and *chaupal sagar* which touch four million farmers in 40,000 villages in ten states. The company's aim is to act as an honest intermediary, which raises its credibility with the community. This is done by helping the farmer increase productivity and keep the cost of production low while increasing productivity with the help of technology and better tools and techniques such as better water management, sun and shade management, etc. The reasoning is that it adds value to all components of the system and everybody, including the company, prospers. It is also involved in areas where there may not be an immediate and direct business link but which has a ripple effect on developing the community on a sustainable basis. Some such initiatives are as follows:

- Sangeet Academy for discovering and promoting talent in Indian classical music;
- Art foundation;
- Education for children;
- Women's empowerment;
- Farmers' production techniques;

- Water cooperatives, watershed management, and resurrection of ponds, help build village wells, etc.

Although tobacco is the mainstay of the company, it has built a colourful rainbow identity for itself. In so doing, it is considered as one of the leading companies and a major force on India's industrial scene, and has ensured increased prosperity not only to the community where it operates but also for all its shareholders, including foreign shareholders. ITC Limited has the distinction of being one of the few companies in the world which is carbon-positive, water-positive, and has achieved 100 per cent soil recycling. It earns on an average Rs 500 miilion worth of carbon credits every year while it helps preserve three times more water than it consumes. It has consciously and consistently built itself into a responsible corporate citizen of the country; for instance, in the 1980s when world tobacco prices were low, it went against accepted commercial wisdom and advice and did not import tobacco but worked with Indian farmers to purchase the produce locally. Today ITC looks with justifiable pride at the 32 million tobacco farmers that the company has nurtured, apart from 2 million retailers that it sustains.

ITC Limited follows a triple bottom line approach in its performance but this does not stop it from losing commercial focus and the company has averaged a commendable 26 per cent return to the shareholders.

This journey of ITC Limited from a British Raj era company to a leading Indian corporate citizen has tied it to the lives and fortunes of Indians over the past many decades and today touches more lives than it ever did in the past.

ICI India Limited

The story of an imperial company which had first-mover advantage in independent India but did not retain that position in changing business conditions within the country

The company traces its lineage to a trading office in Calcutta in 1911 under the name of Brunner Mond & Co., which later combined with three other companies to become Imperial Chemical Industries in the UK and Imperial Chemical Industries (I) Limited in 1929 to market paints and chemicals. ICI Ltd, a trading company, started its first manufacturing in India by setting up Alkali & Chemical Corporation of India Ltd in 1939 in Rishra, West Bengal and became ICI India Ltd in 1989.

Independent India had enormous demand for several products but little access to technology; erstwhile British companies like ICI were ideally suited to fill the gap because of the natural advantages they had in the country. When the government of India invited companies to invest in businesses like oil mills, fertilizers and chemical industries in which the government could not invest, ICI invested in the explosives' business in 1954 and fertilizer business in 1969 to become the largest manufacturer in India at that time. Likewise, ICI entered lines of business that were clearly defined by the government as growth sector: declaration of a goal of self-sufficiency in agriculture saw the company invest in fertilizers, focus on industrial development made it enter alkalis and chemicals, growth of the mining sector led to investment in explosives, etc. Despite the restrictive FDI policies of the government, ICI India continued to consolidate its position by setting up facilities in various industries like polyester staple fibres in 1963. The company chose to remain a FERA company with the parent company continuing to hold 51 per cent of the equity in Indian operations, partly because of fear of IP dilution along with equity dilution but mostly because it wanted to manage its business globally.

The subsequent growth strategy of the company also followed a global path and the Indian company was constrained in exploiting the local growth opportunities fully. For instance, the emergence of Reliance as a progressively serious player in fibres and polymers did not make the company take rebuttal actions either by infusing more funds or getting new technology to retain its pole position. Globally, the company had acquired several different businesses to the extent that its total portfolio had become somewhat cumbersome. Besides, competition in most businesses, at least in India, had become very intense. The parent company in the UK had got stuck in a mire by 1981 'with nobody really looking after the company as a whole—cash was being controlled but not managed, new business wasn't being generated fast enough, creeping centralization was following in the wake of bureaucratic swelling and managers were simply not profit-conscious' (Harvey-Jones 1988).

Most businesses that the company had were technology intensive, for which constant innovation or purchase of newer technology was essential. However, even after the economy opened up in the 1990s, the Indian company, with weak financial position—primarily due to over-dependence on the fertilizer business that was affected by a prolonged period of drought—could not access funds, which increasingly marginalized it as a competitor in the relevant segment. The technology for making explosives, for instance, had become so readily available that it was dominated by the small-scale sector which hit performance of this 'steady-state' profit-earning segment of the company.

Ironically, when the economy opened up on liberalization and gave a fillip to the business environment, it also brought in severe competition. The entire technological paradigm had to be changed and wherever this could be done locally, the business survived in India even when the parent company had divested that business globally and could not procure the necessary new technology.

ICI India, unfortunately, got a double whammy of increasing competition in India and lack of access to latest technology for its local businesses to combat competition. ICI India was involved in research since 1976 through a dedicated R&T (research and technology) centre whose main objective was to engage in and carry out scientific and technical researches and investigations. Later the R&T centre changed focus from exploratory to applied research to better align its research to market needs. The centre also developed a close association with other R&T divisions of ICI globally; within India the company has applied for 119 patents out of which forty-four have been granted and seventy-five are pending approval. Despite such proactive measures of trying to stay abreast of technological change, the company did not possess ground-breaking technology that would help to maintain its leadership position.

On its part the parent company had identified India, China, Russia, and Brazil as growth areas needing country-focused strategy and separate yardsticks but subsequent events overtook this initiative. The company went through a series of acquisitions and mergers and demergers throughout its global operations in an attempt to rationalize its operations, perhaps losing vital energy and focus in the process.

In a major move in 1993, the company decided to demerge its chemical business from the pharmaceutical/bioscience divisions.

Pharmaceutical, agrochemicals, specialties, seeds and biological products were placed into a new and independent company, the Zeneca Group, and the company decided to focus on two core businesses of paints and chemicals. In another major move, the ICI Group acquired National Starch & Chemical Company in 1997 from Unilever as part of a strategy to diversify into the specialty chemical business; globally, National Starch contributes 41 per cent of the total sales.

The Indian operations have also followed the see-saw mergers and demergers of various businesses:

- Forty per cent joint venture with Nalco Chemicals, USA in 1987; exited in 1998.
- Divestment of seeds, fibres, and fertilizers business in 1993.
- Agrochemicals transferred to a joint venture with Zeneca Ltd of UK in 1995, from which the company exited in 1998.
- Started joint venture for Initiating Explosives Systems in 1996 and from which the company exited in 2003.
- Fresh investment in paints and polyurethane in existing factories and building new plants in 1997 and 1998. The company exited from the polyurethane business in 2001.
- Motors and industrial paints' business was first transferred to a joint venture with rival Berger Paints India Ltd in 2001 from which it exited in 2002.
- Flavours and fragrances' business through a joint venture (with majority stake) with Hindustan Lever Limited and Quest International BV in 2001. This was converted into a wholly owned subsidiary in 2006 and the company exited from it in 2007.
- The pharmaceuticals business of the company was divested to Nicholas Piramal (I) Ltd in 2002.
- Catalyst business, started in 1984 was divested in 2002.
- Nitrocellulose and trading businesses were divested in 2004 to Nitrex Chemicals (I) Ltd in which the company holds a minority stake.
- Rubber chemicals business was transferred to the PMC Group, USA in 2005 (retaining a minority stake).
- Uniqema business was divested in 2007 to Croda Group, UK.
- Advance Refinish Paints business was divested in 2007 to an affiliate of the PPG Group.

Thus, the Indian operations were not left unaffected by the global strategy of acquiring diverse businesses, only to exit from most of them. From being an industry leader in many segments, ICI India was in the third position in 2007 in paints, commanding roughly 13 per cent market share. The Indian subsidiary had pioneered the concept of a 'tinting machine' in the 1990s. This empowered the customer to choose a particular shade and also helped increase profitability by lowering stocking costs of the dealer and expanding the shade card in the decorative paints section, the mainstay of the business. It also pioneered financing of this proprietary machine but could not press with its first-mover advantage. This concept, more than anything else, has helped to consolidate the business by raising the entry barriers for smaller players who cannot invest in these machines and restricting the field to big players. However, in 2007, it was still a Rs 10 billion company after divesting various business segments. It has not only increased its market share per se but also had profitable growth and has met most internal expectations.

Ironically, the company had just become debt-free and was well-positioned for some real inorganic growth after emerging from global restructuring when the century-old imperial company was bought in 2008 by the Dutch conglomerate Akzo Nobel. 'Today businesses are like chessboard pieces, to be moved as per global strategy to maximize one's winning chances. Akzo Nobel's acquisition of ICI is an indication of the tremendous value proposition that the company has got' (Sandeep Batra, the former CFO and Executive Director, ICI India Limited; Interview with the authors). The new owners plan to restructure the company further by selling off the adhesives business to Henkel of Germany. This may well be the end of the British-owned brand of ICI but the company is looking forward to a regenerated business identity in the new structure with cautious optimism.

HCL Group

Thirty-five years ago, when India had a total of 250 computers, a group of young entrepreneurs left their secure jobs to follow a dream—to develop a microprocessor that will change the world. HCL (earlier known as Hindustan Computers Limited) was born out of that dream and has its origins in a team of engineers led by Shiv

Nadar, who wanted to start a computer company in India in the early 1970s, but due to lack of funds had to settle with a business of making calculators, for which there was ready acceptance and an established market in India. With the funds generated from this business and a licence from the state government of Uttar Pradesh (UP), HCL was formed in 1976 on the terrace of the house of one of the foundres. It was an era when government policies were hostile towards business and entrepreneurs, and getting government approvals for importing technology, components, or sub-assemblies was the toughest job. This spurred the company to focus on in-house design and home-grown solutions. This innate innovativeness has ensured that it is one of the only three surviving computer companies from the 1970s (the other two are Apple and IBM). HCL claims that its micro computer in 1978, which was launched at the same time as Apple's and prior to IBM's PC (personal computer), gave birth to the Indian computer industry.

In the mid-1970s, the government of India, besides introducing FERA (requiring equity dilution below 40 per cent for foreign companies), made a rule that if a product was to be made in India, its source code had to reside in India. This provision made IBM leave India, leaving the field clear for HCL. The company, however, greeted this development with mixed feelings because it meant having to divert precious resources to create a market for computers in the country— computers, at that time were considered an optional convenience rather than a necessity and this job could have been done better by IBM with its deeper pockets.

HCL soon established itself as an electronics hardware company in India but continued to look for opportunities to keep up with technology change and calibrated its approach accordingly. For instance, at one time it was a significant player in office automation systems like electric typewriters. It also manufactured pagers for Nokia and later became the sole distributors for other Nokia products besides being resellers for a competitor company like HP. Thus, HCL continuously tracked industry trends and moved quickly with global shifts in technology and into newer products and ideas.

HCL Group now comprises two distinct identities, HCL Infosystems Limited which deals with hardware systems and systems integration and HCL Technologies Limited which works on IT solutions including software, services, remote infrastructure, BPO services, etc.

The group believes that in future, several aspects of any company's business will be aligned and redistributed within and across countries in a manner of global sourcing including outsourcing, in-sourcing, off-shoring, near-sourcing, right-sourcing, and the like, and sees itself as an end-to-end solutions provider. It has set up operations in various countries under various ownership forms.

The transformation of a company that was earlier identified with a 'hardware' tag, and relatively low-technology items like calculators or typewriters into a USD 6.5 billion annual revenue global company providing end-to-end solutions employing 80,000 people is one of the biggest success stories in India's modern economic history. The company achieved this through a well-thought strategy of combining growth through organic and inorganic means and optimizing risks by leveraging skills in domain space, geography, and skills.

HCL has often been ahead of its time with ideas that some may call radical and even contrarian. It has also suffered some failures because of this: created a relational database system called Genesis (which was ahead of Oracle), envisaging client–server architecture in the future and preparing products accordingly, writing software themselves to establish credentials instead of banking on the usual route of body-shopping, etc. For all its failures, however, the company has retained its identity and constantly reinvented itself.

HCL has always been the bedrock of entrepreneurial spirit with a heavy accent on innovation. This spirit was translated by a number of entrepreneurs who have worked in HCL during their careers and later turned their own ideas into business institutions. Some of them are Rajendra Pawar of NIIT, Arjun Malhotra of Headstrong, Vineet Nayyar of Tech Mahindra, Neelam Dhawan, CEO of HP India, Saurav Adhikari of Infinet, B.V.R. Reddy of Infotech Enterprises, and Diwakar Nigam of New Gen. There are not many companies around the world, which have a cradle of such entrepreneurial exposition.

HCL Technologies' chief executive officer (CEO), Vineet Nayyar, launched the 'People First–Customers Second' initiative, which is a case study in Harvard and has been reflected in a successful book by the same name. In 2005, HCL was redefining its identity and in order to outperform its competition, it came up with an innovative mantra to use people as the strategy and the differentiator to drive organizational performance. The approach is not embedded in being employee friendly but through empowerment, building trust and 'engaging the whole person'. To demonstrate this, Nayyar put his own 360 degree appraisals on the company's intranet, started a one on one blog with the employees and innovative remuneration systems. Since 2005, HCL Technologies outgrew all its major competitors.

Recognizing the fast changing nature of technology and the need to be at the forefront of change, HCL took up minority stakes in a number of small companies around the world that innovate in cutting edge technology. This will help the company to tap into the transformational force of collaboration which is restructuring all business models around the world. HCL has also set up 'technology cradles' at its facility in India where new, high-potential and cutting edge technologies are incubated and developed, which may enable HCL to not just ride the technology waves but very often mastermind and create the next wave.

In June 2010, Shiv Nadar, the chairman, founder of the group and principal shareholder, made one of the largest contributions to charity in India by donating 2.5 per cent of his shares in HCL valued at Rs 5.8 billion. His foundation, apart from running a successful engineering college in Chennai and starting a university near Delhi, embarked in 2009 on a very unique project of educating some of the brightest students, who are economically weak, in Uttar Pradesh, a state of India, where HCL started its journey. The project called *Vidyagyan* (or knowledge) is a partnership with the UP government and chooses its students after a rigorous test conducted throughout the state and provides free education, mentoring, and nurturing to help them become leaders. In the next five years, the project is expected to enroll 4,200 students.

The journey from 1970s to create a unique proposition and contribution has never lost its fire and continues to create a value and delight for all its stakeholders.

Motherson Sumi Systems Limited

Motherson started in 1975 as a family-owned single-product company in Noida, India and in 1983 entered into a technical collaboration with Tokai Densen (now Sumitomo Wiring Systems) of Japan. In 1986, this collaboration was converted into equity participation with this and another Japanese company, Nissho Iwai Corporation. The new entity went public in 1992 and today the family holding is around 34 per cent, foreign equity holdings is around 37 per cent, public holding around 18 per cent, and the remaining is with institutions and others.

The partnership with both these Japanese companies is thriving in 2011, which is a successful business relationship of over 25 years. In India very few partnerships could stand such tests of time. Sumitomo always had an option to set its own wholly owned subsidiary but decided to stay by its Indian partner. Vivek Chaand Sehgal, the son of the 'motherson', is now on the Sumitomo's board in Japan, which is a reflection of true partnership based on time-tested mutual respect and trust.

Chaand Sehgal started this journey in 1975 along with his mother, S.L. Sehgal, and set up their first cable factory in 1977. Thirty-five years ago—and even today—the male-dominated industry of automobile components and industrial products was not the usual choice of a business owned by a mother and son. The desire to be brave and different was the hallmark of the group and it always took their vision to great heights.

The main business of the group over these years has been to design and manufacture automotive components for the automotive industry. As part of its de-risking strategy, the group has diversified into the manufacture of cooling parts used in computers and other assemblies and products. The company has integrated backwards to produce most of the critical inputs required to cater to its wide spectrum of products. The equity partnership with Japanese companies introduced the company to Japanese auto majors in India like Maruti Suzuki, Hero Honda, DCM (originally, Delhi Cloth Mills) Toyota, etc., and even today it is one of the main suppliers to other automotive and auto components' companies.

The Japanese influence is also evident in the Kaizen management style which includes a strong and constant process upgrade. Plants are located strategically to efficiently service customers' requirements and so as to aid in inventory management and reduce lead time.

It was the first company in India to manufacture integrated wiring harness and Woodstock door trims and currently commands 65 per cent of the wiring harness market in India besides being the largest producer of rearview mirrors in the world. In fiscal year ending 31

March 2011, the business of Motherson Sumi had a turnover of nearly USD 2 billion.

Initially, the company's foray into the global markets was through joint ventures with several international companies so as to acquire technology and maintain a strong product portfolio. However, currently it is in some fourteen businesses with over twenty-five business partners twelve major joint ventures, and operates in twenty-three countries. The company has a reputation for managing some of the most successful joint ventures. . Though the company has followed the path of growing through its natural progression, it simultaneously believes in the power of joint ventures and inorganic growth. Chaand Sehgal believes that in today's world technology for a company like his can be best exploited through joint ventures as the time to invest in technology and take it to market is getting shorter. In the past ten years his footprint of joint ventures has tripled from four to twelve, and in 2009 his company acquired VisioCorp of Germany, the largest manufacturers of rearview mirrors in the world. The fact that some of his partners have entered into multiple joint ventures with him is a reflection of the value he has created for his partners.

The group's competitive advantage that has enabled it to go global, rides primarily on the strength of the India cost advantage besides economies of scale and possessing established technology. Globally, OEMs (original equipment manufacturers) are looking for low-cost locations to better manage their shrinking margins and India offers one of the cheapest locations in the world without compromising on design and engineering capabilities.

Ranbaxy Laboratories Limited

On 12 June 2008, as India's largest drug maker, Ranbaxy Labratories Limited, declared a deal worth up to USD 4.6 billion to sell its control to Daiichi Sankyo of Japan, the disbelief of the Indian business community was palpable.

It was considered very unusual for a research-based pharmaceuticals company from Japan to diversify overseas to purchase one of the largest generic drug manufacturers. Manvinder Singh, CEO of Ranbaxy defended the sale plan, saying '[It will] allow us to transform and go to the next level and the combination will create a mix of innovation and generics' (*Financial Times* 2008). Analysts felt that for a USD 5 billion company to be valued at USD 8.5 billion at the top end of past valuations reflected the inherent value of Ranbaxy as an iconic brand that India was proud to create.

Ranbaxy Laboratories Limited, now called Daiichi Sankyo Limited, is an integrated international pharmaceutical company producing a wide range of generic medicines. Ranbaxy is often called India's first private sector multinational company and operates in forty-nine countries with manufacturing facilities in eleven countries. The company has a multicultural, multi-ethnic workforce of around 12,000 people comprising more than fifty nationalities.

Ranbaxy followed a guiding M&A strategy and a dual growth policy—organic growth through expansion of existing facilities and aggressively following acquisitions to strengthen the front-end in terms of gaining critical size and having a stronger basket of products, additional competencies and skill sets.

Ranbaxy was originally floated by two cousins, Ranjit Singh and Gurbax Singh of Amritsar (the company's name is an amalgam of the two first names), to act as distributors for A. Shinogi, a Japanese pharma company manufacturing vitamins and anti-TB (tuberculosis) drugs. This business was later taken over by Bhai Mohan Singh in 1952 who continued the distributorship but thereafter also collaborated with the Italian pharmaceutical company, Lapetit Spa, and later bought out its business.

It was an era of the licence–permit raj where domestic companies were favoured over foreign ones. This helped the company to grow quickly in its initial years. It made modest investment in R&D and mastered the art of reverse engineering drugs. Ironically, it was a generic version of a sleeping pill sold as Calmpose by the company that shook it awake and the phenomenal success of the drug propelled the company into the big league. As the company grew more prosperous, the founder Bhai Mohan Singh, in line with conventional thinking amongst family businesses at the time, inducted his son, Parvinder Singh, into the company. He later made him the MD, while founding other businesses for two of his other sons. Soon, differences in the style of management between the patriarch and Parvinder Singh cropped up, with the former preferring a family-controlled style and the latter favouring professionalization of the company. Parvinder Singh finally prevailed and was appointed as the chairman cum managing director (CMD), thus paving the way for sustained professional management. In 1999, a few months before his unfortunate demise, Parvinder Singh chose a professional to take over from him as MD rather than promote one of the family members. It may be argued that his sons Malvinder and Shivinder were too young at that time to take over the task.

Perhaps as a means of protecting family interests or out of genuine belief in corporate governance mechanisms at a time when such phrases were not yet fashionable, Parvinder Singh set up various committees to run the company and sought and implemented experts' opinions. In many ways, this conscious style of management has helped the company to rise from a family-owned, mid-sized distributor of drugs to India's largest and one of the world's leading manufacturers of generic drugs. Later, in 2004, Malvinder M. Singh, having climbed up the ladder, was inducted into the board of Ranbaxy. In 2006 he was nominated as the CEO and MD by the Ranbaxy Board. In the same year, Shivinder M. Singh, also a qualified professional manager, was inducted into the board of Ranbaxy.

One of the factors contributing to Ranbaxy's early growth was the patent structure existing in the country till 2005 which only recognized process patents. It enabled Indian companies to reverse engineer drugs and offer pharmaceutical products at some of the lowest prices in the world. This route brought immense success to Indian pharmaceutical companies like Ranbaxy, best illustrated by the performance of the AIDS (acquired immune deficiency syndrome) cocktail of drugs. In 2000, the lowest worldwide price for a triple combination cocktail AIDS drug sold by patent-holding MNCs was around USD 10,439 per patient, per year. Most generic manufacturers quickly learned to reverse engineer this drug and in the same year 2000, Cipla, an Indian company, offered a generic version of this drug to NGOs and least developed countries (LDC) which had few or no effective patent laws for as low as USD 350 per patient per year. This drove the originator's worldwide price to USD 727 per patient per year. Subsequent generic companies brought down the price further. Ranbaxy was amongst the first companies to bring down the prices of basic first-line ARV (antiretroviral) regimens to less than USD 100 a year. It continues to be at the forefront, introducing innovative multi-drug combinations to help the governments in their effort to control the epidemic. According to the World Health Organization (WHO), over one-third of the world's population lacks access to many essential medicines, a figure that rises to 50 per cent in the poorest African and Asian countries. Companies like Ranbaxy that are able to produce and sell drugs for a fraction of the cost charged in developed markets bring hope and succour to millions of sufferers the world over.

Once Ranbaxy decided to be a global company, it consciously tried to replicate the organizational structure of big pharmaceutical companies globally. The business was carved into different regions like the US, Europe, Asia-Pacific, and India so that each market could get the focus it required and deserved individually. Despite increasing complexity following global expansion, the basic structure of regions headed by a regional director with country managers reporting in, remains in place. This requires a balance between delegation and centralization and a high focus on performance.

This strategy was particularly emphasized when Malvinder Singh took over as CEO and MD in 2006 and the company put in place a new set of drivers to achieve its aspiration of becoming among the top five global generics company with global sales of USD 5 billion by 2012. The global business was de-risked by increasing focus on emerging markets like Romania, Brazil, Russia, China, South Africa, and central and eastern European nations. Another significant step was to expand into high-potential therapy areas and specialty portfolios like oncology, bio-similars, peptides, limuses, and sterile products. Ranbaxy has spearheaded partnerships of a strategic nature with companies who specialize in the manufacture of these products, and is leveraging its regulatory expertise and front-end infrastructure to introduce these products across geographies. The move adds significant depth to the existing product pipeline.

It is no small feat that Ranbaxy is the only pharmaceutical company in the world to challenge the world's biggest pharmaceutical company, Pfizer, for its blockbuster cholesterol-lowering drug, Lipitor. This signifies its strength in cutting-edge R&D. The company has been successful in bringing forward the launch of a generic Atorvastatin in the US, by fifteen months with 180 days exclusivity and has made a serious opening in the market for what is today the world's biggest drug.

Ranbaxy was among the few companies which also has a focus on neglected disease areas (the so-called 'orphan' diseases). The company has taken a conscious decision to dedicate its resources (manufacturing and R&D) in developing anti-malaria and anti-AIDS medicines. The company's constant effort in the field of HIV (human immunodeficiency virus)/AIDS has enabled it to become a leading provider of high-quality, affordable, generic anti-HIV medicines (ARVs). Presently, nearly 4,00,000 patients, many of whom are in Africa, benefit from Ranbaxy's ARVs. Ranbaxy at the time of sale was working on developing Arterolane, a new synthetic drug for the treatment of malaria. With the development of this new drug, Ranbaxy aims to address several challenges facing existing malaria drugs.

Indian family-owned businesses, public sector companies or multinational companies find themselves on several common platforms such that it is only of academic interest to classify them into these categories. There is a commonality found in the working of businesses with the result that their identities coalesce into one another. Entry of foreign firms in manufacturing may be followed by an entry of their international suppliers and later by other support services including R&D; this phenomenon is commonly referred to as 'follow sourcing'.

Domestic firms may or may not benefit directly with linkages to foreign firms but are nevertheless forced to move along the average efficiency curve brought on by competition. Over a period of time, local firms supply to the global manufacturers and collaborate in innovating and improving the products in the supply chain. The next wave takes these firms onto the global map with global production and sourcing facilities as independent producers of ancillary products supporting key industries. Some of them would ultimately venture into production. The circle of reverse engineering thus gets completed. This is perhaps the biggest contribution that multinational companies make to the host country. A number of Indian multinationals of today have gone though this cycle and are powerful contenders for global business leadership and Ranbaxy in many ways epitomized this strength.

The Singh brothers, post the sale of Ranbaxy, have moved into two sectors that are under-utilized in India and thus provide the potential of large measures of success—financial services and healthcare. Religare, the financial services company, was listed in India in 2007 and has grown into a company with a turnover of Rs 28 billion by end of March 2011.

In another dramatic turn of events, in April 2010, the Singh brothers stepped down from the board of Religare, their financial services company, to hand over its reins to professional managers of the company and concentrate on the rapidly growing healthcare venture Fortis, an integrated hospital and healthcare services provider that grew through a series of acquisitions in India and overseas. This signals the new wave of Indian businesses which have unshackled themselves from the past to play in the global arena as prime players.

6

Arbitrage of Thought and Innovation

Innovation is now known to be the critical factor which will determine the performance and growth of organizations, businesses, and economies. It means different things to different people but the real worth of an innovation is actually tested in the marketplace—when potential users buy into the belief that an innovation provides greater worth than existing processes or products.

It is equally true that innovation is not always positive for everyone; 'disruptive innovations' often mean just that to many old and established organizational forms and practices, and even their very existence. How quickly an entity adapts to innovation is an indication not only of its ability to survive but also of the worth of the innovation itself.

The Organisation for Economic Co-operation and Development (OECD) report on China—which is equally true for other countries, including India—says: 'Developing [a] country's innovation capacity is a prerequisite for escaping from a pattern of specialization characterized by intensive use of low-skilled labour and natural resources and a low level of technological capabilities' (qtd in *New York Times* 2007).

India has achieved some degree of advancement and prosperity by leveraging its cost arbitrage in several industries. However, several factors are rapidly closing in on labour cost arbitrage—weakening dollar, steady salary hikes in India, improving global competition, new technology that makes coding simpler and lowers entry barriers, etc. Labour cost arbitrage, therefore, is not sustainable as a long-term national advantage.

A sustainable advantage belongs to the group of people who can constantly innovate, improve, and break new ground. In other words, people who can leverage *thought arbitrage* to their compelling advantage.

India as a country has a poor record of being innovative—as opposed to Indians who have gone out of the country and proved their innovative mettle in other environments. It is perhaps a throwback to our deeply-ingrained agrarian and trading culture—live off the land, add a mark-up, and settle for a low-risk low-reward ratio. Even industries where India can truly boast of size and market dominance are linked to commodities and manufacturing processes such as manufacture of steel, petroleum, mines and ores, tea, and sugar. The fact that incremental value-add gives exponential rewards is only now being applied by Indian businesses.

Innovation is not only about new and breakthrough inventions but also about finding better and more efficient solutions. It may lead to a citrus juicer, a pimple remover, or a more efficient transmission system in a jet plane. Innovation must help larger numbers of people to benefit from an idea and do something more simply or efficiently than in the past. Innovation is also about adapting or creating processes that use new or existing technology or ideas.

Arbitrage of thought is a process where the key difference is in having control over an idea or thought to control its access to the ones who do not possess such information. This could be in any space where there is an investment of intellectual capital like electronics, engineering, pharmaceutics, technology, etc. However, arbitrage is not forever, as other companies will de-construct the product or idea and be able to create a somewhat comparable copy. Over a period of time, quality will improve and the copy will be acceptable to consumers. The advantage over thought is not eternal and the innovator needs to improve the product or process and constantly innovate in order to survive and compete.

Essentially it is the quality of human resources that determines an organization's ability to stay abreast and develop innovative

Philips of Holland is arguably one of the most innovative companies in consumer lifestyle and healthcare space. The speed of innovation and the huge investment in innovation, which is about 6.2 per cent of sales, makes them amongst the most innovative companies. Philips gave the world the commercial electric bulb, compact disc player, DVD, cassettes, etc. Though cassettes and DVDs were invented by Philips, the product idea was commercially exploited by Japanese companies, especially Sony, who innovated the product to bring the costs down while making them both usable and portable. Sony actually made cassette players and DVD players reach more people than Philips, the originator of the thought.

ideas. Enterprises look to their workforce to differentiate themselves from competition; talent drives innovation which provides critical differentiation.

A new idea forms only the kernel of a successful innovation. The other components in the value chain of innovation—raising money to commercially exploit the invention, targeting the right production process, identifying an appropriate path to the market, and scaling up—are equally critical in determining the success of innovation.

WHY IS INDIA A LAGGARD IN INNOVATION?

There can be no single factor that can answer this question but a combination of several factors. One reason is that Indian culture has never been comfortable with making money—and innovation is all about commercially exploiting ideas. According to Saurabh Srivastava, founder of NASSCOM (The National Association of Software and Services Companies), the umbrella association of IT companies and now an investor and mentor to a large number of entrepreneurs,

Another explanation is a possible colonial hangover; when a group of people are colonized and made to believe they are inferior to the ruling class for generations, it is bound to have an effect on the innovative psyche and it takes a long time for such people to start believing that they are as good as any other people. India is only recently moving towards having a critical mass of *believers*—people who believe in their self-worth and capability. (Interview with the authors)

The former commerce and industry minister, Kamal Nath, noted in an interview at Wharton School, University of Pennsylvania, that ever since the Indian government's first comprehensive trade policy was drafted in 2004, foreign direct investment (FDI) has increased seven-fold and foreign trade has doubled. '"If there is a place for entrepreneurs to meet, it's India—the rowdiest democracy that produces the most entrepreneurs in the world." Enormous growth is occurring in B-class cities, he added. "In an uncertain global atmosphere, new opportunities are being thrown up for entrepreneurs as centres of economic activity shift"' (India Knowledge@Wharton 2008a).

A third reason is that about 90 per cent of Indian workers are employed in the informal sector and this sector is often characterized by unemployment as well as low-productivity and low-skill activities. Productivity is a good proxy for how well businesses and enterprises absorb existing and new knowledge; when large numbers of citizens are engaged in low-skilled and low-productivity occupations, innovative ability will be difficult to nurture. 'Domestic innovation efforts, R&D spending and diffusion and absorption efforts remain low largely because competition pressures—although strengthening—are not sufficiently widespread throughout the country' (Dutz 2007: 7).

But a far more real reason could be a lack of *institutional innovation* in the country. India invests less than 1 per cent of its gross domestic product (GDP) in systematic research and development (R&D), which is certainly not enough to unleash an innovation culture. Out of this 1 per cent, less than 20 per cent is allocated to civilian applications and the bulk to defence, space and atomic energy. This public R&D support of 20 per cent of 1 per cent of GDP almost entirely goes to government-owned institutions—8 per cent to thirty-eight laboratories under Council of Scientific and Industrial Research (CSIR), 4 per cent to agriculture under Indian Council of Agricultural Research (ICAR), 4 per cent to applied research programmes of the Department of Science and Technology (DST), and 1 per cent to medicine through Indian Council of Medical Research (ICMR) (Dutz 2007: 8). Therefore, institutional innovation, which is critical to incubate and carry forward sparkling ideas from all sections of the society is practically nonexistent in India.

Institutionalizing innovation helps not only in *eureka* moments of earth-shaking innovations every decade or so but—more importantly—to produce steady, disruptive innovations at more frequent intervals that help stir up thoughts and ideas. It is widely acknowledged that only the presence of a robust institutional innovation network makes the US a leader of innovation and not because Americans are inherently smarter than other nationalities.

'R&D by Industry' was developed as a conscious strategy by the government of India to incentivize in-house industry R&D and bring it into sharper focus. In-house R&D units of public and private sector as well as government scientific research organizations can apply for recognition by the DST which makes them eligible for certain incentives. The number of such units has grown steadily from about 100 in 1973 (mostly government R&D labs) to over 1,000 by the year 2000. The amount of money spent by these units has also risen steadily—there were only 65 companies that spent more than Rs 50 million in 2000–1 and by 2009–10 there were 151 such companies. Companies that spent between Rs 10 million to Rs 50 million rose from 218 in 2000–1 to 296 in 2009–10 (DSIR 2001; 2010).

IS THERE HOPE FOR AN INNOVATIVE INDIA?

Perhaps the greatest indicator of innovativeness in India is the state of erstwhile quota/licence companies. These companies should logically have died out in the new competitive environment; however, most of them have adapted and survived, even thrived in the new paradigm— several Birla companies, the house of Tatas, even public sector companies like SAIL, ONGC, BSNL, etc. This also skews prevailing wisdom that innovation does not come from established business houses but only from small, highly-keyed entrepreneurs. The Indian economic boom was being led by IT and BPO companies who were all first-generation entrepreneurs like Infosys, HCL, Patni, and to an extent, Wipro, who shattered the safe path of working in established businesses and turned into entrepreneurs. Today, they have inspired thousands around the world to move away from their comfort zones and fulfil the entrepreneurial promise they held to themselves.

Tata Nano, the wonder car priced at below Rs 1,00,000 will change the way most of the developing world will travel; the house of Tatas is an old and established business house but one which has constantly innovated to remain relevant and even lead in some sectors.

Indians have always been known for their ability of *jugaad*, a colloquial term closely approximating to 'fixing things', a quality essential to survive in the pre-1991 economic regime. This innate 'innovativeness' is quickly being turned around by several enterprises to play by modern global rules. However, this stems from the fact that the country for decades has been an economy of scarcity and the limited resources and availability of technology made people innovate and adapt to survive and make this work. This does not originate from deep thought or research but is to satisfy immediate needs and hence may not be entirely scalable.

A key factor for creating a climate of innovation is to focus on rural and indigenous innovations. Since India is largely an agrarian country with the bulk of the population being the 'base of the pyramid', innovations targeted at this segment will deliver the volumes necessary to sustain the movement. These innovations may not even scale-up enough to migrate to other cultures or countries but perhaps that may be just what will make them workable—by being quintessentially Indian.

Kamal Nath spoke of the enormous challenges facing the government:

> India has 300 million people living on less than $1 a day. We also have 650 million engaged in agriculture that's not commerce but subsistence. That keeps disposable incomes meagre and reinforces a vicious poverty cycle. The driver of growth in India has shifted from the state to the entrepreneur ... and this growth has enabled India to move forward. [India] needs rural entrepreneurship to move 200 million people into industry and services. The rural sector is the new challenge for entrepreneurs (India Knowledge@ Wharton 2008a).

'Faster growth can be facilitated by promoting "new to the world" knowledge creation and commercialization—the traditional understanding of the term innovation—as well as through often underappreciated but even higher-impact "new to the market" diffusion and absorption of existing knowledge' (Dutz 2007: xv). The 'new to the market' concept has been successfully used by countries to scale-up the threshold of the quality of products and services. For instance, the tag 'Made in Japan' which in the 1950s and 1960s was seen to be that of a cheaper imitation of Western products has undergone a complete change. Within a few years and even today the quality of Japanese products is amongst the best in the world, at price points which others cannot achieve and a value proposition which is quite unique. Whether in automobiles, consumer electronics, or in machinery, etc., Japanese entrepreneurs have moved from imitating to enhancing, to innovating new products or service experiences that give them a sustainable competitive advantage. This edge, over a period of time, helped them move into a higher value plane of new ideas, new technology aimed at the future markets, and the advantage of new ideas and technology keeps increasing as competition is often left struggling to defend their falling market share. Following this strategy, in 2007 Toyota Motor Company (TMC) became the largest automobile company in terms of sales in the world and its market capitalization is many times more than Ford and General Motors'—arguably the original automobile makers in the world—combined market capitalization. However, in 2010 Toyota had problems with quality following such growth and had to recall a number of vehicles around the world.

India is trying to systematically cultivate a culture of innovation. The DST set up a National Innovation Foundation (NIF) in 2000 'with the main goal of providing institutional support in scouting, spawning, sustaining and scaling up grassroots green innovations and helping their transition to self-supporting activities'. There are several NGOs which are also working towards developing institutional support for innovators.

There is a lot of innovation currently happening in India but mostly small in scale and attracting little attention; primarily these are aimed at maintaining India's labour cost arbitrage. These are incremental in nature and mostly at the process or business level.

The fact that Indian innovators tend to sell out their ideas early on rather than thinking big and commercially exploiting them is often cited as a drawback to inherent Indian innovative ability. However, the mindset that is required to kindle a business idea is vastly different from what is required to run that big business idea. Besides, 'globally, the rate of conversion of innovative ideas into mega corporations or businesses is only about 1 per cent. Indians are no different and this percentage equally applies to Indian business ideas' (Saurabh Srivastava, interview with the authors).

In today's flat world, innovation is totally location independent, which means that the spark can be lit anywhere and implemented anywhere else. Innovation is rapidly becoming a commodity like any other factor of production except that it is capable of delivering more value. Nations can create an enabling environment and actively promote networks that nurture a culture of innovation. Innovation thrives on competition and economies that provide a cluster to develop a critical mass will achieve enduring value.

The *NASSCOM–BCG Innovation Report 2007*, has identified the following challenges to the Indian innovation ecosystem in the IT–ITES sector but which are equally applicable to the rest of Indian industry:

- Insufficient mentoring and networking support for start-ups and entrepreneurs
- Lack of entrepreneurs focussed on IP development in emerging technologies
- Lack of knowledge sharing between IT-ITES firms and key user industries
- Severe lack of funding at the seed/start-up stage
- No platforms for all stakeholders to interact
- No marketplace for innovation trading in India
- Tenuous partnership between industry and academia
- Lack of meaningful collaborations between industry and research institutes (NASSCOM–BCG 2007: 16)

RESEARCH AND DEVELOPMENT (R&D)—VALUE, SPREAD, AND INDIA'S POSITION IN THE GLOBAL R&D PIE

In the global economy, knowledge assets now comprise a greater share of public companies' valuations than hard assets and this is particularly true of technology companies. Intellectual property is now the most critical component of value creation for companies around the globe (PricewaterCoopers 2007). Indian businesses have been traditionally known to use tried and tested methods and technology—that is, tried and tested by other countries. The obvious advantage of course, is the low rate of failure with proven methods; however, this is overwhelmed by the much greater disadvantage of using technology which may be past its 'sell-by' date.

Most Indian companies spend a fraction of their sales—less than 1 per cent on average on R&D. India is often viewed as a third-world country that gets along by copying or making crude imitations of proven Western technology and products, ably assisted by lax patent protection laws and enforcement mechanisms. However, winds of globalization have ensured that spending on R&D is no longer a matter of choice for companies but one of survival. In the pre-1990s, Indian companies often had a foreign partner from whom they would source technology (even if it was never cutting edge) while they themselves would manufacture, distribute and market the final products. But increasingly, several foreign companies are setting up their own operations in India for a number of reasons and this is forcing local companies to spend their own money on R&D.

One only needs to look at the automobile sector to realize the importance of R&D. For years, Indians put up with inefficient, even primitive, technology in Premier Padmini and Ambassador cars, Bajaj autorickshaws, or Tata trucks which were built on technology at least two to three decades old. The multinational companies operating in India too rarely innovated. The Exide batteries or Leyland trucks were many generations old and customer satisfaction or environmental degradation was not the focus in a protected market. Of course, it is possible to argue that the real blame lay with the regulatory and economic climate prevailing in the country. But that does not absolve the businesses of the blame of neglecting basic R&D. The same inward-looking Indian automobile industry of the 1970s and 1980s is today quite a trailblazer, keeping up, even innovating new and improved technology. R&D spending too has increased considerably. At TVS Motors, the amount has increased from around Rs 120 million in 2000 to nearly Rs 980 million in 2009–10; likewise, the market leader in scooters a decade ago, Baja Auto spent about Rs 1.347 million in 2010–11, from a negligible amount when it ruled the market (*Times of India* 2007a).

Innovation is a key determinant of the competitiveness of an entity. This includes not only new products and services but also newer and more efficient ways of doing things or enhancing the effectiveness of existing products or services. A comprehensive technology innovation system encompasses the range of activities from 'mind' to 'market'.

Also, for too long, Indians have pursued science for the sake of science. The crucial link between science and technology has to be strengthened and pursued:

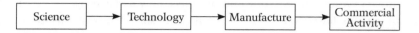

A knowledge economy based on just 'knowledge' in an exclusively intellectual pursuit is bound to be unstable, unless it is anchored through technology into industry and creates real jobs. Commercial activity may not always be the logical progression of science but there must be enough justification of its pursuit to lead to creation of direct or 'satellite' applications and, therefore, national wealth.

There are three levels on which R&D efforts in India need to be undertaken in order to reach any position of reckoning in the global R&D sector:

- At the first level, advanced research and testing of products conceptualized elsewhere should be carried out in several labs in India, particularly in-house labs of multinational companies;
- At the second level, basic research should be carried out as a standalone component or even for sale, that is commoditization of R&D efforts;
- And finally, in a multiplier or cascading effect, as momentum picks up, more and more R&D work should be carried out in India and once a critical mass is achieved, India could well become an R&D hub of the region, if not the world.

The biggest challenge to Indian R&D efforts is scalability—the real challenge is managing the transition from 'doing' prescribed research assistant work to conducting basic research from concept to execution. Technology dynamism of an industry or business forms its competitive backbone. It is now accepted that R&D activities can reap high returns and an organization that reduces its R&D spend ends up clearly compromising its future viability as a profitable organization. Perhaps the prime mover for Indian companies to focus on developing core R&D skills is the realization that having innovation capabilities to create world-class products is essential for a company to be reckoned as a global force.

A big success or two in R&D efforts goes a long way in rejuvenating the research unit and also attracts more funding. A strong R&D infrastructure helps companies feel more empowered to deal with the uncertainties of business. Successful R&D efforts can transform the whole outlook of a business and has a multiplier effect by energizing all components, much like what the iPod did to Apple Computers.

Internationalzation of R&D

The importance of R&D in different countries is revealed by the share of national GDP that is devoted. The major global R&D players are:

Table 6.1 Global R&D Spending in 2010

	GERD PPP (in billion USD)	as per cent of GDP
US	395.8	2.7
Europe	268.6	1.6
Japan	142.0	3.3
China	141.4	1.4
India	33.3	0.9

Source: Batelle and R&D Magazine 2010 [based on data from OECD and IMF]

As in the software industry, India is slowly becoming a hub for global R&D. The same reasons of low capital costs and a large pool of good quality manpower that account for outsourcing in the software sector apply to this sector. As of now, it is the subsidiaries or units of multinational companies that carry out most R&D efforts in India in the private sector. Most big corporations seem to agree that future growth markets are likely to be in countries like India, China, Mexico, and Russia. The vision of such future market needs can, the wisdom goes, be better fulfilled by a local designer than a highly paid designer sitting hundreds of kilometres away.

Shrinking lifecycles of a product require that companies launch products faster; also, as product prices decline, there is a pressing need to bring down costs—and R&D costs form a major chunk of costs for MNCs. Just the cost advantage of shifting to cheaper locations like India provides these companies with substantial savings. The benefits of equally good talent with competence of skills come in later and are an interactive and scalable 'commodity'.

The success of product innovation is in how well it adapts to local conditions and how well it can be adopted globally. The R&D units of global MNCs can indeed fuel sales and profits of their parent companies. The reasons for expanding the international base in research are primarily related to business strategy and aligning it to the changing paradigms of conducting business. Some have simply 'followed their customers'. By locating their development units close to their clients who have migrated to India for various reasons, these units can offer better support and closer collaboration. For some others, locating R&D units in India can cut costs and reduce the 'time to market'. And for yet others, it is a long-term strategy to be located where the most important ingredient is likely to be in the future—trained manpower.

Today, in addition to their roles as suppliers of low-cost manufacturing and technology talent, emerging market economics are themselves poised to become voracious consumers of technology products. Therefore, technology companies have been ramping up their research, manufacturing, and sales strategies throughout a broad range of emerging markets.

Microsoft believes that India's diversity in terms of religion, culture, geography, climate, and language makes it a microcosm of the developing world. Solutions that work in India are more likely to transfer to other locations because they will have been tested across these barriers (India Knowledge@Wharton 2005).

Low capital outlays, cited as a driver for pulling global R&D to India, can actually be a double-edged sword. It is certainly cheaper to set up an R&D unit in India, including hiring quality brainpower, than in developed markets. At the same time, Indian outfits have a low threshold of failure. Research and development is often a slow, long haul, and unless one has deep pockets, it is easy to pack up and make an early exit; it is not something that gives results in a predetermined time so it is difficult to estimate a return on investment. Moreover, R&D requires that skills and capacity are built over time—and sometimes over a series of projects in the case of a corporate R&D unit.

The sectors carrying out the most R&D in India are IT, biosciences, pharmaceuticals, and to some extent automobile engineering. There is also growth potential in areas like waste recycling—of garbage, water, and plastics. Software linked to various service sectors like tourism, banking, education, and testing can be hugely sustainable and can provide a cascading effect.

Outsourcing of R&D is not a new phenomenon; but with the rate and extent of globalization, it has taken on greater momentum. The global trade in knowledge and IP and other forms of R&D are expected to provide benefits similar to other forms of trade in goods and services.

As per a PricewaterCoopers (2007) study, ample talent, lower operating costs, and massive domestic market potential lure technology investment to emerging markets, but there are serious concerns about rampant noncompliance and outright piracy. It is no secret that multinational companies use emerging economies like India, Brazil, or China as sources of cheap labour; therefore officials in these countries tend to overlook several lesser instances of IP infringement. There is also the matter of cultural differences of collective or community ownership (as is prevalent in China) versus individual ownership rights. However, the study also rates India as one of the emerging markets with a better record of IP enforcement; a major reason for this could be that India is proving to be an effective innovator of its own.

Globalization of R&D has also quickened the pace because of increased competition. Location of R&D facilities depends on the speed of innovation and speed of commercial conversion. At the end of the day, however, general economic principles of comparative advantage that operate on other forms of trade are equally applicable to the R&D 'trade'.

The basic component in successful R&D activities, however, is the quality of human capital. This, then, forms the crux of the issue for India. Although much has been written and spoken extolling the sheer numbers of university and engineering graduates in India, the capability of such young people to carry out sustained academic and intellectual work is a moot question, and increasingly a crucial question for the very sustainability of what is rather euphemistically called 'the Indian century'. Adding to this capability is the fact that R&D processes are usually of long gestation and, as of now, do not always command good pay packets. This may cause trouble in attracting talent into the R&D sector.

Also, between 1980 and 2000, the number of scientific papers from India included in the Science Citation Index (part of Thomson Scientific, it assists professionals by providing citation information on scientific and scholarly literature) fell from 14,987 to 12,227, and then rose to 30,000 in 2007 (China's share grew from 924 to 22,061, and in 2010 there were over 1,00,000 scientific papers from China) (Thomson Reuters 2006).

India had the third highest increase in the number of citations in the world after China and South Korea, although this could be because of a small starting base (Thomson Reuters 2006). Since citations measure the effectiveness of a research paper as well as the impact of the individual research, they are an important indicator of the quality of research conducted.

As per data from Elseiver's Scopus, India's share in global scientific publications rose to 2 per cent in the period 2004–8 from negligible contribution (being clubbed under 'other') over the period, 1998–2003 (The Royal Society 2011). Over the same period China's contribution to global scientific publications rose from 4 per cent to 10 per cent. The important feature for development of R&D is the close synergy that academic and university communities can forge with business communities so that efforts are aligned to commercial considerations. This will lead to sparking off clusters of R&D.

There also needs to be a clear demonstration of the benefits of particular research by companies, academia, and the government so that critical mass can be obtained in that particular field and resources can be marshalled to promote a research-led culture. This is particularly important in emotive issues like stem-cell research, use of genetically modified foods, etc.

There is also a global trend towards holding fewer but strategic patents. One is, of course, the cost of patents—a PricewaterhouseCooper study (2007) estimates the cost of a multi-jurisdictional international patent to exceed €200,000. The other is the cost of enforcement and litigation. It is neither feasible nor useful to patent everything. Companies try and evaluate the value of each potential patent before applying for protection.

According to OECD guidelines on international R&D, governments should seek to establish environments that:

- Enable the growth of a knowledge-based economy by providing an effective mix of market-based regulation, fiscal, tax and procurement policies and consistent investment
- Offer a strong public science base and well-educated human talent

- Encourage good connections between the science base and industry
- Provide intellectual property rights that appropriately balance protection and mobility of knowledge
- Achieve a positive attitude among the public towards the value that such R&D can bring and
- Anticipate future trends, skill needs and new opportunities. (BIAC 2005: 5)

A study by Battelle and R&D Magazine revealed that in 2010, China's spending on R&D made it the second highest investor after the US. The difference in investment is still huge as can be seen in Table 6.2:

Table 6.2 Share of Total Global R&D Spending

	2009	2010
US	34.7 per cent	34.4 per cent
Europe	24.1 per cent	23.3 per cent
Japan	12.6 per cent	12.3 per cent
China	11.2 per cent	12.3 per cent
India	2.5 per cent	2.9 per cent

Source: Batelle and R&D Magazine 2010.

Enabling Regulatory Environment

Patents' Regime

An important factor for India to become a global R&D hub is the flexibility and sleekness of its intellectual property rights (IPR) protection regime. Innovation, protection, and enforcement of infringements by patent laws are the foundation for attracting R&D investments to the country. Progressive patent laws actually promote innovation by stimulating investments in R&D in a safe and secure environment.

The patent system provides a framework for protection of innovation and technological development through a delicate balance between providing for an exclusive right to the patent owner to prevent others from commercially exploiting the patented invention for a limited period and a corresponding duty to disclose the information concerning the patented invention to the public. A patent, when granted, is applicable within the geographical boundaries of the country of that patenting office. There is no such thing as an international patent. However, there are two multilateral treaties—the Paris Convention and the TRIPS (trade-related aspects of intellectual property rights) Agreement of WTO, which cover protection of innovations through patents. Signatory nations to these agreements can ensure a reasonable degree of uniformity for patent holders.

India became a signatory of the TRIPS Agreement in 2004, following which it amended its patent laws in 2005. Until the amendment, only process patents were applicable in India. This, of course, has helped India to become a low-cost manufacturing base for multinational companies and much of the strength of the pharmaceutical industry is based on the years spent in learning manufacturing skills.

Although process patents are no longer fashionable today, at the time they were in force, there were genuine reasons for their existence. The process patent policy was anchored by developmental concerns rather than promoting innovation. As in other areas of business-related policy, the official view was to regard patents on drugs especially as 'profiteering from life and death'. An assessment by committees set up to review Indian patent laws (The Patent Enquiry Committee, 1948–50 and Ayyangar Committee, 1957–9) observed that 80–90 per cent of patents in India were held by 'foreigners' for reasons more to prevent competition from rival manufacturers here than to set up manufacturing facilities themselves (or other economic considerations for the host country) and were thus trying to establish monopolistic control over the relevant market segment. Thus, the Patent Act of 1970 came about which was primarily to ensure that patents did not lead to monopoly by foreign companies while keeping prices, particularly of medicines and food items, within the reach of the people of India.

Therefore, the law did not recognize product patents but only process patents in food, pharmaceuticals, and chemical fields, restricted the term of patents and combined with the national licensing policy, tried to ensure that patents were actually for work carried out in India, rather than a grant to the patentee to enjoy monopoly of imported patented items. This policy also inevitably provided protection to domestic manufacturers from global competition.

Multinational companies came to regard Indian generics and formulation pharmaceutical companies as 'pirates'. But these generics and formulations have made medicines more affordable to millions of people around the world—a fact that holds true even today under the present system when India is the world's largest manufacturer of generics and formulations. For example, in Africa, the annual cost of patented HIV/AIDS drugs per patient was USD 15,000 per annum, whereas a generic, made in India, doing the same job was about USD 200 per annum. In other words, one man's pirate is another man's saviour angel.

Gradually, with liberalization and increased economic interaction with the rest of the world, there was a change of thinking among the policymakers in line with the Western concept of 'intellectual property rights'—a system contrary to traditional Indian thinking. The need to attract foreign investments and self-assessment of our capability to innovate and survive, led to a change of thought and also an appreciation of the market as a great leveller to combat the threat of monopoly.

The present system of product patents has helped India to be viewed as a destination with an enabling regulatory environment. Pharmaceutical research, in particular, is dependent on success of new molecules up to the stage of commercial production and this requires deploying huge financial resources. The product patent regime assures the investigator that the final product will be protected by patent so that there is reasonable assurance of recovery of R&D investment. This regime, in itself, will help to attract international R&D investment of a superior grade—greenfield investments, buyout of existing Indian companies, etc. There is, however, an ever-present fear that this may lead to monopoly by giant multinational companies with deep pockets, in the Indian drug market, putting drugs effectively out of reach of poor citizens. Such large players may also direct R&D efforts towards 'glamorous', lifestyle-related diseases which have a better global market rather than mundane, developing-world health concerns. This may divert Indian skills and energies to less effective use to the country.

The Indian patent laws have tried to address some of these concerns. There could be cases which seek grant of patents for old and established drugs, enabling the applicant to hold patent on such product for long periods of time (up to 20 years) and block cheaper, generic versions. This is called 'ever-greening' a product. Therefore, the Indian patent law contains the requirement of 'inventive step' to be shown. For a patent to be granted for a pharmaceutical product it must be different from a known substance or there must be significant increase in its efficacy. In other words, it must be a 'new chemical entity'. The TRIPS Agreement requires that patents should be available for inventions that are new, involve an inventive step and are industrially applicable.

This provision, however, is not without detractors. Several experts feel that since medical innovations are rare in medical research, incremental innovation assumes great significance, especially in commercial terms. There may be a research finding which leads to a better delivery mode or a reduced dosage. While this may pass the 'enhanced efficacy' requirement, it may not clear the 'inventive step' rule.

Then again, determining 'significant increase in efficacy' leaves room for interpretation and arbitrariness and India's severely understaffed patent office does not really inspire confidence for fair dealing. A recent case tried by Indian courts indicates the nuances that must be understood while granting patents. The Indian Patent Office had rejected an application by Novartis AG, a multinational Swiss pharmaceutical company for a beta-crystalline version of its drug under the name Gilvec, used for treating blood cancer. The patent office invoked the newly amended Patent Act (section 3[d]) and held that it cannot be considered a patentable invention since it is a variant of a known substance and there is no significant enhancement of its known efficacy. The company challenged the constitutional validity of section 3(d) in that it did not comply with the TRIPS Agreement of WTO, which the Madras High Court turned down. The company also challenged the section because of being 'vague, arbitrary and ambiguous' and because it did not provide sufficient 'guidance' to the patent controller as to what constituted 'enhanced efficacy' or what was meant by 'differing significantly in properties with regard to efficacy'.

Leaders in academia and industry will likely debate the matter and in the days to come, there should be fine-tuning of the provisions of the patent law so that it is seen to be fair to all parties. It is a moot point whether disallowing incremental innovations will protect the Indian public from expensive patented drugs since several drugs used in the public healthcare system *are* off patent. The central government and various state governments spend only a fraction of the health budget in procuring drugs and salaries account for the bulk of the health sector expenditure in India. While there are huge variations among states in procuring drugs, with Punjab spending as little as less than 2 per cent and Kerala and Tamil Nadu spending over 15 per cent on an average, roughly 10 per cent of the public health budget goes into procuring drugs in India (Sakthivel n.d.: 187). But it will very likely affect the investment mood in pharmaceutical R&D. Companies making heavy investment will not want to rely on the discretion of the patent controller to decide what a patentable invention is but will want very clear guidelines before committing resources.

As R&D spending increases, clearly, companies will also want to see a return on such expensive investments, as with any other investment. They are also likely to get aggressive about the outcome of research with greater possibilities of patent litigations. Therefore, to complete the circuit of an enabling regulatory environment, the redressal mechanism has to improve so that decisions are seen as prompt, fair, and just for companies to continue to invest in R&D. As India acquires its own portfolio of legitimate IP, it will provide an incentive to protect all IP, an example being the software industry where consultants got their start in outsourcing low-end work, learned their trade, built their capabilities, and are now gathering higher-value-added businesses. Since they have their own portfolios of IP assets to protect, there is pressure on the regulatory authorities to improve IP enforcement.

R&D INFRASTRUCTURE IN INDIA

Formal R&D infrastructure in India is largely comprised of:

- A network of state-owned national research laboratories;
- Premier institutes of learning like the Indian Institutes of Technology (IIT) and Indian Institute of Science (IISc), Tata Institute for Fundamental Research (TIFR), etc.;
- Foreign company-owned or promoted laboratories like Intel, IBM, Novartis, etc.;
- R&D cells of some Indian companies.

Government-owned Laboratories

The largest network is the government-owned labs with about 200 national laboratories, an equal number of R&D institutes in the central sector, and about 1,300 R&D units in the industrial sector. India has one of the world's largest chains of publicly funded R&D institutions where the central government is the chief patron of scientific and industrial research with about 74 per cent share of India's total R&D expenditure. How does this compare with worldwide trends? Table 6.3 shows statistics related to ownership of R&D laboratories in various countries.

Table 6.3   Ownership of R&D Laboratories

Country	Industry-owned	Government-owned
US	63 per cent	31 per cent
UK	43.9 per cent	31.3 per cent
Japan	74.5 per cent	17.7 per cent
Korea	74 per cent	23.9 per cent
Spain	48.4 per cent	40 per cent
China	33.4 per cent	57.6 per cent
India	23 per cent	74.7 per cent

Source: Batelle and R&D Magazine 2010.

Looked at another way, the contribution of the industry to total R&D investments in the country is less than 30 per cent of total investments, whereas in industrially advanced countries it is the other way round (Planning Commission 2005).

Government investment in R&D is rather a double-edged sword for India because while there is an emphasis on early stages of basic or applied research, there is a historical disconnect between the activities of national R&D centres and the requirement of the industry. There has also been little emphasis on the commercial viability of R&D efforts. These poor linkages mean that Indian R&D efforts are not harnessed to deliver on their potential.

While it is true that government labs are not exactly trailblazers in their field, they are very fertile ground for 'poaching' of bright scientific talent for the private sector, particularly foreign-owned labs.

In fact, the entire public sector in India has played a very paradoxical role in the country's development. Most PSUs are much maligned for soaking up a bulk of scarce resources—and not producing a decent return on investment most of the time. However, as an incubator of scientific and technical manpower, the PSUs' contributions have usually been outstanding. Several of the country's top brains working presently for the private sector are from the public sector fields as diverse as medicine, oil and natural gas, steel, science, etc. The reason for a lacklustre performance of the government laboratories may also be the HR policy of the government where scientists are bracketed as yet another category of government employees. Also, in premier government R&D organizations like the Defence Research and Development Organization (DRDO), the ratio of scientists to non-scientist staff is a woeful 1:5! Its US equivalent, DARPA (Defence Advanced Research Projects Agency), has a scientist/administrator ratio of 1.4:1, which is perhaps what makes it a first-rate research station (the Internet being one of its better-known products) (*Indian Express* 2007a). Science and Technology (S&T) departments of the government need autonomy and flexibility more than any other government department because they deal with knowledge—which is ethereal—rather than goods and services. Their funding decisions also need to be freed from the standard government audit mechanism.

India's emergence as a global R&D hub in the private sector should see rejuvenation of government laboratories. Working in foreign-owned labs is likely to be a win-win situation—it will help build expertise and depth of skills available in the country and leapfrog the pace of development while providing substantial cost savings to the investor. Competition will also ensure that employers will work harder to provide a stimulating and conducive work environment to retain scientists in much the same way that software companies come up with new and innovative HR (human resource) policies—and in research that means working on the latest and cutting edge technology with the best possible equipment, among other things.

The Centre for Scientific and Industrial Research (CSIR) is the national R&D organization, providing scientific and industrial research for India's economic growth. It has a country-wide network of forty laboratories and eighty field centres covering fundamental and applied research in all fields of S&T (except atomic research which is under a separate ministry).

In 2005–6, CSIR had filed 407 Indian patents (276 granted) and 570 foreign patents (179 granted) (CSIR n.d.). The government's approach to R&D has changed quite radically—the Central Plan Outlay for CSIR labs (under Department of Industrial and Scientific Research [DSIR]) has gone up from Rs 3 billion in 1995 to Rs 10.70 billion in 2007. Apart from this, the Central Plan Outlay under DST is Rs 15.26 billion and the Department of Biotechnology (DBT) had Rs 6.75 billion in 2007–8. The Tenth Five-year Plan had allotted Rs 252.43 billion to promoting research in institutions under scientific departments. The government proposes to increase allocation for science and technology from the current 0.6 per cent to 0.7 per cent of GDP to 2 per cent—which is the world average—over the next five years (starting 2006–7), which means a quantum jump of Rs 640 billion.

The R&D thrust in the chemical and pharmaceutical sector is focused on the development of new drugs and on both innovative and indigenous processes for known drugs. The technologies developed invariably involve indigenous substitutes for expensive imported raw materials, optimizing conventional process routes, and applying novel techniques for product quality and purity.

The government's decision to open some parts of the defence sector for private participation has also helped to uncork the latent scientific talent nurtured in government labs. Although not a deluge yet, several scientists have left government labs to explore defence applications in the civilian world.

R&D in Universities and Educational Institutions

Universities are the cradles of basic research. India has a large network of public-funded universities and higher education institutions, mostly governed by the Ministry of Human Resource Development (MHRD) and some by respective ministries like health, agriculture, and legal. The central and state governments are responsible for major policies relating to higher education in the country and provide funds via the

University Grants Commission (UGC) and state plan and non-plan grants.

Some of India's institutes of excellence like the IITs, IIMs, IISc, IIITs, etc., have an international reputation for quality education, which, however, does not extend to the vastly more numerous universities that ought to be engaged in basic research. The Science and Engineering Research Council (SERC) of the DST has emerged as the single largest support system engaged in promoting basic research in all areas of science and engineering and is the mainstay of open-ended research in the academic sector. In 2009–10, 44 per cent of extramural research funding in universities & colleges was from SERC and the rest from 18 other departments and funding agencies. Research projects supported by SERC in 2009–10 were worth Rs 1.60 billion across institutions in the country and shared by the following as shown in Table 6.4:

Table 6.4 Research projects supported by SERC

Institution	per cent support
Universities (171)	33
IIT/IISc/IISER/NIT (159)	30
National Laboratories (151)	29
Colleges (28)	5
Others (18)	3

Source: Department of Science and Technology 2010.

Leading US universities have a mix of funding sources; MIT, USA derives about 20 per cent of its income from fees, 40 per cent from research projects and technology licensing, and nearly 40 per cent from endowments and investment income. In contrast, an IIT gets more than 85 per cent of its resources from government grants and less than 10 per cent from fees. There are very few instances of technology licensing through collaborations with the industry and faculty is not encouraged to bear responsibility for earning for the institution. There is also a cap on corpus or endowment funds that a government university or technical institution can accept: Rs 5 million for universities and Rs 1 billion for institutes like IITs and IISc.

The most important aspect of the pre-eminence of US universities is that the first phase of impetus to higher education came from the government which also gave land grants besides the initial corpus. After that, institutes were left to develop on their own. In India, it is the politician and the bureaucrat who decide how universities and technical institutes are run—including admission policy, hiring teachers, fixing fees and salaries, and even the curriculum. This is hardly conducive to promoting a vibrant research atmosphere in basic sciences, which ought to be the bedrock of research.

In 1950, around 32 per cent of students who passed the higher secondary examination enrolled in the science stream. This percentage fell to around 20 per cent in 1986 and now hovers around 15 per cent. That is, there has been a 50 per cent drop in science enrolment over fifty years (Department of Science and Technology n.d.). It can be reasonably assumed from the cut-off marks needed to gain admission that there is also a marked downward shift in the quality of students opting for the science stream. A major problem is to attract the right brains to pure sciences. Pure sciences require long years of hard work with very few lucrative employment opportunities at the end of it, and most students apply to undergraduate science courses only if they have failed to get admission into engineering, medical, or other such courses. As per the UNDP *Human Development Report 2006*, only 22 per cent (25 per cent in 2004) of all students enrolled in tertiary institutions are studying mathematics, science and engineering (compared to China's 53 per cent), while the number of researchers engaged in R&D in India was a mere 119/million of population (154/million in 2004). The figures for China, by contrast are 663/million in 2006 and 587/million in 2004.

Falling enrolment rates in the science stream and fewer numbers of published research papers bodes ill for the Indian economy because without constant S&T capability through original research, economic development can get seriously hampered.

The university system needs to be strengthened by augmenting faculty positions so that teachers can devote exclusive time for research. The remuneration system also needs to be streamlined to an incentive-based one where more research papers and publications in peer-reviewed journals will lead to better pay rather than everyone getting clubbed in a single pay scale with minor adjustments.

For R&D to flourish, educational institutions must be places where information can be easily accessible in context, communications easily established with any corner of the world, and intensive collaboration takes place which increases the pace of knowledge creation. Speed and high bandwidth for information exchange is crucial if the Indian innovation system is to compete with global competitors in the field of knowledge creation. Outsourcing R&D work is also largely dependent on network connectivity and dedicated communication networks.

There are currently three major education networks initiated by the government in India:

- ERNET (Education and Research Network): This is India's first NREN (National Research and Education Network) that connects 172 universities, 245 R&D institutions, fifty-two engineering colleges, 251 Navodaya and government schools, 274 ICAR institutions, and 322 other educational institutions. This was set up with the mission to enable the Indian scientific fraternity to match their global partners in access to knowledge and speed of data analysis.
- GARUDA (GRID Computing Network): Garuda is a collaboration of science researchers and experimenters on a nation-wide grid of computational nodes, mass storage, and scientific instruments, linking forty-five institutions in seventeen cities across the country. It aims to provide high-speed and seamless access to indigenously built supercomputers (developed by the Centre for Development of Advanced Computing [C-DAC]) and also enables creation and management of dynamic virtual collaborations and organizations.
- BIOGRID: Research in biotechnology over the past decade has produced a deluge of information. To make effective use of this information, DBT has established a national bioinformation high-speed and large bandwidth network named BioGrid India, with several nodes pursuing bioinformatics activities in various fields. The BioGrid allows exchange of biotechnology information, database and software among researchers in the country.

Involving students in a collaborative virtual network through their schooling years may help to overcome a critical problem of Indian schooling—the majority of students lack communication skills and team-working abilities. Over seventy nations have interconnected their scientific and research communities and educational institutions through high-speed computing networks, where aggregation and advancement of knowledge takes place by collective efforts of researchers across the globe. Exposure to international student communities through such R&D collaborations with innovations such as virtual research laboratories or simultaneous use of distributed virtual databanks by researchers around the world will help raise the standards of performance among Indian students.

A major lacuna of the education system is the lack of science books and journals in Indian languages in which a bulk of Indian students are educated. To awaken scientific temper in the vast numbers of students of the vernacular medium, translations of international papers in Indian languages are essential.

Inadequate access to literature or information is only one part of the problem that scientists in developing countries like India face— the other major problem is that research work conducted here lacks visibility. Few notable research papers report or quote the work and very few papers published in developing countries become citation classics in other research works (Kannan and Khuntia 2006).

India faces a disconnect between research and teaching in universities which has led to a crucial break in the link between research in basic sciences and development. There is a crunch of not only financial resources but also of intellectual resources. This, however, is not something that the country has faced just yesterday rather it is an accumulation of years of neglect of nurturing a spirit of inquisitiveness and enquiry among students.

Collaboration   Innovation does not thrive in isolation or in silos and requires an enabling environment at the national or regional level to create innovation at the firm level. A typical innovation ecosystem provides linkages among the various innovation stakeholders including firms and entrepreneurs, investors, government, and governmental bodies, industry bodies and educational and research institutions, and even among countries. These linkages encourage collaboration for idea generation and transformation of ideas into a business outcome. The degree of participation of the different constituents and the nature and strength of their interactions gives the ecosystem its vibrancy and its raison d'être. Experience across the world has shown that a strong linkage between R&D laboratories and industry along with an enabling environment to commercialize the resultant knowledge are necessary to exploit the science and technology capabilities for economic development.

Industry is the major end user of products of an education system but the extent of engagement with each other differs from country to country. In India, this linkage has traditionally been weak. Because of an increasing mismatch between these objectives, most companies invest heavily in in-house training programmes to bring otherwise unemployable graduates up to the mark. Companies in the information technology sector like HCL, Infosys, TCS, etc., run full-fledged college-style training institutions to make up for the deficiencies of India's somewhat moribund educational curriculum.

Acknowledging the importance of institutional and policy support for software development, the government has intensified its support for R&D activities, starting from spelling out a formal computer policy in 1984, to setting up institutes such as the C-DAC and Electronics Research and Development Corporation (ERDC). 'But it was the creation of a series of software technology parks ... that soon revolutionized the development of the software industry, which led to the mushrooming of several local IT companies' (Taganas and Kaul 2006).

This is ample proof that the government's role ought to be one of creating an enabling environment and letting entrepreneurship develop rather than trying to get into the business of business or worse, setting up controls at every step. Such an environment could include tax incentives to companies and research institutions, rationalizing duty structures to foster the country's competitive edge vis-a-vis rival nations, helping to create support institutions such as venture capital funds since the 1990s, etc.

However, policies of R&D have tended to be ad-hoc and aimed at specific problems, rather than a cohesive national policy framework to adapt to a global innovation system. The capacity of firms, industries and countries to develop and manage knowledge assets is a major determinant of competitiveness and economic growth.

Despite favourable government policies and institutional inter-ventions, the apparent absence of a systemic innovation system characterized by the lack of interdependence between public sector companies, public R&D institutions, universities, and vibrant private sector companies shows that public policy has largely failed to stimulate a culture of innovation within the economy.

Collaboration between educational institutions and companies for R&D offers great scope for increasing innovation. The philosophy behind such collaborations is to separate the research component from the development part; while the research institution may get funds from the company to carry out research, companies benefit from tapping into the academic excellence and other network facilities of campuses. Such tie-ups can even extend to joint patents for new products. Collaborations like these are an extension of the outsourcing concept by getting educational institutions to carry out industry-relevant research, even as companies themselves will consider economic viability, production and marketing.

Networking of institutions and the industry is an essential catalyst for all-round development and progress.

Boston, USA, has eight universities which are considered a leading source of the region's economic vitality and growth. The universities sustain the pace of growth of industry by acting as an incubator of ideas and attract more federal research grants (approximately $1.5 billion a year) in a virtuous cycle, besides attracting national and international students. International companies like CISCO, Merck, Novartis, Sun Microsystems, Pfizer, etc., have located major facilities in areas around Boston to gain access to scientific talent associated with research universities. As per some estimates, the annual economic impact of these research universities is more than $7 billion on the regional economy—equivalent to having the Olympic Games every year. (MIT News 2003)

However, most companies interacting with educational institutions are interested in applied research rather than basic research, in order to commercially exploit the 'seeds' of investment. Even though academicians involved in basic research tend to get too conceptual and far removed from applied research, without a strong base of pure research, applied research may not hold scrutiny. Therefore, interactions between the industry and academia need to find a natural synergy between these two extremes, say, by defining broad expected outcomes but not always firmly fixing a defined outcome.

The Government of India has floated several initiatives and programmes aimed at such networking; perhaps the best managed of them is the network under the name New Millennium Technology Leadership Initiative (NMTLI). This initiative has been set up by CSIR and aims to bring together academia, research institutions, and corporations to work together in areas where India can potentially achieve technology leadership. The effort of the network projects is to organically link the vast competencies developed across laboratories and draw upon the cumulative strength. The NMTLI is perhaps the largest public–private partnership (PPP) effort within the R&D domain in the country. It seeks to consciously and deliberately identify, select, and support potential winners. It claims to be a proactive scheme in the sense that instead of funding a project based on requests and applications, it identifies the areas or projects for development based on national consultation, disassembles the project into components, and invites various institutions and academics in the public and private sector to play a role in the development of individual components. This may sound very similar to Nehruvian-style socialism, where the government would identify areas for public investment; therefore, the initiative is only as good as the quality of its identifying and monitoring mechanism.

Since its inception in 2000, the programme has, during the Tenth Plan period, evolved forty-two R&D projects covering diverse areas and involving 287 partners (222 in the public sector and sixty-five in the private sector). Financial support under the scheme is in the form

The collaboration for an indigenous Hepatitis-B vaccine is a good example of the power of public–private participation (PPP). One of the biggest successes in India's biotechnology industry is the first indigenously developed vaccine for Hepatitis B. Shantha Biotechnics, a private sector biotech start-up, began research for an affordable vaccine in 1993 in a government-sponsored collaborative programme with Osmania University. Scientists from government laboratories (particularly the Centre for Molecular Biology) and various hospitals also joined the project to successfully develop the vaccine called Shanvac-B within four years. This brought down the prevailing cost of imported vaccine from around USD 16/dose to about 50 cents/dose—less than 5 per cent of the original price.

of grant-in-aid to public institutional partners and as soft loan (average rate of 3 per cent per annum) to individual partners.

The 2011 report of The Royal Society titled 'Knowledge, Networks and Nations' finds that the scientific world is getting increasingly interconnected with international collaborations on the rise. Today over 35 per cent of articles published in international journals are internationally collaborative, up from 25 per cent 15 years ago. It is fairly obvious that collaborations improve the quality of research as well as efficiency and effectiveness but the interesting point is that the drivers of collaboration are scientists themselves. Improved communication technologies enable scientists to work with the best minds, institutions, and equipments that complement their own research.

R&D in the Indian Industry

In the Indian industry, R&D is concentrated in pockets like software, pharmaceuticals, and automobile components.

Indian Pharmaceutical Industry The Indian pharmaceutical market is expected to reach USD 20 billion by 2015 and is a flagship section of the Indian economy (McKinsey & Co. n.d.: 11). India is currently ranked fourth in terms of volume and thirteenth in terms of value globally in the pharmaceutical sector. As per a PricewaterhouseCoopers (n.d.) report, the pharmaceutical industry will not be in a strong position to capitalize on opportunities unless R&D productivity improves. The core challenge for the industry is a lack of innovation.

Research is always more efficient if it is collaborative and especially so in drug discovery. Few pharmaceutical majors engage in all the links of the research value chain for reasons of costs, time, skill availability, etc. The trend is to collaborate with research boutiques that work at creating new molecular designs, or outsource clinical trials to recognized CROs (clinical research organizations) and hospitals. Corporations spend as much as 30 per cent of their total research expenditure outside their organizations.

This sector is billed as a growth driver for the Indian economy along the same lines as the IT–ITES industry. Like the IT sector, this sector too is an export revenue earner through the outsourcing route.

Robert Fleming, credited with the discovery of penicillin, used the compound more as an antiseptic to treat wounds rather than as an antibiotic therapy. The major significance of penicillin is its efficacy as an internal medicine against infectious diseases. But Howard Florey and Ernest Chain worked out that bit with their Oxford team, mostly in the US, which turned penicillin into an antibiotic drug. Fleming attributed this to the fact that he was a microbiologist and lacked the chemical expertise to perform the requisite experiments. Here Chain, a biochemist, and Florey, a pathologist, had definite advantages. Justifiably, the 1945 Nobel Prize for penicillin was awarded jointly to Fleming, Chain, and Florey.

The potential size of the pharmaceutical sector in India is huge—India is home to one-fifth of the world's population with only about 30 per cent market penetration; that is, an abysmal 70 per cent of the population is uncovered by healthcare facilities. This is also one sector in which R&D is crucial to growth and survival of businesses. Moreover, R&D also constitutes a major expense of a company's total cost.

Basic research is rapidly becoming a matter of priority for the pharmaceutical industry and several Indian companies have launched intensive efforts to attempt new drug discovery. In part due to a conducive patent regime through the 1970s and 1980s, India has a thriving generics, formulations, and bulk drug industry on such a scale that outside the US, India has the largest number of FDA-approved pharmaceutical manufacturing plants. India has built up world-class synthetic chemistry skills and invested in state-of-the-art manufacturing facilities. On the contrary, India has a poorly developed resource bank of skills that are required to support an innovative R&D-based industry. Making generics and formulations out of patent-free drugs do give volume and provide funding for research to the manufacturers but there has to be deepening of fundamental skills and knowledge to be a serious player in the global research arena.

Medical research is a long-haul process, requiring deep pockets to sustain. Indian pharmaceutical companies typically invest just 2–4 per cent in R&D, whereas multinationals may spend anything between 14–20 per cent. Medical research in India is presently concentrated in the following areas:

- Drug discovery;
- Clinical trials of medical devices;
- Immunology studies—genetic compound;
- Stem cell research.

Indian Council of Medical Research (ICMR) is the apex body in India for the formulation, coordination, and promotion of biomedical research, funded by the Government of India through the Ministry of Health and Family Welfare. The ICMR was set up to foster a research culture in India, improve and develop infrastructure, and foster community support. Its primary role is the development of infrastructure, capacity building, peer review, monitoring, evaluation procedures, and to provide guidelines on various topics. The ICMR carries out its work through twenty-seven permanent institutes/centres and provides an extramural research support system to investigators in various institutes and medical colleges in India besides engaging in international collaboration.

The labs of ICMR serve as a conduit for conducting clinical trials of drugs that are referred by the drug industry regulator, Drug Controller General of India (DCGI). Even drugs that are established or approved for use in other countries have to pass through limited clinical trials in India because of ethnic differences, which may cause a drug to react differently. This mandate also includes conducting human clinical trials on genetically modified foods; the first item being tested presently is the genetically modified brinjal, by the National Institute of Nutrition (NIN), Hyderabad.

The ICMR sends research teams to all sites of national calamities like the Bhopal gas tragedy, tsunami, Latur and Gujarat earthquakes, droughts, cyclones, etc., to document the effect on human physiology, which forms part of the bio-information system.

The dynamics of global biomedical research is still evolving, as is the ideal synergy amongst sponsors, government ethics committees and regulators, and these government-issued guidelines ensure that quality of research that is conducted in the country is at par with research anywhere in the world.

Traditional medicines/indigenous drugs Traditional medicine is regulated by the Department of Ayurveda, Yoga, Unani, Siddha and Homeopathy (AYUSH) under the Ministry of Health and Family Welfare (the Tenth Plan allocation stands at around Rs 7.75 billion). Research in traditional medicine systems is carried out under the 'Golden Triangle' partnership—Department of AYUSH, CSIR, and ICMR—wherein the Department of AYUSH provides the technical inputs regarding the formulations to be used, CSIR carries out the preclinical studies on these formulations, and ICMR conducts the clinical trials. The network is further expanded to include the DBT, gene banks, ICAR for agro-technology, academia–industry collaboration, etc. (Kumar, Muthuswamy, and Ganguly n.d.)

The validation and standardization processes that are used in the testing of chemical or synthetic drugs are done here. According to Vasantha Muthuswamy (senior deputy director general, ICMR), the objective being that a medicine, device, or a treatment method that is generated out of this process, 'forms part of Indian pharmacopoeia and can be prescribed by a medical practitioner trained under Western (so-called modern) medical practices, subject to prescribed guidelines' (Interview with the authors). Testing traditional medicines follows a process that is called 'reverse pharmacology', a technique that is approved by the WHO. In this process, the formulation or medicine is prepared according to prescribed texts and toxicology and limited animal tests are carried out. After this, the medicine, device or formulation is subjected to human clinical trials. If the trials are successful, the researchers work backwards to try and analyse and isolate active molecules or the chain reaction among the several molecules before applying to the DCGI for approval. This process saves a lot of time and other resources as compared to the traditional expensive drug discovery process.

Multicentric trials have taken place in six thrust areas: anal fistula, diabetes mellitus, viral hepatitis, bronchial asthma, urolithiasis, and filariasis. During the course of execution of these studies the apex research body has developed formulations like Ayush-64 for Malaria, Ayush-56 for Epilepsy, 777 Oil for Psoriasis, Ayush-55 for Medoroga, Ayush-82 for Madhumeha, and has standardized special treatment techniques like Kshar Sutra, Panchakarma, and Amashya Shodhan Chikitsa (AYUSH 2008).

Multinational companies have often accused India of piracy for allowing generics and formulations of branded drugs to be made and sold. India, on its part has introduced the term 'bio-piracy' in the international lexicon, meaning piracy of its traditional knowledge base as well as its genetic material. This is to protect traditional knowledge systems that have developed over time and that are either codified in texts or retained in oral traditions. Intellectual property laws are unsuitable for traditional knowledge primarily because IPRs are based on protection of individual property rights whereas traditional knowledge is by and large collective.

There are cases of patents granted in the US on the wound-healing properties of *haldi* (turmeric) and in some countries on the hypoglycaemic (blood sugar reducing) properties of *karela* and brinjal, besides knowledge of Indian Ayurveda. Some 'infringements' are contested by India in courts of law overseas and as a result, patents have been overturned (haldi in the US, *neem* as fungicide in the EU patent office). But such processes are time-consuming and expensive and therefore, traditional knowledge needs to be protected by different legal and institutional means.

In order to prevent grant of patents based on Indian traditional knowledge, the Government of India has undertaken an ambitious project of creating a Traditional Knowledge Digital Library. This is a joint venture of the Council of Scientific Research (CSR) and Central Council for Research in Ayurveda and Siddha (CCRAS). This project is intended to cover about 35,000 formulations available in fourteen classical texts of Ayurveda for conversion of the information into a patent-compatible format. The work has been initiated with a cooperative setup of thirty Ayurveda experts, five information technology experts, and two patent examiners. The digital library will include all details about international patent classification, traditional research classification, Ayurveda terminology, concepts, definitions, classical formulations, doses, disease conditions, and references to documents in a digital format.

The Ministry of Health and Family Welfare has set up an All India Institute of Ayurveda (AIIS) to give impetus to research in the field of traditional medicine. It aims to bring a synergy between traditional wisdom and modern tools and technologies and will offer postgraduate and doctoral courses in various disciplines of Ayurveda. The institute is set up in New Delhi and by 2011 a few out-patient departments are already functioning while the entire college is expected to be operational by 2012. This is in addition to several national colleges that teach other branches of traditional medicine (A. Ramadoss qtd in *Times of India* 2007b: 5).

Biotechnology   Biotechnology is technology that is based on biology, especially when used in agriculture, food sciences, and medicine. The United Nations Convention on Biological Diversity (UNCBD) has defined the term as: 'Biotechnology means any technological application that uses biological systems, living organisms or derivatives thereof, to make or modify products or processes for specific use.'

This rather bland definition does not quite convey the excitement and promise that biotechnology holds out; in fact some even refer to it as 'technology of hope' and the twenty-first century as the 'biotech century'; it is to the current century what information technology was to the last century. It has promising applications in fields as diverse as healthcare—pharmacogenomics (the study of how an individual's genetic inheritance affects the body's response to drugs), drug production, genetic testing, gene therapy—agriculture, industry, and even public concerns like clean air and water.

In India, the government identified the development of biotechnology as a priority area more than two decades ago when DBT was formed in 1986 to become the central agency responsible for policy and promotion of R&D and manufacturing activities as well as for international cooperation. The DBT has five research institutions under its supervision:

- National Institute of Immunology;
- National Centre for Cell Science;
- National Brain Research Centre;
- National Centre for Plant Genome Research;
- Centre for DNA Fingerprinting and Diagnostics.

Biotechnology is a very capital-intensive industry. In the initial stages of investment, physical equipment, and special buildings (confined air, temperature control, vacuum conditions, etc.) constitute a major portion of investment. The industry is also very technical and calls for intensive collaboration and development of scientific networks and cooperation. In fact, the main entry barrier in this industry is the scientific skills of the project leader. The return on investment is longer than in most other industries. The biotechnology industry in India is estimated to be worth Rs 141.99 billion in 2010 (ABLE 2010).

Since biotechnology is such a new industry, regulation is essential to ensure coverage of ethical issues, preserving the country's gene pool, preventing exploitation of India's resources, etc. But if anything, India has a plethora of regulations that end up creating hurdles rather than streamlining the process. Besides rationalizing procedures, what will really give a boost is to have fewer regulatory agencies—ideally only one—with adequate finances and mandate over implementation and enforcement. Several state governments have taken initiatives to provide a conducive environment to the biotechnology industry: articulating a state biotechnology policy, setting up biotechnology parks, setting up task forces comprising experts to guide on policy issues, etc.

The government policy approach towards the biotechnology industry is often accused of being excessively slow and cautious—the price of democracy, as it was—which must accommodate the concerns of all sections before moving to take up positions in unfamiliar territory. After all, biotechnology is such a new industry that its full effects, despite extensive clinical trials, may be felt several years later, by which time changes may become irreversible. Perhaps the biggest hurdle biotechnology has to face is basic human fear about ethical issues like tampering with 'god's creation', a hurdle that few other disciplines have to face. Nevertheless, in the years ahead, R&D in biotechnology should produce genetically improved varieties of rice, wheat, *moong* bean, besides cotton, which has already passed several stages of trials prior to wide-scale adoption. Vegetables like brinjal have also reached an advanced stage of trials, and others like tomato and okra are expected to follow; fruits like mango, citrus, plants like neem, and even saffron can expect better commercial success. A better environment with clean rivers and efficient garbage breakdown through use of microbes is not unlikely. Biotechnology also holds out hope for better vaccines, more targeted drug delivery akin to Ayurveda for better public health.

Biopharmaceuticals The pharmaceutical industry is the largest segment of the Indian biotechnology industry commanding as much as a 61.7 per cent share. Its value at around Rs 882.9 million in

2010. Biologics are essentially living cells (a bacterial strain or human and animal cell lines in culture) that are genetically modified so that they manufacture therapeutic proteins. These proteins are highly sensitive to even minor variations in their environment This process of modification, even under stringent laboratory conditions, can produce variations which affect efficacy and tolerability or both. Even small changes in ambient conditions would mean that the entire production batch may have to be discarded and the process started again with cultivation of new cells.

This requires more extensive clinical trials before a regulator will grant approval to a biosimilar—a 99 per cent purity level is required for most regulatory approval—and the usual protocols for assessing equivalence between generics and the original drug will have to be reworked. Also, biologic drugs are less stable than chemical-based drugs and also have a shorter shelf life, requiring extensive cold chain distribution networks. This makes manufacturing a biosimilar much higher than a chemical or synthetic generic; the estimated cost of a biosimilar is expected in the range of USD 10–14 million as against USD 1–2 million for a conventional generic (Pisani and Bonduelle 2010). Therefore the price differential between an original and its biosimilar is much smaller, increasing the entry barriers due to lower incentives of profitability.

Biologic prescriptions are a fast-growing market; in fact, growing at a faster rate than conventional drugs. This is mainly because of better efficacy. Biopharma drugs also command a higher premium price than conventional drugs. Although biologics may not replace conventional drugs, they are expected to steadily increase their share in the choice of treatment plans of doctors and patients all over the world. Manufacturing of biopharmaceutical drugs is a major technical challenge. The complex molecular structure of biologics requires extreme and precise control of living production systems. Unlike new chemical entities (conventional drugs), material used in Phase 3 clinical trials of biologics has to be produced by using the final manufacturing process that will be employed to commercially supply the drug, including the manufacturing site. This means that construction of a biopharmaceutical manufacturing facility must be completed even ahead of completion of clinical trials. This raises a serious issue of choice for companies to balance risk of product failure with the risk of investment failure.

Companies and countries that can achieve success in biopharmaceuticals can expect immense returns—both monetarily and in terms of better and more efficient healthcare.

R&D in the Defence Sector
(Based on inputs from and interviews with DRDO officials and other duly acknowledged resources)

Defence R&D constitutes one of the largest R&D spending in India in terms of sheer resources. For the year 2011–12, the budget of DRDO was about 102.53 billion, which is around 6 per cent of the country's defence budget (around Rs 1644.15 billion for the year 2011–12). The end users of DRDO's work are predominantly the defence services, although technology developed by the Life Sciences and Special Metals (LSSM) divisions has found users in civilian sectors like food industry, medical devices, and the diagnostics and pharmaceutical industry. The roughly fifty laboratories comprising the DRDO cover a gamut of projects from sophisticated guided missile and aeronautic systems to mosquito repellents, covering in between items like special metals, diagnostic kits, radars and avionics systems, armaments, technical clothing like pilot Anti-G suit, and NBC water purification technology. The DRDO is reported to have a huge human resource strength, which in reality translates into a 2:1 ratio for technical and admin personnel.

Technology transfer or commercial exploitation of patents
The DRDO usually transfers technology to production agencies at token or nil prices. Holding patents for their inventions is not a commonplace activity, with only 550 patents developed over a twenty-year period from 1985 to 2005 (and only 180 of these being sealed over the same period). There is hardly any commercial sale of the patents that are held, which gives little insight into the innovative efficiency of the organization. Most patents developed and sealed are in basic life sciences and materials and not on strategic military programmes, because of reasons of confidentiality. Since most DRDO (a government institution) technologies are given to ordnance units or PSUs (also government institutions), there is no commercial value put

at the transaction, even if it is a notional figure without actual transfer of funds from one government department to another. This means vast amounts of public resources do not really have to prove commercial utility. It is important to have a real valuation of technology so that there is a real seller and a real buyer in order to have some degree of performance pressure. With the defence sector being gradually opened to private participation in India, this is all the more necessary so that public resources spent on defence R&D, produce products that are competitive and can stand the rigour of scrutiny in technology sourcing decisions of private and public companies.

Efficiency and Effectiveness Despite having a dedicated R&D unit for defence purposes, the fact is that nearly 50 years of its existence later, India remains one of the largest importers of defence equipment in the world. However, this is no indication of the success or otherwise of DRDO per se; factors that have hampered Indian industry in general are equally at play in defence production.

The DRDO is a research organization and its role ought to end with transfer of technology to production units. These, till recently, were only public sector units or ordnance factories which do not quite have a reputation for being vibrant and at the forefront of innovation themselves. Therefore, DRDO has to spend substantial time on the production line of these agencies because in most cases, production units do not have an in-house R&D unit to bridge even small production gaps or minor upgradation of existing products.

India has had a weak industrial base for most of its life after independence. When the Integrated Guided Missile Development Programme (IGDMP) was launched in 1982–3, the industrial base of the country was so underdeveloped that even getting locally-made small components was a challenge, which could be overcome either by importing or developing them from scratch; there was simply no capacity to produce even components, let alone larger sub-systems or systems within the country. If DRDO is often accused of losing focus by reinventing the wheel, the fault also lies with the industrial and political environment of the country.

When the first Prithvi missile was launched in 1988, there were only a few industries, mostly public sector units, which were involved. In 2007, some 800 small and medium sector companies are part of a national network involved in defence projects, including some that partner multinational companies which are contractors to produce components and sub-systems. Producing missile systems at home requires intensive development of several related industries, including a vibrant private defence production sector.

In 2006, ahead of the newly defined defence procurement policy, TATA Power and Larsen & Toubro were awarded a joint contract (50:50) by the army to manufacture forty PINAKA Multiple Barrel Rocket Launchers. Although the value of the contract is small, about Rs 3 billion (USD 75 million), it was a landmark event for the Indian private industry, to participate in the challenging but hitherto closed defence production industry.

As India's former President and former head of DRDO, A.P.J. Abdul Kalam said, '…through its efforts, (especially up to the 1990s), DRDO has graduated from an import substitution establishment to a full-fledged system design and development organization' (Kalam 2007).

The development of defence industrial capacity within the country working with DRDO technology ensures that critical defence systems can be produced and integrated indigenously, particularly considering the factor of international sanctions. There are some technologies, components and systems that simply cannot be bought, such as those which go into Agni or Prithvi missiles; these necessarily have to be built indigenously. Association in development of military products has also helped in developing spin-offs that have application in the civilian sector like the automotive and petrochemical industries, refineries, desalination plants, process industry, etc.

Estimating the efficiency of DRDO as a research organization, therefore, is not a straightforward linear equation because there is really no method to calculate the strategic importance of developing indigenous weapons systems or the real cascading impact of knowledge and capabilities that are built in the country in the face of changing geopolitical equations. For instance, electronic warfare equipment manufacture technology was built almost from scratch from the 1980s because of the nature of usage of equipment such as jammers and other surveillance equipment.

Then again, there is sometimes a disconnect between DRDO and its end users, the defence services. Although DRDO product prototypes are usually assured of exhaustive testing by the users, there is no guarantee that that technology will finally be adopted. As mentioned earlier, technology developed by DRDO is transferred to users at little or no cost and, therefore, there is no conventional method in ascertaining the efficiency of fund usage. However, the value of production orders placed by the ministry of defence on production units using DRDO-developed technology over the last fifteen-year period is approximately over Rs 1,000 billion of which 38 per cent is for missiles, 17 per cent for electronic systems, 11 per cent for aero systems, and another 28 per cent for armaments and combat engineering.

Although the production value of orders by the end user is by no means the only indication of the efficiency or effectiveness of the R&D organization, more so because defence procurement is a highly complex matter, it provides a rough barometer of the marketability of DRDO's inventions.

There are several critics who question the rationale of spending funds and energy on areas like life sciences which hardly give any incremental benefits to the organization and for which there are specialized agencies like ICMR, ICAR, etc., which also use public resources. The answer to this lies in the fact that the life sciences group consumes a very small fraction of the R&D budget, although it gets far more than its fair share of public interest, and is mandated to cater to the requirements of the soldier—ranging from their selection, protection, training, and physiological/psychological needs. These therefore become obvious spin-offs to the civil sector.

A success or two is very important to energize a research organization and the recent successes of DRDO in 2007 have certainly been the high points of its achievements: the successful demonstration of the Interceptor missile test in both endo- and exo-atmospheric layers gave a much needed boost to the technological prowess of the country, compounded by the successful test launch of our intermediate range ballistic missile, IRBM, and Agni 3. In essence, these test launches demonstrated India's strategic capability for minimum credible deterrence, ensured India its rightful place in an elite club of technologically advanced countries of the world and became a valuable tool to enable the pursuit of an independent foreign policy.

The DRDO has also invested a considerable percentage of its resources in the establishment of world-class test facilities and related infrastructure, which are critical for its development programmes. The facilities include high-tech simulators, structural test facilities for aircraft and naval systems, missile test launch facilities, automotive and engineering systems, test rigs, etc. The Indian industry has contributed significantly to the establishment of these facilities, which has been a part of the learning curve in the development of high-technology systems. These infrastructures are today national assets, which are slowly being made available to agencies within the country for their common application.

The DRDO is often compared with the US defence agency DARPA, but the comparisons are somewhat skewed because the charters of these two organizations are widely different and amount to comparing apples and oranges. Essentially a funding agency of the US Department of Defense, DARPA, focuses on scouting for cutting edge technology development capability in the industry, academia, etc., and is run by project managers, while DRDO is a *development* agency which works primarily with 'mission mode projects' which have immediate/current requirement—the distinction has to be understood and appreciated in its entirety while comparing the two. Moreover, DARPA is also an agency that has very limited overheads, no laboratories or facilities, and mainly focuses on high-risk, large-payoff projects with future potential. Also, DARPA is independent from other more conventional military R&D and has around 150 technical personnel directly managing a USD 3.2 billion budget; it invests about 97 per cent of its funds in organizations outside DARPA, primarily in universities and the industry. Thus, DARPA operates in a technologically superior environment where leading industries/global leaders of its country/world are available for tapping. In contrast, DRDO invests most of its funds in its own laboratories for development. The DRDO has had to play the role of trainer and educator in the 1980s and has also contributed to lifting the industrial base of India to a reasonable level, through its critical programmes like LCA and IGMDP.

Deepening indigenous expertise in IT (software costs in a complete missile system can go up to one-third the total cost) increases the scope for collaboration with private industry and helps DRDO focus on its core objectives. With opening of the defence sector to gradual private participation, defence R&D is likely to face the pros and cons of competition and market realities—in any case, it will likely rejuvenate a largely secretive, stratified edifice into a nimble-footed research organization, in the process strengthening the industrial base of the country.

R&D IN INDIA ... WORK IN PROGRESS

India was noted for the depth and breadth of grassroots knowledge since ancient times, absorbing and enhancing knowledge of the various influences that came into her domain. The British were the first rulers to systematically undermine India's traditional knowledge and superimpose their own thought processes, systems, literature, and technology to strengthen their control and supremacy over India.

Since independence, the government has consciously and gradually developed institutional technology transfer mechanisms to enhance the potential of people. The protective period of the 1960s and 1970s saw India stress on self-reliance and indigenous capacity-building. Although with hindsight we see a wide gap of where India still is in terms of global R&D and efficient S&T, the period was very important

In 1966, IBM turned down the Indian government's request to share ownership (and technology), holding out the threat of shutting down operations, which it finally did in 1978 when faced with an assertive government. It was left to the state-owned Bharat Electronics Limited (BEL), set up for military use in the 1950s to be the lone producer of informatics equipment of any kind. But although its products were commercial failures, it served as training ground for several thousand engineers. The Electronics Corporation of India Limited (ECIL), which was formed in 1968 to tie up with international companies for local production of computers and gradually increase local value-add to the point of self-reliance, could, in the 1980s evolve into a successful large-scale systems integrator, providing solutions to key developmental domains, such as an automated monitoring system for offshore oil/gas wells at a fraction of internationally quoted figures.

in developing basic infrastructure, confidence, and an incremental bank of knowledge, which was totally absent at independence.

India's exposure to diverse techniques and technologies has its roots in geopolitical realities; India sourced much of its defence requirements from the Soviet Union, as also crude oil and machinery in several heavy industries. To contain the possible rise of communist influence in India, the US and other Western nations encouraged private multinational sector corporations to set up new plants in India. These diverse technologies have been adopted and refined to suit Indian conditions in several disciplines, including capital goods and agriculture.

Ever stronger integration into the global economy has ensured that the importance of R&D is not lost on anyone, from business owners and managers, to educationists and policymakers alike. While large private firms are moving towards larger internal R&D or even buying out firms and companies with strong R&D capabilities rather than buying imported knowhow, the public sector is opening up its R&D knowledge to private players as well.

7

Successful Business Practices of Modern India

India is a country of several paradoxes where many extremes coexist cheek-by-jowl. It is a country of a few stunningly rich people (including three of the world's top ten richest people) and offers hope of a decent life to several tens of thousands of people. It is also home to some of the world's poorest people who live in abject poverty with little hope of ever improving their lot in life.

The onset of the twenty-first century has seen dramatic improvement in the quality of life of many Indians. Although no one can deny or ignore the harsh reality of uneven distribution of income and even opportunities, today more people have a better chance of leading a more prosperous life than previous generations. Business, trade, and commerce make it possible to put the key to unlock destinies in the hands of several million Indians more than any other occupation. Certain economic processes and tools have developed on a continuum over the years and have now reached a critical mass that is ready to deliver results.

In this section, we focus on some of these processes—cooperative movement, micro-financing, and off-shoring. Ironically, the fruits of even such processes are not always fairly distributed and may even end up creating more and rigid divisions. Therefore, at the end of the section we look at the nature of the beast called *digital divide* and some ways at breaking it down.

COOPERATIVE MOVEMENT

In India, the cooperative movement was introduced by the erstwhile British government as a response to the agrarian riots which took place in the deccan in the late nineteenth century. The root of the movement, therefore, was state-sponsored rather than a spontaneous peoples' movement. Farmers were in deep debt to local moneylenders and there was steady increase of landlessness due to the inability to repay loans. Cooperative agriculture lending was an alternative credit mechanism mooted and promoted by the imperial government. The cooperative movement got a formal structure in 1904 when the Cooperative Societies Act was passed and has since undergone several changes to include purposes other than credit.

After independence, the Indian government continued with state sponsoring of the movement through its five-year plans as a chosen instrument of public policy, particularly to deliver credit to the farm sector. This is in contrast to the origins of the movement elsewhere in the world which was a grassroots peoples' movement in response to some of the ills of the Industrial Revolution. In many ways, state sponsorship was needed in the initial years because of the low penetration of commercial banks in the rural hinterland. Experts believe that continuing state involvement in the cooperative movement is one of the crucial factors why the cooperative movement in the country has not been as successful as it should have been.

Cooperatives can be formed for any human endeavour that requires people to pool in resources towards common goals. In India, nearly 80 per cent of cooperatives are concerned with agriculture; farming in India is mostly done by small and marginal farmers with low levels of holdings and hence low per hectare productivity. Under World Trade Organization (WTO) provisions on agriculture, India has opened up several commodities for free flow of imports with the result that products of countries like the US which typically have large farm holdings and very high per hectare productivity can enter Indian markets at very competitive prices. Cooperative farming (or fishing, poultry, dairy, etc.) is the logical answer to problems emerging from this process of liberalization and globalization. The principle of mutual aid, which is the basic idea of a cooperative organization, and the practice of thrift and self-help that sustain it, help to generate a feeling of self-reliance, particularly among the marginalized sections of people. Cooperatives have been successful in places where small and marginal farmers are able to pool in their land to cultivate it as a large farm. Cooperatives also have better collective bargaining power in purchase of inputs and sale of products besides being able to access better technology.

The biggest challenge for cooperatives is to sustain competitiveness in a global marketplace with few geographic boundaries and for this to happen societies must invest in training, professional management, and latest technology.

Notwithstanding its infirmities, cooperatives have spread widely across the country. Today, there are over 0.5 million registered cooperative societies with a membership of more than 200 million and working capital of more than Rs 2,200 billion. According to the National Cooperative Union of India (NCUI), cooperatives contribute as much as 50 per cent of the total production of sugar, 25 per cent of fertilizer production, 43 per cent of agro-credit disbursement, and 11 per cent of milk procurement in the country. Cooperatives have an unparalleled outreach with outlets located in inaccessible areas with about 70 per cent of its clientele drawn from small farmers and other marginal groups. These societies are often used by the government to act as a preferred instrument for execution of public policy as the most effective delivery system. Although the cooperative movement in India has a large coverage, there is a lot of variability in the spread and depth of coverage across sectors, activities, and regions.

In hindsight, it can be said that state promotion has turned into state control—and from bureaucratization to politicization is but a short step. Political participation on the ground level is not necessarily a bad thing if it is used to correct grassroots anomalies between public policy and public need. Trouble creeps in when cooperative institutions are used to promote narrow, sectarian or personal objectives. 'The Registrar and politician intervene in the affairs of the cooperative so much that cooperatives can well be said to have become a part of the government machinery' (Joshi 2007). Bureaucratic and political appointments to cooperatives, poor housekeeping, and management have led to cooperatives suffering an identity crisis of sorts—of being neither private nor government.

Over the years, several committees have been set up to recommend improvements in the working of the cooperative movement. One such committee, the Vaidyanathan Committee, was set up by NABARD (National Bank for Agriculture and Rural Development), the apex agriculture and rural development bank of India, to examine rural cooperative credit structure and to reorganize and increase the viability of state credit cooperative institutions, which include central cooperative banks, primary land development banks, and primary agriculture cooperative banks. Since over 70 per cent of the clientele of the cooperatives in India is drawn from small farmers and other marginal groups, the committee 'found it a strong reason to justify expending public funds for recapitalizing a system that was not just financially impaired but also impaired in terms of governance and management' (Thorat 2005). The committee in 2006 recommended a revival package of Rs 150 billion of the rural short-term cooperative credit structure in India—the package is partly financed by multilateral and foreign agencies. The recommendations deal with the critical issue of financing people's entrepreneurial ambitions, however humble they may be.

In a rapidly globalizing world where large transnational companies (TNCs) have the money and power to alter the landscape of regions, sectors and industries, the cooperative movement needs to be strengthened and developed further as a counterweight who can speak on behalf of the small farmer, fisherman, weaver, milkman—in short, the common man.

The Indian cooperative movement has witnessed several failures but equally there are several spectacular successes, notably IFFCO (Indian Farmers Fertiliser Cooperative Limited) for fertilizers, and AMUL (Anand Milk Union Limited) for milk. AMUL is also a part of Operation Flood, a programme started in the 1970s to create a nationwide milk grid by establishing an extensive system of 70,000 cooperatives, 170 district dairy units, and some twenty-five state level federations. It is a tribute to India's cooperative movement that within a short while, the country has achieved a reasonable level of self-sufficiency in milk production.

The Story of AMUL

Over four decades ago, the life of a farmer in the Kaira District of Gujarat was very much like that of his counterpart anywhere else in India. His income was derived almost entirely from seasonal crops. The income from buffaloes was undependable. The marketing and distribution system for the milk was controlled by private traders and middlemen. As milk is perishable, farmers were compelled to sell it for whatever they were offered. Often, they had to sell cream and ghee at throwaway prices. In this situation, the one who gained was the private trader. The story of AMUL (Anand Milk Union Limited) began in 1946 as an offshoot of the freedom movement with an aim to do away with the exploitation of middlemen in milk collection and give the villagers the best returns for their milk.

The Kaira Union began pasteurizing milk for the Bombay Milk Scheme (BMS) in June 1948. An assured market proved a great incentive to the milk producers of the district. Inspired by the Kaira Union, similar milk unions came up in other districts too. By the end of 1948, more than 400 farmers joined in more village societies, and the quantity of milk handled by one Union increased from 250 to 5,000 litres a day. As the movement spread in the district, it was found that the BMS could not absorb the extra milk collected by the Kaira Union in winter, when the production, on an average, was 2.5 times more than in summer. Thus, even by 1953, the farmer-members had no assured market for the extra milk produced in winter. They were again forced to sell a large surplus at low rates to the middlemen. The remedy was to set up a plant to process milk into products like butter and milk powder. A Rs 5 million plant to manufacture milk powder and butter was completed in 1955. In 1958, the factory was expanded to manufacture sweetened condensed milk. Two years later, a new wing was added for the manufacture of 2,500 tons of roller-dried baby food and 600 tons of cheese per year, the former based on a formula developed with the assistance of the Central Food Technological Research Institute (CFTRI), Mysore. It was for the first time anywhere in the world that cheese or baby food was made from buffalo milk on a large, commercial scale.

In 1973, in order to market their products more effectively and economically, they formed the Gujarat Cooperative Milk Marketing Federation Limited (GCMMF Ltd); GCMMFL became the sole marketer of the original range of AMUL products including milk powder and butter. AMUL is largely credited with starting the dairy cooperative movement in India, which is jointly owned by some 2.2 million milk producers in Gujarat, India. Backward integration of the process also led the cooperatives to advances in animal husbandry and veterinary practice.

AMUL has grown exponentially and the scale of operation of AMUL is inspiring. Every day the union collects some 4,47,000 litres of milk from 2.2 million farmers (many of them illiterate), converts the milk into branded packaged products, and delivers goods worth Rs 60 million to over 5,00,000 retail outlets across the country. A key reason for success is the use of indigenous technology, then developed by H.M. Dalaya for spray-drying and processing buffalo milk which was never done earlier anywhere in the world. This changed the shelf life of milk forever and this innovation to a great extent laid the bedrock of the white revolution in India (Dutta 2008). The range of products has since grown to include ice cream, ghee, cheese, chocolates, shrikhand, paneer, and so on. These products have made AMUL a leading food brand in India.

To implement the vision of sustained long-term growth along with effective management and commercial viability while retaining their focus on farmers, a hierarchical network of cooperatives was developed, which today forms the robust supply chain behind GCMMF's endeavours. The vast and complex supply chain stretches from small suppliers to large fragmented markets.

Even though the cooperative was formed to bring together farmers, the union recognized that professional managers and technocrats would be required to manage the network effectively and make it commercially viable. GCMMF and the unions play a major role in this process and have jointly achieved the desired degree of control. The board is drawn from the heads of all the unions, and the boards of the unions comprise farmers elected through village societies, thereby creating a situation of interlocking control.

Operation Flood, which was perhaps the world's largest development programme, was based on the rich experience gained from the AMUL model, also popularly known as the 'Anand Pattern'. The three-tier 'Anand Pattern' structure consists of a cooperative society at the village level affiliated to a milk union at the district level, and they are further federated into a milk federation at the state level. The above three-tier structure was formed in order to delegate responsibilities at various levels such that there was no internal competition and economics of scale was achieved.

The village cooperative is the primary society under the three-tier structure. Membership consists of milk producers of the village (approximately 200 member milk producers per village) and the main function of this cooperative society is to collect surplus milk from the milk producers of the village and make payments based on quality and quantity. It also provides support services to the members like veterinary first aid, artificial insemination services, cattle-feed sales, mineral mixture sales, fodder and fodder seed sales, conducting training on animal husbandry and dairying, etc.

The district-level milk union is the second tier under the three-tier structure whose membership is drawn from the village societies of the district and it is governed by a board of directors consisting of nine to eighteen elected representatives of the village societies. The district-level milk union processes the milk into various milk products as per the market requirement.

The state-level federation is the apex tier under the three-tier structure. Membership consists of district-level milk unions of the state and is governed by a board of directors consisting of one elected representative of each milk union. The main function of the federation is to market the milk and milk products, manufactured by the milk unions. The federation establishes a distribution network for marketing of milk and milk products and maintains the supply chain network. It also provides support services to the milk unions and members like technical inputs, management support and advisory services.

V. Kurien, ex-Chairman GCMMF, popularly called the 'Milkman of India' had a primary goal of building a strong Indian society through an innovative cooperative network, to provide quality service and products to end-consumers and good returns to the farmer members.

There is also something very special about milk, something which requires that any brand for milk and milk products to act not simply as a seller, but as a trustee. Milk is not a white good or a brown good. It is not something people save their entire lives in order to buy – like a car, or a house. Milk is not a status symbol; rather it is the symbol of nutrition. Milk is a nearly complete food, providing protein, vitamins, minerals and other nutrients so essential to maintaining good health. (Kurien 2001)

AMUL's products compete very successfully against some of the largest private sector and global companies and today are nearly a billion dollar enterprise with forty product categories, 300 stock-keeping units, 1,00,000 retailers with refrigerators, an 18,000-strong cold chain, and 5,00,000 non-refrigerated retail outlets. The sales turnover in 2006–7 was Rs 42,778 million (USD 1,050 million).

Incidentally, in October 2007, Amul's probiotic ice cream won the prestigious International Dairy Federation Marketing Award at the World Dairy Summit in Dublin. This is what makes AMUL so special. A dream of a few villagers, standing up against exploitation and then going on to innovate to bring in the wave of white revolution and changing the rural scape in many states of India forever. (Dutta 2008)

As a direct consequence of 'Operation Flood' and the AMUL model, India is now the leading milk producer in the world, with a milk production of 91 million MTs/annum. The cooperative structure now touches the lives of 11 million farmer households across India. In Gujarat itself, 2.4 million farmer households form a part of the large AMUL family. Dairying has now become an attractive source of livelihood, bringing prosperity and economic development to rural India.

MICRO-FINANCE—A CHANCE OF OWNING THE KEYS TO DESTINY

Millions of poor in India (as indeed, in the world) are largely left out of the banking network and, ironically, they are the ones who need such services the most. Conventional commercial banking norms require a certain profile of a borrower, something that most poor, illiterate people living a subsistence existence can rarely meet. A World Bank study of 6,000 families in Andhra Pradesh and Uttar Pradesh shows that 87 per cent of them have no access to credit, 85 per cent have no access to insurance, and 56 per cent borrow from moneylenders at exorbitant rates of interest.

Out of necessity and enterprise, such disenfranchised people who are shut out of formal banking channels have formed a system of credit—

microcredit. Microcredit is the extension of small loans to people who are below the bar of acceptability as borrowers of mainstream banking for reasons ranging from being landless or with no assets to offer as collateral or practicing uncertain trades (like hawkers, etc.).

The credit for pioneering microcredit is attributed to Bangladesh, in particular Grameen Bank, set up by winner of the 2006 Nobel Peace Prize, Mohammed Yunus. The genesis of microcredit, in fact goes back a few decades to another Nobel Prize winner from Bengal, Rabindranath Tagore, the poet-philanthropist, who started an experiment in microcredit—though not by that name—in Patishar, Naogaon district in present-day Bangladesh in 1905, when he made a huge grant to poor farmers through a specially set up bank called Patishar Bank. The experiment was not a success commercially, failing to recover even 20 per cent of the loans, despite the scheme not charging any interest from the borrowers.

Microcredit in India is largely through self-help groups, in particular women's self-help groups (SHGs). An SHG is a registered or unregistered group of micro entrepreneurs with a homogeneous social or economic background who come together voluntarily to save small amounts of money regularly and mutually agree to use the funds so collected to help each other with financial aid (Reserve Bank of India n.d.)

Grameen System (prevalent in Bangladesh)

A microfinance organization (MFO) or bank identifies potential clients and organizes them into groups of five members, which, in turn, are organized into a cluster or centre consisting of five to seven such primary groups. The members make regular savings with the MFO or bank according to a compulsory schedule and also take regular loans. Regular meetings, usually weekly, are held which are supervised by the MFO where savings and repayments are collected and handed over to the MFO worker who maintains records.

Bangladeshi village communities are generally more socially and economically homogeneous and less divided by caste, etc., than villages in India, which makes it easier for this system of microcredit to flourish. The primary driver in a Grameen system is the MFO or designated bank that exercises tight control over most functional

At these weekly meetings, potential borrowers must learn bond rules and chant '16 decisions' at the start of the session. These are codes of conduct that members are encouraged to follow in daily life such as education of children, use of latrines and safe drinking water, rejection of dowry in marriages, etc. Although these are recommendatory in nature, reports suggest that in practice observance of these rituals, including participation in physical training, is a precondition for grant of loans. This aspect of running a microcredit scheme may have its detractors but is a proven effective method employed by several non-governmental organizations (NGOs) and other agencies to drive home certain messages while gathering for an altogether different purpose.

aspects including recordkeeping and enforcement of rules. Meetings are handled and organized by bank staff that devotes considerable time to nurture existing groups and open new ones—groups are the only reason for the existence of Grameen Bank. (Grameen Bank in Bangladesh is protected from regulatory interference by the country's Parliament.) A Grameen member can, therefore, get by without needing too much technical knowledge about administration or banking matters. The downside is that Grameen-style micro loans tend to carry a high rate of interest to pay for the large staff that the system demands for close supervision.

Self-Help Groups (SHGs) System

A self-help group (SHG) is a flexible system where people come together voluntarily based on groupings of their choice, whether along caste, community, gender, occupation, or other lines. Moreover, SHGs may also evolve from existing groups like chit funds or nidhi funds to scale up operations and SHG members can decide who gets loans, when, and at what rates. The difference between their cost of funds and the interest they charge member-borrowers is retained by the group and is their compensating factor.

Each SHG is expected to handle its own administrative work, with or without help from NGOs (non-governmental organizations) or banks. The members of an SHG are effectively owners and managers of a small bank. Members have an account with the SHG rather than a linked bank—the group as a whole can hold an account with the bank but the bank does not deal with individual members.

Although this may eventually strengthen the SHG, it is only one of several varied customers of a bank linked up with an SHG; the bank, therefore, has little time to handhold individual SHGs. It is a moot point that the typical SHG member—poor, often illiterate women with little time, few skills, or even confidence—can successfully conduct all the management and banking processes required of a successful SHG. But SHGs can be very fragile social entities; it is difficult for them to absorb the shocks of changes in membership and they can easily be destroyed by minor disputes or disagreements. Since they are loosely structured social groups, depending on internal cohesiveness rather than institutionalized structural strength, they can be easy prey for external influences, perceptions of unfair gains or losses among members or even political patronage for block voting, etc.

The distinction between SHGs and Grameen type of organizations is getting increasingly blurred and more a matter of nomenclature. The basic idea behind such groups is simple—save money, pool it together, and give loans to each other. It is really an extension of the nidhi funds (or ASCA—see section on nidhi funds, pp. 49–51) concept except that the absolute sum of each saving or loan is typically very small—hence the term 'micro' and is usually for small periods of time and often for small reasons as well. However, these small loans can jumpstart a long chain of economic activity. Borrowers usually come back into the scheme for larger and larger loans, having cleared their earlier dues and this helps enlarge their business. The group members rely on collective wisdom and peer pressure to ensure proper end-use of credit and timely repayment. Group lending in rural areas rests on the pivot that all villagers know one another and therefore only 'safe' borrowers come together to form an SHG. The Reserve Bank of India (RBI) also recognizes peer pressure as an effective substitute for collaterals for loans. (These parameters, however, change for urban lenders where grouping of like individuals have to find a different mechanism.) The RBI also permits microcredit organizations or SHGs to use their discretion in charging interest from member borrowers instead of having to adhere to prescribed norms for commercial banks. Terms and conditions imposed by microcredit banks for organizations or groups are also allowed a large degree of flexibility, depending on ground realities.

Financing through SHGs reduces transaction costs for both lenders and borrowers—for the lender, it comes from dealing with a single SHG as a unit instead of a large number of small-sized individual account holders; borrowers, on their part, save on time and travel costs and other paperwork in canvassing for loans when they operate through their local SHG.

Approximately 75 million poor households potentially requiring financial services makes the microfinance market in India among the largest in the world. The average size of a loan to an SHG is Rs 22,240 and to a family, Rs 1,316 in rural areas (it goes up to Rs 8,000 in urban areas). This takes the total credit demand to somewhere between Rs 225 billion and Rs 500 billion (Chankova et al. 2004).

In 1991–2, National Bank for Agriculture and Agricultural Development (NABARD) started a pilot project to facilitate smoother linkage of SHGs with banks. There are variations of models of operation of such microcredit lending (figures in brackets indicate the spread of models actually adopted):

- Direct lending by banks to SHGs without any intervention of an intermediary (16 per cent);
- Lending directly to SHGs with facilitation by NGOs and other formal agencies (75 per cent);
- Lending through NGOs and financing agencies (9 per cent).

This indicates that SHGs want active participation in the banking, borrowing, and lending process but are not averse to seeking help to achieve their goals. The SHG linkage programme has emerged as the dominant microfinance dispensation model in India.

The RBI and NABARD have set up a Microfinance Development Fund (MDF) to move to an integrated approach to microfinance rather than a minimalist approach of offering only financial intermediation. The Rs 1,000 million fund (Rs 400 million each by RBI and NABARD, and the balance Rs 200 million by eleven public sector banks) is expected to address institutional and delivery issues like institutional capacity and increasing volumes. It aims to make microfinance play an important role in poverty alleviation by taking a more holistic view of the client including providing enterprise development services like marketing infrastructure, introduction of technology and design development, training SHG members, partner NGOs and other agencies. Its mandate also extends to providing start-up funds to microfinance institutions and to meet their initial operational deficits as also to meet the cost of formation and nurturing of SHGs.

SEWA (Self-Employed Women's Association) is an organization of poor, often illiterate and self-employed women workers of Ahmedabad. The organization's main goal is to serve the invisible women workforce in the unorganized sector by bringing them under an umbrella of collective bargaining power. It is a registered trade union body since 1972 and perhaps the most successful and well-known micro-financing institution in India.

A large part of the SEWA staff is recruited and promoted from among its members.

SEWA's two main goals are:

- Full employment—meaning employment that ensures work, income, food and social security;
- Self-reliance—women should be self-reliant and autonomous, individually, collectively, both economically and in terms of their decision-making activity.

These activities are implemented by the members through a number of different institutions established by SEWA including a total of eighty-six cooperatives (dairy, fodder, grain banks, plantation, ration shops, etc.), village committees for integrated watershed development, water users' group for management and operation of village tanks, ponds and piped water supply scheme, handicraft associations, urban community slum organizations and health workers and child care workers' cooperative (Jhabvala and Kanbur 2004: 298).

The largest of these cooperatives is the SEWA Bank. The profile of a typical SEWA member—poor, illiterate, often vulnerable woman but economically very active—is such that she will never make the grade as a borrower of a commercial bank but she definitely needs a safe place to park her savings. Mahila SEWA Cooperative Bank was set up in 1973 as a response to this need among women. It is perhaps the world's largest poor women's bank and has, over the years, also achieved financial viability. A unique feature of the SEWA Bank is Doorstep Banking. Since its clientele is made up of low-income daily wage/income earners, each day spent in making trips to a bank for making deposits means loss of earnings. SEWA Bank operates mobile bank vans to mobilize collections and also extension counters throughout the city.

In 1992, SEWA set up an insurance programme, implemented by the SEWA Bank. Women paid a small premium and in exchange were covered for death, hospitalization and asset loss. The premium had to be paid annually and keeping in mind the low saving-ability of its members, SEWA bank linked it with savings and the interest generated from such savings of deposit account covered the premium. These insurance schemes were in collaboration with the public sector companies, LIC and GIC (Ibid.: 309).

Scalability

Microcredit is a very appealing idea with the right mix of profit-making and social responsibility that draws a lot of champions to the cause. The United Nations (UN) General Assembly designated 2005 as the international 'Year of Microcredit'. The millennium development goal (MGD) of reducing poverty in half by 2015 relies on microcredit as one of the means. It has also become the flavour of the season with the Nobel Peace Prize 2006 being awarded to a leading proponent of microcredit.

However, SHG schemes appear to work well when groups are small and easy to monitor. The system soon shows signs of complacency and is afflicted with local rivalries and politics. It is one thing to collect money and build a corpus but it is equally important to utilize that money optimally and manage it in a way that provides lasting benefits. Facilities provided by other financial service agencies such as insurance, legal services, capacity-building, opening lines of credit, etc., are necessary for the scheme to sustain itself.

In India, the SHG movement is the strongest in Andhra Pradesh. Fifty per cent of Small Industries Development Bank of India's (SIDBI) entire portfolio is in Hyderabad, the capital. Andhra Pradesh accounts for 26.2 per cent of the total SHGs in India, 38.2 per cent of the total loans sanctioned, and 44 per cent of the total number of federations (CASHE Program Summary of CARE India).

The Amravati District Central Co-Op Bank (ADCCB) has a little over 0.1 million loan accounts, which it lends through primary agriculture cooperative societies (PACS). The loan recovery rate is around 10 per cent (in 2004).

The ADCCB also runs the NABARD-backed SHG scheme—a small savings and loan system begun around the year 2000 and micro-managed by local members. The bank has nearly 4,000 SHGs with around 60,000 members. The loan recovery rate is around 82 per cent.

The bank noticed that several SHG members are good borrowers in SHG schemes but defaulters on other loans, perhaps because they know that prompt repayment will enhance their credit record and get them higher loan entitlement the next time or perhaps because of mere peer pressure.

The involvement of RBI and commercial banks in microcredit is, undoubtedly, a welcome move in as much as it provides the movement with structural benefits and a framework of a regulatory mechanism that is so necessary to streamline the movement. There is a lot of money involved in microcredit and it is essential to prevent malpractices and dishonesty, which can have devastating consequences (think of unscrupulous chit funds).

But the ground level perception among many participants is that the microcredit model has lost its original purpose and now serves only the not-so-poor families, as it is not commercially viable for them to service the poorest. Besides, peer pressure as an instrument of loan recovery often becomes more heartless than banks pressing for repayment. The borrower has to keep up the repayment schedule regardless of genuine exigencies, the standard response of the SHG being, 'Why should she be singled out for generosity?' The SHG–bank linkage system is structured in a way that creditworthiness of the group is downgraded in case of default by any member, which only serves to tighten pressure on borrowers. Thus, economics and profits take precedence and not necessarily wellbeing or real development. It can be nobody's case that money should be given away for free to the poor and deprived—no economy can survive that kind of misguided philanthropy. But the microcredit delivery mechanism has to evolve into a distinct system that clearly differentiates between commercial lending and microcredit. The end goal of microfinance is improved social welfare—a very difficult thing to estimate at any point of time.

A crucial component of extending microcredit is to monitor the end use of borrowings. If the borrower uses such funds to meet medical, educational, or other social costs, it is inevitable that the system of microcredit will suffer. It is important that microcredit is not used as a conduit to shift the burden of healthcare, education, etc., that are clearly the state's responsibility, onto individuals on the plea that as 'entrepreneurs', they can pay for such services. In order that borrowers graduate from low-level incomes to higher levels and even exit from the schemes altogether, national-level programmes of healthcare, social security, education, mid-day meal schemes, and the like must be intermeshed in the system so that the poor can focus on the end use of borrowings. Further, for microcredit to truly empower poor people, the schemes must look beyond change in name to change in fortunes. For instance, 'maids with micro loans suddenly become micro entrepreneurs with their own cleaning service' (Neff 1996), but if micro loans actually imbue such people with a degree of control over their destinies, microcredit would have done its job.

Urban Poor

Urbanization is inevitable, inexorable, and a reality all over the world. But the urban poor rarely find official recognition in poverty alleviation schemes. Many a scheme targets the rural poor, and receives budgetary sanction as well, but the urban poor are often left out of this loop. In many respects, the urban poor are a more wretched lot than the rural poor, more disenfranchised because they do not form a strong enough political vote bank; arguably, their lot is worse than life in the village.

Very few agencies—government, NGOs, etc., even acknowledge the presence of the urban poor, let alone tailor programmes for them. The urban poor have no recourse but to rely on dubious networks of 'support system', including moneylenders or commercial banks at commercial rates of interest. While there is a crying need for extending microcredit to the urban poor, the scheme needs to be modified to deal with the particular circumstances of urban life. For instance, the pivotal role of peer pressure in the success of a microcredit scheme is likely to get diluted in an urban setting, with fewer societal bonds linking the borrowers. Whatever the mechanism, the urban poor are equally in need of microcredit as are the rural poor and equally in need of policy focus as a distinct group by themselves.

A promising start has been made in establishing microcredit as a viable means of lifting the poor out of poverty and there are equal numbers of success stories to counteract the naysayers. The movement certainly needs a few ground rules along with a specially designed regulatory mechanism that will help realize the latent entrepreneurial skills and accumulated savings but the regulator must take care not to crush the spontaneity of the movement. Microcredit schemes find participation mostly from women and, therefore, they are also closely linked to a woman's status in society and her empowerment, especially in times of scaling up, in the extent of control she can exercise over her enterprise and not merely as a conduit for cheap loans meant for the men of her family. However, microfinance by itself has not proven to significantly alleviate poverty and is of limited impact. Poverty

Several NGOs and donor organizations are working to correct various anomalies that have crept into the microfinance sector. CASHE (Credit and Savings for Household Enterprise), CARE's long running and successful microfinance programme has incorporated its hands-on learning back into the project:

- Community Ownership: Microfinance requires sophisticated systems to track vast numbers of loans and repayments, which the poor and often illiterate target audience is ill-equipped to handle. Hiring professional staff will only raise costs, rendering the SHG unviable. CARE works at local and state levels to provide standardized training to create Barefoot Trainees (Orissa) with a common curriculum on the key principles of SHGs and MFIs, which all groups across the state share as a knowledge base. This ensures local flavour as only locals will know their communities and how to serve them best.
- Gender and governance: The experience of NGOs is that creating women-focused SHGs alone does not lead to women's empowerment. Often, assets created through microfinance loans are held in the names of male family members who usually also take large decisions concerning usage of family funds. To tackle this, some NGOs have rigorous gender-sensitizing programmes while some have also started male SHGs to create awareness of the SHG

movement and its intricacies, among men. Some SHGs also take up the mantle of collective justice by taking up cases of domestic violence or official corruption.

- Public–Private Partnerships (PPP): Women in microfinance sometimes improve governance of communities in addition to their own livelihoods. In West Bengal, the government's Panchayati Raj department is experimenting with allowing SHGs to get contracts for government-aided projects. This will help keep the money within the community rather than an outsider contractor, besides deepening the knowledge and skill bank of the community. Hindustan Unilever Limited (HUL) is partnering with SHGs in Orissa and Andhra Pradesh for commodity marketing where the company provides the raw materials and the SHG women repackage the materials for sale and sometimes also sell the finished product.

- Grain Banks: CARE has initiated grain banks for the very poor in West Bengal and Orissa to improve food security for populations who found it difficult or impossible to meet mandatory cash savings. Grain banks allow members to save paddy during harvest season and withdraw during the lean season or in times of natural disasters. During the next harvest season, the loans of paddy are repaid with interest, typically 20–25 per cent. Such grain banks usually become sustainable through member contributions in four to five years.

is multidimensional and issues that contribute to poverty are often integrated in the lives of the poor, especially women, in very complex ways.

Despite microfinance catching on in appeal, only about 10–20 per cent of India's poor are served by any such schemes. However, the sector is growing—one estimate is at 300 per cent per annum—and mainstream banks are aggressively getting into the act. The MFI (microfinance institutions) sector is beset with many problems, inevitable in an industry with Rs 225 billion of outstanding loans and 26.7 million active borrowers. The finance ministry is still working on a bill to address several problems of the sector. The initial costs of creating and sustaining an SHG for the first two to three years are crucial for long-term survival of SHGs and NGOs. Once groups and NGOs mature and have built sufficient capacity, mainstream banks find it immensely profitable to lend to the sector.

Ratings of NGOs by mainstream rating agencies Partner NGOs working in the microfinance sector are streamlining their processes so that they qualify for a good rating from mainstream rating agencies like CRISIL (Credit Rating and Information Services of India Ltd) and M-CRIL (Micro Credit Ratings International Ltd). Microfinance is becoming an increasingly competitive sector and for microfinance institutions to function effectively, it is important that they build capacities sufficiently to be rated through such organizations. These ratings would not only help leverage funds from banks like SIDBI but also provide strong indicators to the long-term survival of the particular MFI.

OFF-SHORING

While the world was occupied with other theatres of world commerce, Indian companies were busy developing a reputation for work efficiency, information technology (IT) capability, and cost-effectiveness. The word BPO (business process outsourcing) has become synonymous with India and has even spawned idiomatic expressions like 'being Bangalored', meaning one's job has been outsourced to Bangalore, arguably the best-known location for the purpose in the initial years of the movement.

Indian companies have been in the business of process deliveries for years and have established Brand India in no uncertain terms. Brand India now stands for commitment, quality, and most importantly, credibility. Off-shoring and outsourcing in India have reached a level of maturity that makes it irresistible to a company shopping for these skills.

Outsourcing has many variants like off-shoring (outsourcing to a distant location), near-shoring (outsourcing to a nearby location), and even in-shoring (opposite of outsourcing, that is bring in a function that was previously performed outside).

The concept of outsourcing is not new and was first used by data-processing companies. Since then, outsourcing has been inextricably linked with the IT industry and in fact, most outsourcing activities do rely heavily on IT for execution and delivery but outsourcing may include both IT management and business operations. Therefore, the term BPO, suggesting a whole range of possible activities, is more descriptive of this hot new industry.

The relocation or contracting out of business processes to an outside provider is mainly to achieve increased shareholder value. An important facet of business process outsourcing is its ability to free corporate executives from some of their day-to-day process management responsibilities and duties.

Unlike in land, fragmentation of business can be quite helpful to growth. Each organic segment can grow faster, stimulating the economy and encouraging prosperity.

Business process outsourcing involves business process management and outsourcing. Business process management uses technology aimed at redesigning the process, reducing unnecessary steps, and removing redundancies. On the other hand outsourcing uses expertise and resources of dedicated outside service providers to perform many of these vital yet non-core activities. Therefore, a BPO performs both the functions at the same time, thereby speeding implementation and ensuring that the intended benefits really hit the bottom line (Brown and Wilson 2005).

There are broadly three groups of people within an organization:

- Core workers for essential and managerial tasks;
- Contract employees for non-essential work;
- Flexible workers, temporary, part-time, and occasional labour.

Companies typically employ an essential core team and, as a corollary, incur the associated structural costs. Around this core team a company will hire contracted expertise for specific time-bound projects. In addition, there will be flexible labour needed for maintenance, running a canteen, sorting the mail and cleaning the office, etc. (Handy 1989). The job of the second group of workers can be outsourced to any cost-effective yet efficient location but the third kind of jobs must necessarily be located close to the company and can only be outsourced within a limited geographical location.

Outsourcing is done either by the company's subsidiary office in another country or by a third party. A company may use a subsidiary company as a captive investment to do some portion of the work for the parent organization. This model helps in knowledge retention within the company and can better protect intellectual property rights (IPR) or business secrets. It also helps in employee mobility globally to any facility and provides speedier ramp-up time for new projects. The downside is that the company has to incur overhead costs at all its locations, including overlapping and duplication of processes.

The real benefit of outsourcing is produced when a contracted company that has no relationship with the client company other than the contract, performs the work. This model provides flexibility to the client company in future vendor or supplier selection by keeping their options open to shop for cost-effective options. It also neatly addresses the problem of employee hiring or redundancy in accordance with business needs. The resources freed up in the process of outsourcing can be used more effectively in improving core processes within the company. A BPO offers a way of achieving transformational outcomes much more quickly and effectively than contracting out only non-core and non-essential work.

The BPO industry is maturing and fast mutating to provide effective business solutions that go beyond saving time and money. The first-generation outsourcing offered low-cost solutions to simple, non-essential work. Today, the BPO industry can offer complex, mission-critical, and strategic applications, while still being cost-efficient. In the process, the wave is creating specialist outsourcing firms, totally focused on particular business processes and serving more than one client organization.

What Can India Offer?

- Numbers: The BPO industry is labour-intensive and India is home to a large and skilled workforce. At last our mammoth population seems to be our biggest advantage. The sheer number of students emerging from the country's education system, most of them equipped with basic skills for a new-age economy, makes India a destination that is hard to beat. With an estimated two million graduates and 0.3 million postgraduates entering the labour market each year, there is almost a constant supply of human talent. The numbers are set to increase as more social classes achieve upward mobility both as a result of natural progression and active government incentives.

- Cost-effectiveness: Indian salaries are typically 25–30 per cent lower than European or American salaries, mostly without compromising on quality. This factor is expected to last for some more time before the society matures and prices rise accordingly. Even so, the increasing influx of people into the middle class will ensure that the price band of services remains competitive for a long time
- Power: The domestic power situation may be pretty dismal but commercial enterprises, particularly those situated in dedicated technology parks—and there are many of those—are usually assured of uninterrupted power supply. Government insistence on private power backup and generator systems has had its share of criticism but at last there seems to be a positive fallout. Foreign client firms factor in a steady supply of electricity in its due diligence before awarding a contract. Large company campuses rarely depend on state-supplied power and generate their own electricity. Increasing business usually offsets the cost of such installations.
- Democracy and its institutions: Our rambunctious form of democracy seems more chaos than a chosen form of governance to the outsider. The fact is that India has been a successful democracy for most of its young life as a nation and the fear of a takeover by anarchists, which is a major fear while investing overseas, is not justified by ground realities. No one will deny that the country's delivery mechanisms like the state of our redressal system or capital markets or role of regulators need improvements; however, these mechanisms do exist and only need to be strengthened.
- Telecommunications: Most outsourced work depends heavily on telecommunications either for execution or delivery or both. Since liberalization and opening up of the telecom sector to private players, there has been a quantum leap in available bandwidth. Telecom penetration is on the rise, allowing more locations to be exploited for setting up business. The cost of telecom services is falling by the day and while this makes telecom companies sweat, it is excellent news for users.

Is This Industry Sustainable?

Most global companies are committed to the idea of off-shoring on purely commercial conditions. Suddenly, the whole world is a marketplace for talent and it is a rare company that carries out all its operations or processes in-house.

Peter F. Drucker in 1996 said about outsourcing:

> I met with a very big company not long ago—around 80 or so on the Fortune 500 list. They expect to be Number 5 on that list in ten years, and I shocked them by saying I don't think that list will exist, so the goal is meaningless. That list basically assumes that everything you do is under your roof and owned by you and run by you. But already in many companies, most work is done through alliances, joint ventures, minority participation, and very informal agreements which no lawyer could possibly handle. (qtd in Kobayashi-Hillary 2004: 175)

Today this statement sounds like reading contemporary news.

Organizations today resemble the team in the Hollywood movie *Ocean's Eleven* (2001), where people with different skill sets get together for a (perilous) task and when that task is complete, disband and each goes his own way, or get together for another job—as in *Ocean's Twelve* (2004)—where they build upon a few deep relationships constructed during the previous jobs. That outsourcing is the most replicated business model is a settled question. What is unclear is the players who will dominate this field.

At the moment India appears to be riding the wave but there are enough countries with similar advantages that can overtake the 'Great Indian Advantage'. As more and more countries join the queue for a share of the outsourcing pie, India may find itself priced out of the market by equally qualified populace in other countries. That is, while we are deeply focused on surviving the global outsourcing/off-shoring industry, it may well be that India becomes so wealthy that it cannot offer a cost advantage. Unbelievable, but not improbable, if we look around the globe and see the growth trajectories of countries like Japan, Taiwan, Singapore—and now, increasingly, China—in the manufacturing sector.

India cannot win this battle on the *cost factor* alone. It is an established economic fact that if you can do a job at a certain price, sooner or later, another person can deliver the same job at a lower price. India already has an edge in the off-shoring industry and by relentlessly focusing on quality and establishing high levels of delivery quality this industry can easily put itself beyond competition.

Most outsourcing contracts dictate that knowledge created within a service provider's organization (SPO) becomes the intellectual property of the client company. This knowledge, however, translates into experience for the SPO, which can be translated into services to different clients or to create scalable improvements, without violating the terms of the contract. There is a gradual build-up of knowledge in multiple layers, some of which can be spun off into new entities.

An example of such an organic SPO is Spectramind. The founder, Raman Roy, was working with GE Capital and handling the company's remote processing centre (RPC), which was an in-house unit. Roy spotted a business opportunity for similar services outside the company that the centre could not accommodate, being a captive unit of the company. Thus, Spectramind was born and later sold to the software giant Wipro. Today, Wipro Spectramind is one of India's leading BPO companies.

This layered nature of knowledge acquisition is the key to moving up the value chain—and herein is the escape route from being mere digital coolies to the world. Jobs that are handled well become systematized into entrenched processes and resources can be released to focus on higher-value tasks.

The focus on quality, however, has to find rapid backward integration into India's education system. For, what is the use of producing millions of engineers and other graduates if, to quote Infosys chief mentor N.R. Narayana Murthy, 'Seventy-five per cent of Indian engineering graduates are unemployable?'

The hunger of the offshore industry boom has to immediately ratchet up the quality of education and training imparted by numerous Indian institutes. The biggest threat today is from countries like China, Philippines, and Mexico. All these countries have large populations, hungry for success and promise to deliver on quality just as well as India. India can pride itself on having a lead in infrastructure, experience, and the largest English-speaking population, but others can rapidly pare down this advantage. For instance, Mexico has a large Spanish-speaking population—and Spanish is spoken in at least 24 countries. Proactive intervention in education by the government may look at teaching more languages in schools to help retain India's edge. This may achieve more to ensure social parity by expanding the scope of employment than perhaps reserving seats in educational institutes.

Training is a critical cost component of the BPO industry. If our education system is retooled and geared up to absorb substantial portions of these costs, we would have a situation where graduates step into the workforce ready to start delivering with minimum resources being spent on additional training. This will reduce investments of companies and help them be more competitive.

Increasingly, immigration laws are getting tight all over the world. Countries like the US, UK, and other western European will continue to employ a few 'cream of the crop' from countries like India, but hardly with a guarantee of permanence. Such countries have strong pressures of unemployment in their own populations and cannot afford to give state benefits to large numbers of new citizens. It is no wonder that governments the world over tacitly support the outsourcing industry as it falls in line with immigration policy because off-shoring necessarily means location of personnel outside the geographical boundaries of the client company with the added benefit of cost advantage. This cost advantage coupled with reduced outlay on public services like health, education, etc., is expected to offset any loss of tax revenues from citizen-employees.

Therefore, the options of migration to developed countries that were available even a decade and a half ago to Indians are rapidly shrinking. The phenomenon of off-shoring has created an immense pressure that attracts jobs to certain locations; presently, India is that destination.

India has a huge stake in this industry to raise the standard of living of its citizens.

DIGITAL DIVIDE

Today, India competes for a share of the global outsourcing pie largely on the cost factor. But what if labour and transport costs, two crucial factors of production that are now cheap, were to become expensive— transport costs through increased prices of oil, and labour through improved wages? Would the competitive edge of India (and China) disappear? Would the production and service capabilities of these countries then disappear? (A few years ago, Bangalore offered coders at USD 2 an hour. In 2006, companies like Wipro and Infosys have moved up the value chain with services like consulting, integration, and architecture, although these still account for less than 5 per cent of their revenues. Coders now command a price of about USD 25 an hour, which is still very cheap by global standards.)

That seems unlikely. Such a situation will call for a restructuring of resources on a national or even regional level. Increased wages in a country will mean increase in purchasing power, which can exert a pull on demand for goods and services. Infrastructure created within the country for catering to an export market can be turned around to deliver results for a growing domestic market, sparking a rising chain of demand and supply.

Moving beyond being digital coolies, consumption of new capabilities within the country will accelerate growth but at the same time may deepen class divides.

India as a 'Poor Country' or India as a Country with Many 'Poor People'?

The IT and IT-enabled industries are, without question, responsible for ushering in unprecedented and *broad-based* levels of prosperity. However, these could just as well become 'enclave' industries, benefiting foreign companies and the rest of the world, with only a marginal or indirect impact upon India itself. This could repeat a historical pattern of some 1,500 years ago that benefited the whole world but bypassed India itself when Indian mathematicians created the decimal system. They and many astronomers then emigrated to Baghdad, the 'Silicon Valley' of that era; their ideas eventually passed from the Arab world to the West, where the decimal system replaced the Roman numerals (Mukherji 2000; qtd in Cohen 2005: 105).

Prosperity is always relative and part of the perception problem is that measurement matrices of poverty (as indeed many other indices) are largely rooted in an Anglo-Saxon or a 'Western' notion of how much is enough.

Standard of living is a highly localized thing based on the immediate environment, and what may be considered poverty in, say, southern California may be a decent standard of living in sub-Saharan Africa or, indeed, in parts of India. That said, information and communication technologies have the power not only to transform lives but are equally capable of deepening the gulf between the haves and have-nots, aptly described as the 'digital divide'.

The digital divide is the gap between those with regular, effective access to digital technologies and those without. It is closely linked to social inclusion and economic advantage. The digital divide is not a clear, single gap that divides a society or community into two groups but more like a layered phenomenon and can take such forms as lower-performance computers, lower-quality or high-priced connections, barriers of access to community-owned resources, including gender barriers, lack of locally relevant content delivered in a local language, or even difficulty in obtaining technical assistance. There are many kinds of digital divide affecting the world today so that it is common to find people talk about a 'continuum of digital divides' rather than a single divide.

Bridging the Digital Divide

It is crucial to bridge this divide in the prevailing economic situation of the country where the share of services in the total gross domestic product (GDP) of the country is steadily increasing. Increasingly, education, jobs, and even economic prosperity are directly related to the Internet, and when some sections of the society are unable to access technology and develop computer-based skills, an entire generation of young people may not be able to realize their potential or contribute fully to society.

Equally, what matters is how technology touches peoples' lives. Unless the much-touted Indian brainpower is yoked to proverbially drawing water from the village well, we may well end up with yet more divisions in society.

Bridging the digital divide, then, is all about bringing up the rear along with the galloping horse. In other words, convert the 'digital divide' into 'digital dividends' (Goh Chok Tong; qtd in Legard 2001). There are several initiatives undertaken in the country, by the government, by NGOs, by corporations and through public–private partnerships (PPP) to try and reduce this divide.

It is important for such initiatives, most of which are started as pilot projects, to scale up their reach and operations. Most projects tend to flounder after the initial success largely because there is a lack of commercial focus and broad objectives. Successful but unviable experiments do not always translate into workable models to become widespread bridges of the divide. Economic viability is essential because the initiatives cannot be sustained on subsidies.

The target audience must be able to perceive a clear value proposition as against general do-gooding. It is well established that even disadvantaged groups are willing to pay for value-added services that also empower such communities. Sustainability of projects is essential for real-time value-add.

Some of these initiatives are presented below—most of them have been in operation for a period of time and have withstood the test of time and commerce fairly well.

ITC's e-choupal

E-choupal is an Internet-based intervention in rural India launched by ITC's International Business Division in the year 2000. *Choupal* is a Hindi word that means a 'village gathering place'.

The Indian farmer is trapped in an endless cycle of dependence—on the vagaries of weather, unscrupulous middlemen, lack of knowledge of better farming techniques, variations between different agro-climatic zones, and, of course, fragmented holdings. These constitute severe challenges to improving the productivity of land and quality of crops, resulting in inconsistent quality and uncompetitive prices. The large number of intermediaries or middlemen also makes agriculture produce overpriced and uncompetitive. The agriculture commodity market in India is based on the village *mandi* (market) system, where the farmer or middleman would bring the produce to the mandi to be sold.

The e-choupal system works by eliminating costs in the supply chain that do not add value. It is a supply-chain management system, reaching up to the producer. It combines a web portal in the local language and PCs with Internet access placed in villages to create a two-way channel between the company, ITC, and the villages. This network provides farmers with market intelligence on prevailing prices in the local and even international markets and also with information on best practices in farming their land holdings. With the e-choupal initiative, the company aims to mitigate two of the big difficulties faced by the rural economy: virtual aggregation of produce at the local or village level disguises the tiny size of most landholdings in the country and better information helps overcome uncertainty by enabling informed risk-taking.

A crucial component of the success of this mission was not to equate eliminating costs in the supply chain with eliminating middlemen. ITC redefined the role of the middlemen by de-linking information flows from physical flows in the supply chain such as logistics and collecting pricing data from local auctions and maintaining records. What is no longer in the domain of erstwhile middlemen is the hold over information. Besides providing the farmer with advice on best farm practices, e-choupal projects itself as a dependable source for critical farm inputs like up-to-the-minute prices, weather forecasts, seed and fertilizer information, and facilitates instant sales.

The farmer needs only to carry a sample of his produce to the kiosk and will receive a spot quote from the *sanchalak* (meaning coordinator, as the erstwhile intermediaries have been renamed), the company's representative farmer who acts as the interface between the computer terminal and farmers. If the farmer accepts the quote, he can drive the produce directly to ITC's collection centre and expect to get paid with the minimum delay. All costs—such as those paid to the sanchalak for services rendered—are open and negotiable, subject to genuine market dynamics. This empowers the farmer with critical information to know where to get the best price besides helping tune his cropping pattern in accordance with market needs.

The company wins by purchasing high-quality, cost-effective farm output, which helps make their end product more cost-competitive. By eliminating unnecessary costs, the company could benefit from lower net procurement, despite offering better prices to the farmer. It also strengthens its relationship with the rural community, winning their abiding trust. Better prices to farmers means more rural purchasing power, which boosts demand for all goods and services, including, of course, the company's.

ITC establishes e-choupals where it is already buying agriculture produce and locations are chosen from 87 per cent of India's 6,00,000 villages with under 5,000 inhabitants (but typically over 1,000) and which are fairly accessible.

E-choupal has several distinct strands which deal with the unique challenges faced by each sector:

- Soya choupal: This is the first e-choupal started by the company to deal with purchasing the soybean crop and forms the building block of the whole initiative. Within a short while of starting the initiative, ITC reduced the cost of procurement to Rs 200 a ton from Rs 700 a ton (Assisi and Gupta 2003: 25);
- Aqua-choupal: This serves the billion dollar shrimp business by providing the aqua farmer with support and knowhow to cope with and manage specific risks and also to keep abreast of food safety norms to compete in international markets;
- Coffee-growing business: Although this sector is well established and enjoys adequate infrastructure facilities, it is at the mercy of fluctuating international prices. The dedicated e-choupal provides an electronic marketplace to help with real-time information on world prices;
- Wheat-choupal: This essentially replicates the model of soya choupal and tries to ensure that information on best farm practices and market intelligence of produce prices and availability of quality seeds and fertilizers helps the farmer to progressively improve the quality of produce. The wheat market is far bigger than the soybean market and any savings in the entire chain translates into a win-win situation on a large scale for all components.

ITC hopes to scale up the e-choupal into a one-stop shop for all the farmer's needs—an e-commerce hub for the village. This may be achieved, for instance by allowing other companies or agencies to use its e-choupal distribution and procurement network for a fee, like state governments wanting to put their services online, consumer goods firms with weak rural distribution networks, microcredit providers who want to profile the creditworthiness of potential borrowers, etc. The company hopes to expand into wider e-commerce by re-engineering the supply chain in respect of commodity procurement for other FMCG (fast moving consumer goods) companies. An integrated and information-empowered rural network will allow all such companies to reduce internal costs.

In order to scale up its operations and leverage this relationship with the rural folk, the company has ventured into rural malls, under the banner of 'Choupal Sagar'. ITC reckoned that when farmers come to the warehouse with their produce and get paid promptly, they have cash in their pockets and an empty vehicle. It simply combined the two ideas and developed rural malls, usually located close to its warehouses. It seeks to monetize the footfalls to warehouses by offering a huge range of products for rural consumption from toothpaste, hair oils, televisions, tractors, farm inputs, etc. Most FMCG companies service areas with populations of 1,00,000 and above, leaving large rural areas underserved. Choupal Sagar combines the company's formidable distribution network with knowledge of local needs to reap collateral benefits.

In another attempt at linear and vertical linkage, the company plans to locate banks, insurance offices, even learning and training centres, so as to ensure continued footfalls even in non-harvest seasons.

The project started in June 2000 in Madhya Pradesh with a pilot of six choupals and by 2008, it had scaled up to over 6,500 choupals across ten states, covering 40,000 villages, and reaching nearly 4 million e-farmers. The company has a grand agenda for the year 2010 by which time it hopes to cover fifteen states with 20,000 e-choupal kiosks covering 1,00,000 villages and reaching out to 10 million e-farmers (from information obtained in discussions with senior ITC officials).

But if this reads like a success story, it was not without many hiccups along the way. A typical Indian village has no or minimal reliable power, telecom connectivity, and poor literacy—hardly an encouraging set of conditions for e-business to flourish. Some of these are:

- Erratic power supply: This was resolved with specially designed hardware which includes a desktop computer with power backup through batteries charged with solar panels;
- Limited bandwidth: ITC initially bore part of the costs of 175 local telephone exchanges to upgrade their equipment to support data transmission. The company also uses a VSAT (very small aperture terminal) connection to supplement telephone connectivity;
- Poor literacy and steep learning curve: ITC recruited farmers at each site to become the human interface between other illiterate villagers and the company. The emphasis was on developing hands-on, working knowledge of the system rather than dull, classroom

teaching of subjects with which rural folk may not connect. Also, it helped to instil a sense of ownership and involvement in the project among the villagers—a kind of social contract that always has more binding value;

• Lack of resources for investing in the system: Each e-choupal costs about Rs 0.13 million and is expected to pay back for itself in four to five years. The important thing is that farmers have accepted the value-add that the system provides and are willing to pay for use of the facility.

A country like India where about 85 per cent of the population lives in villages and draws sustenance directly or indirectly from land needs many such initiatives on a multiplier basis to uplift the rural economy. Although the share of services in GDP is rapidly growing, the underpinning of the economy will foremost be agriculture, both for direct consumption and as an input for industry for a long time.

Bhoomi—Liberating Land Records

The revenue department of the Government of Karnataka in 1999 conceived of a project to provide transparency to land records and bring governance closer to people. Land records enable the state to collect land revenue on the basis of land tenure and also provide data like soil type, irrigation details, tree cover, number and kind of crops cultivated, etc., which are important for planning and advising on a macro level.

The prevailing centuries-old system, which 'Bhoomi' sought to displace, consisted of manual, handwritten records that were maintained by village accountants, many of who were corrupt. Villagers, especially small and marginal farmers, lived in fear of losing their land to someone better placed to pay the necessary bribe to the village accountant who could—and often did—change the name on the deed at will. Records were maintained in a decentralized manner, which made the job of collecting and coalescing data for centralized planning difficult and often inaccurate.

Bhoomi was launched in March 2002 and has since covered 30,000 villages in the state of Karnataka. It has impacted 20 million land records of some 6.7 million landowners. It is a fairly simple project, not requiring very high technology especially since it does not need real-time transactions. Each kiosk runs on a PC and adequate security. Land records, with details of ownership, soil quality, irrigation, cropping patterns, etc. (on an average, at least 45 kinds of details are mentioned for each piece of land), are put on a centralized database with computer terminals at several *taluk* offices. A farmer can walk up to the nearest taluk office and ask for a computer printout of his land record certificate on payment of a small fee (average of Rs 15 per transaction). S/he can also check details of land records on a touch-screen kiosk by inserting a coin (usually Rs 2). Before Bhoomi, the official fee for procuring a land record was only Rs 2 (which rarely reached the department); however, a farmer typically paid Rs 500 to Rs 600 to finally get the village accountant to provide the record. Land is often used as collateral by farmers to raise bank loans and credit lines and with this transparent land record delivery system, time taken to process loans can be significantly reduced.

The whole system envisaged by Bhoomi is very simple in design and execution—and a small matter of administrative reform using information and communication technology (ICT) has positively impacted the daily life of some 70,00,000 villagers. Bhoomi now has a coverage in 177 talukas. Since 2006, by paying as little as Rs 15 per transaction, citizens contribute approximately Rs 250–300 million every year as revenue to the Bhoomi project (Chawla and Bhatnagar 2004). The system has a small but significant safeguard built into it— something akin to FIFO (first in first out) system of accounting of stores. For example, if there are four applicants for say, mutation of property waiting, and a fifth applicant comes along and pays a bribe for speeding up work, the system would only work if the previous applications are disposed off. This, in effect means that an application cannot be left hanging indefinitely for refusing to pay a bribe. Parallelly, once information goes down the line that work can be done for some without having to pay bribes, it reduces the necessity in the population to pay 'speed money' and contribute to a system of bad governance.

The success rate of the project is so good that the central government has adopted the Bhoomi model across all states of India for digitizing land records.

Of course, no project is without its critics and in Bhoomi, the criticism is focused on the use of proprietary software (Microsoft

Windows) as against an open source software (OSS). Besides allegations of collusion and misuse of public funds in using particular software, detractors claim that proprietary software is more opaque and that all citizen-centred services must be in open source, making it possible for the citizen to do a software audit.

Drishtee—A For-Profit Rural Kiosk Venture

Drishtee is a rural network for delivering services and related information to the village community through an ICT centre called 'Drishtee Soochanalayas' or information kiosks. Entrepreneurs selected from the village run these kiosks on a service-delivery-based revenue model (www.drishtee.org).

Rural kiosks are somewhat like Internet cafes for villagers with one or more connected personal computers available for shared use by village residents. Rural kiosks offer a range of user-charge-based services, mostly customized to local conditions and often in the local language rather than plain Internet access and standard applications offered by urban cafes. The software is simple and menu driven, not requiring too many typing skills and usually in Hindi or other local language. A kiosk typically contains computer(s), modem, printer, and UPS, and is wired through an Internet network, besides furniture and stationery. The villager-owner/operator owns the kiosk with either his/her own funds or borrowed funds.

Economic viability is essential in any initiative seeking to bridge the digital divide; these initiatives are not sustainable on a subsidy model for a long period of time. The Drishtee model seeks to create local entrepreneurs, who in turn will produce a new IT-literate generation in some of the most disadvantaged sections of the country. The emphasis is on 'owning' the project and generating independent revenue while contributing to strengthening the intranet network so that more services can be added and the whole project scaled up.

Local content development is as important as providing IT literacy, for what is the use of net connectivity and ability to surf the Web if searches do not throw up relevant information to the user.

The project, in turn, relies on a global network of service providers and business partners. This helps to fine-tune various modules within the platform and also attracts other businesses to partner the project.

Drishtee's original focus was on providing e-governance services to rural village—'…to cause a shift in the government's delivery apparatus … serve the villagers directly rather than through civil services' (from the official website, drishtee.org)

Therefore, it has digitized a number of government services (like birth certificates, vehicle licensing, etc.) in the regions where it operates. This communication backbone is supplemented by a string of services like land records, mailing software, virtual marketplaces, matrimonial alliances, online grievance postings, and other such customized services. While other applications have their use, most kiosk owners report that computer education is a major source of revenue, indicating that even the most disadvantaged groups are willing to pay for services which show a real-time value addition.

The initiative was started in 1999 as The Gyandoot Project in Dhar, Madhya Pradesh and since then, Drishtee has set up ninety kiosks in five different states in India, mostly in the northern and eastern regions. However, sustainability of the project remains an issue. In a survey of these rural kiosks, it was found that the average monthly income at kiosks remains low, at approximately Rs 2,000 per month, well below the target break-even income desired by the project at Rs 3,000–5,000, depending on the terms of the loan (Toyama et al., 2005).

Infrastructure is still a major constraint, particularly erratic power supply and limited bandwidth. Innovations like a hybrid system of wired and wireless network with standard fixed-line telephones at one end and high-technology Wi-Fi system at the other end, or a combination of solar and other alternative energies, despite the feel-good factor about them, distract attention from the core issue of very poor rural infrastructure of basic utilities—attention that can be better focused on issues of business improvement.

C-DAC—Centre for Development of Advance Computing

C-DAC is a research and development institution set up by the Ministry of Communication and Information and Technology, Government of India in 1989. It had an original mandate to design and produce supercomputer systems based on parallel-processing technology as a government reaction sparked by the refusal of the US to sell the Crazy supercomputer to India in 1988. C-DAC has since brought out several generations of PARAM supercomputers with increasingly advanced technologies and computing power. Some of these machines are also in use in other countries like Russia, Singapore, Canada, and Germany.

Its mandate has since expanded to include design, development and deployment of advanced IT-based solutions. A major area of engagement is training—C-DAC's Advanced Computing Training School (ACTS) is dedicated to creating high-quality manpower for C-DAC in particular and the IT industry in general through designing and delivering various courses. The courses are offered through a network of 100 plus Authorized Training Centres (ATCs) in India, besides the C-DAC's own centres in Pune, Delhi, Hyderabad, and Bangalore.

C-DAC is a market leader in India in its language technology mission to create a framework for support to various Indian languages with diverse scripts on standard computers, including software and hardware products. This language support initiative aims to allow application providers to build applications in local languages, thereby extending computing to the masses and helping to bridge the digital divide. A major constraint in popularizing existing solutions in India is that keyboards designed for the English language alphabet must be adapted, with special software, so that their keys can produce Indian texts. This software constructs Indian language characters out of smaller pieces known as glyphs. To complicate matters, researchers working on this issue in India constructed their own sets of glyphs or character pieces. This often meant that text composed on one computer could not be read on another loaded with rival software. This is a great handicap since it is the ability of computers to talk to one another that makes them such powerful tools.

C-DAC has worked towards standardizing many protocols— in 1991, the Bureau of Indian Standards (BIS) adopted the Indian Standard Code for Information Interchange (ISCII). All Gist products are based on ISCII; several companies are developing products and solutions based on this representation, for instance, IBM for PC-DOS, Apple for ILK, etc. This is also mandatory for the data collected by organizations like The Election Commission, and for projects as Land Records Project, etc.

C-DAC has developed a character-slice (glyph) coding standard for fonts, ISFOC (intelligence-based script font code), to ensure good appearance and aesthetics for which Indian scripts are famous. Unlike ISCII, these code charts are different for each script and are represented in 8 bits only. The ISFOC standards are popular with users and vendors for compatibility and wide acceptance.

Linux systems Linux is an operating system that was initially created as a hobby by a young student, Linus Torvalds, at the University of Helsinki in Finland. Linus had an interest in Minix, a small Unix system, and decided to develop a system that exceeded the Minix standards. He began his work in 1991 when he released version 0.02 and worked steadily until 1994 when Version 1.0 of the Linux kernel was released. The kernel, at the heart of all Linux systems, is developed and released under the GNU General Public License and its source code is freely available to everyone. It is this kernel that forms the base around which a Linux operating system is developed. There are now literally hundreds of companies and organizations and an equal number of individuals that have released their own versions of operating systems based on the Linux kernel. Apart from the fact that it is freely distributed, Linux's functionality, adaptability and robustness, has made it the main alternative for proprietary Unix and Microsoft operating systems (www.linux.org).

The idea behind open-source software is rather simple: when programmers can read, distribute, and change code, the code will mature. People can adapt it, fix it, debug it, and they can do it at a speed that dwarfs the performance of software developers at conventional companies. This software will be more flexible and of a better quality than software that has been developed using the conventional channels, because more people have tested it in more different conditions than the closed software developer ever can.

More than a decade after its initial release, Linux is being adopted worldwide primarily as a server platform. Its use as a home and office desktop operating system is also on the rise. The operating system can also be incorporated directly into microchips in a process called 'embedding' and is increasingly being used this way in appliances and devices. Some of the reasons for increased adoption the world over are low cost, flexibility, security, and control. Japan, Munich in Germany, Brazil, and now China, are pioneering its use in various sectors ranging from consumer electronics to computer hardware, education and governance. Several computer companies like HP, IBM, Sun Microsystems, Novell, etc., have adopted Linux and are dedicated to its development.

Though Indian software brainpower provides solutions to most leading global IT companies, most people in India cannot afford to buy the expensive licensed software (or hardware). This leads to cheap assembled PCs (which may not be a bad thing) and pirated software—something that does not sit well with India's aspiration to be a knowledge powerhouse. The answer perhaps lies in the open-source Linux. Most technical education in India is built around the concept of Unix, which is what Linux embodies, and so, most graduates are well trained in that platform. Official adoption of 'open-source software' policy by the government will help project implementation with minimal upload time in terms of training. 'Official' endorsement of an open-source regime has come from no less a person than the former President of India, A.P.J. Abdul Kalam, both as an empowerment tool as well as to offset growing capital expenditure on computer systems (*Times of India* 2003). Several state governments in India have adopted the free/libre and open-source software (FLOSS) as the platform for education, e-governance, and other projects. Kerala, in August 2006 decided that 12,500 schools across the state will migrate to Linux over a period of three years (Varma 2006). Kerala state government has approved by law the setting up of The International Centre for Free and Open Source Software (IC-FOSS) with the vision to become a leading research organization in free and open source model of knowledge development (www.itmission.kerala.gov.in). Open-source software relies on an army of volunteer software writers and its success depends on this community who are passionate about free software and who, in many cases, view Microsoft as 'the enemy'. Open source is not a business model as much as a social movement, akin to club membership or community meetings.

IBM is perhaps the world's largest corporate supporter of Linux. The IBM Linux Technology Centre (LTC) is a worldwide development team composed of IBM engineers who work externally as peers within a variety of open-source development communities as well as internally with every brand and team in IBM. Its goal is to utilize IBM's world-class programming resources to actively accelerate the growth of Linux as an enterprise operating system while simultaneously helping IBM brands exploit Linux for market growth. The LTC works closely with industry teams (such as the Open Source Development Labs [OSDL] workgroups) to help accelerate the expansion of Linux into usage scenarios such as telecommunications, the data centre, the desktop, the embedded space, and anywhere else that the world's most modular and flexible operating system can go (www-1.ibm.com).

India is likely to face a severe shortage of trained and skilled manpower to sustain its IT and IT-related prosperity. Various agencies are trying to bridge this deficit in different ways. West Bengal, one of the states that derives a lot of revenue from IT industries, decided to strengthen the technical skills of middle school and high school students and partnered with IBM. Starting in 2005, IBM Learning Solutions has provided the necessary IT infrastructure, education services, IT support, and project management for 400 schools. IBM will equip each school with ten computers and the schools expect to train more than 1,50,000 students in three years. IBM also selects, trains, certifies, and deploys instructors at every school. Based on a USD 75 monthly fee that each student pays, the programme is expected to be self-sustaining. IBM provides the schools with IBM PCs and IBM Intel processor-based servers running Linux. Linux was a natural choice for the project because it is an open-source software and the Linux platform can 'open up the open-source world to new, budding talent from India' (www-1.ibm.com).

These are only some examples of people who are proactively taking charge of their destinies rather than wait for the state's largesse to reach them. When large numbers of people succeed in achieving even a part of their ambitions, the energy and vitality that this brings to the community is far more than the sum of the small bits. After a long time the common Indian citizen has started to believe that s/he can actually control her/his destiny through personal effort and not be entangled in *kismet* (preordained destiny) or be resigned to fate. This perhaps is the single biggest advantage with which today's youth faces the world, confident that s/he can work towards changing the course of life.

Often the state of the business of a country is a barometer of the changing times and indicative of how well its people are adapting to change. In India, even as policymakers sometimes struggle to understand and deal with global shifts and technological changes that have profoundly altered geopolitical equations, economic participants have adapted faster and are usually much ahead of the curve.

The traditional face of Indian business has changed dramatically in the last few years; tradition and modernity are not distinct compartments among Indian businessmen but work in tandem with each other and also help society with stability in the face of massive social, cultural, and economic change. Modern business methods and advancement in technology have opened the doors to rethink the way to organize business and adapt to a 'new way' of doing business. In the 'new way' or 'new traditional economy', there is an effort to re-examine traditional thinking, disengage from the existing socio-cultural framework, and re-embed a modern economy within the same framework by adopting modern methods and technology. Today, the greatest divide between the 'old' and 'new' economy is in accepting, adopting, and making modern technology more and more accessible. Increasingly, the gulf between village and urban life is getting bridged by integrating rural India into the broader economy, whether due to mutually sustaining market systems, tapping into vast rural human resources, or expanding the theatres of commerce.

There is a strong sense of tradition tied to business dealings in India; at the same time Indian businessmen have historically adapted very well to changing circumstances, usually to their advantage, through interaction of ideas, philosophies, and practices that are exchanged and adapted to local conditions. In the context of the Indian economy, there is a collective sense of the possible in sustaining a growth rate momentum of over 8 per cent p.a. in the coming years.

8

The Indian Story in Modern Times

It is now accepted economic wisdom that the global centre of economic gravity is already moving to large emerging economies such as China and India. The Indian economy is set to grow to 90 per cent of the size of the US by 2050 and the real economic growth would average around 8.5 per cent annually (China: 6.8 per cent, Vietnam: 9.8 per cent) (Hawksworth and Cookson 2008). Goldman Sachs Economic Research says that India's high growth rate since 2003 represents a structural increase rather than simply a cyclical upturn and projects India's potential or sustainable growth rate at about 8 per cent till 2020 (Poddar and Yi 2007).

These projections of a sustainable India Dream are, of course, premised on continuity of business-friendly and growth-friendly policies. Productivity gains in an economy is a cumulative process— higher productivity leads to greater economic and policy confidence and accelerated policy reforms towards a market economy which further produces growth. The Goldman Sachs report further says, 'In particular, policies to enhance Financial sector growth, Openness to trade, Rural-urban migration, Capital formation, Education and environment, which we call the "FORCE" factors will be critical to sustaining growth' (Poddar and Yi 2007). Historically, India has been one of the world's largest economies, in 1770 contributing more than

20 per cent of world output. After two hundred years of colonial rule and relative economic stagnation, India's share of the world economy had fallen to 3 per cent, the lowest in recorded history. Subsequent Indian state policies further dragged the country into a low-performing economy with the annual rate of growth hovering around 5 per cent p.a. Only over the past one and a half decades has the Indian economy moved forward on a growth trajectory and looks set to regain its lost glory in world trade. Since India is starting from a relatively small base, the potential for growth in most sectors is immense, particularly infrastructure and traditional manufacturing. Here, we look at a few sectors that are or can become powerful growth drivers to sustain the economy while providing employment to tens of thousands as they migrate towards a better lifestyle.

INFORMATION TECHNOLOGY AND INFORMATION TECHNOLOGY ENABLED SERVICES (IT–ITES) SECTOR

If there is one industry or sector that can take credit for putting India in global business consciousness, it is the software and its corollary industries.

The Indian economy's 'poster boy' sector has its origins in rather humble manpower supply to Western countries, notably the US in the 1990s. From then to now has been a success story that is nothing short of spectacular; the information technology (IT) sector accounts for 6.1 per cent of gross domestic product (GDP) in 2010, up from 1.2 per cent even a decade ago (NASSCOM 2010). It is one of the sectors in which India has managed to move up the value chain from merely supplying material (manpower) to more value-added services. Companies have seized opportunities and converted them at a faster pace than in other industries. For instance, after IBM's departure from India in the 1980s (because of changed government policies) for a long time there was no single viable computer of any reckoning in India. This forced users to import a wide variety of models and various technologies from manufacturers all over the world. Indian coders and programmers thus learned to work on a variety of platforms, which proved helpful in acquiring contracts for the maintenance of legacy systems. Also, manufacturers relied heavily on Unix (the first portable, machine-independent, multi-user operating system) even as the rest of the world was developing proprietary software at that time. By the 1990s, when Unix became the system of choice for personal computers and workstations, India's programmers had a skill that was extremely scarce elsewhere in the world (Saxanian 2002: 176).

The annual software export has seen a steep rise from USD 24 million in 1985 to USD 164 million in 1992 to USD 7.8 billion in 2002. The annual NASSCOM (IT–ITES industry chamber of commerce) survey has clocked export revenues of USD 31.4 billion in the financial year 2006–7 (up from USD 23.6 billion in 2005–6) and USD 47.3 billion in 2010. This does not include revenue from companies whose headquarters are located outside India and who have not provided India-centric revenue figures. The rapid rise of the information technology sector over the last few years has been a dream story so far.

The interesting thing about the IT business is that not only can it produce value as a standalone product but can be used in just about any industry to improve its efficiency. Moreover, IT is a very powerful engine that not only sustains a growing IT and its sibling industry, information technology enabled services (ITES), but pulls along other industries by sparking changes in several business processes to make them more efficient and streamlined. There are strong complementarities between the IT sector and the rest of the economy because of the all-pervasive nature of IT benefits. For example, use of IT in automating railway ticket reservation has brought in much-needed transparency and made train travel less tedious. Besides, it has released resources within the Railways and rationalized several processes, including freight rates, manpower productivity, and passenger amenities. Likewise, computerizing land records has delivered real-time gains to both users and the government besides putting IT to work for the common man.

A CRISIL–NASSCOM study has found another way in which IT boosts the economy. It says that the high growth of the IT industry has had a sizeable multiplier effect on employment and output in the 'larger' economy—every rupee spent by the IT–ITES sector translates into a total output of Rs 2 for the economy. Apart from the backward linkages with sectors that feed into IT–ITES, the study found that consumption spending by IT–ITES employees has a multiplier effect on the economy. For every job created in the sector, four are created in the rest of the economy in areas like housing, transport, hospitality, and entertainment. The interesting aspect is that these additional jobs absorb people with little higher education, indication that the benefits of a booming economy do reach less privileged Indians and in many more numbers than previously thought (*Indian Express* 2007b). Clearly, the sector did some things that were in sync with what the world was doing and Azim Premji of Wipro, one of India's leading IT companies, articulates this (McCormick 2006):

- Get certified—(Indian companies) invested very early in obtaining leading-edge quality stamps, like ISO and Six Sigma, that attested to the fact that these unknown Indian companies met the West's highest standards;
- Go slow—the industry did not get overambitious. Instead of over-reacting, everyone quietly focused on delivering goods as promised and building up more reference customers—successful work for Motorola leading to work for Intel, leading to work for Sun Microsystems, and so on;
- Make more engineers—as Wipro recruited from engineering colleges and as engineering colleges started to get more and more privatized, more people enrolled, so they were able to keep up with the supply requirements (India added more than 3,50,000 engineers in 2009 to the talent pool);
- Keep 'em trained—the other smart thing the industry did was invest in training to keep on upgrading the skills and of engineers (at Wipro's Electronic City campus, employees pack into courses to brush up on computer operating systems and programming tools. Everyone is drilled in language and culture ahead of shipping offshore on assignment).

Enabling Policies

Perhaps the most recognizable global face of Indian industry is the software sector and most observers agree that it reached the level it did because it was initially largely ignored by the government. When the government did wake up to its potential, liberalization was well under way and the sector benefited from rather progressive government guidelines and policies. These policies are responsible for making

Indian software exports competitive and boosting earning potential such as setting up special technology parks that serve as incubators of ideas and help harness the energy that such clusters produce. Software exports also enjoy substantial tax benefits up to 2011; the industry hopes that these will be extended further to help combat competition from newer low-cost locations like China, Ireland, Israel, etc. There are a broad range of fiscal and procedural incentives given by the government at the centre and state levels to sustain India's competitive edge.

India's success in IT would not have been possible without rapid growth in telecom connectivity for which government policies must be given credit. In little over a decade, liberalization and policy reform have changed this sector from a closed public sector monopoly to a vibrant free-market competition. Inflows of capital into India and depreciation of the rupee around the same time along with government's software technology park scheme added further impetus to growth of the IT sector. Internet penetration is still very low, leaving a huge domestic potential that can jointly be realized by the telecom and IT sector. Also, there is still scope for lowering telecom costs to match international levels, which will further enhance the labour-cost advantage of the IT sector. Policy reform coupled with an efficient regulator has shown that modern government policies are as tuned in to individual needs as industry itself.

The IT–ITES industry has a unique advantage of having a proactive and energetic industry association—NASSCOM—which engages all stakeholders at multiple levels and truly acts as a mentor for the industry.

Is it a Mere Bubble?

As Indian IT becomes the talk of the world, a crucial question arises whether IT can contribute to the economic development in more than a niche, export-oriented pocket? Can it become more fundamental to the Indian economy?

Even more important is the question of sustainability of the IT sector as a major contributor to the economy. Certainly, the global downturn of the economy since late 2007 seems to point to the fragility of the sector. The largest outlet for India's software is still the US—

accounting for 61 per cent of exports. A recession in the US economy could mean lower work outsourced to India. Then again, it could mean more work outsourced to India as US companies further tighten costs. Nevertheless, the Indian IT industry must diversify its reliance on US markets; already the share of Europe and Britain is increasing. The biggest insurance, however, could be closer home—India's huge domestic market, fuelled by economic growth of over 8 per cent p.a. Revenues from domestic IT, including hardware, are estimated to reach Rs 1,200 billion during the year 2009–10. The infrastructure boom in India will also throw up more domestic opportunities for this sector.

Indian IT companies are spreading risk by diversifying manufacturing and setting up shop in other countries like China, Ireland, etc. Some companies are shifting to Tier II and Tier III towns to cut costs by as much as 15 per cent. This will also help spread the reach of the IT industry within India and create a synergistic relationship.

The bottom line for Indian companies, however, is to innovate, innovate, and innovate. With slowdown in exports and shrinking labour cost arbitrage, companies have no choice but to move up the value chain, deliver smarter solutions or bring down prices to penetrate newer markets. In fact, the biggest test of Indian IT capability will be its ability to drive down the costs of products and services from the price points set by Western companies. Western markets have a vastly different price tolerance compared to India and beyond a point companies catering to Western markets see no merit in bringing down prices and often concentrate on improving features. However, there is a vast market awaiting companies which can breach this price barrier.

The intense engagement of the IT and ITES sector with its global counterparts is helping to shape the industry in India. In several aspects this sector is far ahead of others in the economy such as in operating standards, corporate self-governance, environment safeguards, and even work ethics and other labour issues. The industry is proactively tackling the gaps in talent with regular training and skill upgrading programmes. With ambitious increase in hardware manufacture, Indian companies have to manage critical environment issues like handling hazardous waste during manufacture and at the end of the useful life of the product, replacing harmful substances with more eco-friendly substances, etc.

In spite of lingering concerns about the availability of employable talent, infrastructure shortages, international currency fluctuations, and the like, the Indian IT industry is moving beyond exuberance towards a more rational assessment of capability and on the whole the balance sheet appears to be positive. Indian IT and ITES still account for a very small fraction of global IT spending but have all the potential to pull the country forward on the path to becoming a software superpower.

US President Barack Obama's 2010 healthcare references bill expects to extend medical coverage to about thrity-two million additional people who were not earlier insured for healthcare. This historic and monumental legislation is expected to challenge the US healthcare IT systems to cater to the sheer numbers of additional people brought under the umbrella of coverage. A major challenge will be to adopt technology to meet healthcare solutions and create Electronic Health Records (EHRs) for all American citizens by 2014. For Indian IT companies this presents an opportunity to play an active part in the expected outsourcing business to an extent of USD 20 billion.

WELLNESS AND FITNESS

India is a growing economy with rising incomes and evolving, fast-paced lifestyles. Greater disposable incomes, however, bring with them rising stress levels and stress-related lifestyle diseases. The good news is that people are willing to spend time, attention, and money on fitness products and services, geared towards a holistic approach to managing lifestyle disorders. The future shows a trend towards an integrated healthcare approach which could likely see a convergence of healthcare, beauty, wellness, and leisure tourism, often built around traditional medicine systems.

The burgeoning holistic healthcare sector encompasses West-inspired aerobics, traditional grandma's recipes or advice in consumable packages, yoga and Ayurveda interventions, herbal and non-herbal beauty products, and gymnasium and sports facilities.

A PricewaterhouseCoopers report has identified chronic diseases as a growing and costly threat to corporations and their workers (PricewaterhouseCoopers–World Economic Forum 2007). It calls on global CEOs to make wellness central to their corporate business strategy, suggesting that multinational employers have the greatest stake in and best opportunity to prevent chronic diseases. Traditionally, governments have been held responsible for managing major global health risks, with focus and funding on infectious diseases like HIV/ AIDS, malaria, TB, and on maternal and child health, etc. However, the report found that only 3 per cent of all health expenditure was directed at prevention and public health in 2004 in OECD member states. In the report, the challenges businesses face as a consequence of the growing epidemic of chronic diseases were explored, and it was found that approximately 2 per cent of capital spent on the workforce is lost to disability, absenteeism, and presenteeism (in other words, diminished productivity from ill employees who go to work but work below par) due to chronic diseases. Combined, these indirect costs are more than the additional direct medical claim costs that some employers incur.

In an increasing trend, corporate houses initiate wellness schemes for their employees for a host of reasons ranging from employee attraction and retention, motivation, better productivity, lower medical bills, or even as part of CSR to build a better and healthier global community.

A UK study by Unilever measured the difference in productivity between healthy and unhealthy employees. It showed how employees who had a low score on their health risk assessments also performed at a lower level over time. A group of staff helped by Unilever to manage stress, to cope with pain and to sleep more soundly, were 8.5 per cent more efficient at work—and less liable to take time off. (PricewaterhouseCoopers– World Economic Forum 2007: 11)

On an average, corporate wellness programmes have been shown to provide a 3:1 return on investment. Working adults spend an average of one-third of the day at the workplace and therefore the workplace is ideally suited to initiate changes in behaviour.

In the same report, a study of the Indian context revealed the following:

- In 2005, it was estimated that chronic diseases in India accounted for almost 53 per cent of all deaths and 44 per cent of disability-adjusted life years (DALYs). It is estimated that deaths from chronic diseases would register a sharp increase from 3.78 million in 1990 to 7.63 million in 2020 accounting for 66.7 per cent of all deaths;

- India's loss in terms of losing potentially productive years due to deaths from cardiovascular diseases in people aged between 35–64 years is one of the highest in the world. By 2030, the loss is expected to rise to 17.9 million years which is 940 per cent more than the loss estimated in the US;
- In India diabetic nephropathy is expected to develop in 6.6 million of the 30 million patients suffering from diabetes;
- The number of people with hypertension is expected to see a quantum leap from an estimated 118.2 million in 2000 to 213.5 million in 2025;
- The projected foregone national income for India due to heart disease, stroke and diabetes during the period 2005–15 is estimated to be more than USD 200 billion.

Preventive healthcare, rejuvenation, and self-indulgence are taking centre-stage in modern lives. Pharmaceutical, health services, cosmetics, food and beverages, and fitness companies are businesses whose products and services are closely linked to health. The beauty industry alone was worth about Rs 126 billion in 2007 and growing at approximately 30 per cent every year; the global fitness industry is estimated at Rs 9,000 billion and growing at 10 per cent, while the corresponding Indian industry is worth Rs 3 billion but growing at 40 per cent annually (*India Today* 2008).

The beauty industry—despite or because of common wisdom that beauty is only skin-deep—is attracting new customers, particularly the male gender in volumes large enough for businesses to cater to them as a separate segment. Wanting to look good and spending serious money on achieving it is no longer taboo and it is perhaps a mark of a self-confident population that even a teenager demands to be taken to a professional dermatologist for dealing with normal, puberty-related skin ailments.

Marico Industries, a hair care product company, ventured into specialized skin care clinics in an entrepreneurial leap of faith by setting up its brand Kaya Skin Clinics in 2002 through a subsidiary company which offer scientific, unisex dermatological procedures like anti-ageing services, permanent hair reduction, face rejuvenation, etc., using US FDA-approved technology. By 2010, it had 87 clinics in India, 14 in the Middle East, and 2 in Bangladesh. Despite the high cost of capital expenditure for each clinic, in the range of Rs 10 to 15 million per clinic, the company achieved breakeven during FY07 with a Profit Before Tax of Rs 0.4 million. The company considers Kaya Skin Clinics to be a future growth engine for top as well as bottom line growth. (Marico Industries Ltd 2007: 55–6)

Day and residential spas are another growing business segment in India, which combine traditional Indian Ayurvedic treatments with the best global facilities. The credit for putting India on the world wellness map and promoting the country as a destination for holistic health tourism in a large measure goes to Ananda in the Himalayas. Spa is necessarily a people-intensive industry and offers great scope for offering employment; its scope for rural employment is particularly exciting. The biggest challenge for this nascent industry is on the supply side—an acceptable standard of service, constant supply of trained personnel, guaranteed protocol of hygiene, and some sort of accreditation or regulatory authentication to filter out unscrupulous elements and fly-by-night operators. In the absence of an organized structure, there are also 'accredited' training institutes offering courses in fitness and health, including 'overseas affiliations'. For example, Central YMCA Qualifications, UK's health and fitness qualifications-awarding body, has opened shop in India claiming to be among India's first internationally recognized fitness qualifications. While it may be of a good standard, there is lack of regulatory authority in India that carries out screening of such courses.

Acceptance of Western concepts has made introduction and penetration of new technologies easier and are much sought after. It also indicates a trend away from traditional areas towards more global and homogenized activities (like abandoning wrestling *akharas* in favour of gyms). Working out in gyms with or without supervision of a health trainer has become an essential element of urban living and even corporate life. It is no exaggeration to say that gym memberships are on a family's budget enjoying the same importance as paying utility bills or other household expenses.

Today, Tier II and Tier III Indian towns also boast of multiple gyms with modest to good memberships. It is still a highly fragmented market but in the past three to four years, some international chains of gyms like Gold's Gym, Powerhouse Gym International, Reebok gyms, etc., have set up business in India mainly through the franchise route. For the Indian partner a franchise offers a chance of reaching into the bank of expertise with a low rate of failure and significant return on investment rather than struggle for brand identity, and marks the beginning of the corporatization of the domestic fitness industry. Several corporate houses collaborate with such standardized gyms to offer their employees facilities that they themselves cannot build or operate. The gym culture is well and truly entrenched in the Indian psyche and the market will only consolidate hereafter.

SPORTS

India may not be the toast of the world in sports but a small sports goods industry has been in existence for some time and Jalandhar, Meerut, and Gurgaon are major hubs for sports goods, mostly for the overseas market, like cricket bats and balls, hockey sticks, boxing, and fishing equipment, as well as equipment for indoor games like chess and carrom, inflatable balls, protective gear, etc. Nearly 60 per cent of the domestic produce is exported, mostly to well-known international brands. These are essentially goods that are highly labour-intensive which is why India has long been a destination for sourcing. Large sports goods companies also outsource manufacture of sports clothing, shoes and other gear.

However, the Indian sports goods industry is mostly engaged in making low-unit-value equipment; high-unit-value equipment for sports like golf, sailing, racing, or skiing is practically nonexistent. India's share of the global sports goods industry is barely 1 per cent and mostly occupied by cottage and small-scale industries. Therefore, scale of operations is at a low level and there is a lack of funds and other technical and managerial resources for upgradation and breaking into the top league. This is an industry that is ripe for consolidation and setting up new infrastructure to attract global business.

Venkat Sundaram, former test cricketer has remarked that, 'War or sports are two things that really unite our country' (Interview with the authors). Taking a cue from that remark, sports development must be tackled on a war-footing.

One of the biggest hurdles in inculcating a sports culture in the country is non-integration of sports with the formal education system—the Seventh All-India Educational Survey (2002) estimates that more than half of our schools do not have any sports facility at all. This is compounded by the fact that sport is an unstable and insecure choice of career. Given this reality, what parent would encourage her child to focus on sport—which requires complete dedication of time, money and other resources—when there is a reasonable chance of stable earnings by pursuing academics, which again requires an equal degree of dedication.

Like education and public health, sports can contribute to society on various dimensions—community bonding, national pride, development of ancillaries—primarily through patient funding. Sports requires land for building facilities, the facility itself, developing multiple disciplines in a facility, and other recurring bills; these are expenses that do not easily lend themselves to a linear relationship with returns on investment. Therefore, public funding will remain the likely route or some form of public–private partnership (PPP).

The All-India Football Federation and Bharti Enterprises (India's leading telecom company) have launched India's first public–private partnership (PPP) in 2007 to build India's football capabilities. Bharti Enterprises will make significant contributions—starting with Rs 1 billion—to build a world-class residential-cum-educational football Academy, to be called Bharti–AIFF Academy. It will select and nurture talent in different age groups with the help of experts around the world and provide exposure to global best practices and training techniques and hopes to become a supply line for a national team down the years. One modest target of the initiative is to prepare an Indian team for the World Cup 2018.

Sports can be more than only a game when countries host mega events if funds also flow into more conventional regeneration activity. Hosting large events does not automatically translate into economic benefits for an already developed host nation but for countries like India, hosting the Asian Games or Commonwealth Games has sparked off an overall boom like increasing construction activity, pushing through 'bed and breakfast' schemes and unlocking earning potential, boosting local infrastructure to give better quality of life, and improve productivity, and maybe even give a fillip to develop sports as a potential career choice. Sports tourists also generate hospitality revenue and additional sales for local businesses.

For a developed country like Germany, the four-week FIFA World Cup of 2006 earned the domestic tourism industry an extra $399 million in revenue, added 2 billion euros to retail sales and yielded 50,000 new jobs. The government calculated an increase in the following businesses due to the World Cup: tourism, hotel and catering—29 per cent, airline industry—52 per cent, security firms—29 per cent, food industry—24 per cent, media and film companies—25 per cent and advertisers—18 per cent and an overall bottom-line growth effect on the GDP of 0.3 per cent points. (Federal Government of Germany 2007)

After the 1982 Asian Games, the union sports budget was dramatically increased nearly nine times from Rs 265.4 million in the Sixth Plan to Rs 2,074.5 million in the Seventh Plan and to Rs 11,453.6 million in the Tenth Plan. Even so, in 2007, the fiscal allocation to sports was a mere 0.073 per cent of the total Union Budget (Cuba, the size of NCT of Delhi spends 13 per cent of its national budget on sports); out of this, more than one-fourth was allotted to the Commonwealth Games rather than promotion of sports as an integral component of youth development. The ministry of sports has asked for funding of Rs 80,000 million during the Eleventh Plan. India is a long way from providing universal access to sports—out of a population of 770 million under the age of 35 years, only about 50 million have access to organized sports and games. International sport today is a very expensive proposition involving training, coaching, equipment, travel, and participation fees, etc. The government supports high-performing national sportspersons to represent the country and participate in recognized international competitions. However, to reach that level and to sustain themselves beyond their playing years, players are often left to fend for themselves except when some of them are employed with government or public sector companies. Some players manage to find corporate sponsors in return for commercial endorsements; while this certainly boosts the player, it is likely to lead to skewed development of certain sports. Excellence in sports is essentially the outcome of three factors:

 (i) Breadth and depth at the base of the talent pyramid;
 (ii) Rigour of the selection process to move up the pyramid;
(iii) Quality of coaching and training facilities at the top.

Sports can engage and develop large numbers of people not only directly but through ancillary and related fields like coaching institutes, therapists and psychologists, sports medicine, media and multimedia, travel industry, merchandise, facility and event managers, etc. It can open a whole new world of opportunities for a nation raring to perform. As the Indian economy prospers, it is reasonable to expect that society will go through a process of evolution where a leisure activity like sports will attract serious players to a point where sport meets business.

In 2008, Indian sports witnessed something exciting which could be the potential game changer for the nation's sports sector—the birth of the Indian Premier League (IPL), a league dedicated to taking cricket to the size of a mega industry. The governing body first auctioned teams to wealthy Indian individuals and corporate houses—for the first time India saw high net worth individuals like film stars and industrialists come out and spend money on owning cricket teams. The governing body holds periodic auctions of international cricketers where team owners can bid for and buy their dream team. The matches themselves are keenly contested and attract greater interest than matches held hitherto between and among national teams; it helps that IPL teams work very hard to make cricket a true spectator sport with glitz and glamour. This is the first time a sport in India has been exploited to create a commercial value attractive enough for large businesses to own and participate in the industry. It is a significant shift from sponsoring an event or a team which has always happened over the years but a key difference was that the sponsor had no significant involvement apart from putting up the contracted amount and garnering whatever publicity it could. In 2008 when the original eight teams were auctioned, the highest price was about USD 110 million, representing over 300 per cent increase in value in less than three years. The sheer size of the IPL brand is put at USD 4.13 billion in 2010, up from about USD 2.0 billion in 2009 by Brand Franchise Plc, a UK-based organization. Sony Corporation, through its affiliate, entered into a nine-year television broadcast deal at the inception for USD 1.8 billion. The IPL has succeeded in making owning a cricket team an aspiration in India and the list of owners contains some of the biggest business groups and most successful film stars of the country.

And when commercial value is opened and exploited in cricket, can other sports be far behind? For instance, UB Group has (even before the birth of IPL) owned and promoted two iconic soccer teams in India, East Bengal and Mohun Bagan, and made significant contribution to the development of a professional soccer league in India. Kingfisher (part of the UB Group) also co-owns a Formula 1 racing team, Sahara Force India, which is close enough to making a podium finish within two years of existence. Gautam Thapar of the Thapar Group was the brain behind—and bankrolled—the Professional Golf Tour of India (PGTI) a few years back. By 2010, there were three co-sanctioned European Tour events in India and a number of Indian golfers are amongst the top in Asia and some even within the top 100 in the world. Hero Honda (now Hero MotoCorp) has been sponsoring the Indian Open of golf, with prize money of more than USD 1 million and is another key supporter of the game.

Corporatization of the sports industry in India is well under way and development of spectator sport needs to move away from government influence to flourish. India is moving towards a market economy and sports as a business would be an integral part of that growth story, as excellence in sports is a hallmark of a developed economy and a reflection of the health of its citizens as a whole.

PHARMACEUTICAL INDUSTRY, CLINICAL RESEARCH, BIOTECHNOLOGY

Gazing into the Crystal Ball

The pharmaceutical sector is billed as a growth driver for the Indian economy along the same lines as the IT–ITES industry (see discussion in Chapter 6, pp. 182–4). According to a FICCI–E&Y report (2009), the Indian pharmaceutical market will treble to USD 20 million in 2015 from USD 7.1 billion in 2007, with a compounded annual growth rate of 12.3 per cent. Like the IT sector, this sector too is an export revenue earner through the outsourcing route. The potential size of the pharmaceutical sector in India is huge—India is home to one-fifth of the world's population with only about 30 per cent market penetration. This means that an abysmal 70 per cent of the population is uncovered by healthcare facilities.

Medical research is a long-haul process, requiring deep pockets to sustain. Indian pharmaceutical companies typically invest just 2–4 per cent in R&D, whereas multinationals may spend anything from 14–20 per cent. Medical research in India is presently concentrated in the following areas:

- Drug discovery;
- Clinical trials of medical devices;
- Immunology studies—genetic compound;
- Stem cell research.

Drug Discovery

There are few disciplines in which research is so long drawn out or rigorous as in drug discovery. Adding to the uncertainty of success is the historical fact that several major drug discoveries have been accidental. Accidents in laboratories can lead to 'eureka' moments and produce lifesaving miracles for humanity—and Nobel Prizes for the researchers. It is interesting to note that most 'accidents' that led to discoveries took place in laboratories which were designed precisely for discoveries. It is part of a process, a series of 'whys' that must be answered, eliminating and discarding wrong leads, before reaching the 'aha' moment. Pharmaceutical research has since evolved to reduce serendipity, into a rational and planned process with fairly accurate estimates of outcomes. Still, the process of drug discovery contains heavy elements of chance, leading some researchers to use the term: 'taking chance systematically'.

Sucralose is an artificial sweetener that was discovered by scientists in 1976 at the British sugar company, Tate & Lyle, and the then named Queen Elizabeth College London. Shashikant Phadnis, a young Indian scientist, and his mentor, Leslie Hough, were trying to make an insecticide. One evening Hough asked Phadnis to test some powder; Phadnis, possibly because he came from a different linguistic background, thought he was asked to 'taste' it and found the substance ridiculously sweet. Hough was shocked at the process but delighted at its possibilities and even dubbed the substance 'Serendipitose'. The duo worked for a year to develop the final formula—but still could not find any use of it as an insecticide.

Discovery of the drug Viagra came about as a by-product of a failed research for a drug for heart diseases. Researchers at the pharmaceutical major Pfizer were gloomily prepared to consign the work on sildenafil, an enzyme that they hoped will help relax coronary heart muscles, into the mortuary of failed clinical trials (only one in ten projects passes through trials successfully to become a commercial product). But strangely, the participants in the trial were reluctant to part with the unused trial drugs given to them. Investigations revealed that Pfizer had indeed stumbled upon a blockbuster drug, though not for the problem they were working on but for erectile dysfunction.

The time frame involved in the drug discovery process is large, often with a huge failure rate; as a thumb rule, out of 600 possible lead compounds, only about thirty are finally workable compounds that are taken for further testing; to put another perspective, out of every 5,000 compounds that are evaluated, only about five go into clinical trials. These initial steps require strong skills in biology, chemistry, and toxicology.

The volume and complexity of work in international markets that is required to bring a chemical entity to approval is increasing. Rising costs and reduced avenues of patient recruitment are critical issues in drug development. This also tends to extend the time taken for approval, shortening the life of a drug under patent. Clinical trials of new drugs account for more than 40 per cent of drug development costs and out of these costs, some estimates reckon that patient recruitment and cost of medical personnel account for nearly 70 per cent. Performing these studies in India can bring down the price of a drug by as much as 60 per cent. India is particularly advantageously placed to carry out such pharma research and development (R&D) activities—adequate high-quality scientific talent, patent protection laws, and a large drug-naïve patient pool, that is, patients that have not been exposed to modern medicine. Estimates of the size of clinical trials' industry in India vary but most studies agree that it was in the band of USD 1 billion to USD 1.5 billion in 2006 and is expected to grow at a rate that may well equal the IT industry's revenues. In 2006, the Indian clinical trials market was worth about USD 140 million and has been growing at an average rate of 40 per cent (Cygnus Business Consulting and Research 2007)

Over 100 pharmaceutical companies, including Fortune 100 companies such as Pfizer and Merck, are currently outsourcing clinical trials in the country. Besides, India's inherent advantage in IT skills helps in outsourcing of high-end activities like data management, which are important in areas like bio-informatics, pharmacovigilance, etc.

As more and more clinical trials are outsourced to India, there is deep disquiet that Indian patients will be used as guinea pigs in the process. It is true that India offers a large drug-naïve patient pool of a varied genetic composition that is highly valued by several research organizations. Regulatory systems are being strengthened and laws updated to facilitate clinical trials while protecting the population from drug abuse. Efforts are also on to train research professionals and expand the base of investigators and support staff.

The Drug Controller General of India (DCGI) is the central authority to approve all clinical trials in India. It is also training a group of people to act as clinical trial monitors to oversee the progress of trials. A central registry of clinical trials is hosted at Indian Council of Medical Research's (ICMR) National Institute of Medical Statistics (NIMS) since 2007 to better track all trials in the country and also to serve as a resource base for researchers. It started as a voluntary measure and since 2009 is made mandatory. The Indian Council of Medical Research (ICMR) issues guidelines on several topics which are largely voluntary except the guidelines governing clinical trials where the Drugs and Cosmetics Act states that all clinical trials in India *should* follow ICMR guidelines. The Medical Council of India (MCI), which has regulatory powers over the medical profession, states that all research in India carried out by physicians must follow ICMR guidelines. Therefore, there is a fair degree of legal sanctity to these guidelines.

Exposure of the Indian healthcare system to the rigors of international norms of clinical research will deepen the intellectual base in the country and enhance the practice of evidence-based medicine, through record-keeping and issues like informed patient consent, all of which contribute to improving the standards of research. However, the pursuit of scientific knowledge and commercial interests must be tempered with protection of the target population.

Commercial Production of Drugs

The Indian pharmaceutical market is likely to be worth USD 20 billion by 2015 and the bulk of this will be contributed by manufacture and sale of drugs (McKinsey & Co. n.d.). India is currently ranked fourth in terms of volume but only thirteenth in terms of value globally. This is largely because three-fourths of active pharmaceutical ingredients and almost one-fourth of formulations produced in the country are exported. But if India is to aspire to global leadership in pharmaceuticals, the industry must make a paradigm shift in mindset from generics and low-value/high-volume vaccines to inventing and commercializing new molecules and drugs or novel drug delivery systems. The size of the potential market is huge because there is a long way to go before India can reach healthcare penetration levels prevalent elsewhere—India currently has 1.5 beds per 1,000 people, similar to sub-Saharan Africa while the WHO norm is 3.3 beds per 1,000 people. The number is 7.4 beds per 1,000 people in the US, West Europe, and Japan, 4.3 beds per 1,000 people in Brazil, China, Thailand, and South Africa (Ibid.).

India already has a well-developed pharmaceutical industry and is the only country outside the US to have the largest number of Federal Drug Administration (FDA)-approved manufacturing facilities. There are nearly 20,000 pharmaceutical manufacturing units in the country, with several of these in the small-scale sector. However, the industry is highly fragmented where the organized sector comprises 250–300 companies, controlling 70 per cent of the market in value terms.

There is increasing recognition in India that quality is necessary for survival and several pharmaceutical units are complying with manufacturing standards prescribed in highly regulated markets like the US and Europe to secure certification.

Stem Cell Research

Stem cells have the ability to continuously divide and transform into various types of tissues. Stem cells, adult and embryonic, have raised great hopes for improvement in human health. The goal of stem cell therapy is to repair a damaged tissue that cannot heal itself and therefore these remarkable cells have captured the imagination of scientists, clinicians, and laymen alike. Applications of stem cells include:

- Can become magic bullets to cure debilitating diseases;
- Provide deeper insights into embryonic development and improve quality of basic research;
- Can help in developing better drugs with greater efficacy while also bringing down the costs of drug development;
- Help in immune modulation, that is, induce tolerance in transplants and rheumatologic and autoimmune disorders.

Most stem cell 'therapy' around the world is as yet experimental and calls for strict regulation to prevent malpractices and ensure ethical and responsible research.

Ethical and government barriers impede stem cell research in several Western countries. A major reason for this is that according to the church and some critics, stem cells are mostly derived from embryos that have the potential to create life, hence any research involving physical examination of such tissue in a laboratory is akin to murder. India does not experience such ethical dilemmas but there is an official guideline issued by ICMR that deals with most ethical and moral issues.

In India, the Department of Biotechnology (DBT) is the nodal funding agency for supporting stem cell R&D programmes. The DBT's strategy for stem cell research is to promote city cluster programmes at places like Delhi, Vellore, Hyderabad, Pune, and Bangalore. The aim is to share information, collaborate with universities and clinicians, refine policy issues, and carry out clinical research in coordination. The focus is on creating a critical mass of researchers in the country. Apart from the absence of religious opposition to stem cell research, the advantages that India has to develop this area lies in its genetically diverse population which is very important for embryonic stem cell lines, a strong pharmaceutical and biotechnology sector, and a large pool of scientific talent.

A lot of stem cell research work in India is carried out at government laboratories and hospitals like All India Institute of Medical Sciences (AIIMS), New Delhi, and Christian Medical College (CMC), Vellore, in collaboration with DBT, The Centre for Cellular and Molecular Biology (CCMB) at Hyderabad (a CSIR laboratory), and King Edward Memorial (KEM) Hospital, Mumbai. Some private companies are also engaging in this research, Reliance Life Sciences being one of the bigger players and having developed ten stem cell lines. Several laboratories have moved from animal to human studies but it may well take another ten years for stem cell therapy to become feasible for humans and form part of a clinician's treatment line.

Biotechnology

Biotechnology is technology that is based on biology, especially when used in agriculture, food sciences and medicine. Biotechnology is a very capital-intensive industry. In the initial stages of investment, physical equipment, and special buildings (confined air, temperature control, vacuum conditions, etc.) constitute a major portion of investment.

The industry is also very technical and calls for intensive collaboration and development of scientific networks and cooperation. In fact, the main entry barrier in this industry is the scientific skills of the project leader. The return on investment is longer than in most other industries.

There are great expectations that biotechnology will catalyze Indian economy in the same manner that IT did a few years ago. The biotechnology industry is estimated to be worth Rs 141.99 billion in 2010 (www.ableindia.org). However, there are other drivers that need to be addressed to achieve excellence in biotechnology before the success of IT can be replicated. The IT industry's success can be linked to lack of government 'guidelines' in the early years, leaving the industry to develop on its own, a large 'private education sector', engineering colleges, particularly in south India that ensured a steady supply of engineers and relatively low capital investment.

Biotechnology, however, is slightly different. For one, it requires large, often heavy initial capital investment in special buildings and equipment. It also needs large numbers of basic science graduates and PhDs in subjects like biology, microbiology, etc., an area where the country is seriously lagging behind. An immediate ramping up of the education system will still take time to deliver trained manpower. Thirdly, globally biotechnology is subject to a lot of debate, leading to regulations and guidelines, which leaves the industry more constrained than the IT industry to develop.

Biopharmaceuticals

The pharmaceutical industry is the largest segment of the Indian biotechnology industry commanding as much as a 61.71 per cent share, value at around Rs 882.9 million in 2010 (www.ableindia.org).

The move into biopharmaceuticals is anchored by India's strong generic and bulk pharmaceutical manufacturing base which has developed considerable expertise and capacity in manufacturing and process innovations. However, the generics' markets in conventional and biopharmaceutical drugs are totally different and success in one cannot be taken as a format for success in the other. There are several barriers to entry in the biosimilars (generics) market primarily because there is innate variance and lack of established methods to determine bioequivalence, that is, equivalence between an actual tested product and its generic form.

Biocon is India's first biopharmaceutical company that was set up in 1978 as a garage start-up with a capital of about Rs 10,000. It is focused on research-driven global healthcare. Biocon is an integrated company that undertakes work from discovery to development and commercialization of drugs. It also provides custom research—the first company in India to do so—and clinical research services to other pharmaceutical and biotechnology companies through its subsidiaries, Syngene and Clinigene.

Bioinformatics

Although the share of bioinformatics in the total biotech sector is less than 2 per cent (in 2010), it has immense potential for becoming a high-growth industry and to attract outsourcing work. Bioinformatics refers to the science of information, processing information and engineering information systems. It studies the structure, behaviour, and interactions of natural and artificial systems that store, process, and communicate information. Bioinformatics involves creation and advancement of algorithms, computational and statistical techniques and theory to solve formal and practical problems arising out of management and analysis of biological data.

The increase in the demand for bioinformatics as a discipline came about due to the explosion of information coming out of the Human Genome Project (HGP). The HGP's information management challenge involves tracking the sequencing of the entire human genome—approximately 3 billion base pairs of DNA that make up our 23 pairs of chromosomes—and the precise mapping of the 1,00,000 or so genes that are interspersed on these chromosomes (Maria et al. n.d.: 91).

Bioinformatics is closely linked to other biotechnology sectors. The HGP, for instance, signals a paradigm shift for the global pharmaceutical industry in its search for critical drug discoveries. This huge trove of information, more than anything else, has led to a rapid development in biotechnology as a research thrust area. Chemistry, traditionally the anchor of drug discovery, is fast ceding ground to biology, with molecular genetics, genomics, and bioinformatics together promising customized drugs.

After Y2K, bioinformatics promises to be the next big wave for the IT industry. The global bioinformatics industry was about USD 60 billion in 2005 (www.ciionline.org); with proven strengths in IT, India can hope to gather 5 per cent of this market share. Pharmaceutical and biotechnology companies need strong IT support to write algorithms, develop software to improve existing algorithms and, most importantly, manage the complex databases. This presents a fine opportunity for software and IT companies to harness their competence to a new growth sector.

There are bioinformatics centres at various universities, ICAR, ICMR, CSIR, DBT, DST, Department of Atomic Energy, and other central and state government-supported laboratories. Research in biotechnology over the past decade has produced a deluge of information and to make effective use of this information, DBT has established a high-speed and large bandwidth national bioinformatics network named BioGrid India. This grid has several nodes pursuing bioinformatics' activities in various fields such as HR development, R&D in bioinformatics, etc. The BioGrid allows exchange of biotechnology information, database, and software among researchers in the country, besides sharing teaching materials and delivering lectures through video conferencing. As part of knowledge creation, each centre is entrusted with developing a database in an identified thrust area and more than 100 databases have been created till date.

Bioinformatics at ICMR

A huge information base for the medical community is being set up by ICMR. The organization is working on setting Indian normative clinical parameters for laboratory tests for the Indian body type. Around 250 such parameters, ranging from haemoglobin counts, endocrinology tests, urine parameters, blood clotting time, etc., have been identified by ICMR. According to V. Muthyswamy, the project is unique in several aspects, not least because this is the 'first time that such a massive exercise is being conducted to develop clinical standards for the developing world' but also because of the unique challenges of topography in the country—tests will take place over six zones in the country to take into account regional or ethnic differences, namely, north, south, east, west, central, and northeast (Interview with the authors). For some tests like blood clotting time, for example, the nature of the parameter demands instant results and therefore, ICMR has designed six mobile testing units to carry out such tests. ICMR has collaborated with institutes like the Indian Statistical Institute (ISI) at Kolkata to develop the statistical and mathematical model for collating the results of the study. The ICMR has developed 20 databases of clinical and bio-molecular data in 2010 (ICMR 2010).

ENTERTAINMENT AND MEDIA

Entertainment in some form or the other has always been a part of the subcontinent's lifestyle, which is the reason why there is a rich culture of folklore, art, theatre and street plays, music, etc. The immense change that is sweeping this sector for the past couple of decades is due to the impact of technology. Entertainment and media (E&M)

are fast-evolving, changing, and exciting sectors because they have become highly technology-dependent, which increases their volatility and unpredictability.

The number of consumers (audience) is guaranteed in the way few other sectors can boast of but it is not a homogeneous group; consumers are very discerning and do not give their loyalty easily, are constantly adapting to new technologies, willing to try out new ideas and deals. The demography of India is breaking its clichéd mould with nearly half of the population under twenty-five years of age—a segment that has not known want the way a generation or two of the older population has. The Indian youth's relationship with money is also far less emotional and for them it is more of a commodity than a holy cow worthy of worship. This is a segment that more assertively demands to be entertained for the sake of entertainment—where having a good time is not a guilty pleasure.

The biggest force in the entertainment and media sector is convergence. Convergence of:

- Media—broadcast, cable, broadband;
- Devices—television, PCs, cell phones, print, radio.

Walls between and among these media and devices are collapsing to merge and intermingle in a single delivery chain, offering a range of choices for consumers to log on to various nodes or modules as they wish. This convergence also spills over into innovation in non-entertainment areas, such as banking, paying utility bills, travel and tourism, etc. Convergence is causing a tectonic shift among the players, leading to more innovation and the ability to better reach target consumers in a world of unlimited content and limited consumer time and attention span. The acid test of success in this sector is the ability of players to transition smoothly among various media and devices, to spot a trend on its cusp and act on it quickly.

This also means that there is going to be greater integration among sectors of the businesses which are currently fragmented, through organic growth or mergers and acquisitions (M&A); already mega M&A deals are being struck all across the globe. According to Shekhar Kapur, '...the price of failure of a non-integrated or non-aggregated business is fairly low...' (India Knowledge@Wharton 2007) and this is going to change rapidly as more big money comes into the sector. The Government of India is steadily liberalizing this sector and foreign direct investment (FDI) up to 100 per cent is allowed under the automatic route in most E&M sectors: films—100 per cent; radio—up to 20 per cent; print—26 per cent for news media) and 100 per cent for non-news media. The entertainment industry in India is estimated at about USD 10.7 billion in 2011 (www.ibef.org).

The entertainment and media industry consists of creation, aggregation, and distribution of content, products and services, news and information, through various platforms and channels. New technologies like 3G, greater use of 3D, and newer content delivery devices are making this sector as exciting as its content.

The entertainment and media industry is heavily dependent on advertisement revenue for sustenance. The ad–GDP ratio is 1.34 per cent in the US and 1 per cent in the UK, while in India, it is only 0.34 per cent. With the economy growing at 8–9 per cent annually, the corporate sector's growth and spending on advertisement is also increasing.

Animation and Gaming Industry

This sector is usually clubbed with the software sector and is under the banner of National Association of Software and Service Companies (NASSCOM). The global animation market is expected to touch USD 80 billion by 2010 and the entertainment market is projected to be the key driver of this market, contributing almost three-fourths of the revenue generated. Likewise, the global gaming market is expected to touch USD 42 billion, with mobile and online gaming expected to create the maximum impact (NASSCOM 2007). The Indian market share is estimated to be USD 253 million for animation and USD 1.3 billion for gaming (if skilled manpower is available) by 2013, which is still less than 2 per cent of the global market share. Domestic consumption of animation is on the rise in mainstream films and TV, which will help the market to mature and create a market for employment.

India is also a good destination for attracting outsourced work—strong IT skills, large pool of educated, English-speaking young population, an improving infrastructure and regulatory environment (as in IP protection), and a maturing market. This is, however, applicable to non-artistic production work and at the moment India can be an attractive destination for pre- and post-production finishing work and in some cases production support. A NASSCOM report estimates that a typical half-hour three-dimensional (3D) animation TV episode costs up to USD 70,000–1,00,000 to produce in India as against USD 1,70,000–2,50,000 in the US (without major stars for voice-overs); savings in full-length animation are even more—USD 15–25 million in India against USD 100–175 million in the US. To attract global business into artistic production work is a different proposition and requires nuanced skills of the cultural type to write content, create characters and dialogue for an overseas audience—this is where the big money resides. The animation and gaming industry, being regulated under software rules, gets tax benefits as part of software technology parks (STPs) for exports. This creates artificial barriers for the domestic industry and is hardly conducive to deepening local expertise.

The Indian entertainment back office can move up the value chain by evolving from being service providers to solution providers but for that it requires a coordinated effort of all the agencies involved.

The main factors affecting the E&M industry in India can be summed up as:

- Convergence–confluence of media and technology and associated synergies;
- Liberalization and growth of private businesses;
- Consolidation through M&A, sales, alliances;
- New technologies and quick adaptation;
- Global footprint of major players.

The biggest game changer possibly is the roll-out of 3G networks despite all the controversy surrounding it. It can completely change the way consumers experience entertainment.

As Shekhar Kapur puts it, '...the world is going through a certain reverse cultural colonization. Among all new ideas that will generate in the world, E&M are likely to be from Asia-Pacific' (India Knowledge@ Whatron 2007).

It is a sign of a confident population when it starts to re-embrace indigenous culture and rediscover its own art forms rather than accepting and adopting Western culture as global culture.

AUTOMOBILE AND COMPONENT SECTOR

The automobile sector is a key growth engine of the industry and the economy in terms of employment, revenue generation, infrastructure development, vehicle financial sector, creating ancillary industries, etc. As such, it is often called the industry of industries. The Indian automobile industry crossed the historic landmark of 10 million vehicles in 2006–7 including two and three wheelers, passenger cars, and commercial vehicles. According to Society of Indian Automobile Manufacturers (SIAM) data, the cumulative growth of the passenger vehicle segment in 2010–11 over the previous year was 29.16 per cent and exports grew by 29.64 per cent over the same period. According to the ITP (Investment and Trade Promotion) Division, Ministry of External Affairs (MEA), the sector is growing at over 18 per cent p.a., and forms a major focus area of government policies (ITP 2010).

The Automotive Mission Plan 2016 was released in 2007 to provide a roadmap to help transform India into a global automobile player in the next ten years. It proposes to make India the manufacturing and export hub for small cars, multi-utility vehicles, two- and three-wheelers, tractors and components—in short, across all segments of the industry. The plan envisages the following:

- Increase in turnover from approximately USD 35 billion presently to USD 145 billion by 2016;
- Increase exports from the present USD 4.1 billion to USD 20–25 billion;
- Raise investment to USD 40 billion;
- Provide employment to 25 million people.

The sector witnessed real growth when it was de-licensed in 1993 and global Original Equipment Manufacturers (OEMs) set up assembly lines in India. Up to 100 per cent FDI is allowed in the automotive sector. Both OEMs and the component industry are highly competitive with several global giants sharing space with Indian automobile companies. India is the largest manufacturer of two-wheelers and ranks eleventh in the manufacture of passenger cars. The automotive industry in India is going through structural transformation where all players are re-aligning their businesses to be part of the global auto supply chain.

The Indian automobile consumers are a discerning and shrewd lot who expect value for money—a low purchase price, high fuel efficiency, comfortable ride, low maintenance costs, and long-lasting product. Maruti Udyog Limited (MUL) could fulfil all this and ruled the Indian market for a decade and a half in a country that was bereft of real choices before the company came along. Peugeot and Daewoo, however, could not survive, while giants like Ford and General Motors (GM) are still struggling to find a comfortable segment. Asian companies like Hyundai, Honda, and Toyota have managed to understand the Indian market better and occupy an undisputed position in the order.

Indian companies are increasing investments in production capacities in India and are also expanding their footprint overseas by establishing partnerships and joint ventures or even Greenfield manufacturing facilities. But the tipping point of the Indian automobile industry has come with the introduction of Nano by Tata Motors in early 2008.

Tata Motors is already the market leader in commercial vehicles in India; with the introduction of Nano, a USD 2,500 (Rs 1,00,000) passenger car, the company will create a whole new class of consumers—the two-wheeler-owning population. As mentioned earlier, India is the largest manufacturer—and consumer—of two-wheelers; a large number of these consumers are expected to upgrade to a car in this price segment, helped by rising income levels and improving lifestyles. More than that, Nano has brought a surge in the confidence of the Indian manufacture sector. Not very often does a single product upturn perceived wisdom in its industry segment; it has pushed the boundaries of what can be achieved and brought about a paradigm change in the very thinking of the segment. Nano has helped build an entire platform from where add-on, fully-loaded content cars can be built at much lower prices, increasing competitive value to the customer.

Nano is a classic example of how constraints are turned into stepping stones for new breakthroughs and has raised the level of innovation that can be expected from India. In most sectors Indian companies have sourced technology from outside, maybe tweaked it a little for cost-competitiveness but never really challenged the essence of the techniques and concepts involved. Nano has undeniably changed that. It underscores the understanding that India, with its economic, political and business environment, can be a good laboratory for ideas that can succeed anywhere in the world. It has also energized vendors into investing more in projects and entrepreneurs into exploring the idea that is Nano.

Automobile Component Industry

India has strong engineering skills and a thriving domestic automobile industry which is growing at 18 per cent p.a. This, coupled with India's cost-competitiveness, has helped the auto component industry to mature and attract global auto majors to see India as a sourcing destination. India's component industry has the capability to manufacture the entire range of auto components such as engine parts, drive, transmission, steering, suspension and braking parts, electrical, body and chassis parts, etc. The automotive component industry has very deep forward and backward linkages with several engineering manufacture sectors of the economy like machine tools, steel, aluminium, rubber, plastics, electrical, electronics, forgings, machining, etc. and, increasingly, IT sectors.

The total global auto component trade is USD 185 billion and India's share in that is only about 0.4 per cent. Auto Components Manufacturing Association (ACMA) is the apex industry body; the ACMA–McKinsey 'Vision 2015' document estimates the potential for the Indian auto component industry to be USD 40–45 billion (growth of 17 per cent) by 2015 and of this, 50 per cent is expected to come from exports (growth of 34 per cent). This will help raise India's share in the global market to 3–4 per cent. Exports for the year 2009–10 were USD 3.8 billion while imports were USD 8.2 billion (ACMA 2010). This indicates a rising demand in the country which will help to further mature the industry and ramp up industry quality to exacting global standards.

India is increasingly being used as a base for multinational companies to shift automotive design centres here since it has proven to be an excellent place for prototyping, testing, validating and production of auto components. The component of software vis-à-vis mechanical parts is increasing in automobiles and India's strong IT skills are an added advantage for steering work into the country. However, for scaling up, India needs to do a lot more original design and engineering work within the country. Most component manufacturers deepen their expertise by acquiring facilities in foreign markets and learning from international experience. To be a truly global force in this sector, Indian companies need to develop proprietary knowledge within the country.

Some challenges that the automotive sector faces are:

- Infrastructure—power, highways, ports, etc.;
- Rapid technology change;
- Environment issues and how they impact the dynamics of the whole industry;
- Scaling up and handling a greater share of the world auto trade;
- The rupee's appreciation versus the dollar makes Indian products unattractive in the global market as against countries with a regulated currency.

It is an accepted industry fact that companies no longer have pricing power; also, few automotive companies are vertically integrated manufacturers and most have moved to a model where they are assemblers and marketers of vehicles. This de-integration of the industry has opened up large avenues for the Indian automotive industry to step in and try to replicate the success of the IT and ITES industry.

The automobile sector will continue to remain one of India's core sectors and will likely see a lot of activity over the next few years as Indian industries gather strength to become a global player.

GREAT INDIAN ROAD SHOW...

The opening of the economy following liberalization introduced a competitive dynamic that the private sector in particular seized, and restructured itself to become modern and tuned in to the global economy. 'The trigger for growth in India was the turnaround in manufacturing productivity since 2003, more importantly led by efficiency of private sector firms in the face of growing competition' (India Knowledge@Wharton 2008b)

The sectors discussed here can help translate India's promise into reality; the most promising thing about most of these sectors is that they are people-intensive—and manpower is going to be India's single biggest advantage in an ageing world. India's demographics, including an 'urbanization bonus' over the long term actually could work in her favour due to continued movement of labour from rural agriculture to industry and services. Of course, this requires policy planning for urban infrastructure and other public services.

Investment in highways and roads has historically benefited kingdoms and nations making such investment; linking major cities with high-speed highways will help reduce travel times, lower the cost of the critical economic resource of fuel, improve freight delivery times, spread out population pressure on infrastructure and contribute to increasing productivity. However, the metaphorical road is not without bumps; there are several sectors or areas that can act more as roadblocks and these have to be smoothened before the 'Great Indian Road Show' can roll on.

The last forty years have seen a quiet growth of confidence in Indian business; within this is the remarkable rise of entrepreneurs who have seized opportunities that came their way or even created opportunity for themselves and have earned a place in India's business history. It is significant to note that several of these are first-generation entrepreneurs and most of them do not come from traditional business backgrounds or castes. These new entrepreneurs have dared to think beyond conventional boundaries and moved out of the security blanket of regular jobs, along the way also helping to create several independent or inter-related businesses and entrepreneurs.

Every Forbes list of the world's wealthiest contains some additional Indian names—names that were either non-existent or nowhere in the reckoning even in their local environment. Such new businessmen and women have broken free from traditional caste shackles dictating occupational choices, embraced Western influences, and adapted them to suit Indian conditions, and kept up with new global business ideas and practices and perhaps done more to integrate India with the rest of the world than any other agency. Interestingly, most of these entrepreneurs are people who established their businesses in the difficult years of nationalization and dealt with tight bureaucratic control and regulation—conditions ideal to stifle entrepreneurship. Yet they have cut their teeth in the difficult working conditions in India and stamped their presence in the global marketplace.

We are profiling some of these entrepreneurs here who have made the big leap into global reckoning; these stories are truly inspirational and also define benchmarks of success for others to emulate.

Bharti Airtel

Bharti Airtel is India's largest integrated and first private telecommunications service provider with a pan-India presence, a feat achieved by a first-generation entrepreneur with few resources other than plenty of grit and determination at his command.

The founder, Sunil Bharti Mittal, started with a small bicycle components manufacturing business in 1976 at age 18 in Ludhiana, Punjab. Although Ludhiana was an industrial hub of decent size, it was not enough for Mittal who wanted a larger canvas to play on. He, therefore, sold the business and moved to Mumbai to seek his fortune in import and distribution of various products. He traded in diverse products like steel, brass, zinc, plastic, zip fasteners, and generator sets. Electric generators was probably the turning point in his career; apart from the commercial success of this product (made in Japan by Suzuki), Mittal learnt the famed Japanese business techniques including international trade diplomacy and other business concepts in the early 1980s.

However, India was at the peak of the licence–permit raj where items could summarily be put on or taken off a restricted list for production or import. The political climate of the country was hardly encouraging; India faced the Emergency and its aftermath where socialism and anti-private sector sentiment was the norm. Shortly thereafter, electric generators were taken off the permitted list of imports and Mittal's business was left without its star performer. He scouted around the world for a substitute best-selling product—something that did not require too much capital but which had not yet attracted the big players with deep pockets. It turned out to be another turning point in his life when he picked up push-button telephones to manufacture in India in technical collaboration with Siemens AG of Germany. It was his first brush with telecommunications. Once again, government restrictions of capacity and nature of production intervened and Mittal set up a facility in Ludhiana where he assembled semi-knocked-down (SKD) kits within prescribed parameters and capacity. His company, Bharti Telecom Limited, went on to make fax machines and cordless phones in the early 1990s. India's tough working conditions made Sunil Mittal a very hands-on businessman, helping him understand the nuances better. While he was developing his entrepreneurial abilities, the country was steadily moving towards liberalization, and when opportunities were thrown up in the early-1990's Mittal was primed and ready to unleash his potential.

In 1994, India's teledensity was around 0.8 per cent against a world average of 10 per cent when the National Telecom Policy called for a major increase but noted a resource gap of about Rs 230 billion and recommended private sector participation for basic and cellular services. The country was divided into 20 circles for basic telephony and 18 for mobile services. Each circle was opened for bids to the private sector and the government-owned Department of Telecommunications (DoT). One of the conditions the government put forth was that the bidder must have experience as telecom operators.

In yet another inflexion point in his career, Sunil Bharti Mittal decided to make a bid and to meet prescribed conditions, tied up a deal with the French telecom group Vivendi—he won the bid for the Delhi circle and in 1995 set up Bharti Cellular, which launched the Airtel brand of cellular services in Delhi. The telecom sector in India (as indeed the world over) was not an easy one, requiring huge investments, long gestation periods, dominated by state-owned behemoths, and subject to frequently changing regulations.

Mittal had to contend with competition that had deeper pockets, some backed by family businesses, and of course the entrenched government companies. With little else but determination to succeed, Mittal dug in and proved his worth in the only circle he had then— Delhi. Perhaps his lack of business house backing proved a blessing as he learnt to capitalize every little opportunity that came his way and explore unconventional ideas. Telecom—particularly mobile phones— was a new area and in a sense it was a level starting point for everyone. Tying up alliances and entering long-term partnerships became the hallmark of Mittal's working style and a major factor of the spectacular success of the business. The Bharti group of enterprises tied up with Telecom Italia in 1996 in exchange for 20 per cent equity and with British Telecom in 1997 for a 21.5 per cent stake. The company also expanded into Himachal Pradesh in 1997 and by buying out other companies or their licences had moved into three major circles in south India by early 2000. In perhaps the biggest alliance ever, SingTel, Asia's largest telecom company, bought a 15 per cent stake which was its largest investment outside the country and enabled Bharti to gain access to knowledge and technology from the global telecom world. The two partners have since partnered in other ventures for various projects such as the submarine cable link between Chennai and Singapore, besides bidding for major projects around the world. It could not have been easy for a small company like Bharti with little recall value to tie up these alliances with large multinationals. But the Indian telecom market was opening up and many global companies wanted a piece of the action with the result that Mittal's record of successful deals just kept going up.

Therefore, the very handicap—lack of resources or expertise, which could have hampered growth—was turned into an advantage by strategic alliances and partnerships and this released management resources and energies to focus on other business ideas, approaches, and practices; for example, replacing the revenue-per-customer model with the revenue-per-minute model which is better suited to Indian conditions, particularly the vast rural market, introducing music instead of a regular ring tone (an idea adapted from Korea) which became hugely popular and raised visibility, tying up with TV game shows to increase traffic, etc. Most players, certainly the large state-owned companies and several other private companies set up their own towers for mobile telephony; Bharti went against the trend and sewed up long-term partnerships with companies like Nokia and Ericsson to build and maintain networks under a revenue-sharing model, a trend which others soon copied. Network leadership was a critical driver in Airtel's success story and these partnerships helped to roll out cost-efficient, on-demand capacity.

As Sunil Mittal puts it, 'When faced between a choice between perfection and speed, choose speed; perfection will follow' (India Knowledge@Wharton 2008b). Following that logic, Bharti has strived to enter the market ahead of competition—rolling out networks, putting out new products, attractive packages, innovative services—in short, being a market leader. A leader who is not perfect initially perhaps but has made enough of an impact with first-mover advantage; in business there is rarely a happy thing called perfect positioning—one moves in, improvizes, and learns sophistication.

Bharti went ahead and outsourced several other aspects of the business, including backend and office operations and call centres for mobile services (an Indian company outsourcing to other companies in India, creating more entrepreneurs in the process) to companies like Nortel, Mphasis, Teletech Services, IBM Daksh, etc. It has a ten-year information technology alliance with IBM (worth USD 750 million) for its group-wide IT requirements. Bharti group companies and the founder Sunil Mittal have justifiably received several awards and been voted 'most successful', 'most innovative', 'most many-things' several times.

Since he started in business as a teenager, Sunil Mittal has been very successful in entering uncharted territory, accurately anticipating trends and change, and encashing them whether it is changing market dynamics, change in tariffs, assessing competition, stitching up alliances, exiting shaky partnerships, etc.

The first ten years of Bharti Televentures have been, relatively speaking, easier in terms of growth, considering the near zero base from where India's telecom revolution had begun. The next few years will likely face a different kind of challenge—intense competition in a crowded market, expanding rural network, increasing customer demand for segmented and value-added services, rapidly changing technology, convergence among various media, etc. There will also be pressure to expand into markets beyond India to sustain growth or even to move beyond telecom. One of the reasons Sunil Mittal often cites for his phenomenal success is that he had only one business to concentrate upon and he put all his attention to it. Most other private players had other businesses to run and telecom was only one of the new things they were trying out. However, that singular focus is set to change, with the Bharti Group having already moved into the retail sector, once again through its hallmark of strategic alliance, this time tying up with one of the biggest names in global retail, Walmart. Retail promises to be the next big wave on par with telecom in India but the two sectors could not have been more different; a primary difference being that in retail speed is a distant secondary requirement to detailed, slow and meticulous planning. Building supply chains is likely to be different from building airwave networks. But one thing will remain the same and that is Sunil Mittal's cornerstone business model—lowest cost with highest quality.

Mittal has many firsts to his credit—the first push-button phone, the first cordless phone, first fax machine, first answering machine, and the first private mobile network. It has been a long journey from a young boy in Ludhiana making bicycle crankshafts to India's complete telecommunications solution provider with more than one billion minutes of traffic passing through its networks per day and with over 60 million subscribers (fixed and mobile).

Sunil Mittal's Bharti Airtel is the market leader in mobile services in India with over 20 per cent share and together they have earned a place for themselves in India's business history. But their real and sustainable contribution to India is the big push a small hand phone has given to business and entrepreneurship across the board, from senior leaders, CEOs, politicians, and executives to the small-time self-employed like the plumber, carpenter, driver, fruit and vegetable vendor, domestic help, etc. The keen competition among state-owned BSNL/MTNL and private players like Airtel has continually made mobile technology cheaper and more sophisticated and increased the reach of this powerful medium. This, more than anything else, is the lasting imprint of an innovative first-generation entrepreneur and his company.

In March 2010, Bharti Airtel Group created a new growth path for itself with the acquisition of Zain Telecom of Kuwait in a deal worth USD 10.7 billion, with the combined company having a turnover of USD 13 billion, the fifth largest telecom player in the world. The acquisition opens up the large market of Africa to the company (after the failed acquisition of South African telecom major MTN), even lending strategic depth to India as a whole as apparent from the country's External Affairs Minister S.M. Krishna's statement following the deal: 'We are helping African people to improve the quality of their lives by building a win-win partnership for us' (Shukla and Mukherjee 2010). The Indian industry has also endorsed the deal with Dr Amit Mitra, secretary general of FICCI saying, 'This move by Bharti Group will enhance India's brand equity and add a new dimension to the Indian growth story' (*Indian Express* 2010).

Info Edge India Limited (better known as Naukri.com)

This is the story of one man's abiding belief in turning a germ of an idea into a business opportunity and going all the way to turn it into a Rs 840 million enterprise in less than a decade.

The business as it stands today developed slowly through exploring some of the several thousand ideas churning in the mind of the principal founder, Sanjeev Bhikchandani. After giving up the security of a good multinational company (MNC) job, Bhikchandani and a partner began literally as a garage start-up and examined several interesting options thrown up in a steadily liberalizing economy in the early 1990s. The fledgling venture started out with rudimentary salary surveys—a standardized non-customized survey report of entry level salaries of MBAs (Master of Business Administration) and engineers, which they sold to a few companies as human resource (HR) data— and trademark searches, wherein they gathered information about trademarks already registered with the trademark registry in respect of a few hundred pharmaceutical compounds and sold a computer-generated check report to companies seeking to register a trademark. What made this project a success was that the software delivered near instant results, whereas the government reviewer used to take on an average five years to accept or reject a trademark application, by which time a company would have invested a lot of money in that trademark. It was perhaps the country's first database search, not exactly online but close enough. However, the partnership did not last long and Bhikchandani concentrated on the salary survey portion that was left with him.

In the mid-1990s a very interesting idea called the Internet came to India, albeit in a rudimentary form. The servers were located in the US and businesses in general had not caught on to the notion of speed and the power of the medium.

One of the ideas that Bhikchandani had been pondering over for a long time was the habit people had of obsessively looking at job classified advertisements in magazines and newspapers even if they were employed in a good job. He reckoned that everyone wants to look *at* new jobs even if they were not looking *for* one. Thus, a web-based job search mechanism seemed like a winning proposition. So, with a server in the US (whose monthly subscription was paid by his brother in return for a percentage stake in the start-up company), a programmer-partner who wrote the first software for the website (for a 7 per cent share), and a few other core people (in exchange for more percentage shares), the company launched its first website—Naukri. com—in April 1997.

It was India's first job site that was targeting Indians in India whereas the competition, such as it was, was offering overseas jobs to overseas Indians. The site became a big hit and with the added first-mover advantage, it brought a lot of traffic to the website. The initial strategy was to let people log on for free; the jobs offered were mostly free and the company made a little money from other work, including salary surveys. This mix steadily altered, visitors had to pay for membership and to apply for jobs. The strategy clicked so well that business revenues which were Rs 2,35,000 in the first year of operations jumped to Rs 1.8 million in the second year and then to Rs 3.6 million in the third year; the company was looking at making Rs 5–6 million shortly, with a profit of Rs 1 million. Although the promoters were very happy with the way business was going, money was still very tight and they had no choice but to be very frugal. In fact, Bhikchandani took up a second job at a newspaper to earn some money because Naukri.com still could not pay him. As luck would have it, the newspaper changed hands and he found himself the owner of a quarter of a paper which had huge debts, mounting bills, unpaid wages, and no money in sight. The new owners of the paper fought hard to survive and pull back from the brink, and lessons of those bootstrapping days have stayed with Bhikchandani and helped him run a tight ship at Naukri.com.

Then suddenly the nature of the game changed with the arrival of big-budget venture capitalists (VCs) who were looking for promising new ideas to back or even buy up. The promoters realized that the scale of the field was going to go up so dramatically that unless Naukri thought in terms of ten times its current business size, it may as well not be in the reckoning. So, putting sentimental misgivings aside, Naukri.com took a hard-headed decision to accept VC funding (in return for a 15 per cent stake) in April 2000. The timing of the funding was somewhat fortuitous, coming as it did just before the global dotcom meltdown which not only dried up VC funding but made companies use their money far more wisely than if it had come in an atmosphere of plenty. On its part, the company spent money cautiously, and invested in servers, technology, product development, sales offices, top-quality consultants, and people. Hitesh Oberoi, one of the main promoters, was instrumental in propelling the company into a high-value chain with innovative and lucrative additions like banners, microsites, home page links, and other high-value products. Despite 9/11 and its effect on global business, Naukri.com kept moving ahead steadily and carefully, improving products and delivering value. It broke even after two years of losses and in the following year posted a Rs 10 million profit. The company estimates that it handles some 60 per cent of job traffic in India, with a 50 per cent market share of revenues. A one-stop information clearinghouse about jobs and careers, it was the first to consolidate a hugely fragmented market and deliver results in real-time to people besides significantly reducing lead time of successful matching.

The underlying business logic of the company is to create a platform where complementary needs of people are satisfied and the company charges money for the prospect of completing the deal, a platform ticket, as it were. The core proposition of the company is fairly simple—greatest aggregation (of hunters and seekers) and intensive focus on technology to deliver a valuable experience. The company has become India's leading portal for jobs, matrimony, property, education classifieds, etc., within a decade of setting up operations. It achieved this in an environment that was most unlikely to throw up any winners—Internet penetration was sketchy, bandwidth was poor, most clients were not net-enabled, HR departments of companies still operated on the system of snail mail, hardware and software capability in the country was rather rudimentary, etc.

And yet, perhaps the biggest threat to the company's sustainability is the very nature of the Internet medium, fast changing, ever evolving, and continually falling prices. For instance, Naukri.com's pay-for-use model faces a challenge from the highly popular social and business networking websites like Orkut, Facebook, Linkedin, etc., which are not only global but also work as an 'old boys' club' to the disadvantage of a plain vanilla job site. The Internet is increasingly getting more competitive and the company needs to 'think younger' in order to flourish in the years to come.

Technology is perhaps the single biggest expenditure in a web-based company; in 2006–7 alone, the company changed its search algorithm about twenty times to take into account the changing needs of the expanding client base. Naukri.com uses open-source solutions rather than proprietary software which would have substantially raised costs.

Although the company focuses on the virtual world, it is also involved in actual contact with potential customers. One of the nine businesses of the company is purely offline, called Quadrangle, an executive search unit which started in 2000 as a means of hedging bets in a tough online world. It bills on success fees, unlike the model of its online streams, and contributed 6 per cent to company's revenue in 2007–8. Also, the Indian psyche and ground reality is such that while an online contact system may be good enough for Naukri.com, it may not succeed in Jeevansaathi.com or 99acres.com because of the target audience and the nature of the transaction. In both marriage and property matters, the direct clients (an older generation or other non-technology-savvy parties) will find physical contact more reassuring.

Info Edge India Ltd has had a good run in the one decade of its existence, propelled by sharp insights of promoters, ability to spot unmet needs of potential clients, scaling up at the right time, and of course its first-mover advantage. It grew with the growth of Internet penetration in India and engineered a change in the way searches across a broad spectrum of activities take place. Along the way, it rose from a small garage setup to one of India's fastest growing companies employing over 1,000 people working at its forty-five offices across thirty Indian cities and an overseas office at Dubai.

What is more significant is the high degree of ethics practiced by the owners even when it hurt their meagre financial resources such as paying taxes although the demand was contestable or buying legal copies of software and getting all their machines audited. The promoters practice the philosophy of sharing their wealth, having shared 45 per cent of stock (apart from IPO [initial public offering] and VC dilution) with people who made their dream happen.

Info Edge India Ltd aims to be the leader in whichever segment it is in and to be the smartest company in the world. It believes that there is enough growth opportunity in India and will continue to focus on the Internet while growing internally and by investing in similar businesses.

NDTV

It seems unbelievable in today's world of several 24-hour television channels that just about twenty-five years ago Indian viewers had no choice but to watch programmes for a few hours a day on one or two channels run by state-owned Doordarshan (DD). Indian viewers would wait for a whole week for the weekly news-based programme called *The World this Week* to catch up on the news around the world. Competition was not allowed either from local private sources or from foreign news agencies because news was something of a holy cow and only the government's version was permitted (even today foreign companies can only have minority ownership in a news channel).

It was in this atmosphere of state stranglehold on news that a couple, Radhika Roy and Prannoy Roy, along with some friends set up a TV production house in 1988 as a start up called New Delhi Television (NDTV). NDTV bagged a contract with DD to produce an international news program, *The World This Week*—the first ever privately produced news bulletin—which became an instant hit with viewers. (A few years ago Times of India Group, a large media conglomerate, rated this programme amongst the top five programmes produced since Independence.) The face of the production house, co-founder Prannoy Roy, with no previous experience in journalism, quickly established a reputation for reliable, authentic, and sophisticated news stories. At a time when such concepts were unheard of in the country, NDTV pioneered detailed coverage and analysis of elections—psephology—and further consolidated its reputation with accurate forecasts. It is no exaggeration to say that Prannoy and Radhika Roy are responsible for changing the face of election reporting in India.

NDTV was the partner of choice for foreign news agencies like BBC and STAR Network when satellite TV helped break DD's grip on national access to news and allowed more private participation. Ten years of building credibility saw NDTV enter into a five-year contract with STAR Network in 1998 to produce all of its news content. The company got a great opportunity to work with a globally recognized brand while promoting its own editorial capability. Business and economic news remained the company's core competency and it was not without justification that one if its advertisements said, 'If it is news, it must be NDTV'. The credibility of its news bulletins is what made NDTV a pioneer in getting news channels as wide a viewership as entertainment channels. While Prannoy was the face of the channel, its back end was run by Radhika with the same principles of honesty and integrity as in news broadcasting. In NDTV, the method to determine whether an action or a transaction meets the expected standards is by making it pass an imaginary test called 'Radhika's smell test'.

Early in its life NDTV was able to have equity capital from global investment banks of impeccable reputation and known for their quality of investments like Goldman Sachs and Morgan Stanley. In 2004, when NDTV went public its board had people like Narayana Murthy of Infosys, and Tarun Das, the chief mentor of CII, as independent directors. If a man is known for the company it keeps, NDTV always had a great reputation!

However, the very principle of editorial credibility, impartiality, and independence became a stumbling block in the relationship with the Murdoch-owned STAR Network. Star wanted complete control over news content, whereas NDTV did not want to let go of its editorial independence. The alliance with STAR had provided the funds for creating the necessary infrastructure and the company already had production experience. Therefore in 2003 after parting ways with STAR, NDTV became a broadcaster with two news channels, the Hindi-language NDTV India and English NDTV 24x7, and continue to be leaders in the chosen strata.

Life as a broadcaster was quite different than as a content provider and NDTV had to learn to prove its credibility all over again to viewers and advertisers. In fact, NDTV had to pay hefty carrying charges to cable operators to even allow its channels to be aired, which till date plagues independent broadcasters in India. Luckily, the following year, 2004, witnessed India's most televised general elections. Prannoy Roy's formidable reputation as the best psephologist in the country gave the channel a great opportunity to sustain scaled up revenues. This helped the company to show profits in the very first year of existence as a broadcaster and within a year and a half of parting ways with STAR Network, NDTV emerged as a frontrunner in English news, while the Hindi channel was doing decently.

The ability to sustain revenues without big-ticket events like elections is, however, crucial; the years after liberalization have seen a proliferation of channels across all spectrums. Increased economic prosperity, rising literacy levels, demand for customized news, not to mention participative democracy have made Indian viewers avid consumers of news programmes; these very factors are responsible for splitting up the advertisement and sponsorship pie. To remain relevant in a crowded market place and get on the curve of cutting edge technology, all the while not compromising on content quality is something NDTV does on a daily basis by creating new shows, innovative content, in-depth analysis, and hard-hitting journalism. NDTV is one of the few companies that has a codified code of conduct for its journalistic content and one that is treated with reverence within the company.

NDTV has successfully pursued the strategy of promoting TV anchors as stars, both to create brand equity for the channel and as a policy of talent promotion and retention. In fact, NDTV is widely acknowledged for creating a whole new category of media professionals of high credibility, some of whom have branched off to start successful ventures of their own or even to rival channels. Radhika and Pronnoy Roy believe in sharing wealth with people who helped build the value and the company has over 200 employees, which is about 15 per cent of the total work force, who have stock options that have been valued over Rs 10 million. The other barometer for measuring empathy and concern for the employees is reflected in the fact that about 28 per cent of its work force has been with NDTV for over ten years, which is unprecedented in the electronic media, where the average length of the service period is less than four years.

In January 2008, NDTV Networks sold a 26 per cent stake to NBC Universal, the US broadcaster for USD 150 million and in turn expected to gain access to the TV formats of NBC's shows. The valuation of nearly USD 600 million for a general entertainment channel by NBC, solely based on a business plan on paper and that of a channel which was in a drawing board stage was unique. This allows an insight to the value that companies like NBC, which is owned by GE attribute to the capabilities of NDTV and its team.

NDTV has always been good at turning events into winning opportunities for itself from its early days: it covered seminal events like the fall of the Berlin Wall and China's Tiananmen Square incident for DD; accurately gauged India's need for accurate reporting of news and even made a dry topic like elections very exciting and glamorous; it had established a reputation when foreign agencies came shopping in India; found the most opportune time to lauch itself as a broadcaster; and still keep a finger on the pulse of change in the media and entertainment world.

But running NDTV was not always easy. In 1997, Rathikant Basu, the man who had a major contribution in ushering in the current television age in India as the director general of state-owned DD, left and joined the multinational rival, Star Network, resulting in several of his decisions to come under scrutiny. NDTV came under a protracted dispute relating to allegations that the rates paid to them by DD, during Basu's regime were arbitrary and caused loss to the exchequer. Central Bureau of Investigation (CBI) and Public Accounts Committee (PAC) of the Parliament had looked into the matter and, subsequently, it took over fourteen years till 2011 for the government to decide that there was no evidence of wrongdoing by NDTV. Prannoy Roy maintains that over these years, the experience he has gone through in dealing with CBI, PAC, and other regulatory agencies has never let him or NDTV give up their belief in their own integrity even if it took fourteen long years to get vindicatd.

What is remarkable is that the company began in an era of bureaucratic control and worked within those constraints to hone the skill of being at the right place at the right time and create favourable situations for growth. The entrepreneurial talent of the founders has transformed a start-up production house into an internationally renowned and acclaimed news broadcaster—a long way to come for a company just over twenty years into life.

Shahnaz Husain—Beauty is Skin-Deep

'I do not sell products. I sell an entire civilization in a jar.' That statement by Shahnaz Husain, entrepreneur and founder of the Shanaz Husain range of beauty products succinctly sums up the USP of the group and its core strength. An enterprise that is only about three decades old, known for exclusive, upmarket products with a loyal albeit small client base, the Shahnaz Husain Group has, nevertheless, firmly marked its place not only in India but also in several countries around the world.

The story begins in the 1970s when the founder, Shahnaz Husain (belonging to an aristocratic Muslim family of India that traces its lineage to Central Asia, Afghanistan, and the Mughals) trained in modern cosmetic therapy in several Western beauty institutions for over ten years. However, Western beauty products and solutions were based on synthetic chemicals and Shahnaz Husain was troubled by the potential harm these could cause to the human body. On her return to India, Husain studied the ancient Indian system of Ayurveda, which is a holistic treatment that looks at beauty as a composite, both within and outside, and uses only natural ingredients. She created a few herbal formulations based on Ayurveda in her kitchen and ran her first clinic from the balcony of her home. This was the beginning of the legend of Shahnaz Husain and her hugely successful business enterprise which lakhs of women—and now some men—swear by.

However, the beginning was not easy, particularly since the beauty products in India comprised a highly fragmented market that was not only unorganized but also of dubious hygiene standards and somewhat dodgy products. Husain went about steadily establishing a reputation for quality that included word-of-mouth recommendations and hosting a show on India's only TV channel, Doordarshan, teaching do-it-yourself makeovers called *Shahnaz Husain on the Kitchen Shelf*. Her products gained popularity and their premium pricing has only helped in adding to the mystique of the brand. Most of Shahnaz Husain products and treatments are proprietary and do not lend themselves to easy duplication; increasing awareness about the benefits of natural products has turned customers themselves into brand ambassadors. Combining Ayurveda ingredients with modern techniques to create premium and niche therapeutic products and treatments for skin and hair has delivered to the private company an indelible place in India's beauty segment.

Shahnaz Husain's products have also set benchmarks and helped to consolidate the market. The company operates on a successful franchise model and has over 200 franchise beauty clinics and outlets. The company supplies Shahnaz products and proprietary treatments to the franchisees besides sharing knowledge and providing support (including finance with a tie-up with State Bank of India [SBI]) and has helped create thousands of entrepreneurs.

Perhaps the greatest contribution that Shahnaz Husain has made to the Indian beauty business is to pioneer the concept of vocational training in cosmetology. The only available training option in the Indian beauty industry was through apprenticeship—mostly fragmented, non-standardized, and somewhat whimsical. Husain created a series of programmes which include both classroom-type theoretical studies combined with practical training at various levels. The company offers training at three levels: a Diploma in Beauty Therapy (200–300 hours over three to four weeks), Postgraduate Diploma (for holders of basic Diploma, comprising 100 hours over two to three weeks, including diagnosis, therapy, salon, and business management), and several short-term vocational courses in various aspects of beauty treatment. These programmes have helped to achieve a certain standardization in terms of hygiene, skill, and service that is so important in a service industry such as this. An alumnus of the institute commands a premium wage in the market and can leverage a better brand value while setting up self-owned salons.

The beauty and wellness business in India is growing at a fast pace. Euromonitor International (a global market intelligence firm) estimates the Indian skin care industry at Rs 12.72 billion, *The World Beauty Report 2006* had put the Indian healthcare and services industry at Rs 22.8 billion, and CII had estimated that the beauty and cosmetics market in India was worth Rs 45 billion in 2005, out of which Ayurvedic herbal care products were worth Rs 25 billion and herbal cosmetics were worth Rs 4.5 billion (Yahoo India News 2008). This huge market is attracting several international players as well; German personal care giants Beiersdorf and Nivea are targeting emerging markets like China and India to increase market share and expect double digit sales growth from such growth markets. Bodyshop, the premium international cosmetics brand has set up several stores across the country and poses direct competition to products like Shahnaz Husain and is backed by financial muscle and global brand recognition.

In the light of growing competition, for the first time the Shahnaz Husain brand is aiming for volume and has launched a range of products for the mass market under the brand name 'Shahnaz Forever' in 2006. The company has invested Rs 50 million in this segment and plans to compete in the price-sensitive mass market which is valued at over Rs 20 billion (*Hindu Business Line* 2005). In 2005, the group had extended its geographical reach and launched a highly successful fairness cream in Chennai in partnership with Elder Pharmaceuticals Ltd. The mass product is expected to provide synergy to the brand's premium products. Besides the mass market, the group is focussing on other exclusive services, particularly day spas under the brand name

'Sparlours'; the spa business alone is expected to be worth about Rs 500 million in 2008 (*Economic Times* 2006).

The group is also aggressively looking at overseas markets to grow globally; Shahnaz Husain products have been sold at some of the leading stores of the world, although as a niche brand. The group is going global in a determined manner; it is setting up liaison offices in Dubai—to serve as a base for Africa—and Malaysia—to serve southeast Asia, including Japan and Thailand. The UK subsidiary has been in existence for a few years and in 2007 the company entered into an eleven-year contract with a large trader in Korea, HAIM, to distribute Shahnaz herbal products in that country. The first year has already clocked sales worth USD 11 million (*Economic Times* 2007).

All these expansion and growth plans require a lot of investment and Shahnaz Husain has always been a 100 per cent private company. The group is now examining private equity options to build and promote various brands and ventures. The family business also seems to have a succession plan in place and the third generation, grandson of the founder, Sharik Currimbhoy, as vice president of the group, is at the helm of company affairs. He is actively working to raise the size and profile of the business to transform it into a professional and global organization and has taken on board professionals from the industry and has a bigger risk appetite than the company has ever had before. Clearly, the business is poised for growth on a global scale in the high-growth global industry of looking young and feeling good.

9

Is India a Sustainable Dream?

The Indian economy is poised at a tipping point; the world—and Indians in particular—is waiting with bated breath to see whether the country will indeed fulfil its potential and promise in the coming years. Although all sectors of the economy have an impact on its functioning, there are some areas that can truly become the engines that power India's growth. Equally, these are the very sectors that are potent enough to turn the roar of the elephant into a whimper.

The Indian economy is going through its most remarkable phase of growth—an average compounded growth of 7.6 per cent p.a. in the Tenth Plan period (2002–3 to 2006–7). This growth is projected to reach 8 per cent p.a. over the Eleventh Plan period. A faster economy needs a robust infrastructure to run smoothly and this is something that is not top quality in India. Economic infrastructure—roads, railways, ports, airports, communication, energy—may turn out to be the biggest constraint in the effort to reach 9 per cent plus growth. Social infrastructure—education, hospitals, quality of life—is also not something that India can currently look upon with pride. Infrastructure, then, is the critical input that must be addressed. The World Economic Forum (WEF), in its *Global Competitiveness Report 2010–11*, has listed infrastructure as one of the twelve elements crucial to a country's productivity and competitiveness.

According to the Planning Commission, infrastructure investment requirement in the country is about USD 502.88 million over the Eleventh Plan period (Planning Commission 2008: Chapter 12). Infrastructure development has largely been the government's job through departments, agencies, or public sector companies but given the colossal nature of development that is required and the limited resources at its disposal, the government is increasingly using the public–private partnership (PPP) route for infrastructure creation. The PPP model is seen as an important tool for producing an accelerated and larger pipeline and catching up with the infrastructure deficit in the country and about 20 per cent of requirement over the next five years is likely to come from this route. Most PPP projects currently under way are in airports, roads, and bridges.

Some areas or sectors that have the potential to push the economy on either side of the tipping point are profiled below.

Government in a Modern Economy

Adam Smith in *Wealth of Nations* (1776) states that the main tasks for a government are allocation of resources, redistribution of income, stabilization of economic activity, and promotion of growth and employment. The degree of governmental intervention will be governed by the level of achievement in all these tasks and by certain external circumstances.

A market economy—the so-called free market economy—is an enterprise system in which goods and services are traded or distributed through the mechanism of free markets. Decisions of what and how much to produce and at what price are made collectively by producers and buyers and not mandated by the government as in a planned economy.

Pure market economy, however, is a theoretical concept. There are various degrees of governmental intervention in all economies, including the US; as Milton Friedman in *Capitalism and Freedom* (1962) puts it, 'Absolute freedom is impossible'. The existence of a free market does not eliminate the need for a government. Economists like Friedrich Von Hayek and Milton Friedman go so far as to hold that economic freedom is a necessary condition for the creation and sustainability of civil and political freedom. But paradoxically, Indians, who by and large fiercely protect grassroots political freedom, have been exposed to shades of the free market only for the past decade and a half.

The commonly held view of the role of the government in a market economy is largely that of creating an enabling environment—establishing clear rules and institutions to enforce such rules, providing a legal and regulatory framework so that operations are conducted efficiently, providing public goods and infrastructure, and largely promoting macroeconomic stabilization to ensure more equitable distribution of wealth among all sections of the society. Joseph Stiglitz, economist and Nobel Laureate, has defined the government's role as providing public services such as education, health, pension, and other social safety nets, and enabling the market to function well.

The stage of development of an economy in a large measure determines the extent of governmental interference in the economy where the degree of development is inversely proportional to governmental involvement. There is, however, the category known as public goods in which the role of the government is indispensable. Public goods are consumed by the public at large where no discrimination can reasonably be made between one individual and another or, for that matter, between a payer and a non-payer. An example of such public goods is providing defence services for the people residing in the country. Here, the beneficiaries are homogeneous and indistinguishable (payers and non-payers) and hence these services have to be paid for through general taxation.

There are not too many examples of truly public goods. However, often governments, especially those proclaiming a middle-of-the-road or a socialist philosophy, expand the notion of public goods to include large areas of commerce—building roads, setting up heavy industries, petroleum products, radio or TV signals broadcast over free-to-use airwaves, or even sports activities. Where governments overreach their proper role in economic life ... the result is increasingly an erosion of competitive energy, economic vitality and social stability (Lesher 1997). This has great relevance for India, which is constitutionally committed to the 'socialist' philosophy. Moving from a socialist, welfare state towards a market economy requires recalibration of the role of the government. This is particularly relevant in today's political environment of coalition governments; policies that require more time to implement than the political horizon of the government introducing them require careful drafting and a set of failsafe guarantees built into them such as reducing business–government dependence.

Since independence, the government has vastly expanded its own footprint across the business landscape, often even erecting barriers for entry of non-government players. Investing time and other resources into managing business enterprises deflects attention from the fundamental job that is expected of the government, namely creating an enabling environment for business to flourish. In many instances, the government acts as a competitor to other players and can also create for itself an unfair or undue advantage while framing rules or committing resources to foster a level playing field.

For example, consider the amount of investible funds in the economy. India's twenty-seven state-owned banks control about 70 per cent of banking loans and deposits. In addition, the government owns nearly all of approximately 600 rural and cooperative banks, many national, state, and local level development banks, financial institutions, and even venture capital funds (WSJ–Heritage Foundation). The government's investment in nationalized banks is approximately Rs 168.09 billion; considering perpetual securities issued over the years, the total net capital support of the government to the banking sector stands at Rs 228.08 billion. In line with its policy of liberalizing the economy, Budget 2006–7 proposed to wind up the special arrangements between the government and banks by converting non-tradable special securities into tradable, SLR (statutory liquidity ratio) Government of India dated securities. This is expected to release additional resources for lending to productive sectors to cater to the increasing credit needs of the economy (Chidambaram 2006). The Reserve Bank of India (RBI) governor, Y.V. Reddy, in a speech said that,

> The transactions between the de facto joint balance sheet of the government, the Reserve Bank of India and the commercial banks were governed by fiscal priorities rather than the sound principles of financial management and commercial viability. The Indian financial system in the pre-reform period ... was thus characterized by segmented and underdeveloped financial markets coupled with paucity of financial instruments. (Reddy 2007)

Central bank interventions are needed more in economies which do not have robust financial markets but that does not stop Indian exporters, including new-age software companies, from demanding

RBI intervention to adjust unfavourable foreign exchange rates. Private industry must understand that free market principles must be applied consistently and without prejudice.

Since the reform period began in the 1990s, the government has consistently ceded space to private and foreign business interests. In a democracy like India there will always be strong voices both for and against government intervention in economic matters; however, receding government presence from business has been vindicated by phenomenal growth figures of the past few years and unleashed the latent entrepreneurial potential of people.

Citizens have a right to expect all government institutions to run in a well-synchronized manner and to create a supportive environment which will harness the energies of all elements. In India, we may reasonably expect the government to continue to be a direct shareholder in several sectors of the economy. We may also dare hope that private industry and citizen groups are strong enough to assert themselves and demand their rightful dues.

Early in 2009, the Government of India was faced with a unique situation which called into question the credibility of the regulatory mechanism and by inference, the strength of government writ on the economy. The triggering event was the shocking admission by the founder-chairman of Satyam Computers that the accounts had been inflated and fudged for several years and profits (as well as stock valuations) were fictitious; the extent of fraud admitted was around Rs 70 billion. The admission sent shock waves across the economy and India's corporate image took a severe beating.

Using its (rarely used) statutory powers, the government swung into action promptly, dismissed the existing board and appointed an interim board which was charged with stabilizing the company in the immediate aftermath of the shocker and to find a buyer for the beleaguered company. This was perhaps the first time the government took such a proactive role in using its powers under the Companies Act to set matters right in a private company in a short span of time, apart from its role of investigating the corporate crime and proceeding with the prosecution. The government's role was widely lauded for being unique and innovative—the new board had a clear mandate to run the company on commercial lines and there was no bailout or infusion of funds using the tax payers' money. There was a clear vision of separating the company from the consequences of fraud—distinguishing between the business of the company and the fraud of the promoters. The government-appointed board focussed on putting in place interim systems to stabilize the company and then floated it as an attractive investment opportunity—in April 2009, three months after the scam broke out, the company was sold to Tech Mahindra through a transparent bidding process. What was unique about the handling of the Satyam challenge was a sense of ownership by the government of the *cause*—and not the *machinery*.

It was the first high-profile PPP of its kind where the obvious government concern was for the shareholders, employees, clients, and the very global image of corporate India that was at stake. According to Anurag Goel, Secretary, Ministry of Corporate Affairs, 'The vision of the Ministry of Corporate Affairs is to be a leader and partner in initiatives for corporate reforms, good governance and enlightened regulation, with a view to provide and facilitate effective corporate functioning and investor protection' (Narendranath 2009).

Later in 2009, the economic wisdom and sense of fair play of the government was tested again in a dispute over natural gas among two large private sector companies (owned separately by the Ambani brothers), public sector oil and electricity companies, and concerned ministries. In many ways, this was a test not only of the strength of property rights and sanctity of written contracts but also of the government's maturity and coming of age in corporate and economic matters.

The role of the government in the Indian economy is evolving along with the economy towards more nuanced and refined processes. At the same time, citizens are getting more aware of rights and displaying public-spiritedness in demanding better governance—something unheard of a decade or two ago. The relationship between the rulers and the ruled is constantly changing. In the months and years to come Indian businesses can hope to have a truly enabling regulatory environment in which to operate.

ENERGY SECTOR

Energy is recognized as one of the most important inputs for economic growth and human development. There is also a strong two-way synergy between economic development and energy consumption. In India, a rising population, expanding economy, and a quest for improved standards of living will drive up the per capita energy consumption.

Coal, oil, and natural gas are the three primary commercial energy sources. Coal has always been the largest energy source; however, India's primary energy mix is changing over time. Presently, coal is the most important source of fuel in India, accounting for about 42 per cent of energy need, followed by petroleum products (23 per cent), natural gas (5.7 per cent), electricity (only 1.6 per cent), and combined renewable and waste at 26.4 per cent. Even where coal is not the primary source of energy as in the railways and some industries, it is the primary input for producing electricity. In the domestic sector, particularly the rural sector, energy requirement is met in a large measure (nearly 40 per cent) by non-commercial energy sources like firewood, crop residue, and animal waste. As the country progresses and its people prosper, this will change towards more modern sources like LPG (liquefied petroleum gas) and LNG (liquefied natural gas). There are five major end-use sectors of energy—agriculture, commercial, residential, transport, and industrial sectors. Various sectors use different forms of energy at different pricing and efficiency levels—the transport sector accounts for nearly 70 per cent of total petroleum consumption, whereas around 70 per cent of coal is consumed for power generation. Energy consumption by the agriculture sector and its pricing in India is an issue dictated by state politics rather than economics. Indian industry is compulsorily required to generate a part of their power needs rather than rely on electricity from the national grid, for which they consume scarce petroleum resources to run generator sets.

The Energy and Resources Institute (TERI) has mapped out various scenarios of energy requirements in the country over a thirty-year period up to 2031. In the business-as-usual scenario, total commercial energy consumption is estimated to increase by 7.5 times (considering economic growth at 8 per cent per annum). In case of a low-growth scenario (at 6.7 per cent per annum), energy consumption would increase 5.5 times, and in the case of a high-growth scenario (at 10 per cent per annum), the increase in energy consumption is expected to be around 11.75 times over the 2001 levels (TERI n.d.). As per TERI's projections, the likely growth in energy demands means that the maximum annual production potential of all forms of conventional energy will be fully exploited by 2016. The country would then need to increase its imports of coal, oil, and gas in the future. For the total energy requirements to reduce, it is imperative to increase the end-use efficiency in each of the consuming sectors through use of appropriate technology, conservation, reducing transmission and distribution losses, etc. Supply-side initiatives are equally important, like increasing the use of renewable energy sources, use of nuclear power, and working towards affordable new technology like fuel cells, plant-based fuels, hybrid technology, etc. The two sides—demand and supply—have to be integrated to provide a credible energy management policy.

With economic growth projected at an average of at least 8 per cent p.a. over the next few years (revised downward to about 6 per cent p.a. due to recession in 2009), energy security is rapidly a core focus area in the country. Several sources of energy are bound in geo-political issues such as the gas pipeline from the Middle East, nuclear power agreement from the US, etc. Energy security is also linked to development of other infrastructure such as roads, ports, railway tracks, etc., to prevent leakages and increase efficiency in the entire energy value chain. This requires an integrated policy development so that there are cross-linkages among various government policies and segments rather than cross-purposes. Increasingly, we can expect greater autonomy in energy pricing, particularly oil and electricity. Simultaneously, we can expect increased market activity leading to better developed and organized energy markets which attract more investment.

Challenges Facing the Power Sector in India

Indian citizens are used to treating water and electricity as free resources, a situation brought about by successive governments that have considered electricity, in particular, as a political commodity. Besides, power is a state subject in the Constitution, which means that there is no unified central policy focussing on various issues. Tariffs generally have a ceiling which means that rising costs cannot be passed on to the consumer and are absorbed by the state electricity boards. Therefore, most state electricity boards are in dire financial straits. In recent years, most state boards have unbundled the three main segments—generation, transmission, and distribution—into separate entities or lines of business. Private sector investment and participation is allowed in all three segments. These reforms have helped in plugging losses to some extent (as per one estimate from 33 per cent to 16 per cent) besides stimulating the market with fresh investments, players, and ideas. In fact, some states (for example, Andhra Pradesh and Karnataka) have even reported profits in distribution.

Although there is a Central Electricity Regulatory Commission (CERC) and an Electricity Act which has evolved from 1936 to 2003, an integrated electricity policy is urgently needed.

Renewable Energy

Conventional energy sources like fossil fuels and hydroelectricity continue to be the dominant energy source but renewable energy sources like solar, wind, tidal, bio-mass, etc., are all set to play a more prominent role in meeting energy needs. Till the middle of 2008, global banks and commodity brokers and leading magazines like *The Economist* were speculating whether the price of crude petroleum will rise to USD 200. Luckily for the world, oil prices came down from USD 160 per barrel before settling down at a more acceptable level of around USD 100 a barrel. This triggered the focus on the use of alternative energy around the world to reduce dependency on fossil fuels. Car manufacturers are competing globally for a viable car that runs on alternative energy while other energy-intensive industries are investing heavily in clean energy. Renewable energy is not only inexhaustible but also clean with no lasting damage done to the environment. Renewables presently contribute around 18,842 MW, which is roughly 10.94 per cent of total installed capacity. India is one of the few countries in the world that has an exclusive ministry that deals with renewable energy sources, known as the Ministry of New and Renewable Energy (MNRE).

The Government of India offers subsidies and other fiscal initiatives for promotion of renewable energy technologies in the country like:

- Income tax holiday;
- Accelerated depreciation;
- Concessional customs duty/duty-free imports;
- Capital/interest subsidy.

Wind and solar power are areas that are well-developed and are seeing a lot of investments. Wind power accounts for 13,184 MW of India's 18,842 MW of renewable electricity generation capacity as of 31 January 2011, or about 70 per cent of the total capacity. This corresponds to a contribution of about 4.13 per cent in the electricity mix (MNRE 2011: 3). Through a series of organic and inorganic growth globally, the Indian wind energy industry has gained sufficient technical and operational experience in handling wind power projects. Other renewable energy sources like tidal or ocean energy, geo-thermal energy, etc., are still in the early stages of development, awaiting commercially viable technologies; the proposed research and development (R&D) outlay in the Eleventh Plan for renewable energy is Rs 15 billion. Most renewable energy projects in India are mainly targeted at replacement of coal rather than oil.

Small hydro power (below 25 MW) is another source of renewable energy that is gaining prominence within the country. These run-of-the river projects, allowed only on tributaries, small rivers, and even irrigation canals, are ideally suited to India's geography and as per some estimates have a potential of generating 15,000 MW. By January 2011, 790 small hydro power projects aggregating to 2,939 MW have been set up in various parts of the country (Ibid.: 12). The turbine technology needed for running these kind of projects is proven technology and readily available in India, capable of delivering up to 90 per cent efficiency. However, success of this kind of power to augment total capacity is crucially dependent on grid connectivity. A small hydro plant that is connected to the main grid can achieve a plant load factor (efficiency) of 45–60 per cent, depending on the season but an unconnected plant will waste surplus power. Karnataka is the leading state in small power projects and there is immense potential in states like Uttarakhand and Himachal Pradesh, particularly for rural and remote area electrification. The northeastern states are also suited to these projects, although grid connectivity is yet underdeveloped.

The present stage of technology of renewables is at a level where per unit cost of this energy is much more than that of conventional energy. Also, a conventional energy unit can expect 100 per cent capacity utilization whereas most renewable energy projects can only expect 20–30 per cent capacity utilization. This then is a premium that is required to save the environment.

The average cost comparison of different kinds of energy is given in Table 9.1:

Table 9.1   Average Cost Comparison of Different Kinds of Energy

Type of Energy	Commissioned Cost/MW (in Rs)
Thermal Power Plant	35 to 45 million
Large Hydro Power	40 to 50 million
Small Hydro Power (renewable)	50 to 65 million
Wind Power (renewable)	60 million
Solar Power (renewable)	250 million
Fuel Cell Power (new technology)	1250 million

Source: MNRE 2011

The Indian government has resolved to try to achieve 10 per cent installed capacity of the country's energy mix through renewable energy sources over the next few years, although the Eleventh Plan paper targets a more realistic 5–6 per cent of the total energy mix. Various state governments have made different commitments to renewable projects. This means that a 4,000 MW conventional energy plant must be balanced with a 400 MW renewable energy project; at a 1:5 utilization capacity ratio between conventional and renewable energy, 400 MW capacity generation will require a 2,000 MW renewable energy plant. This translates into a huge business opportunity in this sector.

Carbon Credits

Burning fossil fuels causes emissions of harmful carbon gases which, in turn increase the earth's ability to trap infrared energy. This leads to global warming and climate change that endangers all life forms and the very planet. In the global village of today, pollution in one geographical area quickly affects the environment in places far removed from it. It is therefore very important to have a global system in place to control carbon emissions. Such a mechanism was framed among countries through the Kyoto Protocol in 2005—an international agreement to which India is also a signatory. The Kyoto Protocol laid the path for a market-based approach. As of October 2010, 191 states and the European Union (EU) had ratified the protocol; industrialized countries thirty-six developed countries (called Annexure 1 countries) are required to reduce greenhouse gas emissions, and 137 countries (including India), although ratifying the protocol, have no obligation beyond monitoring and reporting emissions. The Kyoto Protocol expires in 2012 and talks are on to finalize a future treaty to replace it. The rationale behind this differential treatment and the limited period of operation is that the largest share of historical and current emissions of greenhouse gases has originated in developed countries and also because per capita emissions in developing countries is still low; as a developing country's economy grows, its share of global emissions increases and this calls for a fresh assessment of country-wise emissions after a point. India's greenhouse gas emissions have increased by a whopping 55 per cent over the period 1990–2004, while China's have increased by 47 per cent.

The protocol has set 'caps' or quotas on the maximum amount of greenhouse gases for various countries depending on their stage of development. Annexure 1 countries have to reduce their emissions by a collective average of 5 per cent below their 1990 levels. Countries, in turn, are required to maintain national registers and fix quotas for individual businesses called 'operators'. Each operator has to work within its 'allowance' which gives it the right to emit a certain quantity of greenhouse gases. This allowance is a tradable commodity wherein an operator can sell its unused quota as 'carbon credits' or buy credits from the market to cover its excessive use. This trade can also be carried out among nations. The system allows an operator to manage emissions in the most cost-effective manner—either by investing in appropriate technology or by purchasing carbon credits. In short, the system puts a monetary value for polluting the air.

The carbon credit market operates much like other commodities or futures market and is based on price fluctuations based on demand and supply. The leading markets are European Climate Exchange and Chicago Climate Exchange and carbon credits are usually denoted in euros, perhaps because EU is actively pursuing the commandments of the Kyoto Protocol since its inception. While the scheme looks simple and elegant and seems like an answer to combat global warming, it can only succeed in its mission if adopted by all countries and implemented strictly. Emissions can now be quantified and unless they are kept within check by appropriate methods, they can become a rising cost of business. If the scheme is implemented in letter and spirit, there will be greater effort in research to adopt cleaner technologies and improve everyone's quality of life.

Carbon credits or CERs (Carbon Emission Reductions) are issued by the CDM (Clean Development Mechanism) Executive Board, which is the internationally-mandated body under the Kyoto Protocol to register projects. One CER is equivalent to one tonne of carbon dioxide reduced. India, being a developing country, is exempted from adherence to the protocol. However, Indian businesses investing in carbon-free technology can earn carbon credits for sale to countries or businesses who need to buy credits to cover the shortfall. The nodal agency for climate change issues in India is the Ministry of Environment and Forests (MoEF). India's response measures contributing to the objectives of the UN Framework Convention on climate change are mainly in twelve sectoral initiatives such as coal, oil, gas, hydro power, renewables, afforestation, residential, power, transport, industry, agriculture, etc.

The system of carbon credits can help developing countries practice sustainable development in their respective economies by helping underwrite costs and making it economically viable. It also helps by transferring clean technology to new projects and injects more global funds into developing countries. However, several community and local real sustainable projects are small in size and do not have the wherewithal to encash its value. Such projects can be bundled together so that they can increase their bargaining power to tap their real value and thus have the incentive to stay the course vis-à-vis giant corporations and governments of developed nations.

Carbon credit sales have brought in unexpected gains to developing countries but the fact remains that these credits are bought by businesses and countries that continue to emit greenhouse gases, thereby continuing to threaten the global climate. Indian companies have quickly discovered this as an additional revenue stream. A good example is that of Gujarat Fluorochemicals. It agreed to sell carbon credits worth Rs 10 billion over three years to Noble Carbon Credits of Singapore. In the first year, the deal was expected to rake in Rs 3.5 billion which is double its sales of Rs 1.82 billion of 2004–5 and more than three times its corresponding net profit of Rs 0.96 million (*Times of India* 2006). While this gives a good windfall to companies, Indian businesses must invest in clean technology even without expecting to be paid, keeping in mind the changing scenario from 2012 when the protocol expires.

Demographic Capital

Lifecycle hypothesis of Modigliani and Brumberg (1954) and human capital theories of Schultz (1960) and Becker (1964) suggest that the economic behaviour of an individual will change with age; at some stages of life, a person will be a net borrower and at others, a net saver. Since people's economic behaviour and needs vary at different stages of life, changes in a country's age profile can lead to significant effects on its economic performance. By aggregating these behaviours over a whole society, it is possible to estimate a country's economic growth. A relationship between age structure and gross domestic product (GDP) is therefore a useful tool that can help forecast GDP and shape public policies in a coherent manner.

Countries with a higher proportion of very young or very old people have low or negative savings ratios and also tend to consume more public goods and services (like primary and senior healthcare and pension payouts) while not contributing, in general, to production. A country with a higher proportion of working age population generates greater revenues than it consumes by means of tax contributions and savings.

A study of twenty Organisation for Economic Co-operation and Development (OECD) countries supports this theory that children and retirees have negative or relatively less positive effects on GDP than productive age groups (Österholm 2004) . This is borne out by the experience of Japan where the number of total households exceeds the number of individuals in the highest earning and savings years (thirty to fifty years). Although Japan is considered a frugal nation of supersavers, in line with the Asian ethos, its savings rate has already fallen from nearly 25 per cent in 1975 to less than 5 per cent in 2007 and is projected to hit 0.2 per cent in 2024 (Farell et al. 2005). In today's globalized world, this has serious ramifications. For instance, the US—the greatest absorber of global capital flows even with current account deficit of approximately 6 per cent of GDP—will need to continue consuming at the same rate as in the 2000s in order to sustain the growth pace of China's economy. However, if the rate of savings and wealth generation falls drastically, the entire global equation can become unbalanced.

The population of India presently is approximately 1.210 billion (2011), which is about 17.5 per cent of the world population. It is also one of the few countries of the world with a declining age-dependency ratio (there are more people in the working age group than very young or very old people). Deutsche Bank estimates that in Germany, 29 per cent of the average worker's salary goes towards supporting pension payments for retirees, which is a very high figure (Muralidhar 2005). Post-independence India has seen a population explosion of almost threefold—from 360 million to over a billion. The rate of population growth is today around 1.344 per cent (2011), fuelling hopes of stable growth by the middle of this century.

The huge population of India is somewhat a fixed factor; India has already scrapped any attempt at population control by forceful government policies about two decades ago. The present-day non-coercive population policy—emphasizing healthcare of girls and women and improved female literacy levels, for instance—is the policy that will continue for a long time. The decline in population, therefore, is likely to be slow and more a result of macro factors than micro management. For the next decade or two, the biggest natural resources available with the country will be its human resources. Table 9.2 shows indicators of ageing in India and a few other countries.

India is entering a phase of demographic dividend. Demographic dividend refers to a period—usually twenty to thirty years—when a greater proportion of people are in the working age group, boosting economic growth. There will be massive new entrants in the job market, giving GDP growth a major push. The flip side is to find around 15 million new jobs every year to harness this latent labour force.

This dividend is reaped in two phases: the first dividend is the obvious one when growth of the labour force is less than the dependent population. The second dividend is more subtle and comes about as a consequence of financing consumption for the retired and aged. If financed by accumulated capital during the working life of the retirees, the positive impact of this capital accumulation on economic growth is a source of the second dividend.

Table 9.2   Indicators of Ageing in Some Countries

Country	Median	Age	(Yrs)	Old Age Dependancy*		
Year	2000	2025	2050	2000	2025	2050
India	23.7	31.3	38	8.1	12.1	22.6
Mexico	23.3	32.5	39.5	7.6	13.8	30
USA	35.5	39.3	40.7	18.6	29.3	34.9
Australia	35.2	40.5	41.9	18.2	29.3	37.9
China	30	39	43.8	10	19.4	37.2
UK	37.7	44.5	47.4	24.1	34.8	47.3
Germany	40.1	48.5	50.9	24.1	39	54.7
Japan	41.2	50	53.1	25.2	49	71.3

Source: CII, http://www.cii-skillsdevelopment.in/skill_development_
in_india/india_demographic_dividend.htm
* Old Age Dependency ratio is the ratio of population aged 65 and
above to the population aged 16 to 64 expressed per 100 people.

A significant information that can be gleaned from the United
Nations Development Programme (UNDP) *Human Development
Report 2010* is the spread of population over urban and rural areas
(30:70) and corresponding literacy levels. Data suggests that a major
bulk of new entrants into the labour force is and will likely be unskilled
labour. To convert this unskilled force into skilled labour, commanding
progressively incremental wages requires investment in training at
different levels, closely linked to market needs. Covering the distance
between providing employment *to* and employability *of* the population
requires tremendous attention to enhancing skill levels and promoting
skills that are likely to be needed by the industry.

A peculiar concern for a developing country like India is that
standard theories of human capital have to be modified to glean
meaningful information. For instance, consider the two kinds of
demographic dividends mentioned earlier; the real situation in India
is that the low level of wages most people earn during their working
years does not leave enough savings with which to finance their old
age. In the absence of institutionalized old age health and pension
care, a large proportion of Indians rely on family support for old
age consumption, thus eating into the productive assets and savings
capacity of the working members.

The 'Approach Paper' to the Eleventh Plan recognizes that the expected advantages of a low population dependency ratio would be conditional upon investing in human resource development (HRD) and providing gainful employment opportunities for those joining the working age group. Greater economic prosperity means more money in people's hands, which leads to more consumption. This is likely to kick-start another cycle of productive growth; just sustaining the demands of the growing middle class will improve the dynamics of production and consumption. Of course, economists would argue that the kinds of consumption—whether on productive assets or simply consumerism—will largely determine whether such a cycle is vicious or virtuous.

As mentioned earlier, post-independence India has seen an almost threefold increase in its population. However, there are hardly any new urban centres that have been built to accommodate the growing migration of rural people to urban areas—except Chandigarh and Gandhinagar. Clean, well-planned modern cities are more than just a good place to live. They can act as powerful triggers to increased economic activity with exponential benefits. Existing cities certainly need modernization and updating, but creating new urban centres has a lot more potential to sustain progress in the economy, starting from spin-offs of the construction industry, which provides employment and starts a cycle of consumption of its own.

The window of opportunity opened by India's large and young population needs to be kept and enlarged by suitable policy initiatives. Reforms like deregulation and divestment and generally freeing up the economy have transferred a large chunk of the burden to keep the economy surging (or at least at an even keel) from the government to the business sector because it frees the energies of the government from micro management to matters of macro economics.

Economic development and equitable social development, however, are the key watchwords in enjoying the demographic dividend. Raising skill sets of people to match industry requirements is as important as investing in an institutional support system for the old, while creating an enabling environment for exponential growth of the economy.

These factors will determine whether India's demographic capital is a sterling asset or a non-performing asset.

EDUCATION SECTOR

It is now accepted wisdom that knowledge has become one of the major factors of production, up there with land, capital, and labour of the classical economic theory. The experience of the industry and corresponding policy planning are focussed towards making the country a knowledge economy. Therefore, it is imperative to ensure that there are no shortages of this essential input, that is, ensure that there is minimal 'knowledge gap'. 'Knowledge gap' is defined by the World Bank as unequal distribution of know-how across and within countries. Along with the digital divide, knowledge gap is a major impediment to economic development.

The Indian education system was designed by erstwhile British rulers to serve its purpose as the ruling class; successive Indian governments have seen little reason to deviate from the original script of controlling the supply of education. Universal primary literacy—which ought to be a government's goal—was never a goal for the British because it suited them to have a small 'elite' class of Indians educated in the British mould to serve them and help them to continue to rule. This goal seems to be implicitly carried forward, even endorsed, until recently by the government of the day. Public expenditure on education (as percentage of GDP) was only 3.7 per cent in 1991; in 2000–7 it was even lower at 3.2 per cent (UNDP 2010).

A country aspiring to super-power status, however, will need to drastically rework its approach to education and try to develop a system that will produce strong, confident and analytically-inclined student-citizens.

The UR Rao Committee has projected that India needs well over 10,000 PhDs and twice as many MTech degree holders for meeting its huge R&D needs; currently India produces barely 400 engineering PhDs a year.

Primary Education

Primary education is literally the foundation upon which the entire knowledge economy rests. The success or failure of the primary education system has a direct bearing on the expansion of the upper primary, higher, and even non-formal vocational education systems.

An inefficient primary education system will send fewer numbers of primary graduates in pursuit of further education.

There are several versions of the net enrolment ratio of children in primary classes, depending on the agency which publishes the data; according to UNDP data, a conservative estimate hovered around 89.8 per cent over 2001–9 (UNDP 2010). It is also important to focus on the nature of learning being imparted in primary classes—actual learning in an age-appropriate manner rather than mere enrolment. Experts point out that the official set of enrolment data is beset with deficiencies, inconsistencies, and overestimation, not the least of these problems being an agreed and acceptable definition of 'literacy' and its measurement yardstick. As per the statistics of the Human Resources Development Ministry (HRD), the gross dropout rate declined from 39.03 per cent in 2001–2 to 28.49 per cent in 2004–5. However, the UNDP *Human Development Report 2010* maintains the drop-out ratio of all grades at 34.2 per cent over 2005–8.

The primary education sector in the country is largely run by the government; however, over sixty years and several schemes later, India still has not achieved 100 per cent literacy levels. The primary education system suffers on account of several factors like infrastructure, pedagogy, irrelevant curriculum, staffing, etc. There are several studies to show the pathetic state of infrastructure of schools like lack of proper classrooms, separate toilets for boys and girls, and teaching aids like blackboard, etc. Government-employed teachers spend several hours of the academic year in non-teaching work like poll duty, census duty, government-sponsored health drives, etc., worsening an already adverse teacher–student ratio.

The quality of teaching that is imparted in most government-run schools is often so poor that there is widespread proliferation of 'private schools' across the country and any parent who can eke out money from his/her earnings would rather put the child into a private school rather than government-run schools. When a student appearing for school final or professional examinations takes private coaching, it may indicate extra effort and input that s/he purchases to improve the chances of success. But when a primary school student habitually takes private coaching—and this is a trend across the country, urban and rural—it is symptomatic of a deeper malaise. It is a sad reflection of the quality of teaching in our schools that private coaching for all ages is a flourishing business. Regulation of private schools is, however, fairly nebulous and most of these private schools would rather stay out of the gambit of 'recognition' or 'affiliation' and continue to be able to run their establishments as they wish.

Curriculum ought to be more suited to the Indian values and ethos. Much of what is presently taught in schools and colleges is grounded in Macaulay's prescriptions for a 'colonial people'. Besides, the way the curriculum is taught—pedagogy—is in most part uninspiring. Cramming and rote learning seem to be the preferred route for most students and schools, with a focus on passive absorption of vast quantities of data (as opposed to knowledge), thus leaving little energy to bring out a child's creativity and encourage participation.

The ailments that affect our primary education system, however, are not insurmountable and other than costs of upgrading infrastructure, other shortfalls can be tackled by a judicious mix of loosening state control on education and improving regulatory discipline. The bigger challenge, however, is to sustain the enrolment rates into secondary school so as to improve chances of children getting a higher education.

Higher Education

There are about 350 universities in India and some 17,700 undergraduate colleges which are affiliated to these universities, and they constitute the largest component of India's higher education system (about 85 per cent of all enrolled students as per Government of India estimates).

Higher education has significantly contributed to the economic and political development and helped in spreading the gains of social progress. It is on the foundation of higher education that India has gained global recognition as a knowledge society. However, this strength of the Indian higher education system is very fragile and only a crust covering the deep malaise that runs through and across the system. Much is made of the potential of India's economic success riding on the back of knowledge. However, a lot of this perception is based on the extrapolation of data of a handful of elite institutions and their successful candidates. The ground reality is that a bulk of the country's education system is of substandard quality, churning out—when it reaches that stage—substandard and scarcely employable graduates. On an average each university has 100 affiliated colleges, with some having up to 400 colleges. This makes universities not only administratively cumbersome, slower to adapt and innovate or evolve, but also dilutes standards because a centralized examination automatically tends to settle at the lowest common denominator among all constituent colleges to ensure minimum standards of excellence.

For a large developing country like India, in order to spread the fruits of a booming economy over a large number of people, participating in the knowledge economy is one of the most promising routes. And this requires a manifold increase in enrolment rates in higher education without diluting standards. Although a major chunk of higher education institutions is owned or run by the government, there is de facto privatization in at least three disciplines—engineering, medicine, and management—to an extent of two-thirds to three-fourths of total seats.

The new economy demands a new set of skills and other competencies which include, besides the base ICT skills, other skills such as proper communication, analytical thinking, team work for working on projects and in groups, etc. These skills will be required to a greater degree all along the line and not just for managers. Preparing a child to possess such skill sets requires fundamental changes to the present rigid and theoretical system, making it more flexible and responsive to students' needs.

Rigid compartmentalization of the curriculum at all levels of education is one of the deep-set problems of our education system in that it does not help a student to fully explore his/her range of talent. It does not recognize knowledge as a continuum wherein if a student has chosen, say, commerce, in high school, it excludes him/her from studying, say fine arts, later (in higher education). These clear-cut—and somewhat artificial—boundaries between and among disciplines must be blurred and diluted so that concepts and principles in one may be tried out in other areas to promote innovation.

As a society, we must reflect upon what we need out of a college education. A vast majority of school-leaving children go into under-graduation because it has become the minimum qualification required for facing life—married life, family business or to 'keep up with the Joneses'. A number of students also drift into under-graduation as a 'standby', while also enrolling into vocation-oriented training like a computer course or preparing for other public examinations like banking, administrative, or defence services.

The value of a general graduation education, in India, therefore is very low and unsurprisingly, produces unmotivated students. Teaching as a profession does not give sufficient commercial rewards to attract and retain the best talent. The value of top-quality teachers and professors who go on to train young minds cannot be overemphasized—they not only make a university great but are, in fact, *the* university. Good infrastructure does help but it is people power that makes a college or a university. India has seen a brain drain in every sense of the word with the hollowing-out of Indian universities with a number of brains lost mostly to US universities after grappling with bureaucratic education machinery and mindset. And when good teachers go, can bright students be far behind? As per one estimate, around 15 per cent of the faculty at the Harvard Business School (HBS) is of Indian origin as were thirty-eight of the 900 students (4 per cent) in 2007 (Naithani 2007). Indian universities tend to score self goals by restricting professors from taking up assignments outside the university or collaborating with industry; remuneration is rarely linked to the number of published papers in peer-reviewed journals, so there is no incentive to sharpen skills and improve their own quality of understanding and teaching. In recent months some of these challenges have been critically appraised and, at least in a few leading academic institutions like IIMs and IITs, either modified or improved upon.

The quality of undergraduation studies in India is highly variable and although central universities and various state universities receive similar funding, the quality of education imparted is vastly different. There is a small island of world-class educational institutes in a vast sea of substandard 'teaching shops'.

University–Industry Linkages

The matter of raising standards and reducing the knowledge gap is a mammoth task and cannot be done by any one institution, even if it is the huge government machinery. Industry is the major end user of the products of India's education system but is not sufficiently engaged with it to help raise standards. A holistic development of the economy can only be carried out when there are strong PPP, with inputs from many more agencies than just a particular, even partisan, segment.

The backward integration of the corporate world into the education system need not be purely out of altruistic motives. When companies reach out to the youth through the education system, it creates a lasting sustainable value in terms of aligning education with marketable skills. For instance, newer disciplines like IT, biotechnology, genetics, fibre optics, etc., require touching base with the industry for educational institutions to even know what curriculum to draw up. Since the Indian economy is—at least in recent years—driven by IT and IT-enabled businesses, it may be no coincidence that the number of engineering education institutions far outweighs any other professional discipline; as mentioned earlier, a major chunk of these institutions are run by the private sector. If medical tourism picks up pace in the country to become a major segment of the economy, it should come as no surprise if several new medical and nursing schools are set up—the industry will only be adjusting the demand and supply side.

One of the biggest hurdles in upgrading the education infrastructure is access to funds. The kind of scale that is required to sustain the country's advantages requires commitment of huge resources.

In the US, it is not just the elite institutions which receive donations but also smaller and lesser known schools and colleges. There is a whole culture of giving back to the alma mater or other educational institutions to support laboratories, sports, buildings, libraries, gymnasiums, etc., depending on the support choice of the donor. This is through ingenious schemes like paid dinners and other fund-raising events and also by allowing provisions in bequests and wills, etc.

Value of endowments at a few US universities are given in Table 9.3:

Table 9.3 Value of Endowments at US Universities (2010)

Description	Endowment (in $)
Harvard	27.56 million
Yale	16.65 million
Stanford	13.85 million
Princeton	14.39 million
MIT	8.317 million

Source: NABUCO Public NCSE Tables, www.nabuco.org

Some industry initiatives in India:

- The Tata Institute of Fundamental Research (TIFR) attempts the complex task of balancing the demand and supply side of its main input—scientists—by extrapolating available numbers of scientists in the country, matching these numbers with their requirements and attempting to proactively bridge the gap. It has started an integrated PhD programme for students—a grand cradle-to-grave programme for students from Class 12 upwards; one of the basic ideas is to retain bright young minds in basic sciences rather than allow them to drift to IITs, etc., which are decidedly more lucrative (Bhattacharya n.d.).
- Shiv Nadar, one of the founders of the HCL group of companies, manages the trust that runs the SSN group of engineering colleges in Tamil Nadu. The colleges, rated among the best in the state, provide a stream of talented engineers who are given the first right of refusal to work in HCL group companies. The Trust also provides scholarships to underprivileged students. The Shiv Nadar Foundation has, in 2009, opened the first of a series of residential schools for underprivileged students in Bulundshahar in Uttar Pradesh to identify 100 brightest children of neighbouring districts and provide them with free, top-quality education.
- The Indian School of Business (ISB), Hyderabad, is one of the exceptions in the general apathy of the business class towards education. Considered as one of the top business schools of the country, ISB is promoted by a consortium of private businessmen including the Ambani, Godrej, and Birla families, with a sizeable investment of USD 55 million (Rs 2.2 billion).
- The Technology Business Incubator (TBI) is programmed and implemented by the Foundation for Innovation and Technology Transfer (FITT)—the industry interface unit of IIT-D (Indian Institute of Technology, Delhi) since 2000. FITT and FICCI (Federation of Indian Chambers of Commerce and Industry, an industry association) have signed an MOU in 2006 to facilitate greater university–industry linkage.
- Indian Institute of Science (IISc), Bangalore has several projects with universities, colleges, and national research institutions in aerospace, IT, defence, and space research. Other explicit university–industry

linkages are between IISc and foreign and domestic companies such as Nortel, Motorola, BPL, etc. In 2007, IISc entered into partnership with Texas Instruments (TI) for research on semi-conductors, in the process becoming the first university outside the US to be affiliated with the company. Over a five–year period, IISc will receive USD 4,00,000 towards support for various research projects. The partnership is expected to provide IISc enhanced access to TI teams worldwide and an opportunity to work with TI's other leadership universities globally on TI-funded programmes (*EE Times-India* 2007).

Globalization of Education

Education is the only proven way to develop free and open societies where ideas and exchanges flow in an unfettered manner in the course of abstract development of a student's mind and character. Won't involving the corporate world in education then violate the autonomy of students and institutions by unduly influencing young, impressionable minds with the corporate world view of the sponsor, thereby defeating a fundamental tenet of education? Detachment and critical thinking is vital to growth and companies without vast resources to dedicate towards making a significant impact may end up supporting ventures with a narrow commercial focus.

Many businesses have found that partnering with non-governmental organizations (NGOs) and other such organizations can help them develop a corporate philosophy that addresses social obligations in line with their economic outlook. And for those companies who do find this delicate balance, the rewards are immense and sustainable. It may also help reduce the social tensions that big businesses often face, being accused of pursuing commercial interest over community interest; businesses, with their commercial background, can help put community projects on a fast track by using their communication channels with various agencies.

This tenuous industry–academia link is very important to maintain, requiring a lot of hard work to sustain the link.

Under World Trade Organization (WTO)-mandated GATS (General Agreement on Trade in Services), there are four 'modes' of trade in services:

- Mode 1: Cross-border trade—Services flow from one country to another across national borders. Services that can be transmitted electronically or through regular mail (like education, healthcare, etc.);
- Mode 2: Consumption abroad—Physical purchase of services (like education, medical treatment, etc.);
- Mode 3: Commercial presence—The service provider establishes an agency to deliver services (like a foreign university or a hospital setting up a branch in another country);
- Mode 4: Movement of natural persons—The service-consuming country allows a foreign national to enter and render services (like a professor or a doctor).

India is one of the countries that has agreed to open up its higher education (primary and secondary education are presumably too sensitive in terms of patriotism and character-building, etc., to allow foreign participation), though local laws still have to be amended to give effect.

India's participation in global trade in education comprises Mode 2. Indian students are often the largest contingent of foreign students in US, UK, and Australian universities, spending several billions annually in foreign exchange payouts (in 2008–9, this amount was about USD 2 billion). Indian parents are culturally inclined to spend generously for their children's education and if there are good education options in India, it is that much money retained within the country.

Internationalization of education is a growing global trend; countries like Singapore, Dubai, and Australia are working very hard to promote their countries as an education hub in the region. Singapore is being especially proactive and has entered into collaboration with a number of reputed foreign universities to set up campuses in the country. It has also accorded recognition to some Indian universities in order to attract Indian students. Universities from the US and UK are already setting up offshore campuses in several countries to expand the pool of student intake. Education and industry make a mutually beneficial association, more so because there is hardly a discipline which does not require a constant upgrading of skills and nothing ignites a mind more than an association with the student community. At the least, leading companies, hospitals, professional firms, etc., must incorporate the value of 'giving back' in their internal HR assessments of their staff; it is only with our collaborative efforts that we can raise the standards of our own education system.

The Indian education sector is turning out to be an investor's most preferred destination, balked as it is by favourable demographics and a great business opportunity. The education sector received USD 182.2 million worth of private equity investments in 2010 which is 38 per cent more than the previous year. The K-12 segment is most popular with investors and this is expected to give a push to more investments in higher and professional education.

All of us have a collective responsibility to guard and polish what may well be our best insurance against missing the development bus— the quality of the country's brainpower.

Since 2009, the government has started taking the education sector very seriously. Apart from passing the Right to Education Bill (which will make education the fundamental right of every child), the dedicated ministry is working hard to set right the several anomalies in the system, such as revamping the regulatory mechanism, taking a re-look at the examination system, establishing rules and framework for entry of foreign educational institutions, etc. One piece of legislation in particular, Foreign Educational Institution (Regulation of Entry and Operation) Bill, 2010, recently passed in the Parliament is of great interest and could be the game changer in the education sector. While it is unrealistic to expect the world's top universities to queue up to open full-fledged campuses in India, nevertheless it is likely that there will be increasing partnerships and collaborations of foreign universities with Indian institutions. There could be greater student and faculty exchange programmes, collaborative research projects with foreign universities, or establishing research and executive centres in India. The new bill is also expected to encourage Indian universities to improve standards to keep from getting marginalized or rendered irrelevant.

The various changes in legislation also create a value proposition for private participation in the education sector which is much needed because the task of upgrading the education sector is too big for just the government to undertake.

After milk, food, and telecom, India needs a revolution in education to move to the next level.

LEGAL FRAMEWORK FOR INDIAN BUSINESSES

India adopted its Constitution in 1950 and existing British-enected laws were largely allowed to continue as long as they were in conformity with the letter and spirit of the Indian Constitution. The Indian justice system is centralized, with the Supreme Court at the apex, followed by High Courts of various states, and subordinate courts. There are also specialized tribunals established under various acts under the superintendence of a High Court, such as the IT Tribunal, Consumer Forum, Debt Recovery Tribunal, etc. Independence of the judiciary forms the basic structure of the Indian Constitution.

In a paradox for a country whose biggest advantage is the number of people, India's population–judge ratio is the lowest in the world (according to the *120th Law Commission Report*). This translates into a huge backlog of cases awaiting trials or judgement—over 29 million cases pending across hundreds of subordinate state-level courts, twenty-one High Courts, and the Supreme Court (according to rtiindia.org—a portal dedicated to the cause of citizens' right to public/official information). It can take anywhere from five to fifteen years for a case to be decided in an Indian court, including a long-drawn appeals procedure. This long gestation period of litigation leads people to circumvent the justice delivery system and opt for conflict resolution through legalized arbitration and conciliation procedures, and very often through improper means.

As in other aspects of the economy, liberalization of the 1990s influenced the legal system as well. Domestic laws such as those dealing with intellectual property rights (IPR), banking, exchange controls and even the Code of Civil Procedure were amended to give effect to the integration of Indian economy with global commerce. Independent regulatory authorities have been created in specialized fields such as telecom, capital markets, electricity, and insurance. These regulatory authorities carry out the functions of the executive, legislature, and judiciary in their respective sectors. This is good for business because it provides clarity of law and speedy resolution and shares the burden of compliance with the executive, legislature, and judiciary.

Perhaps the greatest need for legal and judicial reform from an economic point of view is in the body of labour laws in India. There are around forty-five laws that regulate labour and employment in

India, ranging from Factories Act, Maternity Benefit Act, Beedi Workers Welfare Fund Act, ESI Act, Industrial Disputes Act, etc. Such laws make it difficult for firms to have flexibility in hiring and firing various levels of employees. Manufacturers often set up several plants instead of a single large one to get or rely on smaller labour forces complemented with contract labour to get around restrictive labour laws. Not only does this make manufacturing processes uncompetitive but also drives labour out of the protective umbrella of the law, with few rights. The current rigid labour laws actually end up hurting employment opportunities; the manufacturing sector employs less than 15 per cent of the workforce whereas small, informal firms employ 40 per cent of the country's workforce (Ahmed and Devarajan 2007).

In India, labour is nearly four times more productive in industry and six times more productive in services than in agriculture, where there is a surplus of labour. In a country where a majority of the citizens are poor and marginalized, and for whom labour is the principal asset, the formal employment rate with benefits must rise from the present miniscule level. Indian businesses urgently need a thorough revamp of labour laws to give them the competitive edge in global trade.

The growth of international business is providing more opportunities for greater success and prosperity for Indian businesses than at any time before in history. Businesses are looking for a unified set of laws and regulations so that dealings in India are smoother and less expensive. Such laws throw up challenges to existing national redressal systems to streamline with global rules and also provide opportunities to a whole breed of lawmakers, enforcement agencies, consultants, and the like. A system of overly complex laws and multiple regulatory agencies increase the cost of compliance and also the cost of capital. The redressal mechanism through courts is a cumbersome and long process; McKinsey & Co., in a study in 2005, estimated that a premium on capital up to 25 per cent is put in by investors as an adjustment to such risks.

Some global laws, rules, and regulations that Indian businesses need to focus on are:

Arbitration Laws

The growth of international trade is bound to give rise to international disputes that transcend national frontiers and geographical boundaries. Mediation and conciliation which provide an alternate dispute resolution system and the more formal, quasi-judicial arbitration process are hailed as the next revolution in the judicial administration in India.

Arbitration has a long history in India. In ancient times, people voluntarily submitted their disputes to a group of wise men of a community—called a panchayat—for a binding resolution (Kumar n.d.). However, modern commerce needs much more than a panchayat-like arbitration mechanism.

There is no international court to deal with international commercial disputes and, therefore, international arbitration is the preferred option. Arbitration is also favoured over litigation in national courts; firstly because arbitration is always a better option than the more time-consuming litigation mode and secondly because the international element is better handled in an international arbitration than in a domestic litigation through domestic courts where there is always a suspicion of leniency towards national interests. Arbitration reduces costs and delays that are often unavoidable in litigation. International arbitration provides a neutral forum that is a convenient, fair, and expeditious way of solving disputes that cannot be settled by negotiation.

The United Nations Commission on International Trade Law (UNICTRAL) has drafted a law that is designed for universal application called the UNICTRAL Model Law. It attempts to promote harmony and uniformity by ensuring arbitral autonomy along with impartiality of the process through an arbitral tribunal comprising competent and impartial members.

India has enacted a law in 1996 based on the UNICTRAL Model Law called The Arbitration and Conciliation Act. It is a comprehensive piece of legislation that is equally applicable to domestic disputes, bringing synergy between domestic and global rules. The salient features of this act are:

- To comprehensively cover international and commercial arbitration and conciliation as also domestic arbitration and conciliation;
- To make provision for an arbitral procedure which is fair, efficient and capable of meeting the needs of the specific arbitration;
- To minimize the supervisory role of courts in the arbitral process.

The effectiveness of arbitration as a legal institution is judged by the efficacy of its award enforcement regime and the rate of enforcement in India is high—till 2007, 78.41 per cent domestic cases were accepted by various High Courts and the Supreme Court, while only 2 out of 24 international awards were rejected (Sarma et al. 2009).

Intellectual Property

Intellectual property (IP) relates to new ideas, new technology, new products, and evolution of knowledge, and forms a key element in sustaining a successful competitive edge in a particular industry segment. Intellectual Property Rights (IPR) is a right to control the invention and derive economic benefits thereon granted to the inventor, creator, or author of certain kinds of work like designs, music, literature, proprietary knowledge, etc. This right or 'monopoly' is for a finite period and is enforceable through legal mechanisms. IPR is a legal buzzword that gained prominence from the 1990s onwards. It seeks to provide a fair chance to the owner to recover R&D and innovation costs through exclusive rights in the intellectual property and thus provides incentive to increase investment in R&D.

Like any other property that can be traded, owned, bequeathed, sold, etc., IP is notable by being intangible and inexhaustible by consumption. It can reasonably be called a new global currency and is the foundation of a knowledge-based economy and an important factor of differentiation and competitiveness among businesses. They are usually of three kinds:

- Patents, designs, and trademarks (also called industrial property);
- Copyright and neighbouring Rights (includes paintings, musical works, broadcasts, sound recording, etc.);
- Emerging forms (like traditional knowledge, domain names, geographical indicators like Darjeeling Tea, Alphonso Mangoes, Scotch Whisky, Basmati Rice, etc.).

The Agreement on Trade-Related Aspects of Intellectual Property (TRIPS) is an international agreement administered by the WTO. It was negotiated in 1994 and sets down minimum standards for many forms of IPs. India is a signatory to the TRIPS agreement and has already made necessary changes to the patent laws to give effect to the prescribed standards. The TRIPS agreement is the most comprehensive international IP agreement till date. World Intellectual Property Organization (WIPO), an agency of the United Nations (UN), was founded in 1967 to encourage respect of intellectual property throughout the world and ensure that IP rights are maintained and enforced. The WIPO is essentially a technical body with limited political clout; therefore, issues of patent harmonization have moved to WTO to apply greater political pressure for implementation.

Patents and IPRs have become important tools in the hands of transnational companies and even countries to enforce favourable market access, direct investment, and sometimes even development assistance. Strong patent and IPR protection is absolutely essential for transnational companies when they increasingly move their factories to poorer countries; there are several instances of companies selling only the IPR content and not the products themselves—in such cases, IPR becomes more valuable than physical factories. In fact, companies are increasingly being valued on the basis on their IPR content than conventional fixed assets. Although one may argue that a globally harmonized system of patents and IPRs are unfairly skewed towards developed nations at the cost of developing and poor nations, the fact is that WTO has managed to successfully get several countries to adopt the TRIPS-mandated patent laws. There is no option for businesses but to adjust to the new global realities. The government of India has set up a National Institute for Intellectual Property Management (NIIPM) at Nagpur to conduct training, education, research, and think-tank functions. In India, eight separate laws have been enacted to deal with patents.

It is important for a company to understand what rights it owns, if protection is adequate, whether all rights are protected properly, whether there is a system in place to minimize the risk of infringing third-party rights, and to periodically evaluate the commercial value of IPRs. An IPR evaluation for impairment and enforcement is necessary to carry out all these tasks and to check infringement and uphold IPR and also to examine the IPR process to ensure that investment is in the right direction. It requires a good knowledge of the myriad laws that make up the IPR bouquet of laws, including filing applications correctly, searching enormous databases, and securing registration of rights.

Anti-Money Laundering Laws

Money laundering is the process of disguising the illegal origin and criminal nature of funds (like drug or human trafficking, smuggling, illegal arms dealing, prostitution rings, etc.) by moving them untraceably and investing them in legitimate businesses, securities, bank deposits, trusts and charities, etc. When a criminal activity generates large amounts of money, the individual or group involved in it routes the funds to safe havens by disguising sources, changing the form or moving funds to a place where they are less likely to attract attention.

Most money laundering takes place within the banking system. But if idle and non-productive criminal money enters the formal economy and is put to use in legitimate businesses, why is money laundering such a bad thing? This is because, firstly, money laundering allows the underlying criminal activities to continue, even flourish; secondly it corrupts government and banking officials; and thirdly has an adverse effect on capital and money flows by crowding out legitimate money, making money supply volatile and unpredictable, increasing cross-border capital movements, and therefore increasing volatility of exchange rates. KPMG's 'Global Anti-Money Laundering Survey 2007' has estimated that 2–5 per cent of global GDP is laundered annually; for India, the figure goes up to as high as 20–40 per cent of GDP.

Global attention was more directly focussed on money-laundering activities in the aftermath of 9/11, which brought about global tightening of financial rules and regulations and moved several disclosure requirements from voluntary to compulsory or mandatory. Banking secrecy laws have been diluted and bankers have had to don the garb of enforcement officials, responsible for verifying identities of foreign clients, origin of funds, etc. The US has enacted The Patriot Act which, among other provisions, exposes bank directors to personal liability for money laundering in their establishments. Anti-money laundering (AML) policies necessarily need to be global in nature for them to have any impact; OECD has set up the Financial Action Task Force (FATF) as an inter-governmental body which sets standards and develops and promotes policies to combat money laundering and terrorist financing. These standards are recognized, endorsed, or adopted by many international bodies as international standards for combating money laundering.

Tools against money laundering in India:

- The Prevention of Money Laundering Act, 2005: In line with the UN's Special Session declaration in 1998 calling upon member states to adopt national money laundering legislation and programmes, India has enacted The Prevention of Money Laundering (Amendment) Act in 2005 and amended again in 2009 and 2010;
- Foreign Exchange Management Act, 1999: It sets out various restrictions on how much money and assets Indians can hold in foreign countries;
- Financial Intelligence Unit (FIU): It is a part of OECD's global FATF, and is a unit within the finance ministry to check money laundering and finance of terrorism. The FIUs of different countries share information to make anonymous movement of funds across borders more difficult. The FIU functions as an intermediary between banks and the Enforcement Directorate (ED); information from different banks is collated and analysed for irregularities and passed on to the ED for further action.

Banks all over the world are charged with greater responsibility in their functions to detect instances or suspicions of money laundering. KPMG's 'Global Anti-Money-Laundering Survey 2007' found that, in turn, banks rely on vigilant staff as their first line of defence. With more and more banking transactions going online, the focus—and expenditure—of banks is on investment in sophisticated IT monitoring systems. As per the survey, transaction monitoring incurs the greatest expenditure and is likely to remain a key component of AML costs over the next three years (KPMG 2007).

In India, the RBI requires all banks to:

(i) Set key indicators for accounts, bearing in mind the background of the customer, type of transactions and other risk factors;
(ii) Put in place a proper policy framework on 'Know Your Customer' (KYC) guidelines and AML measures;

(iii) Submit a report on solutions and infrastructure and put in place a system of periodical review of risk categorization of accounts.

Non-banking agencies are required by Securities and Exchange Board of India (SEBI) (as per guidelines issued in 2006), the stock market regulator, to put in place AML policies and KYC norms and procedures.

This also creates business opportunities in AML software solutions—USD 2 billion by one estimate—and for accountants in audit of KYC policies, due diligence, handling vast amounts of data, building effective AML programmes for banks, financial institutions, and companies.

International Financial Reporting Standards (IFRS)

Different accounting standards deal differently with certain subjects such as valuation of assets, amortisation, stock options, etc. This creates a lot of confusion for the user to understand the basis of financial statements … [and] such disparity makes it difficult, expensive and time-consuming for investors and other users to compare financial statements and make informed decisions. Development of a truly global capital market demands consistency in accounting standards so that financial statements speak with one voice. (Kaushik & Dutta 2005a: 94)

Progress towards a global GAAP (Generally Accepted Accounting Principles) is largely the effort of the International Accounting Standards Board (IASB), an independent, privately funded accounting standard setter that works with standard setters all over the world and is committed to developing a single set of high-quality, understandable global accounting standards, called International Financial Reporting Standards (IFRS). These standards are fast becoming the global accounting and financial reporting of choice of companies all over the world, because:

- Is a high-quality, principles-based framework;
- Has fewer rules and exceptions (compared to many national systems, notably the US GAAP);
- Allows exercise of more professional judgement;

- Brings transparency to the economics of transactions. (PricewaterhouseCoopers 2006)

Globalization of business and finance has led to mass adoption of IFRS by more than 12000 companies in over 100 countries (PricewaterhouseCoopers 2006). Australia and New Zealand have been on IFRS standards since 2002 and EU countries and Russian public companies since 2005 (Kaushik & Dutta 2005a: 96). The US is the largest market of the remaining holdouts but IFRS is fast gaining acceptance within the US and may even be designated mandatory for US listings by the SEC. US GAAP, with its decade-long 'guidance' and advisories has made the US reporting environment very complex and threatens to become a competitive disadvantage, particularly for foreign issuers. However, if the rest of the world is on IFRS, the US may soon have no choice but to introduce it for US listings as well.

India had planned to adopt IFRS for all listed entities from the year beginning 1 April 2011. However, this has been postponed partly due to unresolved taxation issues. For Indian companies, this would mean a single set of GAAP for statutory as well as global reporting and in the medium to long term means lower costs, particularly if the company wants access to global funds.

Adopting IFRS has benefits that go beyond the obvious approval of potential investors or meeting compliance deadlines. IFRS harmonizes internal and external reporting by creating a single accounting language across a global business, which puts an end to problems of interpretation when different accounting standards are used by units operating in different countries; it may even call into question the viability of some business processes or even units.

Environment Laws

The term 'environment' is broadly defined to include water, air, land, and the interrelationships which exist among them and human beings and other living creatures, plants, microorganisms, and property, as also handling hazardous waste and its management. Environment law is a body of law which is a system of complex and interlocking statutes, common law, treaties, conventions, regulations, and policies which seek to protect the natural environment which may be affected, impacted, or endangered by human activities.

In pre-British India, natural resources were under the nominal control of rulers whereas people, through village panchayats and such institutions, had rights and access to resources for their livelihood. Local governance institutions had de facto authority in matters of the use, exploitation and arbitration of shared and common natural resources. This fabric of village social life slowly whittled away when the British introduced concepts of commodification and exerted direct state control over such resources through legislations such as The Indian Forest Act, 1865. This alienated the local community from the decision-making process in their own locality. As in other aspects of governance, this mechanism was continued by Indian rulers after independence. In fact, this concept of central ownership of resources paved the way for accelerated economic growth in the country through setting up central public sector units, giving the central government (and its bureaucrats) total power over resources to be used by the public sector undertakings (PSUs). In India, thus, there is a centralized approach to environment issues. Industrialists often have to 'lobby' only the 'right' sections of the government machinery—several industrialists also form part of the government—to get their projects cleared. Objections to industrial projects on environmental grounds are often left to NGOs and activists rather than to an institutionalized and empowered local governance mechanisms which can take better care of issues in its own backyard.

Of course India has armed herself with an impressive array of environment laws dealing with different natural resources like forests, wildlife, water, hazardous wastes, noise pollution, coastal zone protection, etc. There is also the Environment Protection Act, 1986, which is an umbrella legislation designed to provide a framework for coordinating the activities of various central and state authorities established under previous laws like the Water Act, Air Act, etc. However, the devil is in the implementation. Environment laws are closely linked to the industry through the concept of sustainable development. London-based Vedanta got various government approvals for its aluminium-linked bauxite refinery to be set up in protected forest lands of Orissa; this linkage was later made as central to the economic viability of the project. However, since some part of it was proposed to be set up in ecologically sensitive forest lands, it was challenged in the Supreme Court, which struck down the project. ArcelorMittal's proposal to set up steel plants in Jharkhand also had problems over a mining lease. Similarly, South Korea-based POSCO's (Pohang Iron and Steel Company) venture in Orissa is dealing with a string of environment, land acquisition, and livelihood issues. Issues of e-waste disposal and other hazardous materials, for example at the Alang shipyard, face strong activist pressure. These are matters that should be given intense thought in the policy stage and consensus should be reached to evolve an official industrial policy which recognizes that we have only one planet to live on. The Indian government has projected an average annual GDP growth at 8 per cent over the next few years; this requires rapid infrastructure creation to achieve and sustain the rate of growth.

It is important for Indian businesses to make a fundamental shift in technology towards cleaner alternatives and design production systems that follow environment protection laws in both letter and spirit.

The Energy and Resources Institute's (TERI) report titled *Sustainable Investment in India: Sustainable Development of Portfolio Investment in India's Publicly Listed Companies* (2009) says that foreign institutional investors (FIIs) now routinely follow the criteria of 'responsible investing', that is, investing based on Environment, Social and Governance (ESG) standards (Siddy and Kumar 2009). Standard & Poor's (S&P) has designed an index for Indian companies specially measured by ESG criteria called 'S&P ESG India'. It is the first effort to measure companies on ESG parameters based on quantitative rather than subjective factors.

Doing business while taking care of the environment is not merely an imperative but can also be an equally profitable route to take. Thus, social and economic constraints in the country are the biggest hurdles presently facing Indian businesses. Overcoming all of these will require massive resources and several years of institution building, neither of which the country has in abundance. The interim solution to the deep and overall reform that the economic system needs has been found in the form of Special Economic Zones (SEZs).

An SEZ is a physical or geographical area which is governed by certain economic laws that are more liberal than the regular laws of the country. The concept of SEZs was first successfully developed by China and replicated with varying degrees of success in several countries around the world.

In India, SEZ entered formal policy in the year 2000 and has legal sanction in the form of Special Economic Zone Act, 2005. This signals commitment to a SEZ policy regime to enable generation of greater economic activity and employment besides promoting exports of goods and services and developing much needed infrastructure. More than 220 SEZs have been created in India since 2000. These SEZs are expected to boost economic activity by providing incentives to attract investments of a certain size and scale, both domestic or FDI. This may accelerate integration of the Indian manufacturing sector with the global economy by creating world-class infrastructure within a small area. Apart from access to good infrastructure, units operating in SEZs can also expect concessions on import duties and other tax concessions on export income, minimum alternate tax, sales and service tax, besides easier terms for borrowing funds from recognized banking channels.

Creating SEZs may seem like an ideal solution for India but its creation faces several protests. One of the major protests against SEZs in India is by owners of fertile farmland on account of land acquisition as SEZs require huge tracts of contiguous land to make it viable. Revenue loss to the exchequer over the years by way of foregone taxes is another strong objection, which, however, is expected to be offset by the expected benefits of increased economic activity. Moreover, since SEZs are designed and intended to provide a boost to economic activity by creating large, contiguous enclaves which will provide economies of scale and be able to deliver world-class goods and services, critics insist that they will become islands of affluence in a sea of deprivation and only exacerbate India's already lopsided regional imbalances.

The underlying objection to the creation of such enclaves is that SEZs penalize industries in areas outside the zone who have been held back from reaching their potential by restrictive labour laws, administrative procedures and other infrastructure constraints. There is no getting away from the job of bringing about deep and sweeping reforms across all areas of economic activity and link all disparate threads into a unified command system for all economic participants.

ETHICS AND CORPORATE GOVERNANCE

Corporate governance is perhaps one of the most important differentiators of a business that has impact on the profitability, growth, and even sustainability of business. Corporate governance is in the best long-term interests of a wide group of stakeholders—customers, suppliers, community, shareholders, and now increasingly the environment. In fact, corporate governance and the economic development of a country or region are also intrinsically linked. Effective governance systems help to develop strong financial and legal systems which lead to a positive effect on economic growth and poverty reduction. This correlation works at several levels—when firms demonstrate transparent and effective governance, they can have access to more extended financing, leading to higher growth trajectory, improving employment levels, leading to more consumption-led growth in the economy, which, in turn, expands the economy. Therefore, corporate governance is a subject of immense importance in a developing country like India because it is so central to the financial and economic development of the country.

Corporate governance is a multi-level and multi-tiered process which is distilled from an organization's culture, its policies, values, and ethics, especially of the people running the business and the way it deals with various stakeholders. As N.R. Narayanmurthy, chief mentor of Infosys says, 'The primary purpose of leadership is to create wealth legally and ethically' (www.infosys.com). And therein lies the crux of the issue of corporate governance and the way its framework is created by regulators and capital markets, and followed or observed by companies and other constituents.

The important thing about ethics and corporate governance is that these are actions that must be demonstrated at every level, in various ways, and an obsession with ethics, morals, and entrenched values practiced over several years leads to the company being known to practice good governance. Creating value that is not only profitable to the business but sustainable in the long-term interests of all stakeholders necessarily means that businesses have to run—and be seen to be run—with a high degree of ethical conduct and good governance where compliance is not only in letter but also in spirit. Codifying and writing down expected behaviour helps people to work closer to the ideals set out and expected and do justice to the spirit of the principles.

General Electric (GE) has a global code of conduct named 'Letter and the Spirit' which deals with GE's value system in conducting business. In India, companies like the Tata Group have such codes written down and it has demonstrated commitment to the code for several years. Over a period of time, the brand recall of a name like 'Tata' or 'GE' is one of trust and faith in its inherent value systems by the public at large. But sometimes, a written code of ethics or corporate governance is a mere smokescreen to cover up the moral turpitude of the owners, promoters, or management—a case of form over content. This was amply demonstrated in the case of Satyam Computers where the management successfully led the world to believe in their statements, figures, and assertions, creating an elaborate sense of illusion of greatness and lofty ideals through what appear to be fabricated evidences. The company was so successful in getting the world to believe in its story that it even won several prestigious awards for corporate governance. Good corporate governance is something to be practiced for years in both letter and spirit—not just for better credit rating or winning awards.

As far as codification goes, India has one of the best corporate governance codes anywhere in the world, modelled as it is on some of the world's best regarded codes such as the iconic 'Cadbury Code' of the UK and other codes of the US and OECD.

Framework of Western Corporate Governance Theories

However, corporate governance code provisions and prescriptions in the US, UK, and Europe are based on the premise of widespread ownership of companies, leading to a gulf between the management and owners, which is known as the 'agency gap'. Management then, so goes the logic, is in danger of becoming self-perpetuating and capable of misaligned interests with shareholders and hence there is a need for a strong board of directors to oversee management. Besides, there is a broad global consensus that the objective of good corporate governance is to maximize long-term shareholder value. Since shareholders are residual claimants to a company's resources, the premise follows that any policy that maximizes shareholder value has first taken care of the interests of other claimants like creditors, vendors, employees, and the community at large. Theoretically, if shareholders are dissatisfied with the management of a company, they can vote with their feet and dispose off their holdings. If this happens in sufficient numbers, the share price of the company goes down and it becomes a takeover target, whereby the existing management can be thrown out by the new owners. Thus, fear of takeover and consequent management change, so the theory goes, is essentially what keeps the management on its toes and makes it work for maximizing shareholders' gain.

Corporate Governance and Indian Economy

The mechanism of market forces in the West presumes the existence of a deep and liquid market in shares, which is not a reality in India. In any case, stock markets have proven to be only partially successful in enforcing good corporate governance even in developed and mature economies.

The primary difference between corporate governance enforcement problems in India and most Western economies (on whose codes the Indian code is largely modelled) is the approach in contemporary corporate governance literature which in essence consists of disciplining the *management* and makes them more accountable. However, In India, the problem—since the inception of joint-stock companies— is the stranglehold of the dominant or principal shareholder(s) who monopolize the lion's share of the company's resources to serve their own needs. In 2010, the average holdings of promoters in Indian companies across various sectors listed in the NSE (National Stock Exchange) was 56.46 per cent, while individuals held 11.97 per cent, and institutions held 13.63 per cent (NSE 2010).

Secondly, much of corporate governance norms globally focus on boards and their committees, independent directors, and managing chief executive officer (CEO) succession. In the Indian business culture, boards are not as empowered as in more advanced capital markets; since the board is subordinate to the shareholders, if a resolution is passed by the majority of shareholders, there is little the board can do to reverse any abuses. Therefore, most corporate governance abuses in India arise due to conflict between the majority and minority shareholders. This applies across the spectrum of Indian companies with dominant shareholders—PSUs (with government as the dominant shareholder), multinational companies (MNCs) where the parent company is the dominant shareholder, private sector family-owned companies, and business groups.

In PSUs, the board's role as an independent monitoring or regulatory mechanism is open to question. The CMD (chairman cum managing director) and other director appointments are usually done by the concerned ministry (after papers are passed through the Public Enterprises Selection Board [PESB]) and often PSUs are led by bureaucrats rather than professional managers. Often many strategic decisions are also taken at a ministerial level while appointment of auditors is done by the Comptroller and Auditor General (CAG). This makes the provisions of corporate governance codes merely a compliance exercise wherever it is applicable. Therefore, PSU boards can rarely act in the manner of an empowered board as envisioned in corporate governance codes. These issues will acquire greater importance as the disinvestment process rolls on.

Multinational companies in India generally have a better record of corporate governance compliance in its prescribed form. However, in the ultimate analysis, it is the writ of the large shareholder (the parent company) which runs the Indian unit, even if it may be at variance with the wishes of the minority shareholders. The compliance and similar functions in an MNC is always geared towards laws applicable to the parent company and compliance with local laws is usually left to the managers of the subsidiary who may not be skilled or motivated for such a role.

Family businesses and business groups as a category are perhaps the most complex for analysing the corporate governance abuses that take place. Firstly, the promoters' shares could be spread across several entities, friends, and relatives so that it is difficult to determine ownership and identify a dominant shareholder. In such cases, the operational control, however, remains with one or two persons or a group who may or may not be a dominant shareholder. Promoters can be dominant shareholders in terms of operational control by holding a small stake because of large blocks held by passive shareholders. Such passive shareholders could be state financial institutions or other entities that may be effectively controlled by the dominant shareholder.

Rewards are expected not only from dividend or capital appreciation but from a large number of related party transactions between firms controlled by the dominant shareholder. Such transactions are sometimes called 'tunnelling' or 'pyramiding'. 'Tunnelling' is a term coined in the Czech Republic to describe the transfer of assets out of a company (through a metaphorical tunnel) to the detriment of minority shareholders. This phenomenon is very often used by some business groups in India through a network of related companies. Such companies may be arranged in a pyramid or web-formation with a main company or controlling stake-holding in the entire network or pyramid. Often the managerial control is in the hands of a small group of people, even a family, who may or may not own a majority stake but exercise control through friends, relatives, other controlled entities, or block-holding passive financial institutions. Pyramiding need not necessarily be done with malafide intentions—the venerable Tata Group, through the holding company Tata Sons, holds shares in all Tata companies. Likewise, the house of Birlas before the family separations also had such an arrangement.

When pyramiding is combined with tunnelling, serious corporate governance issues may arise. Interlocking and pyramiding of corporate control within these groups make it difficult for outsiders to track the business realities of individual companies in the pyramid or network. The problem gets compounded if some or most companies in the pyramid are private companies whose financial statements are not open to public scrutiny. Assets may get transferred within the structure through a number of schemes, usually to the detriment of 'outside' shareholders. Decisions like restructuring the business, transfer of assets between group companies, preferential allotment of shares to promoters, payment of royalties or other charges to group companies or dominant shareholders are some actions that must be fair to all shareholders so that the company is perceived to practice good corporate governance.

Corporate governance processes presently in convention are designed with a view to serve the shareholders and protect them from managerial excesses. In this system, the board is really accountable to the shareholders and if there is a dominant shareholder or group and if there is a conflict of interest between the company and the dominant shareholder(s), the very purpose of setting up an elaborate corporate governance network will have been defeated. A corporate governance regime which involves strengthening board processes alone would be rather irrelevant to solve problems of governance abuses by dominant shareholders.

There are some major challenges to corporate governance reforms in India, such as:

- Power of the dominant shareholder;
- Lack of incentives (in the light of diffused returns from putting expensive systems in place);
- Underdeveloped external monitoring systems;
- Shortage of real independent directors;
- Weak regulatory oversight.

An Indian Institute of Management, Bangalore (IIM-B) study recommends that the problem of governance abuses can only be solved by forces outside the company and lists the regulator and the capital market as two such forces (Varma 1997).

Regulatory mechanisms to protect shareholder interests operate at two levels—*de jure* and *de facto*. India has some of the best corporate governance codes in the world (de jure); however, there is a substantial gap in the extent to which they are practiced or enforced on the ground (de facto).

In the 2004 World Bank *Report on the Observance of Standards and Codes* studying the evolution and challenges in corporate governance in India, the researchers have used two indices— 'a shareholder rights' index ranging from 0 (lowest) to 6 (highest) and 'a rule of law' index ranging from 0 (lowest) to 6 (highest)—to measure the effective protection of shareholder rights provided in the different countries studied (Chakrabarti n.d.). The first index captures the extent to which the written law protects the shareholders while the second index reflects the extent to which the law is enforced in reality.

In the report India had a shareholder rights index of 5, one of the highest in the sample contained—equal to that of the US, UK, Canada, Hong Kong, Pakistan, and South Africa, and better than countries like France, Japan, Germany, and Switzerland. In the rule of law index, however, India had a score of only 4.17, ranking forty-first out of forty-nine countries.

Thus, we may conclude that Indian laws provide great protection to shareholder rights on paper while the application and enforcement of these laws are lax. The government is making structural changes in laws through the proposed Companies Bill (to be introduced in its present form) and other codes in direct taxes, etc., to bring in a shorter timeframe to enforce justice for illegal and inappropriate corporate acts.

Regulatory intervention needs to be finely calibrated because it poses a problem of micro management of a company by regulators. Corporate governance codes must necessarily be written in a way so as to avoid being highly regimented, while still providing a suitable control mechanism that the government can exercise over the corporate sector, because control of an overly wrought nature is at odds with the demand that the government should stay out of business so that it does not stifle free enterprise.

The Madoff Fraud

The Madoff fraud exposed in 2008–9 had no elements of the financial sophistry or creative wizardry of earlier scandals but was a simple century-old Ponzi type scam that most investors believed the system was protected against. A Ponzi scheme (named after Charles Ponzi) is a fraud where a promoter gets people to invest money in a scheme that promises a very high rate of return and uses that money to pay off earlier investors. The repayment not only raises the promoter's credibility but also increases investors' greed with more and more people coming into the scheme till there are no new investors to drag into the scheme and the whole pyramid-like structure comes crashing down.

At the centre of the estimated USD 50 billion fraud was a respected pillar of the American stock market, Bernard L. Madoff, who ran separate broking and investment businesses, regulated and unregulated. Over the years he used his social contacts—and consistently high returns paid for by new investors—to build a network of conduits and an aura of infallible financial acumen. Madoff used the simple technique of maintaining multiple sets of accounting books for different interest groups; he provided little information and demanded a lot of trust. Madoff's scheme had drawn, not just gullible and ill-informed individual investors but sophisticated financial pundits including global banks, investment banks, financial institutions, and even charities, perhaps because US capital markets are perceived to be fundamentally strong, a belief reinforced by quick-reaction laws like Sarbox. Investment banks invested heavily into US markets through Madoff's funds directly or indirectly through custodians with or without tracing the ultimate destination of funds. Perhaps Madoff's client list of reputed financial institutions was a reason investors assumed that someone must have done due diligence on the fund or maybe the intricate inter-linkage of global financial institutions actually makes it difficult to track funds from source to destination.

With 20/20 hindsight, there were enough indications that things were not quite right at Madoff's fund and somebody ought to have followed up on the several red flags that were raised: (i) the firm posted improbably consistent returns, regardless of market volatility, (ii) it claimed to employ sophisticated strategies that should have produced highly visible movements in the options market but remained undetected, (iii) the fund had USD 17 billion in investor assets under Madoff's personal management in a small family-held firm without using an independent bank custodian to hold the money, and (iv) for such a large outfit, the fund used an obscure and tiny outfit as auditor, etc. Should regulators have looked into an unregulated affiliated business as part of its supervision of the regulated broker-dealer business? This also calls into question the regulator's 'scope of examination' practices that Madoff took advantage of. It is a telling commentary on the justice delivery system of the US that Madoff was brought to trial speedily, judicial punishment prescribed and regulatory closure was quickly obtained while valuable lessons were learnt and incorporated.

Satyam Computer Services Limited

Investigating agencies are still grappling with the mechanics of this fraud ever since the staggering admission of the founder in January 2009 that cash was nonexistent in the business as on the date of collapse. The founder, B. Ramalinga Raju, built up a software company from scratch that went on to become one of the jewels of the Indian economy and part of an elite group of stocks that make up the Indian stock indices. He built up an aura of infallibility through several national and international awards for corporate excellence while diversifying into other businesses, including real estate and infrastructure business.

Raju claimed that the books of accounts had been routinely fudged for several years and that the cash position was grossly overstated going back many time periods and that revenue had been overstated hugely to include fictitious clients. The confession letter raises more questions than it answers; for instance, Raju has stated that the operating margin was only around 3 per cent as against an industry average of 20 per cent. Does this mean there were fictitious clients and fictitious employees? This must mean an elaborate system of creating the complete trail of sales agreements, manpower allocation, billing, etc., except that all of it would be fake. This may point to roundtrip money which would bolster the company's balance sheet but in essence be a smokescreen for siphoning money out of the business. But where was this money deployed?

The genesis of the Satyam problem apparently lies in the infrastructure and real estate group business mainly because land is still an unreformed sector of the economy and purchasing large tracts of contiguous land for big infrastructure projects requires a lot of money, a significant portion of which may have to be so-called black money. Investigations are still at a preliminary stage and not much is known in the public domain about what really went wrong but we can infer a few things. Satyam is in the software export business operating out of a Software Technology Park (STP). Its revenues were closely monitored by RBI as were sales agreements by STPI (Software Technology Parks of India) authorities which authenticated the company's revenue figures. Provident fund contributions and statements were filed regularly, giving comfort on employee numbers. The company's financial statements were audited by an international firm known for its strong systems and processes; expectedly, auditing details are not known in the public domain because of client confidentiality. However, it is understood that the audit firm has undergone extensive inspections of its files by internal and external teams, including those relating to Satyam and this too did not pick up red flags. There are several corroborating evidences like TDS (tax deducted at source) certificates and bank confirmation statements. If none of these check posts raised significant red flags, it raises a most disquieting suspicion of forgery of documents and that on a huge level. However, India may have to wait for some time before regulatory closure can be obtained in this case and lessons learnt because of the slow judicial process in the country.

Discipline by Capital Market

If there is a well-functioning capital market, minority shareholders can keep a check on the activities of the dominant shareholder by the effect of their actions on the share price. If sufficient numbers of minority shareholders sell their shares or do not subscribe to new issues, it is likely to depress the share price, theoretically making the company a ripe takeover target. In many ways, a well-functioning capital market is likely to be a better enforcer of corporate governance than regulations.

An OECD study says that it makes imminent sense for stock exchanges to establish themselves as a source of corporate governance-related regulator; 'by raising transparency and discouraging illegal or irregular practices, exchanges are able to accumulate an amount of reputational capital' (Christiansen and Koldertsova 2009). In several OECD member countries, the responsibility for company listing is shared between the stock exchange and the securities regulator. In countries with more extensive self-regulation (like the US), the listing authority is often delegated to exchanges, whereas in more controlled economies (like India), most authority is concentrated in the securities regulator.

Contrarily, stringent listing norms of stock exchanges are a reason for a loss of numbers of companies listed on that exchange. For example, a report commissioned by the mayor of New York City cited the Sarbanes Oxley Act as one of the reasons for a loss of competitiveness of the US capital markets (McKinsey & Co. 2006). The report criticized the US regulatory framework and the 'flawed implementation of the 2002 Sarbanes Oxley Act', citing these as key behind the rapid growth of EU capital markets revenues (20 per cent annually), compared to 7 per cent in the US. It also noted the falling share of the US in the global initial public offering (IPO) markets (a decline from 57 per cent in 2001 to 16 per cent in 2006) at the same time as EU IPOs have increased by 30 per cent.

The power of stock exchanges to enforce compliance, anywhere in the world, pertains to those standards which are also incorporated in the listing requirements. India has had a fair share of corporate governance scandals—the Harshad Mehta stock market scam of 1992, several instances of fraudulent IPOs, improper preference issue to promoters at deeply discounted prices, and perhaps the king of all scams so far, the Satyam shocker, where the promoter is alleged to have shown nonexistent money in the books of accounts or to have siphoned off monies from the company to other channels.

Then again, the corporate governance structure in India is constantly responsive to global trends and their adaptability to local business realities. The past few years have been a period of enormous change in the business landscape of the country:

- Economic reforms have improved growth prospects and companies need to access capital markets continually;
- Tax reforms have made tax burden less punitive and increased the incentive for owners to declare real profits;
- Cultural change in the mindset of owners which makes them plough back funds into the business and grow it rather than take out all possible monies from it;
- A flat world and worldwide recession combine to create a situation in which global funds will find better return in growth economies like India. This in turn will demand better disclosure and compliance;
- Greater regulatory oversight and better information sharing is teaching companies that honesty and transparency are virtues that are encashable at the bourses.

Perhaps the single most important development for improving corporate governance practice in India has been the establishment of SEBI in 1992 and its gradual empowerment since then. It has played a critical role in establishing minimal rules of conduct for corporate India, later codified as corporate governance rules such as Clause 49 of the Listing Agreement. SEBI's role as the market regulator has also evolved over time and its regulations substantially add to the requirement of the Companies Act, particularly regarding standards of information disclosure although its record of bringing defaulters to book still needs to be strengthened. As the OECD maintains, 'the credibility and utility of a corporate governance framework rest on its enforceability'.

Besides, each financial fiasco brings about a spate of new regulations that demand compliance from other players, globally and in India. Yet the regulator usually gets away with little official censure and practically no accountability; after all, businesses never work in a regulatory vacuum and failures could be as much a breakdown of regulatory oversight as the fault of other gatekeepers. Strangely, it is a global phenomenon that regulation is a few steps behind financial product innovation. There are also instances of gaps in or between regulatory regimes through which certain players or products can slip. Enron was a watershed moment for the industry, investors, and regulators which brought about sweeping changes to the way business would be conducted henceforth. However, as subsequent frauds have shown, while Enron has raised the cost of compliance globally, the lessons of Enron have, sadly, not been learnt. Such gaps need to be plugged on a regular basis by the regulator and not only as a response to a financial crisis.

Financial Crisis Caused by Credit Default Swaps

The nudge factor of the market crash of 2008 was the credit crisis that erupted in the summer of 2007 in the aftermath of the US sub-prime tsunami; the root cause of the crisis was an obscure financial instrument called Credit Default Swaps (CDSs) started in the US, which created a new originate-and-distribute model of transferring risk. CDS is a contract that provides insurance against a bond issuer defaulting on its debt and is supposed to provide peace of mind to the buyer to cover the risk of default and when these instruments began to get popular a decade ago, they typically applied to municipal bonds, corporate debt, and mortgage securities. In a booming economy, there was little perception of danger of corporate default and CDSs began to be regarded by banks, hedge funds, and traders as an easy source of money because while these agencies were tightly regulated, the credit swap market was not and was free to operate without restrictions. The CDS market then expanded into other, riskier instruments including the secondary market where speculative investors would buy and sell CDSs without any connection with the actual underlying instrument. In fact, the market got big because of speculators who, in a display of gallows humour, took bets on whether or not a company would go bankrupt. The CDS market exploded over the past decade to more than USD 45 trillion by mid-2007, about twice the size of the US stock market. Further, this and similar financial tools were kept out of reach of scrutiny by the Securities and Exchange Commission (SEC) and the Commodity Futures Trading Commission (CFTC) (both market regulators) through the Commodity Futures Modernization Act of 2000. The CDS contracts could be traded or swapped without anyone overseeing or regulating trades to ensure that the buyer had resources to cover the losses if the security defaults; in fact, no one even knows how much the issuers are liable for. Worse, these were securitized and distributed to investors globally after obtaining mostly false prime and Triple-A ratings from well-known rating agencies. This was not confined only to the US market but had spread all over the world with several global banks having large exposure to these so-called toxic assets.

This is uncannily similar to the unregulated energy trading markets that led to Enron's collapse that triggered a chain of corporate collapses followed by intensive regulation. After Enron and the spate of corporate failures, stringent regulations were put in place all over the world; Sarbanes Oxley and its global clones required companies to develop robust internal control systems, have real independent boards, and increased personal liability of directors and auditors but also raised compliance costs for the entire corporate world.

The crisis of 2008 reached a tipping point because of the liquidity crunch faced by banks and the entire financial sector in the US following the sub-prime mortgage crisis. Investors in CDS markets took a hard look at whether parties insuring the instrument would, or more importantly, could pay up in the event of mass defaults. There was a steady write-down in the value of CDS holdings among banks, insurers and re-insurers. Rating agencies woke up to the impending threat and began to downgrade financial institutions. Downgrading rating of insurance companies was particularly devastating for market confidence because it called into immediate question the insurance coverage of banks and other corporates who had bought insurance covers from them, setting off a domino effect on the entire market. The US government even had to take over the management of two mortgage agencies, Freddie Mac and Fannie Mae to ensure their financial soundness.

But the takeover of these two companies did not stem the bleeding; one by one, the seemingly solid institutions either went bankrupt or were forced to sell cheap like Bear Stearns, Merrill Lynch, etc. Lehman Brothers Holdings, one of the largest investment banks of the US has the dubious distinction of filing the largest ever bankruptcy protection at USD 600 billion in September 2008; it had large exposure in sub-prime and other lower-rated mortgage tranches when securitizing the underlying mortgage, and investor confidence in Lehman's financial soundness continued to get eroded because of lower results, company announcements of layoffs, or simply rumours. America International Group (AIG), a US insurance behemoth with presence in over 130 countries and several million investors all over the world, had to be rescued by the US government but only because its failure would have been disastrous not only for investors but for the very credibility of the US capital market in global perception.

Markets today are linked globally in such an intricate manner and major banks and investment agencies have a stake in so many global markets that a crisis that primarily originated in the US engulfed the whole world. The sheer size of the US market and its liquidity crunch sucked in money from all over the world as institutional investors rushed to liquidate their foreign holdings to ease the pressure in their home countries. The root causes of the current crisis are due to factors such as: new and unregulated financial instruments which propagate an originate-and-distribute model of transferring risk; inadequate understanding of financial nuances by players; allowing speculative investors to operate without stakes; and the role of regulators and rating agencies. In short, there was a complete breakdown of corporate governance and management incentives in financial institutions.

As US SEC (Securities and Exchange Commission) Chairman Mary L. Schapiro said, 'The core principles that must guide capital market regulators are: (i) protection of investors, (ii) ensuring markets are fair, efficient and transparent, and (iii) reduction of systemic risk (Schapiro 2009).

However, as corporate events across the globe have shown, the best of systems can be circumvented or hoodwinked by a determined rule-breaker. The capitalist system is based on the premise that people work most efficiently when they work for maximizing personal gain. This also has intrinsic checks and balances through conflicting interests of participants. However, there is a thin dividing line between acceptable personal gain and plain greed. Leakages and breakdowns are bound to happen as in any other system. Like democracy, capitalism may be the worst form of economic ideology except that alternative systems around the globe have proved more inefficient and definitely not immune to abuse and fraud.

The responsibility for corporate oversight is multilayered, both internal and external. Within a company, the internal audit department is the proverbial foot soldier to detect and prevent fraud on a day-to-day basis while the board of directors including independent directors have the ultimate responsibility for in-house oversight. External agencies have several components such as SEBI, the capital market regulator in India, and SEC in the US, external auditors, direct and indirect tax authorities, banks and financial institutions, besides several investor interest groups and analysts.

A strong culture of corporate governance norms may not be able to prevent frauds occurring altogether but it can certainly contain the fallout to a limited area, conduct speedy inquiries and fix responsibility and incorporate learning from the experience into regulations or practice. It is critical in the aftermath of scandals to desist from knee-jerk regulatory responses; codes can and must provide only guidelines. The environment in which business functions is not static but constantly evolving. In such a dynamic environment, a compliance-based corporate governance regime only adds to the layer of bureaucracy rather than powering the engine of growth as it is meant to do.

In Continuum ...

India has consistently kept up the pace of integration with the global economy through proactive state interventions. Today, India epitomizes hope—for its people for a better lifestyle, for the world as a place very likely to deliver new and cost-effective ideas, and for global industry as a vast new marketplace. The vast landscape that India provides, however, is not homogeneous, or one that lends itself to simple strategies.

The Indian market is multilayered and complex, consisting of a small urban base upon a large rural base. The dispersal of rural markets, low purchasing power, infrastructure constraints, and smaller absolute quantities of purchases makes the world wonder whether India is a poor country or a country with many poor people. One significant point to remember is that prosperity is always relative. A part of the perception of poverty is that measurement matrices are largely rooted in a Western—American—standard of how much is enough. Thus we have statements like 'people live on less than USD 1 a day'; there is no disputing that at the currency equivalent of USD 1 such people are still living in poverty (as per *UNDP Human Development Report 2010*, 51.4 per cent of employed people live on less than USD 1.25 per day in India over 2000–8) but it is the perceived magnitude that gets distorted. Standard of living is a highly localized thing based on the immediate environment. It can be nobody's argument that people should not aspire for more or better material gains—that would surely kill human endeavour. The critical part is in broadly knowing what one wants and being able to achieve it, or rather, being allowed by social and government circumstances to achieve it. (The US Constitution guarantees the *pursuit* of happiness, rather than telling its people what to achieve.)

A shrinking global space is generally good news for business and trade as it shrinks borders and provides a bigger marketplace. But the rules of trade and existing management constructs and approaches are rapidly undergoing change. Shorter product cycles, intensive R&D, and speed and access to information have rendered the term 'latest technology' something of an oxymoron.

Over the past 150–200 years, India has largely been absorbing knowledge from the Western world and most of our institutions and systems have been modelled on a Western perspective. Only in the last decade there has been a steady and perceptible change and today there is clearly a two-way exchange of ideas and knowledge.

India can be the most baffling country to most people, including Indians themselves. It is a land of contrasts where a wide range of views, customs, and habits coexist, each creating space for itself. The immense energy that rural India brings to largely urban business sensibilities is revolutionizing several practices and reshaping conventional wisdom, whether it is rural electricity, mobile phone packages, distribution strategies, or healthcare delivery.

It will take a lifetime of study to fully understand the dynamics of India. We hope this book is a small step towards that goal.

Bibliography

ABLE, 2010, 'BioSpectrum-ABLE Industry Survey 2010', http://www.scribd. com/doc/41267610/Biospectrum-Able-Biotech-Industry-Survey-2010

ACMA, 2010, 'Growing Capabilities of Indian Auto Component Industry & Its Sustainability', http://www.acmainfo.com/pdf/Status_Indian_Auto_ Industry.pdf

Ahmed, Sadiq and Shantayanan Devarajan, 2007, 'Labor Laws: To Create Good Jobs, Reform Labor Regulations', Op-ed Special, *Economic Times* (20 February), http://www.worldbank.org.in/WBSITE/EXTERNAL/ COUNTRIES/SOUTHASIAEXT/INDIAEXTN/0,contentMDK:212 35163~menuPK:295589~pagePK:2865066~piPK:2865079~theSit ePK:295584,00.html

Archibald, G.C., 1987, 'Theory of the Firm', in John Eatwell, Murray Milgate, and Peter Newman (eds), *The New Palgrave: A Dictionary of Economics*, London: MacMillan.

Arora, Ashish and Suma Athreye, 2001, 'The Software Industry and India's Economic Development', Wider Discussion Paper No. 2001/20, Social Science Research Network.

Assisi, Charles and Indrajit Gupta, 2003, 'ITC's Rural Symphony', *Businessworld* (20 January), pp. 30–5.

ASSOCHAM, 2007, '2008 Likely to Witness 35% Attrition Rate in Energy Sector' (11 December).

Athukorala, Prema-Chandra and Kunal Sen, n.d., 'Liberalization and Business Investment in India', Working paper, Crawford School of Economics and Goverenment, Australian National University, http://www.crawford. anu.edu.au/acde/asarc/pdf/papers/conference/CONF2001_02.pdf

AYUSH, 2008, 'Ayush in India 2007', Department of Health and Family Welfare, http://indianmedicine.nic.in/index3.asp?sslid=127&subsubli nkid=52&lang=1

Bagchi, Amiya Kumar, 1972, *Private Investment in India 1900–1939*, South Asian Studies No. 10, Cambridge: Cambridge University Press.

Bala, Madhu, 2006, *Economic Policy and State Owned Enterprises: Evolution Towards Privatisation in India.*

Balasubramanyan, V.N., 2001, *Conversations with Indian Economists*, New Delhi: Macmillan.

Bardhan, Pranab, 1999, *Understanding Underdevelopment: Challenges for Institutional Economics from the Point of View of Poor Countries*, Berkeley: University of California Press.

—, 1984, *Political Economy of Development*, New Delhi: Oxford University Press.

Bartels, L. and H. Brady, 2003, 'Economic Behaviour in Political Context', *American Economic Review*, Vol. 93, No. 2, pp. 156–61.

Bartlett, Christopher A. and S. Ghoshal, 2002 (1989), *Managing Across Borders: The Transnational Solution*, Boston, MA: Harvard Business School Press.

Basu, Champak, 1988, *Challenge and Change, The ITC Story—1910 to 1985*, Calcutta: Orient Longman.

Batelle and R&D Magazine, 2010, *2011 Global R&D Funding Forecast* (December), http://www.battelle.org/aboutus/rd/2011.pdf

Bayly, C.A., 1983, *Rulers, Townsmen and Bazaar: North Indian Society in the Age of British Expansion, 1770–1870*, Cambridge: Cambridge University Press.

Becker, G.S., 1964, *Human Capital: A Theoretical and Empirical Analysis, with Special Reference to Education*, Chicago: University of Chicago Press.

Beena, P.L., Laveesh Bhandari, Sumon Bhaumik, Subir Gokarn, and Anjali Tandon, 2004, 'Foreign Direct Investment in India', in Saul Estrin and Klaus Meyer (eds), *Investment Strategies in Emerging Markets*, London: Edward Elgar, Chapter 5, pp. 126–47.

Bellah, R, R. Madsen, W. Sullivan, A. Swidler, and S. Tipton, 1985, *Habits of the Heart: Individualism and Commitment in American Life*, Berkeley: University of California Press.

Berle, A. and G. Means, 1932, *The Modern Corporation and Private Property*, New York: Harcourt, Brace and World.

Bhagat, Rashida, 2006, 'HR Challenge Looms, especially in Public Sector (An interview with Mohandas Pai, HR Chief, Infosys)', *Hindu Business Line* (6 September).

Bhattacharya, S., n.d., 'Fanning the Spirit of Frontier Science', http://www. tata.com/ourcommitment/articles/inside.aspx?artid=5c2Dyfh3pLY=.

BIAC, 2005, 'Internationalisation of Research and Development', Discussion paper, Business and Industry Advisory Committee (BIAC) to the OECD (March), http://www.biac.org/statements/tech/FIN05-03-Globalisation_RD.pdf

Blackwell, Michael and David Seddon, 2004, *Informal Remittances From the UK: Values, Flows and Mechanisms*, A Report to DFID, http://www. apgml.org/frameworks/docs/8/UK_Remittances.pdf

Boston Consulting Group, 2006, 'Harnessing the Power of India: Rising to the Productivity Power in Biopharma', *BCG Focus*.

Brown, D. and S. Wilson, 2005, *The Black Book of Outsourcing*, New Jersey: Wiley Publishers.

Business Today, 2005, 'Family Values' (30 January).

Businessworld, 2007, 'Private Sector Can Transform India's Defence Industry' (17 September).

CAG, 2007, 'Commercial Audit, No. 9', in *Report 2007*.

Chakrabarti, Rajesh, n.d., 'Corporate Governance in India—Evolution and Challenges', http://unpan1.un.org/intradoc/groups/public/documents/ APCITY/UNPAN023826.pdf

Chankova, S., N. Goldberg, G. Melford, H. Tazi, and S. Tomlinson, 2004, 'India Microfinance Investment Environment Profile', Princeton University—Woodrow Wilson School of Public and International Affairs, http:// www.microfinancegateway.org/gm/document-1.9.41961/36.pdf

Chaudhary, S., 1995, *From Prosperity to Decline—Eighteenth Century Bengal*, New Delhi: Manohar.

Chawla, Rajeev and Subhash Bhatnagar, 2004, 'Online Delivery of Land Titles to Rural Farmers in Karnataka, India', Scaling Up Poverty Reduction: A Global Learning Process and Conference, Shanghai (25–7 May), http:// info.worldbank.org/etools/docs/reducingpoverty/case/96/fullcase/ India%20Bhoomi%20Full%20Case.pdf

Chen, M., 1995, *Asian Management Systems—Chinese, Japanese and Korean Styles of Business*, London: Routledge.

Chidambaram, P., 2006, 'Excerpts—Speech: Budget 2006–07' (28 February), http://indiabudget.nic.in/ub2006-07/bs/speecha.htm

Christiansen, Hans and Alissa Koldertsova, 2009, 'The Role of Stock Exchanges in Corporate Governance', OECD Conference Centre (20–1 April), OECD Directorate of Enterprise and Financial Affairs, Corporate Affairs Division, Paris.

Cohen, Stephen P., 2001, *India: Emerging Power*, New Delhi: Oxford University Press.

CSIR, n.d., 'Annexure I: Intellectual Property from CSIR During 2005–6', http://www.csir.res.in/csir/external/heads/aboutcsir/annual_report/2005-2006/ANNEXURE-I.pdf

Cygnus Business Consulting and Research, 2007, 'Industry Insight: Clinical Trials in India, 2007' (May), www.cygnusindia.com/pdfs/TOC_Clinical%20trials_Feb-2010.pdf

Das, Gurcharan, 2002, 'Indian Business Families', *Seminar*, Vol. 4, No. 11 (11 September).

———, 1999, 'The Problem', Family Business: A Symposium on the Role of the Family in Indian Business, *Seminar* 482 (October).

Davis, Lance E. and Robert A. Huttenback, 1993, 'Mammon and the Pursuit of Empire: The Political Economy of British Imperialism, 1860–1912', in B.R. Tomlinson (ed.), *The Economy of Modern India*, Cambridge: Cambridge University Press.

Department of Public Enterprises (DPE), 2010, *Public Enterprises Survey 2009–10*, Vol. 1, http://dpe.nic.in/newsite/survey0910/Survey01/Overview.pdf#pratio

Department of Science and Technology (DST), 2010, *Annual Report 2009–10*, http://dst.gov.in/about_us/ar09-10/annual_report_2009-10.pdf

———, n.d., 'Executive Summary', *Report of the Steering Committee of Science and Technology Departments/Agencies for the Tenth Five-Year Plan (2002–7)*, http://planningcommission.nic.in/aboutus/committee/strgrp/stgp_st.pdf

Dhar, Biswajit, 1988, 'State Regulation of Foreign Private Capital in India', Working Paper 1988/06, Institute for Studies in Industrial Development (ISID), New Delhi.

Donally, Gene, 2008, 'Asian Brand Buyers Learning from Their Purchase (18 April), www.newperception.com, p. 7.

DSIR, 2010, *Annual Report 2009–2010*, New Delhi: Ministry of Science and Technology.

———, 2001, *Annual Report 2000–2001*, New Delhi: Ministry of Science and Technology.

Dutta, Kaushik, 2008, 'I Admire', *Financial Express* (23 March).

Dutz, Mark A. (ed.), 2007, *Unleashing India's Innovation: Toward Sustainable & Inclusive Growth*, World Bank Report (October).

Economic Times, 2007, 'Shahnaz Husain Group in Distribution Pact with HAIM' (20 October), http://articles.economictimes.indiatimes.com/2007-10-20/news/28412567_1_distribution-pact-shg-shahnaz-husain-group

———, 2006, 'Shahnaz Husain to Go for "Mass" Makeover' (31 January), http://economictimes.indiatimes.com/shahnaz-husain-to-go-in-for-mass-makeover/articleshow/1393590.cms

EE Times-India, 2007, 'TI taps Bengaluru-based IISc for R&D, Chip Innovation' (6 April).

Farell, Diana, Sacha Ghai, and Tim Shavers, 2005, 'The Demographic Deficit: How Aging will Reduce Global Wealth', *McKinsey Quarterly* (March).

Federal Government of Germany, 2007, '2006 World Cup: Final Report of the Federal Government' (with a Foreword by Dr Wolfgang Schäuble), http://www.bmi.bund.de/SharedDocs/Downloads/EN/Veroeffentlichungen/WM2006_Abschlussbericht_der_Bundesregierung_en.pdf?__blob=publicationFile

FICCI–E&Y, 2009, 'The Glorious Metamorphosis, Compelling Reasons for Doing Clinical Research in India'.

Financial Times, 2008, 'Shock in India Over Ranbaxy Sale' (11 June).

Financial Express, 2007, 'PSU Banks Hit by High Attrition Rates' (25 August).

Forbes, Naushad, 2002, 'Doing Business in India: What has Liberalization Changed', in Anne O. Krueger (ed.), *Economic Policy Reforms and the Indian Economy*, Chicago: University of Chicago Press, pp. 129–68.

Foss, K., H. Lando, and S. Thomsen, 2000, 'The Theory of the Firm', in Boudewijn Bouckaert and Gerrit De Geest (eds), *Encyclopaedia of Law and Economics*, Volume III, Cheltenham U.K.: Edward Elgar Publishing Ltd.

Friedman, Milton, 1962, *Capitalism and Freedom*, Chicago: University of Chicago Press.

Gadgil, D.R., 1954, *Industrial Revolution of India in Recent Times 1860–1939*, London: Geoffrey Cumberlage.

Gang, Ira N. and Mohammad I. Ansari, 1999, 'Liberalization Policy: "Fits and Starts" or Gradual Change in India', in *Comparative Economic Studies*, Vol. 41, pp. 23–46.

Gehlbach, S., K. Sonin, and E. Zhuravskaya, 2006, 'Businessmen Candidates', Working paper w0067 (16 July), Centre for Economic and Financial Research (CEFIR).

Ghemawat, P. and T. Khanna, 1998, 'The Nature of Diversified Business Groups: A Research Design and Tow Case Studies', in *Journal of Industrial Economics*, Vol. XLVI, No. I.

Gould, D.M., 1994, 'Immigrant Links to the Home Country—Empirical Implications for United States Bilateral Trade-Flows', *Review of Economics and Statistics*, Vol. 76, No. 2, pp. 302–16

Government of India, 2006, *India Budget 2006–2007*, New Delhi: Ministry of Finance, Chapter 74.

———, 1902, *Financial and Commercial Statistics for British India*, Calcutta: Government Printing Press.

Greif, A., 1992, 'Institutions and International Trade: Lessons from the Commercial Revolution', *American Economic Review*, Vol. 82, No. 2 (May), pp. 128–33.

Gupta, Vipin, Kamala Gollakota, and R. Srinivasan, 2007, *Business Policy and Strategic Management: Concepts and Applications*, New Delhi: Prentice-Hall of India.

Haksar, A.N., 1993, *Bite the Bullet*, New Delhi: Penguin India.

Handy, Charles, 1989, *The Age of Unreason*, New York: Arrow Books.

Harris, F.R., 1958, *Jamsetji Nusserwanji Tata: A Chronicle of His Life*, Bombay: Blackie and Son.

Harvey-Jones, John, 1988, *Making it Happen*, London: HarperCollins.

Hawksworth, John and Gordon Cookson, 2008, 'The World in 2050: Beyond the BRICs', PricewaterhouseCoopers Research Paper (March), http://www.pwc.com/gx/en/world-2050/pdf/world_2050_brics.pdf

Hazari, R.K., 1967, *The Structure of the Corporate Private Sector: A Study of Concentration, Ownership and Control*, London: Asia Publishing House.

Hindu Business Line, 2005, 'Shahnaz Husain's Fairness Cream Hits South India' (29 April).

Hurd, John M., 1983, 'Irrigation and Railways: Railways', in D. Kumar and M. Desia (eds), *Cambridge Economic History of India, Vol. II*, Cambridge: Cambridge University Press.

ICMR, 2010, *Annual Report 2009–10* (compiled and edited by Sudha Chauhan), http://www.icmr.nic.in/annual/2009-10/english/ann_report.htm

IIPS, 2007, *National Family Health Survey (NFHS-3), 2005–06*, Vol. I. Mumbai: IIPS.

India Knowledge@Wharton, 2009, 'Avantha Group's Gautam Thapar: "I See Myself as an Entrepreneur"' (12 February), http://knowledge.wharton.upenn.edu/india/article.cfm?articleid=4351

———, 2008a, 'Despite the Rocky Terrain, an Entrepreneurial "Ecosystem" Takes Root in India' (21 February), http://knowledge.wharton.upenn.edu/india/article.cfm?articleid=4264

———, 2008b, 'Bharti Group's Sunil Bharti Mittal on Lessons of Entrepreneurship and Leadership', http://knowledge.wharton.upenn.edu/india/article.cfm?articleid=4306

———, 2007, 'Shekhar Kapur Bets Big on Asia as Global Entertainment Hub' (26 July), http://knowledge.wharton.upenn.edu/india/article.cfm?articleid=4211

———, 2006, 'How Indian Companies Fund their Overseas Acquisitions', http://knowledge.wharton.uppen.edu/india/article.cfm?articleid=4131

————, 2005, 'R&D in India: The Curtain Rises, the Play has Begun' (21 November), http://knowledge.wharton.upenn.edu/article.cfm?articleid =1278

India Today, 2008, 'Fortune in Figures' (14 January) [In the supplement, *Aspire*].

Indian Express, 2010, 'India Inc Cheers Bharti–Zain Deal' (31 March).

————, 2007a, 'Guns, Not Butter' (4 September), p. 10.

————, 2007b, 'IT Sector has a Huge Multiplier Effect on Economy' (21 February), p. 17.

ITP (Investment & Technology Promotion Division), 2010, 'India in Business—Auto Industry', http://www.indiainbusiness.nic.in/industry-infrastructure/industrial-sectors/automobile.htm

Jain, L.C., 1929, *Indigenous Banking in India*, London: Macmillan.

Jain, P.C., 1971, *Labour in Ancient India*, New Delhi: Sterling Publishers.

Jhabvala, Renana and Ravi Kanbur, 2004, 'Globalization and Economic Reform as Seen from the Ground: SEWA's Experience in India', in Kaushik Basu (ed.), *India's Emerging Economy: Performance and Prospects in the 1990s and Beyond*, Cambridge, Mass.: The MIT Press. pp. 293–312.

Joshi, Sharad, 2007, 'Leave the Cooperative Movement Alone', *Hindu Business Line* (25 July).

Kakani, Ram Kumar, 2001, 'Explaining Diversified Business Groups Failure & Focused Business Groups Success in India', Working Paper Series No. 2001–07 (July), XLRI Jamshedpur.

Kalam, A.P.J. Abdul, 2007, 'Speech', Defence Metallurgical Research Laboratory, Hyderabad (July).

Kannan, Gopika and Jibananda Khuntia, 2006, 'High Performance Computing Networks for Research, Education, Science and Technology in India', GARUDA, Pune, India.

Kaushik, Kshama V. and Kaushik Dutta, 2005a, *Corporate Governance: Myth to Reality*, New Delhi: LexisNexis Butterworths.

————, 2005b, 'Too Important to be Left to Political Compulsions', *Hindu Business Line* (6 October).

Kerr, William R., 2009, 'Breakthrough Inventions and Migrating Clusters of Innovation', HBS Working Paper number 10-020 (September), Harvard Business School Working Knowledge.

————, 2008, 'Ethnic Scientific Communities and International Technology Diffusion', *Review of Economics & Statistics*, Vol. 90, pp. 518–37.

Khanna, T. and K. Palepu, 2000, 'Is Group Affiliation Profitable in Emerging Markets? An Analysis of Diversified Indian Business Groups', in *Journal of Finance*, Vol. 55, No. 2 (April), pp. 867–91.

Kobayashi-Hillary, Mark, 2004, *Outsourcing to India: The Offshore Advantage*, New York: Springer.

KPMG, 2007, 'Global Anti-Money Laundering Survey 2007: How Banks are Facing up to the Challenge', http://www.kpmg.com/UK/en/IssuesAndInsights/ArticlesPublications/Documents/PDF/Advisory/AML2007APPENDICES.pdf

Krueger, Anne O. and Sajjid Chinoy, 2002, 'The Indian Economy in Global Context', *Economic Policy Reforms and the Indian Economy*, New Delhi: Oxford University Press.

Krueger, Anne O., 1974, 'The Political Economy of a Rent-Seeking Society', *American Economic Review*, Vol. 64, No. 3, pp. 291–303.

Kumar, K. Ravi, n.d., 'Alternative Dispute Resolution in Construction Industry', International Council of Consultants (ICC) papers, www.iccindia.org

Kumar, Nandini, Vasantha Muthuswamy, N.K. Ganguly, n.d., 'Initiatives of Indian Council of Medical Research in Scientific Validation of Traditional Medicine', *Health Administrator*, Vol . XX, No. 1&2, pp. 115–19.

Kumra, Gautam, 2007, 'Upgrading India's Energy and Transportation Networks', *Building a Better India* (Special Edition), *McKinsey Quarterly*, http://www.mckinsey.it/storage/first/uploadfile/attach/139925/file/upin07.pdf, pp. 57–63.

Kurien, Verghese, 2001, 'The Amul Saga', *India-Seminar 498* (February), http://www.india-seminar.com/2001/498/498%20verghese%20kurien.htm

Lagace, Martha, 2008, 'Billions of Entrepreneurs in China and India, Q&A with Tarun Khanna', *Harvard Business School Working Knowledge* (28 January) [Interview with Tarun Khanna, author of *Billions of Entrepreneurs: How China and India are Reshaping Their Futures-and Yours*, http://www.hbswk.hbs.edu/item/5766.html

Lal, Deepak, 1999, *Unfinished Business: India in the World Economy*, New Delhi: Oxford University Press.

Legard, David, 2001, *Computerworld* (28 June).

Leibenstein, Harvey, 1968, 'Entrepreneurship and Development', *American Economic Review*, Vol. 58, No. 2, pp. 72–83.

Lesher, Richard L., 1997, 'Democracy's Promise: Building a Modern Economy', *Economic Reform Today*, No. 1, http://www.cipe.org/publications/ert/e23/E23_01.pdf

Madhavan. N., 2010, 'Sibling Rivalry is the Biggest Challenge for Indian Family Businesses: Interview with John L. Ward', *Business Today* (7 March).

Majumdar, Sumit K., 2005, 'The Role of Foreign Firms in India over the Past Half Century: Retrospect and Prospect', Working Paper Series (31 May), Department of Information Systems & Operations Management, University of Texas at Dallas.

Maria, A., J. Ruet, and M-H. Zerah, n.d., 'Biotechnology in India', http://www. cerna.ensmp.fr/Documents/AM-JR-MHZ-BiotechReport.pdf

Marico Industries Ltd, 2007, *Director's Report 2006–7.*

Markovits, Claude, 2001, *The Global World of Indian Merchants, 1750–1947: Traders of Sind from Bukhara to Panama*, Cambridge: Cambridge University Press.

McCormick, Joel, 2006, 'The World According to Azim Premji', *Stanford Magazine* (May/June).

McKinsey & Co., 2007, 'Indian Banking: Towards Global Best Practices— Insights from Industry Benchmarking Surveys', *Financial Services Practice* (November), http://www.mckinsey.com/locations/india/ mckinseyonindia/pdf/India_Banking_Overview.pdf

————, 2006, 'Understanding Supply Chain Risk: A McKinsey Global Survey', *The McKinsey Quarterly* (September), http://www.ismsv.org/library/ SC.Risk.pdf

————, n.d., 'Indian Pharma, 2015', http://www.mckinsey.com/locations/ india/mckinseyonindia/pdf/India_Pharma_2015.pdf

Miles, David and Andrew Scott, 2005, *Macroeconomics: Understanding the Wealth of Nations*, New York: John Wiley & Sons.

Ministry of Finance, GoI, 2003, 'Disinvestment Manual—February 2003', http://www.divest.nic.in/chap5.asp

Ministry of Power, n.d., 'Power Sector at a Glance "ALL INDIA"', http://www. powermin.nic.in/indian_electricity_scenario/introduction.htm

Mishra, P., A. Subramanian, and P. Topalova, 2005, 'Policies, Enforcement and Customs Evasion: Evidence From India', IMF Working Paper 07/60 (March).

Misra, Om Prakash, 1978, *The Economic Philosophy of Pt. Jawaharlal Nehru*, New Delhi: Chugh Publications.

MIT News, 2003, 'Boston's 8 Research Universities provide $7 bln Annual Boost to the Regional Economy' (11 March).

MNRE (Ministry of New and Renewable Energy), 2011, *Annual Report 2010–11*, New Delhi: MNRE, http://www.mnre.gov.in/annualreport/2010_11_ English/index.htm

Modigliani, F. and R. Brumberg, 1954, 'Utility Analysis and the Consumption Function: An Interpretation of Cross-section Data', in K.K. Kurihara (ed.), *Post-Keynesian Economics*, New Brunswick, NJ: Rutgers University Press.

Mohan, T. T. Ram and Subhash C. Ray, 2003, 'Technical Efficiency in Public and Private Sectors in India: Evidence From the Post Reform Years', *Economics Working* Papers, Paper 2003-22 (22 July), University of Connecticut.

Moody's–ICRA, 2007, 'Corporate Governance and Related Credit Issues for Indian Family-Controlled Companies' (October), *Corporate Finance Series*, http://www.moodys.com/sites/products/AboutMoodysRatingsAttachments/ 2007000000448489.pdf

Moraes, F. R., 1967, *Sir Purshotamdas Thakurdas*, Bombay: Asia Publications.

Morris, Morris David, 1983, 'The Growth of Large-Scale Industry to 1947', in D. Kumar and M. Desai (eds), *Cambridge Economic History of India*, Vol. II, Cambridge: Cambridge University Press.

———, 1979, 'South Asian Entrepreneurship and the Rashomon Effect, 1800-1947', *Explorations in Economic History*, Vol. 16, No. 3, pp. 341–61.

Mukherjee, P., 2006, 'Speech', FICCI seminar (24 October).

Mukherji, Joydeep, 2000, '*Information Technology in India: Yet Another Missed Opportunity?*', Standard & Poor's *CreditWeek* (12 July).

Muralidhar, Omkar, 2005, 'Slow Population Growth Strains Western Economies', *The Standard Review*, Vol. XXXIV, No. 5 (22 April).

NABUCO, 2007, 'Endowment Study', www.nacubo.org/Research/NACUBO_Endowment_Study.html

Nafziger, E. Wayne and Andrew Ojede, 2007, 'Software Entrepreneurs in India's Silicon City: Tigers, Copycats, and Mixed Breeds', Seminar paper, Institute for Social and Economic Change, Bangalore, India (26 November).

Naithani, Ambika, 2007, 'Indian Students Dominate Harvard Business School', *Economic Times* (16 November).

Nanda, Ramana and Tarun Khanna, 2010, 'Diasporas and Domestic Entrepreneurs: Evidence from the Indian Software Industry', in *Journal of Economics and Management Strategy*, Vol. 19, No. 4, pp. 991–1012.

Narendranath, K.G., 2009, 'Right Decisions on Time Saved Satyam', *Econiomic Times* (5 May), http://articles.economictimes.indiatimes.com/2009-05-05/news/27643120_1_ministry-process-partnerships

NASSCOM, 2010, *IT-BPO Sector in India: Strategic Review 2010*, New Delhi: NASSCOM.

———, 2007, 'Indian Gaming and Animation Industry come of Age', *Nasscom Newsline*, no. 63 (January), http://www.nasscom.in/Nasscom/templates/NormalPage.aspx?id=50994

NASSCOM–BCG, 2007, *NASSCOM-BCG Innovation Report 2007: Unleashing the Innovative Power of Indian IT-ITES Industry*, New Delhi: NASSCOM.

Nayak, Amar K.J.R., 2006, 'Globalization of Foreign Direct Investment in India: 1900s to 2000', Paper presented at conference of The Historical Society (THS), Boston, University of North Carolina, Chapel Hill, USA (1 June).

Neff, Gina, 1996, 'Microcredit, Microresults', *Left Business Observer 74* (October).

New York Times, 2007, 'China Needs Innovation, says OCED' (27 August), http://www.nytimes.com/2007/08/27/business/worldbusiness/27iht-oecd.1.7267796.html

NSE, 2010, 'Indian Securities Market, A Review (ISMR - 2010)', p. 31.

OECD, 2007, 'Economic Survey of India, 2007', *Policy Brief* (October).

Ohmae, K., 1990, *The Borderless World*, London: HarperCollins.

Österholm, Pär, 2004, 'Estimating the Relationship between Age Structure and GDP in the OECD Using Panel Cointegration Methods', Working Paper 2004:13, Department of Economics, Uppsala University.

Pande, Shamni, Suman Layak, K.R. Balasubramanyam, and Anusha Subramanian, 2010, 'The GenNext Cometh', in *Business Today* (7 March).

Parthasarthi, Ashok, 2007, *Technology at the Core: Science and Technology with Indira Gandhi*, New Delhi: Pearson.

Pisani, Jo and Yann Bonduelle, 2010, 'Opportunities and Barriers in Biosimilar Market: Evolution or Revolution for Generics Companies?', www.ableindia.in/admin/attachments/reports/reports14_biosimilars.pdf

Planning Commission, 2008, *Eleventh Five Year Plan 2007–12*, New Delhi: Oxford University Press.

———, 2005, *Mid-Term Appraisal of Tenth Five-Year Plan, 2002–07*, http://planningcommission.nic.in/plans/mta/midterm/english-pdf/chapter-02c.pdf, pp. 126–48.

Poddar, Tushar and Eva Yi, 2007, 'India's Rising Growth Potential', Global Economics Paper No. 152 (22 January), Goldman Sachs Economic Research, http://www.usindiafriendship.net/viewpoints1/Indias_Rising_Growth_Potential.pdf

Poirson, Hélène, 2007, 'Country Study: India', *IMF Research Bulletin*, Vol. 8, No. 2 (June), pp. 6–8.

Pradhan, Jaya Prakash, 2007, 'Trends and Patterns of Overseas Acquisitions by Indian Multinationals', Working Paper 2007/10 (October), Institute of Study of Industrial Development, New Delhi.

Prakash, Om, 2006, 'Cashless Payment Mechanism in Mughal India: The Working of the Hundi Network', paper presented at Session 2 of the International Economic History Congress, Helsinki, 21–25 August.

PricewaterhouseCoopers, 2007, 'Working Towards Wellness: Accelerating the Prevention of Chronic Diseases', http://download.pwc.com/ie/pubs/Working_Towards_Wellness.pdf

———, 2006, 'Adopting IFRS', www.pwc.com/gx/en/ifrs-reporting/pdf/adopting_ifrs.pdf

PricewaterhouseCoopers, n.d., 'Pharma 2020: The Vision—Which Path Will You Take?', http://www.pwc.com/gx/en/pharma-life-sciences/pharma-2020/pharma-2020-vision-path.jhtml

PricewaterhouseCoopers–World Economic Forum, 2007, 'Exploiting Intellectual Property in a Complex World' (June), http://www.pwc.com/en_GX/gx/technology/pdf/exploiting-intellectual-property.pdf

Radhakrishnan, S., Prahlada, S., and Parimal Kumar, n.d., 'Leveraging Offsets for Self Reliance in Defence Technologies', DRDO.

Rajakumar, J. Dennis and John S. Henley, 2007, 'Growth and Persistence of Large Business Groups in India', *Journal of Comparative International Management* (June).

Ramesh, M., 2007, 'Government Panel Raises Hopes for Nidhis', in *Hindu Business Line* (19 February).

Randall, Morck and Bernard Yeung, 2003, 'Agency Problems in Large Family Business Groups: Entrepreneurship Theory and Practice', *Entrepreneurship: Theory and Practice*, Vol. 27, No. 4 (June), pp. 367–82.

Rao, K.S. Chalapati and Atulan Guha, 2006, 'Ownership Pattern of the Indian Corporate Sector: Implications for Corporate Governance', Working Paper No: 2006/09 (September), Institute for Study of Industrial Development.

Rau, B. Ramachandra, 1925, *Present-day Banking in India*, Calcutta: University of Calcutta.

Ray, Rajat, 1979, *Industrialization in India—Growth and Conflict in the Private Corporate Sector, 1914–47*, New Delhi: Oxford University Press.

Reddy, Y.V., 2007, 'Speech: Glimpses of Indian Economy and its Financial Sector', Central Bank of the Russian Federation, Moscow, Russia (2 July).

Reserve Bank of India, 1998, 'Evolution of Payment Systems in India' (12 December), http://www.rbi.org.in/scripts/PublicationsView.aspx?id=155

———, n.d., 'Micro Credit: A Lifeline for the Poor', FAQs, Priority Sector Lending, www.rbi.org.in.FAQs

Rodrik, D. and A. Subramanian, 2005, 'From Hindu Growth to Productivity Surge: The Mystery of the Indian Growth Transition', *IMF Staff Papers*, Vol. 52, No. 2 (March), pp 193–228.

Rouch, J.E., 2001, 'Business and Social Networks in International Trade', *Journal of Economic Literature*, Vol. 39, No. 4, pp. 1177–203.

Rouch, J.E., and V. Trinidade, 2002, 'Ethnic Chinese Networks in International Trade', *Review of Economics and Statistics*, Vol. 84, No. 1, pp. 116–30.

Roy, Tirthankar, 2000, *The Economic History of India, 1857-1947*, New Delhi: Oxford University Press.

Rugman, Alan, 2005, *The Regional Multinationals: MNEs and 'Global' Strategic Management*, Cambridge: Cambridge University Press.

Sakthivel, S., 'Financing and Delivery of Health Care Services in India', Section III, Access to Essential Drugs and Medicine, in *Financing and Delivery of Health Care Services in India*, New Delhi: Ministry of Health and Family Welfare, pp. 185–212.

Sarkar, Jayati and Subrata Sarkar, 2000, 'Large Shareholder Activism in Developing Countries: Evidence from India', *International Review of Finance*, Vol. 1, No. 3 (September).

Sarma, Krishna, Momota Oinam, and Angshuman Kaushik, 2009, 'Development and Practice of Arbitration in India—Has it Evolved as an Effective Legal Institution', CDDRL Working Papers No. 103 (October).

Sasi, Anil, 2008, 'Coal Ventures Invite Merchant Bankers for Global Mine Hunt', *Hindu Business Line* (2 January).

Saxanian, Anna Lee, 2002, 'Bangalore: The Silicon Valley of India', in A. Krueger (ed.), *Economic Policy Reforms and the Indian Economy* Chicago: University of Chicago Press.

Saxenian, A, 2006, 'The New Agronauts: Regional Advantage in a Global Economy', Boston: Harvard Business School Press

———, 2002, 'Local & Global Networks of Immigrant Professionals in Silicon Valley', Public Policy Institute of California.

Schapiro, Mary L., 2009, 'Remarks', IOSCO 34th Annual Conference (11 June), Tel Aviv, Israel, http://goliath.ecnext.com/coms2/gi_0198-593258/REMARKS-BY-SECURITIES-AND-EXCHANGE.html

Schultz, T.W., 1960, 'Capital Formation by Education', *Journal of Political Economy*, Vol. 68, pp. 571–83.

Schumpeter, J.A., 1934 [1912], *The Theory of Economic Development* (1912 [In German]), Cambridge, MA: Harvard University Press.

Shah, Atul K., 2007, 'Jain Business Ethics', in *Accountancy Business and the Public Interest*, Vol. 6, No. 2.

Sharma, D., 2006, 'Historical Traces of Hundi, Sociocultural Understanding and Criminal Abuses of Hawala', *International Criminal Justice Review*, Vol. 16, No. 2, pp. 99–121.

Shirley, Mary, 1998, 'Why Performance Contracts for State Owned Enterprises Haven't Worked', *Public Policy for the Private Sector*, Note No. 150 (August), n. pag.

Shukla, Saurabh and Nivedita Mukherjee, 2010, 'The African Safari', *India Today* (1 April).

Siddy, Dan and Ritu Kumar, 2009, *Sustainable Investment in India: Sustainable Development of Portfolio Investment in India's Publicly Listed Companies*, New Delhi: TERI Press.

Singh, Manmohan, 2007, 'Inaugural Speech', CII Annual General Meeting (24 May).

Singh, Manohar and James A. Goodrich, 2006, 'Succession in Family-Owned Businesses: A Case Study of Reliance Industries-India' (1 September), *Social Science Research Network*.

Sinha, Jai B.P., 2004, *Multinationals in India: Managing the Interface of Cultures*, New Delhi: Sage.

Smith, Adam, 1776, *An Inquiry into the Nature and Causes of the Wealth of Nations*, London.

Srinivasan, T.N., 2000, *Eight Lectures on Indian Economic Reforms*, New Delhi: Oxford University Press.

Subramaniam, Laksmi and R.K. Ray, 2004, 'Merchants and Politics: From the Great Mughals to the East India Company', in Dwijendra Tripathi (ed.), *The Oxford History of Indian Business*, New Delhi: Oxford University Press.

Swaminathan, S. Anklesaria Aiyar, 2005, '"Swaminomics": Rahul vs. Rajiv, The Bajaj Saga', *Times of India* (18 June).

Taganas, Rey A.L. and Vijay Kumar Kaul, 2006, 'Innovation Systems in India's IT Industry: An Empirical Investigation', *Economic and Political Weekly*, Vol. XLI, No. 39 (September).

Taparia, K.K., 2005, 'Parta Management System', lecture delivered at IMDR (The Institute of Management Development and Research), Pune (March).

TERI, n.d., *National Energy Map for India: Technology Vision 2030* (in collaboration with the Office of the Principal Scientific Advisor, GoI), New Delhi: TERI Press.

Thapar, Romila, 2000, *Asoka and the Decline of the Mauryas*, New Delhi: Oxford University Press.

Thaplyal, Kiran Kumar, 2001, *Guilds in Ancient India: Antiquity and Various Stages in the Development of Guilds up to 300 AD*, New Delhi: Munshiram Manorharlal Publishers.

Times of India, 2007a, 'Costly R&D leads to Patent Fight' (4 September), p. 23.

———, 2007b, (29 August), p. 5.

———, 2007c, 'Hindustan Lever is Now Unilever' (21 February).

———, 2006, (10 August).

———, 2003, 'Take on Gates, Kalam Tells Indian Techies' (29 May).

The Royal Society, 2011, 'Knowledge, Networks and Nations: Global Scientific Collaboration in the 21st Century', RS Policy Document 03/11, London: The Royal Society.

Thomson Reuters, 2006, 'Thomson Honours Leading Indian Scientists' (27 July).

Thorat, Usha, 2010, 'Global Economic Prospects and the Indian Economy', PRMIA Singapore Chapter Meeting (22 September).

Thorat, Y.S.P., 2005, 'Keynote Address', Roundtable on Cooperative Banking, Centenary of Indian Cooperative Movement & Banking Institutions, Pune (10 December).

Tomlinson, B.R., 1993, *The Economy of Modern India 1860–1970*, New Cambridge History of India, No. 3, New Delhi: Foundation Books.

Toyama, Kentaro, Karishma Kiri, Deepak Menon, Joyojeet Pal, Suneet Sethi, and Janaki Srinivasan, 2005, 'PC Kiosk Trends in Rural', India Seminar on Policy Options and Models for Bridging Digital Divides (13–14 March), Tampere, Finland.

TRAI, 2010, *Annual Report 2009–10*, New Delhi: TRAI, http://www.trai.gov.in/annualreport/AnnualReport_09_10English.pdf

Tripathi, Dwijendra, 2004, *The Oxford History of Indian Business*, New Delhi: Oxford University Press.

UNCTAD, 2005, *World Investment Report: Transnational Corporations and the Internationalization of R&D*, New York and Geneva: United Nations.

UNDP, 2010, *UNDP Human Development Report 2010—The Real Wealth of Nations: Pathways to Human Development*, http://hdr.undp.org/en/media/HDR_2010_EN_Complete_reprint.pdf

———, 2006, *UNDP Human Development Report 2006—Beyond Scarcity: Power, Poverty and the Global Water Crisis*, http://hdr.undp.org/en/media/HDR06-complete.pdf

Varma, J.R., 1997, 'Corporate Governance in India: Disciplining the Dominant Shareholder', *IIMB Management Review*, Vol. 9, No. 4 (October–December), pp. 5–18, http://www.iimahd.ernet.in/~jrvarma/papers/iimbr9-4.pdf

Varma, M. Sarita, 2006, 'Kerala Logs Microsoft Out', *Financial Express* (26 August).

Vyas, Yash, 1992, 'Regulation of Monopolies, Restrictive Trade Practices and Prices in Ancient India', *Central India Law Quarterly*, Vol. 5, No. 2.

Wasserman, Noam T., 2006, 'Stewards, Agents and the Founder Discount: Executive Compensation in New Ventures', in *Academy of Management Journal*, Vol. 49, No. 5 (October), pp. 960–76.

World Economic Forum (WEF), 2010, *The Global Competitiveness Report 2010–2011* (edited by Klaus Schwab), Geneva: WEF.

WSJ–Heritage Foundation, *Index of Economic Freedom* (updated annually), http://www.heritage.org/index/Country/India

Yahoo India News, 2008, 'Ready for a Makeover' (24 July), www.in.news.yahoo.com

Index

366 « *Index*